ON MY OWN SIDE

Transform Self-Criticism and Doubt Into
Permanent Self-Worth and Confidence

Dr. Aziz Gazipura

Printed by B.C. Allen Publishing and Tonic Books
144 N 7th St. #525
Brooklyn, NY 11249

Now taking manuscript submissions and book ideas at any stage of the process:
submissions@tonicbooks.online

Printed in the United States of America

Editor: Krista Munster
Cover Design: Zeeshan Haque
Interior Design: Susan Veach
Production: Jade Maniscalco

ISBN: 978-1-950977-96-3

DEDICATION

For Candace, my beloved half-side.
I am eternally grateful to spend this life with you, learning,
laughing, and loving as we tumble ever-deeper into this Great Mystery.
Thank you for being the unseen force that helps my light shine brighter
in the world. Thank you for your deep devotion to our boys.
Thank you for loving, teaching, and guiding us to be strong,
empathic, heart-centered men.

ALSO BY DR. AZIZ GAZIPURA

Books:

The Solution To Social Anxiety

The Art Of Extraordinary Confidence

Not Nice

Online:

Confidence University

Shrink For The Shy Guy Podcast

Get More Confidence YouTube Channel

CONTENTS

My dear friend,
You are already whole, complete,
worthwhile, powerful, and capable.
Any thought or voice in your head that
says otherwise is mistaken.

Prologue:
Do You Remember?

When was the first time you turned on yourself? Do you remember? My guess is that it wasn't recently, but rather a long, long time ago. I'm not talking about the first time someone else turned on you or was cruel to you, but rather, the time you were first cruel to yourself.

When I was eight years old, I went to spend a few summer days at an "all sports" camp. We cycled through various sports, including soccer, which was my favorite.

Except I didn't enjoy this soccer or this camp at all because most of the two days were filled with a group of boys hounding me because of my name. While I don't remember all the details of what they said, I know "Aziz the disease" was a favorite. One would say, "Aziz the disease," as others stood by cackling. Soon, one would just say my name, and they would all laugh. The sound of my name was the punch line.

I remember the pain, hurt, and helplessness I felt. I remember walking away from the soccer field, tears burning my eyes as I heard their laughter rolling across the open field. I hated them. But I didn't hate myself. Not yet.

Three years later, when I was eleven years old and starting my
first day at a new middle school where everyone knew each other
but me, I felt nervous. I was afraid I wouldn't fit in and that the
other kids wouldn't like me.

During recess, when all the boys climbed to the top of the
monkey bars to lounge and talk, I did not. I'd never climbed up
something like that and was not able to. Or maybe I could if I kept
at it, but I didn't want to try too many times lest I draw more attention to myself. Instead, I stood in the sand below, leaning against
a cold metal post, feeling horrible inside. Different. Weird. Less-
than.

But I didn't hate myself. I mainly felt scared—scared they
would do this every recess and that I would be different, and then
the teasing would start. I was scared that I wouldn't fit in and that
I wouldn't have any friends in this new school, this new city.

I'm sure you can recall hundreds of moments like these from
different times in your life, moments where you felt scared, anxious, or inferior. Moments where you hoped people would like
you, that things would go well, that you'd be good enough.

But these moments are not the ones I'm talking about. I'm
asking about the moment you stopped simply being in yourself
while interacting with the world out there. The moment when
you started to look inward at yourself and harshly judged what
you found there.

For me, it was when I started to get acne. I found it repulsive. I
felt intense surges of anxiety bordering on panic when I looked at
myself in the mirror. I was already barely hanging on by a thread.
Somehow, people hadn't caught on to the fact that my name was
different than theirs, that my skin was darker than theirs, or that
my dad was a different religion than theirs. Somehow, I was fitting in. Maybe it was because I was athletic and could run and
jump and play basketball and four square. Maybe it was because

I instantly changed my musical tastes to mimic those of the kids around me. Whatever it was, I was fitting in. And now this.

Each new pimple was bringing me one step closer to the edge of ruin. You may smile at how a dramatic twelve-year-old mind can work, but don't we all do this now, still? Won't the world end if you don't get that next sale or make a good impression on your boss' boss at the next big meeting? Won't you just die if that person doesn't call you back after you spent the night together? Isn't your world regularly on the edge of death and ruin?

That's when I started feeling total revulsion toward myself. I hated looking in the mirror. I imagined everyone was thinking less of me—girls in my class, other boys, my cousins, family, and even strangers. Everyone would find me as gross as I found myself.

The anger, revulsion, and hatred intensified as boys in my class started making connections with girls. They were somehow meeting up, going on dates, or spending time together at school dances. None of this was happening to me, and I knew why. It was because I was gross, repulsive, and bad.

That's when it all began, The Great Betrayal. I stopped wanting to be me and started wanting to be somebody else. I stopped loving me for who I was. How could I? How could I love someone who looked like that? Whose family had accents like that? Whose skin and eyes looked like that?

I wonder, my dear friend, when you first turned on yourself. When did you become your own enemy? When did you decide that who you are wasn't worthy, good, loved, or lovable? Can you pinpoint some of the moments of that early transition?

It may have occurred much younger for you. I've had clients who've told me about chastising themselves out loud as early as five or six years old. One man I worked with started telling himself he was "bad" and "awful" dozens of times per day when he was in first grade. What on earth was a six-year-old doing that was so unforgivable, so bad, and awful? He couldn't even recall. All he remembered was the feeling of complete badness he felt. "I felt like I had a rotten core, like a bad apple you'd throw away once you found out what was inside it."

Maybe the betrayal happened in one distinct moment, or maybe it was a gradual shift that occurred over months. Maybe it was after the third time your family moved when you were a kid, and you had to go to yet another new school. Maybe it was when your mom and dad divorced, and you felt the support you once relied on shatter beneath you.

Can you remember when you first turned on yourself? Whether you can or can't doesn't matter. It's the search that counts, the empathic inquiry that causes your mind to relate to yourself in a dramatically different way. It reminds you that there was a time, no matter how long ago, when you were on your own side.

Introduction:
What Are We Doing Here?

You may not realize it, but the clock is ticking for you and me to be together. Here's the unfortunate truth. You are deciding over the next ten pages whether you're going to read this book or not. Most people don't finish more than a few pages of the self-development books they buy. It's not your fault or some major problem you have. It's just that the book doesn't grab you. You love the title and want the result, but the book doesn't grip you and starts to feel like a bunch of new information to study and apply. It sure sounds good, but it's a lot of work, and life is busy. And so it goes on the nightstand, or in your digital library, under your mental category of "I'll get to this one soon, I swear."

Well, good news! This book is different. It's different than all the other books I've written and most likely different than other self-development books you've read. It's not a list of how-tos and rational techniques to eradicate your inner critic and live life from the rational thoughts of your neocortex. It's not full of the latest research of neuroplasticity and the neurobiological regions of the brain associated with self-compassion.

It's not a book for your brain. It's a book for your heart.

Don't get me wrong. You will find powerful solutions in the

pages that follow, solutions that have helped hundreds of thousands of people from all over the world make lasting changes in their confidence and self-esteem. But the solution might look different than you imagine.

If you're not on your own side, and you've turned against yourself or lost touch with who you are, then you don't need more rational techniques to apply. You don't need more research on the brain. You need to come back into yourself and return to your center. You need to journey to the center of your heart and discover why you are not right with yourself. You need to uncover why you attack yourself, judge and condemn who you are in the world, and constantly pressure yourself to be more, better, and different.

You need to crack open the walls around your heart and feel that vibrant, tender, sweet, wild little kid in there and let her or him come out. You need to smile, laugh, be moved, cry, and remember who you really are. Not who you should be. Not what you're supposed to be to get success, wealth, or recognition. Not who you're expected to be in order to get acceptance and approval. Who you really are.

That's what you and I are doing here together. That's the journey we're about to go on. I don't know if you'll be with me in ten pages, but I sure hope so. This journey to the center of your heart is the most valuable one we could possibly undertake.

In Part I of this book, you are going to get clarity on how you've been treating yourself up until this point. If you're like most people, it's not that great. It's certainly less loving, patient, and encouraging than you are with your spouse, friends, or colleagues. You'll also discover why you have this critic in the first place and what it's *real* purpose is. Discovering this allows you to go beyond surface-level symptomatic solutions, such as affirmations or "positive self-talk," and helps you completely resolve this problem at the root.

In Part II, you will make one of the most important decisions of your life. When I made this decision, my life took a significant turn for the better, and I haven't looked back since. This section will energize and inspire you and provide the explosive force to reach terminal velocity in your O.M.O.S. journey.

Part III is where you will get all the techniques, tools, and ninja moves you're seeking, like how to respond to your inner critic, sidestep self-judgment, and return to being centered, confident, and on your own side, no matter what. You will not only get specific strategies; you'll get a chance to see those tools in action with direct accounts of people I've worked with and their critics. By the end of this section, you will be in control inside our own mind. You will be the captain of your own ship. And it will feel amazing.

In Part IV, you'll go beyond neutralizing the critic and discover how to change the way you approach all key areas of your life, including work, relationships, parenting, and more. You will transform the underlying mindsets and patterns that are a breeding ground for self-hatred, such as perfectionism and constant comparison. Our goal here is to help you repeatedly return to a state of permanent O.M.O.S., so your center of gravity is on your own side, in any situation, no matter what.

There is so much good in store for you, so much freedom, joy, and true happiness that can only come from being authentically yourself and loving that self unconditionally. Your future is bright, my friend, and this is just the beginning. All you have to do is stay with me on this journey beyond ten pages!

Are you ready?

Dr. Aziz Gazipura
Portland, Oregon, 2020

To get bonus audio and video trainings that will greatly enhance what you learn from this book, visit: www.omosbook.com

PART I: INSANITY

Chapter 1:
The Bizarre Normal

I don't remember what came first, the magazine or the poison from my friend. I think it was the poison. I was fourteen years old, and we were driving into a Safeway parking lot in the early evening hours. The dusk sky was turning dark, and it was a Friday night. I felt excited and happy—the kind of feelings that only come on a Friday night when you are out with friends. Elation, joy, and energy pulsed through my body. I loved being with my friends, and I loved being me.

But what I didn't know in that moment, was that, seconds later, one of my friends would say one simple sentence that would poison my mind for ten years. That one sentence that would create hundreds of hours of suffering, self-hatred, and loneliness.

Heck, I don't know if he had that much power. Maybe the seeds of self-hatred were already germinating inside of me, and his words were just the drops of water they needed to explode into a fully-fledged sapling. In any case, here's what happened.

As we pulled into the parking lot, two young ladies were walking into the supermarket. Undoubtedly, they could feel the eyeballs of four teenage boys looking at them as we drove past. One of them turned and looked at us through the car windows and smiled.

"Did you see that?" I said to the guys in the car. "She wants me."

It was teenage bravado for sure. Behind it, as with all bravado, was a deep insecurity. At this point in my life, I already felt generally awkward and uncool around women. I hadn't completely turned on myself yet, but I felt a growing insecurity as if I were about to fully discover the awful truth that there was indeed something about me that made me permanently undesirable to women and undeserving of love and connection.

Then, my friend answered my unasked question.

"Yeah," he sneered. "She's thinking, *Who's that Pakistani kid in the back seat with those gross bags under his eyes?*"

Woah.

Just to write that, I had to take a deep breath. I can feel the hatred and rejection in those words. There was no lightness in their tone, no feigned gaiety or humor. They were delivered coldly and directly, dripping with sarcasm, racism, and buried pain.

One of my other friends gave a single, short snort of laughter and said, "Dude, that was harsh." My other friend remained silent, as did I.

I didn't know that my friend carried a reservoir of self-loathing behind those words, or that his father disdained him for not measuring up, not being the son he always wanted. I didn't understand the unspoken, unconscious resentment his dad felt for him, and he, in turn, felt for his dad. I didn't realize the inferiority and inadequacy he was drowning in daily, despite having cool clothes, hair, piercings, and a car—all the trappings of success in high school repertoire. I didn't know that he was drowning and needed to push off of my shoulders to get himself up for a breath of air. I just thought he was right.

In that one moment, everything became clear. That's why the young women in my class didn't respond to me like they did Chris, or Adam, or Josh. They were white. They had no complexion change around their eyes, no gross bags.

In the seconds that it took to find a parking spot, my world had changed. I had changed. I understood everything clearly now, and I knew what I had to do. Or rather, I knew what I could not do, and that was to attract women, get dates, have a thriving social life, be popular, or fall in love. All of that was off-limits to me because of those disgusting bags under my eyes.

As if to seal in the self-hatred, the next week I was at Supercuts, awaiting my monthly haircut. I picked up a magazine to kill time. The first page I flipped to had a full-page close-up of a woman's eyes. They had dark circles underneath them, and she looked tired, bedraggled.

"Tired of Those Disgusting Racoon Eyes?" the caption read. Okay, maybe it didn't say the word "disgusting," but it may as well have. There it was, in print. Dark circles under your eyes are ugly, unattractive, and gross. I was doomed.

YOU AND YOU

Fast forward a decade.

Ten years of criticism, self-judgment, and dislike. Has it been that long for you? Has it been longer?

I had just ended the evening with a lovely woman I'd dated several times. The date went quite well. We seemed to be connecting, laughing a lot, and enjoying each other's company. In the moment, I felt pretty good. Until the next day, that is...

"It's over. You'll never see her again," said the critical voice inside my head. "You ruined it with that stupid joke you made right before she left. Why on earth did you say that? That was so stupid."

The words penetrate right to my core, and I feel my lips tighten as I cringe inside. I replay the scene again in my mind. *Yep, that voice is right. That joke was so bad. Why did I say that?*

"Remember?" my inner critic continued. "She just looked at you, not sure what to say. She thought you were serious. Oh my god, that was so awful."

More cringing inside as I replay the scene again and again. My critic is right. She's not going to respond to my message. Almost an entire day had passed, and I hadn't heard anything back. I felt a familiar combination of sinking despair and anxiety.

My critic picked up steam, launching into a tirade against me. "You always find some way to mess it up. You keep doing this. And it's going to keep happening. You're so awkward, nerdy, weak, and soft. You're nothing like Chris or Sam. That's what women want, not you."

That last word contained so much depth, in only the way an internal dialogue can. As my critic said the word "you," it referenced a sense of inferiority that was made up of hundreds of data points from my past—moments where I failed, was less-than, or otherwise unworthy.

I didn't say anything. I didn't respond. What was there to say? My critic was right. And so, I sat there, immobilized, listening to its tirade continue. Eventually, it would stop, once the message was complete and the inner fire of hatred was expressed sufficiently. Then, my critic would recede into its cave, like a dragon backing into its lair waiting for it's next moment to strike.

For many years, this kind of self-treatment was normal for me. I didn't question it or react to it with shock or indignation. I didn't share it with others because to do so would reveal an endless list of insecurities and other weaknesses, which I imagined would bring on ridicule or aversion. I also thought others didn't deal with such a thing because they were better than me, so there was no need for an inner critic to highlight of all their flaws. So this brutal inner tyrant remained hidden, and I thought it was completely unique to me.

After so many years, it just felt...normal. I went to school, went to work, had some friends, went on a date here and there, and I appeared pretty typical. Outside of my circle of friends, I was shy and didn't speak up much in groups. With people I knew well, I laughed and smiled and seemed confident enough to others.

But inside was a different story. Inside was a madhouse. Inside was a freaking war zone.

Can you relate? If you're anything like me, you have a polished exterior that you show the outside world, your carefully crafted and cultivated persona or "mask." You put it on for dates, business meetings, work, meeting new people, and an evening at the dinner party. You try your best to be warm, engaging, funny, thoughtful, intelligent, capable, and interesting. And often, you are many of these things, and no one would be the wiser.

But inside, what is it like? What is it really like? Don't worry; this is just between you and me. No one else has to know right now. Do you have a dragon in there? A beast that emerges from the depths to attack you with vicious criticisms, demeaning judgments, and mockery?

Here's a tiny window into that dark inner world that no one wants to talk about openly. These are things people have told me their critic says to them.

After an intimate dinner with a dear friend, connecting, discussing life, the critic hisses, immediately upon departing: "You messed that up. He hates you. You are such an ass. He feels sorry for you, and it's only a matter of time until he never wants to see you again."

I glance in the mirror as a shirt goes over my head: "Ugh. Look at that fat. Disgusting. Weak. Ugly. Gross. I hate it. I hate myself."

A new project comes at work, one that is big and promises to be exciting, challenging, and potentially rewarding: "You can't do this. It won't work out. You're going to fail. Everyone is going to see this, think less of you, see you for the fraud and failure you are, and you'll never have another opportunity like this again."

A feeling of sadness and grief arises inside: "This again? Ugh, what's wrong with me? I'm too sensitive, always moping around. Come on! Get over it!"

I open a window on the computer to watch a video online: "You should be working right now. Come on. What are you doing? What's wrong with you? You're so lazy. You have no will-power. Come on! Stop doing this right now and get to work!"

How many of these scenarios can you relate to? One, two, three, or perhaps all of them? When people talk deeply with me and reveal what's really going on underneath the mask, it's often all of these and more, much more. This is the case regardless of their outward level of success, status, career accomplishments, income, appearance, or anything else. In other words, it seems like everyone has this inner critic, even those who don't appear to have a reason to because they are beautiful, smart, and successful.

In fact, for most, this dragon isn't an intermittent presence that infrequently emerges to terrorize the town. Instead, it is a constant presence, looming in the skies above as it slowly circles above your head. Sometimes, it reigns down brutal jets of fire, attacking your character, lovability, core worth, and value. It leaves you demoralized and sickened with no joy or energy left to create anything meaningful, only enough energy to flick on your TV or swipe open your phone. Of course, your critic attacks you for this as well, creating a background of tension and pressure, telling you that you should be doing something better than this.

And then there are moments of relief, sweet relief, like stepping out of an icy snowstorm into a cozy, warmly-lit house. The critic is gone for a moment. You are here now. You feel alive, present, and aware. You are engaged, excited, and inspired to act, create, connect, and live. Maybe this happens when you're with a good friend, connecting with a partner, spending time with your kids, or working on an engaging, meaningful project at work. There is no self-judgment, evaluation, or berating going on. Things are good.

But then, in a few minutes, an hour, a day, or a week, that critic comes back, repeating the cycle. Around and around we go, never questioning it, never thinking about it too deeply, and certainly never having our inner alarm bells go off, shouting inside, "What is this? This is unacceptable treatment, and I won't stand for it anymore!"

Are You Right With Yourself?

We spend so much time worrying about how we come across to others. We plan what we're going to say, think of ways to make others feel positively toward us, and strive to impress and be adored. We put on nice clothes, prepare our presentation, and act friendly, even when we're feeling tired or irritated inside. We put so much effort into our relationships.

Except, we neglect the relationship with ourselves, which we completely ignore or put low on the priority list. Isn't this so? Let's take a moment to reflect on this right now in your life. Imagine that you are in a relationship with yourself like you would be with another person. Just like any relationship, you talk to each other, spend time together, do activities, and so forth. Reflect on the last few days or weeks of your life and ask yourself, *How do I treat myself?*

What do you notice? How do you talk to yourself? How do you listen to yourself? Do you respond to yourself with empathy and compassion? Do you value what you want and need? For most people, the answers to these questions are not affirmative. In fact, most likely, you attempt to treat friends, colleagues, and loved ones in these positive ways, because it feels wrong to do otherwise. When someone you know is sharing, you listen. You respond with curiosity, support, and empathy. If they are struggling or suffering, you feel compassion and desire to help them in some way, even if it's only with a kind ear and words of encouragement. You may also point out their strengths or what you appreciate about them. You care about what they think and feel. You are curious about what they want and need, and try to help them get it, as best as you can.

How much of this do you do with yourself? Most likely, you do less, a lot less. Responding to yourself in the same way might seem strange, foreign, self-indulgent, dangerous, or somehow inappropriate as if you're doing something wrong by treating yourself this way.

But let's take a step back for a second here. I'm simply describing how we naturally treat the people we care about and love. Yet it seems that we often don't treat ourselves this way. What does that mean? Does that mean we don't love ourselves? It seems that way to me. What do you think? Do you love yourself?

Nonchalant

It's fascinating what we humans can get used to. Whether it's something amazing or something awful, if it happens for long enough, we adapt to it. More specifically, we habituate to it, which means that a particular stimulus does not produce so much of a reaction in our nervous systems. If you ate a sugar-frosted cocoa cream bomb cookie right now, it would make your blood sugar start doing jumping jacks in a few minutes. You'd feel a little buzz, a little energy, a little excited. But if you ate one of those every few hours, you wouldn't feel much at all within a few days. That's when you need to up your game to four cream bomb cookies every hour on the hour.

If a loud jackhammer starts firing off outside your office window, it would be highly distracting at first. But, after an hour or so, you'd be typing away at your computer, barely focused on the abrasive noise.

We also habituate to the daily experiences of our life circumstances and environment as well. Case in point, are you blown away when you walk into the produce section of a supermarket that is packed floor to ceiling with vividly colored fruits and vegetables shipped in daily from all over the world? My guess is probably not. You might barely notice the miraculous abundance and ease of access to all these foods that exceed any other time in human history. You probably don't even think about how you have more access to luxurious foods than even the richest nobles and royalty from five hundred years ago. Pretty sweet, huh?

Whatever. I just need to get some bananas and get out of here. I hate stopping by the store. It's such a hassle. Plus, I didn't find a parking spot close by, so now I'm way over on the other side of the parking lot.

You've habituated to the store being there because it's been there your entire life. Your nervous system is not shocked or delighted by the experience, and it's no big deal.

So what does all this have to do with your relationship with yourself? Most likely, you've habituated to the negativity with which you treat yourself. Much like that jackhammer outside the office window, you have gotten used to this abrasive, unpleasant sound permeating your life. So much so, that when your inner critic berates you, or you feel awful about making a mistake, you perceive this as normal.

Worse still, it may feel so normal because it seems like everyone else is doing the same thing. Your aunt is casually saying how much she hates her cheeks after seeing herself in the family photo. Your friend frets about his poor performance at his job, bracing himself each day to be brought into his boss's office for "the talk." This strikes you as strange as your friend is quite brilliant and has been doing this kind of work for years. Your sister is torturing herself for recently breaking up with her boyfriend, feeling horribly guilty because he's so sad and hopeless now. She feels selfish and cruel and keeps asking herself why she's doing this to him.

Just like you, most of the people in your life treat themselves with harsh indifference. They don't treat themselves like they would a dear friend or a beloved partner. It's normal to be hard on yourself, normal to constantly pressure yourself to get more done, faster, with fewer breaks. It's normal to blame yourself for problems at work, to demand you be further along professionally and personally, to regularly tell yourself you're not doing enough, to dislike many aspects of your life and yourself, to dislike the sound of your own voice, parts of your own body, and your general appearance, to hate looking older and to view getting older as gross, unattractive, and maybe even a personal failing, to be absolutely enraged with yourself after you make a mistake, especially if that results in someone getting upset with you.

This is the bizarre normal. It creates a strange sense of casual nonchalance about something that is extremely problematic and unhealthy. In other words, you may be habituated to treating yourself poorly. And because you're so used to it, you may not even see it as poor treatment. You may be completely oblivious to all the ways you are not right with yourself, all the ways you turn on yourself. Or you may be aware that you are hard on yourself at times, but see it as a necessary evil if you want to succeed and be a "good person" in this world. Or, you may even have a dismissive or defensive quality about the subject, as if even thinking about it is pathetic or worthy of ridicule. Your mind may scoff: *Oh, I'm just a snowflake who needs to be treated with kid gloves. Grow up!*

Let's take another step back here. What if a man was treating his wife in the same way? He regularly criticizes her in a casual manner, saying things like, "You look fat in that outfit," "You're looking so old and gross," "Why aren't you doing more? You're so lazy" and "What's wrong with you?" When his wife doesn't live up to his expectations, displeases him, or god forbid, makes a mistake, he is livid. He launches into a lengthy, loud tirade about her incompetence, stupidity, and selfishness. He breaks down her flaws one by one, comparing her to her friends and colleagues, and explains why she's inferior to everyone. If she tries to get away or ignore him, he follows her from room to room in the house, yelling several inches from her face.

When she does achieve something, accomplish a task, or win some recognition, he dismisses and deflates it instantly. "So what? Anyone could've done that. What's the big deal?" Or, "Yeah, you did that. But what's next? You still haven't gotten to that next project. Hurry up." Worse still, he may snatch defeat from the jaws of victory and turn her triumph into an apparent failure. "That recognition at work? They just gave that to you because they feel sorry for you because you're so pathetic, they needed to prop you up."

How does it feel to read this? Would you want to be married to that guy? Would you want him in your house, in your head? My guess is probably not…but, is he? Right now, do you have a voice in your head that does all that and more? The voice in your head may make this guy look like a kitten.

Most people would perceive this relationship as toxic and view this guy's behavior as abusive. If this were portrayed in a movie, you'd want the woman to find her self-esteem, stand up to that S.O.B., and leave his ass. When she did, everyone in the theater would cheer at her liberation and victory over his tyranny.

That's exactly what you will be doing throughout this book. You are going to wake up to all the unfair, uncaring, and cruel ways you treat yourself and see them as unhealthy and ultimately, unacceptable. You will then find your inner courage, self-respect, and self-worth, staging a revolution inside of yourself to overthrow your own inner tyrant. And then, you will discover what it's like to live life on your own side, discovering and enjoying who you are, day by day.

But first, we have to start where you are. We have to rapidly raise your awareness of how you're currently treating yourself and activate your sense of indignation at how long you've been letting yourself live like this.

HOW O.M.O.S. ARE YOU?

O.M.O.S. is an acronym that stands for On My Own Side. It describes a way of being in which you treat yourself with the same kind of care, respect, and kindness that you would someone you love. In just a bit, you will get much more clarity on what O.M.O.S. means for you and exactly what it will look like in your life to be on your own side.

But first, we have to see where you stand now. To increase your self-awareness and clarity, you will need to take a brief self-assessment to measure your level of being on your own side. This will be a great "before" snapshot so that you can compare it to your score upon completing each part of this book.

If you'd like to get a digital version of this assessment to print out to take at regular intervals, go to the book website at omosbook. com.

I suggest you create an O.M.O.S. Journal. This can be a new paper journal that you buy, or a note file in your phone or computer dedicated for notes, insights, exercises, and anything else related to your journey toward unconditional self-love.

O.M.O.S. Self-Assessment

For each row below, read both statements and rate which one feels more true to you. If the statement on the left feels accurate most of the time, circle 1. If the statement on the right feels more accurate, then circle 10. If it's somewhere in between, circle the number that feels most accurate to you. Don't overthink your answers. Complete the form quickly and go with your first gut response.

1 2 3 4 5 6 7 8 9 10	
I am hard on myself. I often judge, dislike, and feel impatient with myself.	I am on my own side. I don't criticize, attack, or berate myself.
Deep down, I wish I could be somebody else.	I love being me. I am so grateful to be me. I'm awesome.
I often feel inferior, less-than, or inadequate in some way.	I'm aware of my strengths and values, and I trust that I'm enough.
I often feel embarrassed and worried about what others think of me.	I rarely feel embarrassed. I have nothing to hide, and I'm okay with who I am.
When I hurt someone's feelings, I replay the moment for hours or days and feel so guilty.	I quickly forgive myself for making mistakes and being human and apologize if needed.
I often criticize myself for not being motivated or driven enough.	I don't pressure myself. I do the things I really want to do and let go of the rest.
I quickly blame myself if others are disappointed or disapprove of me.	I remain open and relaxed, even if someone is upset. I know I'm safe, and that being upset is an inevitable part of relationships.

1 2 3 4 5 6 7 8 9 10		
I focus on my physical flaws when looking at photos or a mirror.		I see myself as a beautiful, amazing creation. I am grateful to be in this body.
I often invalidate my own feelings, telling myself that I shouldn't feel the way I do.		I regularly move toward my feelings with curiosity, patience, acceptance, and love.
I avoid feeling my feelings by overthinking, distracting myself, or using rich foods, drugs, or alcohol.		I create time and space to fully feel my feelings, including the uncomfortable or vulnerable ones.
I drive myself hard to get more done, even if I'm tired or sick.		I slow down, listen to my body, and know when to take breaks.
No matter what I achieve, it's never enough. I don't feel satisfied with my accomplishments.		I enjoy my success and am inspired to help others experience the same.
I have a clear idea of how I "should be," and I try my best to make myself that way.		I love discovering who I am and what makes me thrive.
I need to drastically improve myself before I'll be worthy of the life I want.		I am worthy of love, deep connections, and enriching work right now, just as I am.

To determine your O.M.O.S. score, add up all of the numbers, and divide by 14.

What number did you get? How O.M.O.S. are you?

Do not get too focused on what your number means. This assessment is meant to be used as a tool rather than as a hard science data point. It gives you a general sense of where you are in this moment. Depending on what's happening in your life this week or this month, your score may be impacted. Even during the course of one day, your score might be different. And sometimes, your answers would be different if you are thinking about how you relate to yourself at work versus in your personal relationships. In that case, you can take the assessment once focused on how O.M.O.S. you are in your work life and then take it again for your personal life.

The point is to use this tool to get more clarity on how you tend to treat yourself. Notice which items raised your score and which ones brought it down. What were the two or three items that really tanked your score? These are important to note because getting fully on your own side will require you to upgrade the way you relate to yourself in these specific ways.

I suggest you write down your score somewhere with today's date next to it. Then, come back after you've read Part I of this book, and take the assessment again to measure your progress. You can then take the assessment again upon completing Parts II, III, and IV. Better yet, you can take this assessment once per week for eight weeks. Not only will you start to see trends about what triggers you to turn on yourself, but you'll also naturally start to become more on your own side simply because you are keeping this goal top of mind.

Oh, and watch out for turning on yourself for turning on yourself. Notice if you are judging yourself for your score as if you are failing at doing this O.M.O.S thing. Watch out for that perfectionism, and smile at all the sneaky ways we can block simple love and appreciation of who we are.

In fact, let's turn our attention now to just that. Let's uncover the main ways you tend to turn on yourself so that you can break through the indifference and start getting upset about all the ways this inner tyrant makes you feel bad. Let's get indignant.

Quick Note: Puppies & the Secret to Rapid Results

Throughout this book, there will be short activities and exercises that you can do in order to radically increase the speed of your results and boost your confidence. As with anything in life, if you put in a bit more effort now, your results in the long term will be dramatically different. Think compounding interest or puppies.

Last week, our family got two eight-week-old puppies, as if managing a three and five-year-old wasn't enough for my wife and me. As I was doing a crash course in dog raising, I discovered something amazing. If you spend just a few minutes each day doing training sessions with your puppy, amazing things happen fast! Within two five-minute training sessions, I had each puppy sitting. After two more sessions, they could respond to their names, sit, and stay. My mind was blown.

The same is true for you and me! So when you come across those exercises, take just a few minutes to do them. The difference in your self-confidence and life results will be noticeably different.

Chapter 2:
Straightforward,
Sneaky, And Savage

Remember that fellow from the last chapter who's always being a jerk to his wife? Imagine you approached his wife and asked her about their relationship.

"How are things going?" you ask.

"Well," she hesitates. "He's gotten a lot better with his temper. He rarely yells at me anymore."

Yikes. That doesn't sound like the big breakthrough moment that we're waiting for in the dramatic liberation scene of our imagined movie.

But, you might be doing the same thing. You may think of being "hard on yourself" as simply criticizing yourself in your head, like calling yourself "stupid" when you make a mistake or "awkward" when you have a social interaction that makes you nervous. You might say, "Well, it's not that bad. I used to treat myself way worse than I do now." And maybe that's true. But it's an awfully low bar to have your standard for a relationship to be "less harsh verbal abuse than before," isn't it?

To be on your own side, we want to go above and beyond that, way beyond. To support you in doing this, let's take a moment to uncover all the big ways you may be turning on yourself right now without even knowing it. In fact, you may not even think of these as self-attack. They might just seem like what you're supposed to do, what you've always done, what anyone would do. They might just seem...normal.

Yet even if they are common, they are not healthy. As the Indian philosopher, Jiddu Krishnamurti, famously said, "It is no measure of sanity to be well-adjusted to a profoundly sick society." So let's take a look and see what's going on in your relationship with yourself.

Below you will find the top ten most common forms of turning on yourself. Take note of the ones you tend to do most, as you will then be able to catch this happening in the moment and interrupt it.

THE WORST TOP TEN EVER

Most top ten lists are fun...like the top ten places to live in the world, top ten foods to eat for health and longevity, and the top ten strangest things billionaires have spent their money on. I'm afraid the following list is anything but fun. It's a hard look at the wide variety of ways we treat ourselves with coldness and cruelty.

As you read it, you may feel a mixture of discomfort and relief. It can be uncomfortable to see all the ways you harm yourself, especially when it's something you've been doing for years without even knowing it. This level of honesty with ourselves can make us squirm.

At the same time, you may also feel a deep sense of relief, the relief that comes from knowing that you're not alone, that you're not messed up in some way. You'll discover that everyone is doing some of the things on this list, and most people are doing most of them, most of the time. You'll realize that, sadly, it's quite normal to dismiss your accomplishments, constantly compare yourself to others, and feel somewhat dissatisfied with who you are.

Fortunately, uncovering this is just the beginning, and we aren't going to stop there. Over the course of this book, you'll learn how to become abnormal in a good way. You'll start to become a person who owns your accomplishments, feels proud of what you can do, quickly learns from mistakes and setbacks, and enjoys being you. But the pathway to all of that starts right here with this list.

Number 1: Direct Self-Attack

"I'm such an idiot."
"Why did I do that??"
"My stomach looks disgusting."
"You're so nervous and submissive. Pathetic."

These are just a few of the ten thousand sweet nothings we whisper in our own ears—each one a barbed arrow, dripping with poison. And we volley one round after another toward ourselves. This is the most obvious, and often the most overtly painful, method of turning on yourself: direct self-attack. This is when you directly, and often brutally, criticize yourself. The critical focus can be on virtually any aspect of you, including your appearance, choices, actions, habits, personality traits, feelings, and even your thoughts. Anything is fair game for the critic.

Sometimes, there may be a trigger for this onslaught of attack, such as a mistake, rejection, or failure. These inevitable experiences in life can often bring on intense and direct storms of self-hatred. Have you ever taken a step back and listened to what your critic says to you after you get rejected? Here's a surprisingly common inner monologue after a rejection:

Of course, he doesn't want to see you. You're so pathetic, weak, desperate, and needy. Disgusting. And look at you. Your arms are so fat. Your thighs are disgusting. Do you think someone like him would ever want you? Did you actually think that could happen? Come on.

This is direct self-attack. Yes, it may be how you've always reacted to rejection, and no, it's not healthy, even if it's unfortunately common and maybe, in the insane world we live in, almost normal. *You got rejected? Of course, you should hate yourself for a while! We all would. How else are you going to get motivated to fix your broken, unlovable self?*

Regardless, it's still toxic. Even if your critic's direct attacks don't have as harsh of a tone, they can still be damaging. Sometimes, for example, the critical remarks can come across as simple statements of fact or "telling it like it is":

That wasn't a good presentation. Did you see how several people were looking down? They were bored. Your voice was too monotone. The material was not engaging. Sigh. You're just not very good at presenting.[1]

While this might sound less harsh than the first example, it can have just as corrosive of an effect on your confidence.

And more important than the exact words your critic uses is the general feeling or attitude you have toward yourself. Often, you aren't even aware of a specific thought stream or inner monologue in your head. Instead, you're aware of an overwhelming sense of frustration or dislike of yourself. You feel disgust, aversion, or even hatred.

---

1   In this example of critical self-talk, the second-person pronoun, "you" is used, as if the critic is speaking directly to you. Some people experience negative self-talk in this way. Others have thoughts that include the first-person pronoun, "I". As in "I'll never be good at public speaking." Pay attention to which one your critic uses more.

Isn't this true? Think of something right now that you don't like about yourself. Perhaps it's an ongoing quality or trait, such as your hair or your height. Maybe it's your current life circumstances, such as your income or relationship status, or maybe it's certain behaviors, such as overeating, blowing up at your kids or partner, or cowering in big meetings. Notice how you feel toward yourself when you focus on this. Do you feel frustrated or upset with yourself? Dislike? Hatred? How intense does it feel?

How do you feel when you focus on it? What do you feel in your body? What expression do you have on your face?

When I do this with clients in my events and group programs, they almost always unconsciously have the same expression on their face. It's the kind of expression you automatically make when you smell something offensive or take a bite of something that tastes bad to you. It's the look of disgust. In some, it's more subtle, in others, it's obvious for all to see. But regardless, it's there.

Common triggers for this direct attack include: rejection, mistakes, setbacks, failures, not reaching targets (or not reaching them in the time frame you want), someone being upset with you, forgetting something, not being able to do a task, losing your temper, becoming anxious, weighing yourself, feeling sad or down, eating foods you view as unhealthy, seeing pictures of yourself, not knowing what to say in a conversation, witnessing others' success, or not receiving a call back from someone.

If you struggle with self-esteem, strong feelings of social anxiety, or episodes of depression, then you are no stranger to direct self-attack. In fact, these criticisms can go way beyond temporary reactions to adverse life circumstances and devolve into ongoing chronic patterns of abusive self-talk.

I spent the better part of a decade residing in chronic, daily, direct self-attack. During these years, I did not need any specific trigger to set off a harsh recounting of my failures and inadequacies. For years, every time I looked in a mirror, my inner critic unleashed a flurry of attacks about my appearance, telling me I was inferior to other men and undesirable to women.

This kind of brutal self-treatment can occur as distinct bursts of intense criticism or be dripped in steadily throughout the day like an intravenous blood drip. It's not at all uncommon to be simply thinking about your day ahead or reflecting on a recent interaction and have your critic slip some poisonous messages right into your ordinary thought stream:

> *I wonder if Eric is going to have his report done before we meet at 3:00. He seemed pressured yesterday, so who knows. Oh, I have to remember to bring my car charger today. I always forget things, I'm so spacey and forgetful, such an idiot. I also need to remember my gym bag too.*

There amongst your harmless, haphazard mental planning, your critic throws an explosive attack on your character and intelligence, like slipping a stick of TNT in your tuna sandwich.

How much do you engage in direct self-attack? Is it a daily occurrence? An hourly occurrence? Does it only happen after something goes wrong and you get rejected or fail at a task? Do you frequently use criticism to motivate yourself to take action?

Interestingly enough, you may not fully know the answer to these questions. A large amount of our self-criticism is outside our standard awareness, flying below the radar. Only when you pay attention over several days, noting when you turn on yourself and what your critic says, do you begin to see the extent of the madness.

To raise your awareness and lay the foundation for being able to regain control from your inner critic, I highly recommend this exercise. Record hatch marks on a notecard or keep a running tally in a note file on your phone, adding to it each time you notice a critical thought of yourself. As you learn more about the other forms of turning on yourself below, you can also include those in your tally. Do this for one week and notice how many daily self-criticisms you can catch.

I've had numerous clients who estimated they criticized themselves several times per day at most try this exercise. They were often shocked to discover this can happen *several dozens of times per day or more!* When they also include other forms of turning on themselves, beyond direct self-attack, the number can be truly alarming.

"*This* is how I'm talking to myself?" one client exclaimed to me after doing this exercise for a week. "I had no idea I was so terrible to myself. No wonder I feel so anxious at work."

In fact, I encourage you to go beyond simply tallying the frequency of these self-criticisms. Instead, make it a deeper study of your relationship with yourself. How is that relationship? What does it feel like to be in this kind of relationship day in and day out? Is it healthy, the way you're treating yourself?

The goal isn't just to notice the volume of the self-attack but to be moved by what you witness, to awaken a sense of aversion, revulsion, or indignation at the injustice of this kind of treatment, like when you watch an upsetting documentary about children or animals being mistreated or exploited, and there's that growing sense of outrage and an impulse for action. This is your heart awakening. This is the force of compassion moving within you. This is what you want to awaken inside yourself for it will provide the fuel needed for your upcoming inner revolution.

Number 2: Diminishing

di·min·ish - make (someone or something) seem less impressive or valuable; belittle; disparage.

Diminishing is your critic's attempt to convince you that you are small and incapable. Whether it's a project at work, a goal in your life, or a person you are romantically drawn to, your critic's diminishing message is the same: *No, you can't.*

You can't complete that project. People won't sign up for that. You can't start your own business. You can't earn good money in the world doing something you enjoy (or at all). She wouldn't want to talk with you — she's way out of your league. Someone like him has so many options; he would never want to settle down with someone like you. And on and on.

The deeper message behind this diminishing is: *You aren't good enough. Who do you think you are?*

When diminishing, the critic can target specifics, such as belittling your attempt to look professional or dress your best. It can also just adopt a general attitude of disdain and mockery. Like a cruel older sibling, your critic can create a constant sense of feeling small, inadequate, and not quite grown up enough yet. When you are believing this and seeing yourself through the eyes of your critic, you frequently feel this disdain for yourself.

Quick confession — diminishing is happening right now! As I'm writing this section, my critic is telling me: *What you're writing isn't good enough. It's too long and boring. This book won't be as good as your last. People won't like this one. You have no good stories. And besides, no one wants to hear your stories anyway; they are self-indulgent and sad attempts to make points from little life experience.*

I am well equipped to handle that critic, so I keep typing away, despite his claims. Those specific criticisms about my stories are directly drawn from the content of negative reviews of my previous books. This is a beautiful demonstration of the inner mechanics of how the critic works. We'll uncover this more in the next chapter.

The critic does not want external rejection or criticism, so it tries to get you to stop taking any risks that might lead to that. It stores memories of past rejecting statements and then uses those against you to make you stop. It may seem just as bad as the external rejection, but, according to the critic's logic, it's better and safer. While these internal slams may sting and diminish your self-esteem, they are under your control. When you put yourself out there in the world, you don't know what will come back your way, which is way more vulnerable. In fact, that's part of the definition of vulnerability—putting yourself out there and giving it your all when the outcome is uncertain. Who knows what can come back your way from the outer world and how it would feel? It could be criticism and rejection similar to what you've experienced before, or much bigger, much worse rejection. Yikes!

The more you believe this stream of belittling predictions about what you're not capable of, the more demoralized you feel, which is exactly what your critic wants! If you are convinced that new business venture couldn't work because you're not good enough, then you'll never risk failure. If you're convinced that person would never date you, then you don't face the risk of rejection. If your critic tells you that your writing sucks and no one will like your book, then you probably won't finish and publish that book.

Or, perhaps you do. Perhaps you find a way to disbelieve the critic's claims and take bold action in the face of its predictions. Perhaps you take the risk and find out your critic is completely false, and its big, scary prediction is just smoke and mirrors, smoke that you can walk right through to reach your goals and create the life you truly want. But, I'm getting ahead of myself here. Let's keep uncovering our sneaky friend's tactics.

Number 3: Discounting & Dismissing

Sadly, this form of self-treatment is exceedingly common, despite it being quite toxic. Discounting and dismissing describes an invalidating way of relating to our feelings, thoughts, and perceptions. Instead of approaching ourselves with curiosity, warmth, and empathy, we often meet our inner world with a harsh, impatient coldness.

For example, imagine you had a full and hectic day. You were rushed to get to multiple places, had some challenges at work, and then you got an upsetting phone call from a family member on your way home. You finally make it home at the end of the day, and you're exhausted. Then, you feel your phone vibrate. You glance down to see a text from a friend reminding you of a get-together you had planned. Ugh, you had totally forgotten about this, and you don't feel like going.

Enter your critic: *You can't bail out now! You can't let him down. He'd be pissed. Just pull yourself together, and get out there. Why are you so tired, anyway? It's not like you've done that much. You need to keep better track of your calendar; you're so disorganized.*

This attitude toward yourself can be so familiar that it might not even seem that critical or harsh. In fact, you may have grown up in a household where discounting and dismissing were the norm.

When you were a child and feeling something challenging, a well-intentioned (or frustrated) parent may have said something like:

"You're scared? Scared of what? Don't be scared."

"Oh, there's nothing to be sad about. Who cares if Johnny doesn't like you? You have other friends."

"Why are you feeling sorry for yourself? There are children starving in Africa."

This is just a small sample of statements that my clients' parents said to them on a regular basis. Even well-meaning parents who love you can easily convey the message: *Don't feel that way. You don't have a reason to feel that.*

The less emotionally mature your parents were, the less space they had for your emotions as a child. They were challenged enough to try to manage their own emotions with the limited level of maturity and self-awareness they possessed. When you experienced emotions and let them show, it may have felt like too much for one or both of your parents. They said or did whatever they needed to do in order to make that feeling go away and to manage their own emotions.

As adults, we carry this attitude forward to our own inner experience. When my wife experiences a challenging day as a mother, I can hear the exact phrases and even the tone in which she was spoken to as a child. She'll describe a full parenting day, including breaking up fights, cleaning up poop, and finding a way to keep the kids awake while driving in rush hour traffic, so their bedtime schedule doesn't get messed up.

As she tells me this story, I often think: *Good God, your day job is 1,000 times harder than mine.* I feel curiosity and empathy. I've been in those situations with our boys, and I know how challenging they can be. In other words, I am meeting her with love and understanding.

However, this can be absent as she relates to herself. She's telling me this story after the kids have gone to bed. She's feeling agitated and discouraged. Part of her wishes parenting was easier, that life could be a little lighter or more fun. Then, she'll say in a specific tone that doesn't sound like her at all: "Well, if I wanted it to be easier, I shouldn't have had kids. Besides, there are moms who have to do all this while working a full-time job."

What's the core message behind that? You have no right to feel upset, sad, tired, or down. In addition, you shouldn't feel anxious, scared, or overwhelmed. You should handle things better, and just feel happy, damn it!

When this discounting style doesn't make you feel better (shocking!), then your critic uses that as yet another reason to denigrate you. *Why are you always so anxious? You're always so mopy and depressed. What's wrong with you?* Then we're beating ourselves up for not feeling better after we beat ourselves up. I'm telling you, it's insanity. But as long as it's operating beneath the surface in our subconscious, it can go on undetected for years. Once you see it, however, your natural drive toward health and wholeness kicks in to clean up this whole mess.

In addition to discounting your emotional world, your critic can have a habit of discounting your strengths, successes, and wins as well. It often does this so automatically that you don't even know it's operating. You just don't seem to notice your accomplishments much. You spend almost no time focusing on what's going well, how you are showing up in powerful or inspiring ways on a regular basis. If you or someone else does call attention to your strengths or what you're doing well, your critic turns up the volume on the discounting and dismissing track.

> *So what? That wouldn't have been a big deal for someone else to do.*
> *That other business does ten times the amount of sales we do.*
> *I'm fitter now, but my body still doesn't look good enough yet.*
> *Sure, I did it, but I was nervous the entire time.*

The general tone of this kind of dismissing is it's no big deal; it's not worth focusing on or even mentioning. If your critic wants to shut this down, it can even throw some moralizing in there about how focusing on your wins is egotistical and makes you a bad person, which, in reality, is complete cockamamie.

Sports psychologists, animal trainers, teachers, parents, and research scientists all know that success builds on success.

When you can help someone achieve some small victory, they feel empowered and are more motivated to try even harder, thus succeeding more. You'll learn all about how to use this to achieve extraordinary results with more fun and less tension in the chapter on Optimal Fuel. In the meantime, watch out for that strength-smashing your critic likes to do.

One final type of discounting worth highlighting is when your critic dismisses your perspective. This leads to a pattern in which your thoughts, your assessment of a person or situation, and even what you think is right can all be immediately discounted. Imagine you just had a conversation that was somewhat unenjoyable. Perhaps it was a first date, and you were straining to find things to talk about. Or maybe you got stuck talking to someone at the dinner party who wasn't that engaging. Your simple, authentic experience might be: *Whew! I'm glad that's over. That person wasn't fun to be around at all.*

But then your critic starts to work away at you: *Why didn't you like that person? You had such a hard time coming up with things to say. You need to be a better conversationalist. Why are you so judgmental anyway? He was a nice guy, and you're too critical.*

Taken to an extreme, this form of dismissing of your own experience can lead to a total disconnection from yourself, including your desires, preferences, and even your values. You may end up going on a second date or spending more time with that potential friend that *you don't even like* because your critic discounted your own gut feelings.

Have you ever done this? Lord knows I have.

Insanity.

Number 4: Projected Dislike

This one is a doozy. For some, this is their primary method of self-criticism. Worse still, they might not even know they're criticizing themselves because they think it's "those people."

Projected dislike involves imagining others are judging you negatively, having critical thoughts, and feeling disapproval, anger, dislike, disdain or even contempt toward you. This kind of self-attack can range quite a bit in its intensity, depending on how frequently you're doing it and how strong you imagine others' dislike to be.

If you occasionally imagine others are judging you in mild ways, such as for having wrinkles in your shirt or for being slightly disorganized in a work meeting, you will only feel mild anxiety in these situations. If you imagine everyone is harshly judging you for being incompetent, and that they think you're a pathetic fraud who lucked into your position, you may feel anxiety all day long at work and be on the verge of panic before meetings.

In some cases, this projected dislike can lead to an almost delusional level of self-absorbed self-consciousness. This is the "everyone is watching me" kind of paranoia you can get when you're feeling extremely uncomfortable about something.

I've heard multiple clients describe this scenario, which captures this feeling quite well. They're walking on a sidewalk by themselves, and a car drives by. They see people in the car laughing. They're convinced with one hundred percent certainty that those people are laughing at them, and they feel a sense of embarrassment, shame, or anger.

This form of self-attack is so insidious because it often presents itself as cold hard observational science—as truth. This isn't a distorted self-criticism; this is just reality. *Those people really are judging me. They really do think I'm incompetent. They really are upset at me.* We can be utterly convinced, and it can be hard to loosen our grip on that certainty.

In fact, if a friend or loved one tries to reassure you by telling you, "Perhaps people thought your presentation was good, and they aren't harshly judging you," you may have an internal reaction of anger. It's as if your friend doesn't get you. They're not listening to you. They don't understand at all. The truth is you did a terrible job, and people think you're an idiot, end of story.

Why on earth would we cling to this perception? Why is it so hard to dislodge that sense of certainty that others dislike us? It's yet another one of your critic's sneaky tricks. It's found a backdoor to climb through, and it continues to undermine your confidence and self-esteem through a continual demoralization campaign: *others think you suck.* With that ongoing influence, you are, yet again, more hesitant to take risks, put yourself out there, and be the biggest version of you.

I've found this form of self-attack to be particularly hard to shake. For one reason, our certainty that others dislike us can cause us to act in ways that bring about more distance, thus confirming our fears. This occurs all the time in social anxiety. If I am convinced you are judging me as boring, I will tend to either hold back, change the subject, or not share fully. This constriction of my energy and lack of warmth and openness tends to be less engaging to others. Then, when you excuse yourself to speak to someone else, my critic pounces on that as confirming evidence. *Ha! You see! I am boring. Just as I suspected…*

Projected dislike, and other sneaky forms of self-attack are extremely valuable to be aware of. Because you'll soon discover that using the tools and techniques in this book, addressing and stopping direct self-attack will become surprisingly easy. But your critic will not simply stop there. Instead, it will go subterranean and start to use less direct methods, including projected dislike. Thus, I will be sharing specific techniques to catch and cease this form of self-attack as well. For now, we must cover the few remaining forms of self-criticism so you can be prepared to catch and dismantle them.

Number 5: Perfectionism

Be better.

Do more.

Accomplish more.

Oh, and do it all faster too.

This is the mantra of perfectionism. It's insidious, all-pervasive, and sometimes difficult to identify. To you, it may just feel like ambition, drive, and a desire to succeed. It may just be the natural way you approach projects, problems, and life in general. You may think it's something beneficial that sets you apart from others, gives you your edge, and makes you superior. Or, it may just seem like a necessary way to be in order to remain competitive, get ahead, and earn money to take care of yourself and your family. In fact, many perfectionists have never thought of themselves as perfectionists.

I personally never thought of myself that way. I imagined a perfectionist was someone who needed their desk to be perfectly clean and organized, and they had to rewrite an email five times before sending it. I did neither of those things—my desk is often disorganized, and I can't be bothered to proofread my emails even once. But, what I didn't realize is perfectionism is not about doing everything just right. It's a sense of pressure you place on yourself to make something happen, be a certain way, or reach a certain goal. This pressure can be summed up as: *I must do X, or else…*

The X is often something large, lofty, or ambitious. Instead of small, easily achievable goals, the perfectionist tends to set ambitious, extreme, or impossible goals, often with unreasonably short timelines. Despite this unreasonableness, most perfectionists don't see their goals as out of reach. They can have a surprisingly matter-of-fact tone as they describe all the superhuman things they should simply get done every day.

Even worse, the pressure to achieve more in less time is combined with a sense of danger or threat if these expectations are not met. The dangers are usually fabricated in our minds, sometimes citing potential threats, such as job loss, poor reviews, or rejection. Other times there is no real threat we can point to, just a sense of: *if I don't get this all done now, bad things are going to happen.*

These high expectations often run rampant at work but are by no means limited to this area of our lives. We can bring the same sense of urgency, pressure, and danger to socializing, hosting a party, or parenting "just right." We can demand flawless perfection socially so that everyone adores us and is duly impressed by our charm and wit. We can pressure ourselves to be emotionally perfect, only feeling the positive end of the emotional spectrum in life, and never feeling sad, down, scared, or stuck. We can demand perfect performances in all we do, ranging from work projects, to music and art, to even casual hobbies and games. We can be perfectionists about learning something new, expecting ourselves to leapfrog through the beginning stages and be significantly more advanced than we possibly could be. And we can demand that we be the perfect parent who never gets upset, always knows what to do, and has perfectly behaved little children that impress your friends and family with their polite manners.

Many people don't realize this, but social anxiety and the demand to be socially perfect often go together. Social anxiety is born out of a deep feeling of insecurity, a sense that I'm not okay as I am, so I'd better interact with people just right so that I don't mess it up.

When I struggled with intense social anxiety, many situations would challenge me, but nothing came close to those good old fashion group introductions. You know the ones I'm talking about, where you go around the room, and each person says something about themselves — where they're from, what business they're in, something unique about themselves, whatever.

In these situations, my mind would be on hyperdrive before it was my turn. I would be planning and preparing the absolute best introduction that any human has ever given. As each person before me introduced themselves, I didn't pay attention to the content of what they were sharing; I focused intently on how they were presenting it. Were they charming, funny, and confident? Did others seem impressed? If not, they're a loser, and I was better than them. If so, then I had to up my game, so I'd beat them. Sound crazy? It sure was.

As it got closer to me, I couldn't even pay attention and rate other's performances. I was fully self-absorbed, rehearsing my "off-the-cuff" charming intro. And then, it was me–showtime. I'd introduce myself in the way I had planned. Sometimes, I'd pull it off with all the external confidence I imagined, and other times I could detect a tremor or hint of anxiety in my voice. If so, I considered myself a failure. Even if I did pull it off just as I'd hoped, at best I'd experience a sense of relief as if I'd just passed an exam. Perfectionist? Who's a perfectionist? Certainly not me...

As a result of all these internal demands, we're always on guard and can feel a relentless sense of pressure to be "ON," do it better, and somehow be better than we are. This kind of attitude can quickly expand from a situation-specific problem into an entire way of approaching the world and our lives. When in the grips of this form of self-attack, we can live in a perpetual feeling of inadequacy, not-quite-enough-yet, and discontent. There is a chronic background noise of criticism cataloging our endless inadequacies. Setbacks, failures, rejections, and even minor delays in our plans for perpetual, rapid progress can bring on intense bouts of pessimism, discouragement, and self-loathing.

But, hey, this is the price of success, right? Isn't this just what it takes to get ahead? Maybe...

Number 6: Relentless Busyness

This form of turning on ourselves is closely related to perfectionism. When we set unrealistic time frames for our unrealistic goals and combine that with a sense of danger if we don't meet our inner demands, we create a breeding ground for relentless busyness. This form of self-attack is so commonplace and so subtle that we may not even initially see it as a form of turning against ourselves. In fact, you may be celebrated at first for your productivity, ambition, and ability to get things done. You are a mover and a shaker. You're also a stressed-out, tense, anxious, basket-case inside. But who cares? You're making money, keeping your house clean, getting all the meals made for the family, staying in great shape, becoming a sought-after socialite, and whatever else is on your list.

So when does being busy and productive turn into a form of self-attack? When it becomes perpetually stuck in the "ON" position. When you are getting signals from your body that you are gunning the engine too hard and you don't slow down, stop, and listen. You think to yourself: *I don't have time for this right now, I have too much to do!* And so you keep blazing ahead at maximum speed, as fast as your engines can handle.

Even when there are potential moments of downtime, such as in between projects or tasks, or at the tail end or beginning of your day, you don't slow down. There is no slowing down, no gaps. Or the gaps are filled with subprojects and mini-tasks, or frantic, aimless fiddling with your phone, social media, games, or email.

While it may not seem like it at first glance, this kind of relentless busyness is a subtle act of harming yourself. Your autonomic nervous system, which is in charge of your fight-flight-freeze response, is in perpetual go mode. Your adrenal glands are firing off adrenaline and cortisol all day long, without a chance to rest and recover. Over time, your body will break down from this kind of stress, especially when early warning signals of tension, fatigue, anxiety, stomach pain, headaches, or body aches are ignored. When this pattern continues long enough, more significant health issues can occur, including heart disease, peptic ulcers, colitis, and even cancer.[2]

In addition, this kind of constant busyness keeps our focus on the external world. We can go through a day, or even an entire week, without really feeling what is happening inside. Our desires and mixed feelings, the longing in our hearts, and all the richness of our inner world are swept aside as we barrel forward toward external achievement. This can lead to increased feelings of anxiety, difficulty sleeping, a depressed mood, or just a general feeling of emptiness inside that is hard to pinpoint.

Within modern-day, economically dominant, competitive societies, such as the U.K., Japan, China, Australia, the United States, and increasingly in more and more countries all over the globe, this kind of relentless busyness is generally accepted as the norm. Of course, you are constantly on the go, working long hours, and glued to your devices when you're supposedly off of work and spending time with your family. How else are you gonna get ahead in the corporation, or grow your own business?

This is a complex topic because accelerating in your career to impact more people and create a more rewarding financial future for yourself and your family is a worthy goal. Creating and growing your own business is a lot of work, but also one of the most beneficial risks you can ever take in your life. So the answer is not to simply avoid all the stress and busyness or avoid ambitious goals and dreams. The answer, as you might have already guessed, is to learn how to take on more while remaining on your own side. It's to prioritize being on your own side *first* over completing that next task or reaching that next monetary milestone in your career

---

2   For a fascinating and eye-opening look at how your physical health is impacted by your psychology, emotions, work, and life choices, I highly recommend Lisa Rankin's book: *Mind Over Medicine*.

at breakneck speed. We will discuss this in much more depth later in this book in the chapter on Optimal Motivation.

Number 7: Should City

What's it like to fall short every day? To work all day long with minimal breaks, being as productive as you can and then feel like it's not enough? To go out on a date and feel like you're not measuring up? Your clothes aren't good enough, you don't know enough about the right topics, your stories are not exciting enough, and you aren't as glamorous, beautiful, or cool as the person you're talking with. What's it like to not be a good enough son or daughter, to fail at giving your parents what they want and need? To fall short as a father or mother so many times?

Is it exhausting? It sure feels that way to me. Even just reading this last paragraph is exhausting. Because living in Should City is brutal. Should City is the world you've constructed for yourself in which there are a hundred and one rules of how you should be to be a good, worthwhile, lovable person. A world of right and wrong, good and bad. These constructs create your criteria for measuring your self-worth. For example:

I should be funnier.
I should never yell at my kids.
I shouldn't be irritable.
I should get more done.
I should want to spend more time with my parents.
I should be thinner.

I could go on. In fact, in my previous book, *Not Nice*, readers create the list of all the shoulds they tell themselves on a regular basis. If you haven't done this, it's a valuable exercise and one that will greatly help you build the skill of being on your own side.

Write out everything you tell yourself you should or should not do on a regular basis. Start by thinking of each of the major areas of your life, including work, friendships, romantic relationships (including sex), fitness and health, money, parenting, and family. What do you tell yourself you should be in these areas? How should you never be?

Then, over the next week, notice when you feel stressed, anxious, irritable, or down during the day. Pause and take a few slower, deeper breaths, listening to the stream of thoughts in your mind. What shoulds are passing through? Undoubtedly, you will discover even more than your original list, which, surprisingly enough, is a good thing!

Each should you discover brings it out of your subconscious programming and into the realm of awareness, where you can let it go. It's possible to completely free yourself from the toxic shoulds that your critic has been beating you with for years. Over the course of this book, you will find those dissolving, deconstructing, or being destroyed. And as each restrictive rule turns to debris and dust, you will feel lighter and lighter, more free to be you.

Because, as you'll see in the next chapter, we all learned early in our lives how we are *supposed* to be in order to be a "good" person who's worthy of love and belonging. The shoulds provide the guidelines that you must live by in order to earn this worth. This is highly problematic, however, when the rules you've been given are extreme, unrealistic, conflicting, or simply not right for you.

When this happens, all the unexamined shoulds you try to live by become extremely life-restricting. It's not you being you. It's you trying to contort yourself to fit into a mold that parents, family, school, and others have constructed for you. It's you spending a great deal of your precious life force trying to smash yourself back into that mold, even though it's clearly not the right fit for you.

A big part of O.M.O.S. is letting go of who you think you're supposed to be to discover who you truly are. And then, you'll use your courage to act on what you discover, to take the small and big risks to be who you are, and see what comes back to you from the world at large.

Number 8: Catastrophizing

This form of self-attack consists of you freaking yourself out. When you're doing this, you are the writer, director, and producer of your own horror show, which you regularly screen for yourself throughout the day.

You habitually predict worst-case scenarios as imminent, which leads to high levels of anxiety, fear, stress, and dread. An upcoming presentation at work could be a traumatic moment that leads to utter public humiliation and your termination from the company. You don't hear back from the person you recently started dating, which is clear evidence that he felt nothing for you and is currently out on a date with someone better than you. Things are going well in your life now, but the economy could turn, your children could get sick, and death and ruin may be right around the next corner.

You may attempt to deal with these impending calamities by kicking into hyperdrive, over-preparing, rehearsing, planning, ruminating, and otherwise trying to protect yourself. Or you may reside in a stew of bubbling anxiety that squeezes your stomach and chest all day, wakes you up at four in the morning, and makes it hard to smile or find joy in life. Either way is brutally unpleasant and can go on for days or weeks surrounding a stressful event.

And then, somehow, you are graced with the wings of the eagle! You survive that meeting! Better yet, you do quite well. In fact, come to think of it, you typically have done well in that kind of environment before. You spoke clearly and convincingly, and the big wigs with their fancy shirts, uncomfortably tight shoes, and sharp haircuts nodded and seemed impressed. Your new lover called you back and is excited to invite you on a weekend getaway to Snowy Mountain cozy cabins.

What a relief! It was all in your head. How silly of you to get so lost in fear. You heave a sigh of relief, smile, and enjoy your life again...for a few moments. But then, remember, you have that report due at the end of the month. And it's unclear if division B is on track to hit their numbers by the end of the year. If they don't, that would be pretty bad for you. It just might be the very thing that turns the top brass against you, leaving you fired, jobless, and penniless under the Burnside Bridge. Oh, no!

We repeat this pattern of catastrophizing, rumination, and worry endlessly. Each new situation seems truly unique, alarming, and worthy of stress and worry. And yet, the issue is not the situations in our lives. The real problem is the mental pattern of creating catastrophic and painful events and then living them hundreds of times in our imaginations.

After practicing this negative mental rehearsal countlessly, our minds don't even need to imagine worst-case scenarios anymore. Instead, we simply feel stressed or anxious most of the time, bracing ourselves against whatever unfortunate event might befall us that day. Instead of it being a series of truly scary fantasies, it becomes the background tension of anxiety and doom that darkens your mood and sucks the joy out of your life.

This is an act of turning on yourself. It's harmful to your mind, emotions, and nervous system. It damages your sense of security, safety, trust, and self-esteem, which, in turn, hinders your creativity, drive, and capacity to engage in meaningful work. It makes it nearly impossible to enjoy the present, relax and be with loved ones, and appreciate your life as it's happening.

Gaining control over this mental pattern is a key step in remaining on your own side and is something we will cover in this book.

Number 9: Self-Sabotage

"But I learned fast how to keep my head up 'cause I
know I got this side of me that
wants to grab the yoke from the pilot and just
fly the whole mess into the sea."

- "Young Pilgrims" by the Shins

There are two major kinds of self-sabotage, and as the name implies, they are forms of turning on yourself. One is good old-fashioned do-nothing-ism. This involves not getting started, not taking consistent action, procrastinating, avoiding, and otherwise not doing the steps needed to make progress or create the life you want. As a result, your health, or your love life, or your work situation, or whatever would benefit from a chunk of focused effort doesn't improve.

We often don't start because we believe some toxic, limiting story about how we won't be able to achieve what we want (a.k.a. diminishing). Or, we imagine we need to do it all at once and feel overwhelmed and confused, and before we know it, we've spent the last forty minutes lost in a wormhole on the internet.

The other side of self-sabotage occurs once you're in motion. It kicks into full gear when you are starting to achieve awesome results in one or more key areas of your life. Instead of nodding your head and smiling because you know you're awesome and enjoying the fruits of your labor, some part of you grabs the yoke from the pilot and jams the plane straight toward the mountain.

Gay Hendricks has a brilliant book about this subject called *The Big Leap*, which describes the "upper limit problem." This is when we exceed the upper limits of what we think we deserve in any area of our lives. If we've lived under the guidance of the critic for many years (as most of us have), then we tend to see ourselves as mediocre, at best. Who are we to stand out, shine, earn money, receive recognition, be deeply loved for who we are, or receive great things in life?

As an example, I'm writing this section while flying first class on an airplane to Florida. I've flown first class only one other time in my life, and that was about twenty-five years ago as a kid. There's a strong voice in my head that tells me I don't need that, and so I never do, even though I can afford it.

But one month ago, when I was booking my travel accommodations, I saw a first-class upgrade for an additional $300, when typically it's $1,000 or more. The thought of spending six hours on a plane in first class was too enticing, so I bought it.

Flash forward a month later, to the day before departure. I haven't told anyone I'm flying first class, not even my wife, who I share everything with. I imagine she will judge me. "You don't need that, Aziz. Why are you wasting money on that?"

In addition to "wasting money," I imagine others being angry at me for having good things in life. "Ooh, look at you in your fancy first-class flight. That pisses me off. You piss me off. I don't like you anymore."

This is a demonstration of the upper limit problem in action. Some part of me feels that I don't deserve the good things in life and that getting them will make others dislike me. Can you relate to this? Where do you hold back, limit yourself, or otherwise play small out of the fear that others will dislike you? What do you hide? Do you restrain happiness, joy, excitement, enthusiasm, possessions, hobbies, or stories of your travels out of a fear of upsetting others?

Discovering this form of self-attack is a major step in liberating yourself from it. This fear of the rejection of others can lead to significant self-sabotage in business, career, and finances. We can hold ourselves back from taking risks, earning more, or stepping into leadership positions to avoid these unexamined fears and uncomfortable feelings.

This doesn't just happen with money and work. We can feel undeserving of any significant thing we want in life. For example, you may not feel worthy of being loved for who you are, so you gain weight and use that as a reason to not date (i.e., I have to lose it first, *then* I'll start dating), or struggle to find suitable dating partners, or enter into romantic relationships where you are not treated well.

Basically, when things get good, we get uneasy. Something's not right here. Something bad is going to happen. This feeling of unease can come from your personal experiences growing up, including what your parents taught you about life—explicitly and implicitly. We will discuss this more in the next chapter, but for now, it's important to see that sabotaging ourselves when things are getting better is another form of sneaky self-attack.

Number 10: Critical Comparisons

No matter how good your life is or how amazing you truly are, in less than a second, your critic can take control of your mood and make you feel instantly demoralized. All it has to do is find another person who is "better" than you.

Better in what way? That depends on your measuring stick.

What metric you use for comparison varies based on your culture, gender, and values. For example, if you are a young woman in a society that places high value on a specific ideal body image (such as the United States or South Korea), then you will most likely compare your beauty to women around you and in the media, finding yourself lacking in comparison. If you value being financially successful in your business, then you might compare your revenue from last year to someone else's and feel worthless.

In a heartbeat, all your strengths, hard work, and positive qualities are wiped away in your mind. None of that matters. She is prettier than you. He is smarter and a better businessman than you. You are nothing.

This is the nature of these critical comparisons. They all plug back into your worth as a human being. It's not just that he earns more money than you (which may be factually accurate). It's that he earns more money than you and therefore is a superior human. You are not as intelligent, bold, outgoing, or valuable as him. And therefore you are nothing.

It sounds extreme when you read it here, but this is the mental game we play with ourselves all day long. And by game, I mean a form of sadistic torture. When I was in high school and beginning my decade-long peak of social anxiety, I engaged in this horrible anti-confidence morning ritual.

I would take long showers in the morning before school, during which I would spend a great deal of time just standing there, letting the hot water hit my back. I would mentally catalog every single way my good friend Chris was better than I was. He was taller, more athletic, more muscular, better looking, richer, better with women, way better at drawing and artistic creations, and knew more about movies and pop culture. And he was way better at soccer too.

My mind carried on like a prosecuting attorney making an extended closing argument. Furthermore, ladies and gentlemen of the jury, not only is Aziz inferior to Chris across all of the afore-mentioned qualities; I'm afraid it gets worse. You see, there is not one thing that Aziz is as skilled or accomplished at as Chris. Even Aziz's best qualities and skills come nowhere close to Chris'. And so, that is why it is clear as the sky is blue, that Aziz is an inferior human to Chris. Thus forth, I suggest to you that he is not worthy of love, connection, dates, or a sense of confidence.

That prosecutor had my number. The crazy thing is I would regularly do this in the shower. Why on earth would I keep doing this to myself? How could I possibly think that was a helpful morning ritual before school? It turns out, I didn't. I wasn't thinking about it at all. This kind of self-abuse operated behind the scenes, underneath my conscious awareness.

Cartoon by Travis Kotzebue 2019

WORST TOP TEN RECAP

1. **Direct Self-Attack:** Chronic, often intense direct criticism of any aspect of yourself, including your character, choices, actions, feelings, or physical appearance.

2. **Diminishing:** Habitually seeing yourself as small and incapable of accomplishing, learning, and doing what it takes to create the life you want.

3. **Discounting & Dismissing:** Ignoring your feelings and preferences, disregarding your strengths and values, and generally treating yourself with little or no empathy.

4. **Projected Dislike:** Imagining that others frequently experience a strong dislike of you and feeling like their negative view of you is somehow warranted.

5. **Perfectionism:** An intense, fear-driven pressure to achieve more and excel at work and perform flawlessly in relationships, love, hobbies, or emotions.

6. **Relentless Busyness:** Living at full speed with minimal time for breaks, reflection, slowing down, or feeling your body, emotions, heart, and spirit.

7. **Should City:** Trying to adhere to all of the rules you have for yourself in order to be a good person who is worthy of love and belonging.

8. **Catastrophizing:** Freaking yourself out by imagining bad things, pain, and misery are just around the corner and that you can't handle it.

9. **Self-Sabotage:** Feeling discomfort when things go well in your life due to an underlying sense of being undeserving. It can lead to never starting, procrastination, or stopping the effective action that leads to positive results.

10. **Critical Comparisons:** Comparing yourself to others who you perceive as better than you based on specific metrics and then feeling demoralized, dissatisfied, or inadequate.

How many of these can you relate to? We might be doing all of these at some point during the week, month, or year. And this list is by no means comprehensive in covering every single way we can turn on ourselves. What about excessive guilt for minor infractions and an inability to forgive yourself? Or staying in a toxic situation in which you are getting bullied? Or eating disorders and body dysmorphia? The list goes on, my friend. But the ten big ones seemed sufficient for our purposes. We're not here to create: *301 Ways to Hate Yourself, a List.*[3] We're here for liberation.

Part of that liberation requires increasing your awareness to be able to notice when you are turning on yourself, so you can intervene and shift to a better way of relating to yourself. Which of these top ten do you do most often? What are your go-to methods of turning on yourself? Start to become familiar with the most common ways in which you turn on yourself, for this will help you break free faster.

Soon, you'll learn how to interrupt these toxic habits and relate to yourself in a much more compassionate, empathic, loving, and sane way. You will also dismantle the underlying demands, pressures, and fears that create all that self-criticism in the first place. But before you learn those tools, there is one very important question we must answer: Why?

Why do you do it? Why are you so hard on yourself?

Why is everyone so hard on themselves? Why are self-hatred and a chronic feeling of inadequacy the norm? What's happening here?

---

3   If you ARE interested in a more comprehensive list of ways we hate ourselves, I recommend Dr. Theodore Rubin's book *Compassion and Self-Hate: An Alternative to Despair* for a deep study in the mechanics of self-hatred. It's an uncomfortable and slightly alarming read but also extremely liberating. But it's not more liberating than this book because Teddy's not better than me. He's not!

Chapter 3:
Origins

Why are you so hard on yourself? Have you ever thought about that in-depth? Let's take a look. Why do you pressure yourself to do more, criticize yourself for not being enough, and berate yourself when you make a mistake? Why do you treat yourself with so little empathy and so much impatience? Take a moment to reflect on this now and see what the first answers are that pop into your mind.

When I ask clients this, they usually give me one of two answers. First, people will say without hesitation, "It makes me a better version of me." Being hard on myself is like using the whip to make sure I perform better, look better, work better, exercise better, socialize better, have sex better, smile better, talk better, and generally be an impressive human, ideally better than most other people. At the very least, this harsh treatment ensures that I perform adequately. That way, I'll "get there" and finally "be somebody." I'll get respect, affection, love, and approval from others (and ideally a little envy or awe thrown in for good measure).

Secondly, people are hard on themselves because they believe this ensures they'll be a "good person." They have this chronic, painful feeling in the background that they are inherently selfish, lazy, or somehow not okay as they are. As a result, they have to be vigilant and constantly criticize or punish the "bad" parts of themselves to keep them in line. Otherwise, they fear they'll say whatever, do whatever, eat whatever, and be an out-of-control, hurtful, bad human. This will lead to a loss of relationships, jobs, and affection and approval from others.

Do you relate to one or both of these? Is that why you do it? Is that why you treat yourself with harshness, cruelty, and a lack of warmth and empathy? Is that really the best way to motivate yourself to achieve more of your potential? Is that how you motivate children, team members, or loved ones? Do you constantly police your partner and point out how bad she is when she falls short of your "good person" standards?

Once again, we see that we are not treating ourselves like we treat the people we love. In fact, our answers to "Why do you do it?" have a strangely defensive tone to them, like the partner of an abusive husband explains his unacceptable behavior. "He only acts that way because he gets so worried about us." "He is hard on the kids because he just wants them to succeed so badly."

Why do we defend the way we treat ourselves? Why do we think it's reasonable and wise to keep doing it? Or, even if we don't think it's helpful, why is it so hard to stop?

The answer to that lies in the origins of your inner critic. We are going to explore these in this chapter briefly. There is so much depth we can go into here that we could spend the entire book just exploring the genesis of your inner critic. But, we don't want to get lost in the weeds. We just want you to discover how this critic was created. Because if it was created, then it can be destroyed, dismantled, and released.

Hence, we will strike back in time to uncover the origins of your critic. This will help you get instant clarity on why you treat yourself this way and what keeps the pattern running. This will help you as you learn the tools to combat your critic because you'll already know why it's there and what it needs to calm down. Are you ready? Let's begin.

Where Does It Come From?

To put it simply, your inner critic is born out of pain. You have had countless moments throughout your life when you experienced painful emotions like grief, abandonment, betrayal, anxiety, despair, helplessness, guilt, fear, hatred, humiliation, jealousy, and panic.

Your critic is a mental pattern that your psyche created to respond to this pain in an attempt to minimize or control it. It's an attempt to solve a problem that felt too overwhelming to address at the time it occurred in your life. This "solution" ends up perpetuating the pain and trapping all these old emotions inside of you, under a lid of self-judgment. No, it's not a good solution. But it was what came to you at the time, and it served a purpose. Soon, you will not need it anymore, and you can release it with love and gratitude.

There have been many sources that contributed to these painful emotions over the years. We will be exploring three of these sources in this book: Family, Peers, and Culture.

FAMILY

"Children swim in their parents' unconscious
like fish swim in the sea."
- *In The Realm of Hungry Ghosts*, Gabor Maté

Your first source of emotional pain was your family as you were growing up. No matter who you are and how amazing your parents may have been, you still experienced pain growing up.[4] This is an unavoidable aspect of the human experience.

Your parents, like all humans, are a mixture of things. In moments, they can be loving, caring, and deeply devoted to you and your development. In other moments, they can be impatient, emotionally distant, dismissive, controlling, or harsh.

When they expressed upset, disapproval, judgment, or hostility toward you, this impacted your mind, heart, and nervous system. You may have felt fear, overwhelm, sadness, or great pain in these moments. You also may have felt uneasy or insecure that you might lose their love and approval forever.

If your parents were self-aware, mature, and capable of creating deep attachment bonds, then they would quickly come to their senses after an outburst or rupture. They would move toward you after being distant or critical, take ownership for their behavior and sometimes discuss what happened or apologize. This can instantly repair the rupture and create a sense of being seen, respected, and valued. Your nervous system relaxes, and all is well.

But what if your parents lacked the capacity and emotional maturity to make this skillful repair? After my dad exploded in anger at my brother or me, the end of his outburst was signaled by a hand over my shoulder and a change in his demeanor. I could tell the storm had passed, and he was no longer upset. This was his way of repairing the rupture and reassuring me that all was well.

However, this kind of communication is usually not fully received in a child's nervous system. He or she still has quite a few unresolved and unfelt feelings rolling around in there. She might still feel scared, hurt, or angry.

4   If your initial caretakers were someone other than your parents, then mental swap the word "parent" for whoever initially took care of you, such as a grandparent, foster parent, or relative.

Furthermore, all of us have a capacity to absorb emotions from others. Have you ever been around someone who's anxious and stressed out and barking at others? How long does it take before you start to feel agitated and on-edge yourself? The energy of our emotions is not contained within our skin but rather emanates outward.

Young children are quite receptive to absorbing other's emotions, especially those of their parents and other family members. This means that the young child might also absorb her parent's anger, overwhelm, guilt, or rejection.

That's a lot of feelings happening in that moment. Wouldn't it be nice to talk about them, share them out loud, breath deeply, be hugged and heard, and allow the energy to be released in that moment? I'm guessing that's not how things went down in your house growing up. Mine, neither. Although now, that's exactly what my wife and I do with our children to prevent the build-up of trapped emotions and inner criticism.[5]

Instead, you may have received a pat on the back or some minimal communication indicating that your parent was no longer upset. In many families, not only is there no space for residual emotion to be acknowledged, but these feelings are actively dismissed and discouraged.

"Stop crying, or I'll give you something to cry about!"

"Aww, are you sad? Poor baby."

"Are you still upset about that? It was just a joke. You're so sensitive."

It's okay. Your parents are not bad or even to blame. They were doing the best they could with the level of self-awareness and emotional maturity they had at that time. They were under the programming and control of their own upbringing and carrying out patterns that were imposed upon them as children. They

---

5   If you're a parent and interested in bringing O.M.O.S. into your parenting, there's an appendix at the end of this book dedicated to that!

are terrified of their own emotions and unable to handle them, feeling overwhelmed. Thus, they had to keep all emotions to a minimum, including those in their children.

This kind of relating has a big impact on us because we remember pain and use our brains to try to avoid pain again. We rapidly and unconsciously assess the situation, trying to determine what brought on the pain so that we can prevent it from happening again. The only problem is we don't have that kind of control over other people. But that doesn't stop us from coming up with all kinds of strategies to prevent pain and get us the love we have always wanted.

~~

"Come on, Aziz!"

My dad's booming voice echoed across the open soccer field as I chased down the ball. I panted as I ran as fast as I could, my legs burning with exhaustion. Then, there was the moment of impact. I grunted as we collided, scrambling to gain control of the ball. He won. He was stronger and faster.

My dad made a hissing sound with his mouth, indicating frustration, exasperation, and disappointment. The other player took off back down the field, and I gave chase. But he remained in front of me, then passed the ball off. The skirmish was over, and I had lost. My dad or my coach may have then yelled something about me needing to try harder or have more intensity. Then, we repeated the cycle a dozen more times that half of the game.

Fortunately, during the second half, we switched directions, and I was on the side of the field opposite my dad and the coach. Whew, what a relief! From that distance, I could only hear when they yelled out across the field at me. From that distance, their disappointment in me was less palpable.

I struggled like this for years on the soccer field. My dad would often get heated during games and shout out his desires for me to perform better or vent his anger at my failures. He often kept it to the field, but sometimes, his disappointment was too much to hold inside, and the car ride home would be a frustrated lecture about my lack of effort.

As a kid, I had no idea why my dad acted like this. As an adult, I have some pretty good guesses. Getting deeply invested in the game and yelling was the culture of competitive youth soccer, and many other coaches and parents did it. Also, as a spectator of professional soccer, fans yell, boo, and celebrate with great emotional intensity based on the moment to moment developments on the pitch. My dad may have been swept up in the game and rooting for his favorite player—me.

He also may have been unconsciously using the soccer field as an outlet for his pent up emotions. He had a stressful job running a small tech company and didn't have many tools for processing fear, anger, and other emotions. The sidelines of the soccer field were the perfect place to rant and yell in a socially acceptable way, thus discharging some of the tension in his nervous system.

As a young kid, I didn't consider any of this. I only saw my dad extremely disappointed and frustrated with me, and I felt terrible inside. Several days before Saturday, which is when we had our games, I felt a mounting sense of dread. As we drove to the game, all the other kids would talk and laugh in the van, but I would sit in silence. Right before the whistle blew to signify the start of the game, I would feel an intense form of anxiety that bordered on panic.

This carried on for years, weekend after weekend. What was there to do? Speak up for myself and tell my dad I didn't want to play anymore? Tell him I hated the way he spoke to me at the games? Quit the team and refuse to play? All reasonable options, but I lacked the assertiveness and courage to stand up to my dad or disappoint him further. Instead, I created a fantasy self.

YOUR FANTASY SELF

In order to deal with emotional pain when we are young, we create an unconscious fantasy in which the pain stops, and we finally get the love and attention we so deeply need and desire. We take cues from our parents' preferences to see what we must be like in order to live out this fantasy. For example, I began to create a fantasy that if I were just faster, stronger, and a better athlete, then I would get my dad's love and approval. And all that pain would disappear. Instead of feeling frustrated and disappointed, he'd feel proud and excited. He'd praise me during and after the game, and I'd feel happy and proud. Furthermore, he'd also magically develop more capacity for presence and focused attention on me, have a deep interest in getting to know me, and take delight in looking into my eyes and being together.

All of this is unconscious, of course. Our minds figure it out the same way we figure out how to hold an object in a comfortable way after picking it up a dozen times. Our hand just goes into the right position without us even consciously figuring anything out.

I wonder what fantasy version of yourself you concocted in response to the pain in your childhood?

When I begin to explore this with clients, there are often a few obstacles that arise. First, they might feel some resistance to exploring their childhood—they question the point or judge it as self-indulgent. They see it as criticizing or blaming their parents or betraying them in some way. When this happens, I remind clients that we're not here to blame anyone; we're here to uncover the origin of their poor treatment of themselves, so we can heal it at the root, once and for all. I know how complex our relationship with our parents can be and that they were not "all good" or "all bad." They were just human beings, like you and me, doing the best they could at that time in their life.

As far as it being self-indulgent or somehow a waste of time to reflect on specific aspects of your childhood in order to grow, this is the voice of avoidance speaking. It has a dismissive and critical aspect to it, doesn't it? In fact, it may be the voice of your inner critic! It doesn't want you to go poking around in there, exploring pain from the past. That's the exact thing your critic is designed to protect you from, and the last thing it wants is for you to uncover some pain that you need to heal.

Finally, one other major obstacle that blocks people from uncovering the origins of their critic is the "everything was fine" stance. I had this stance for many years of my life. It goes something like this: *I had a good childhood. My parents loved me, we had a stable home, and no one was drinking or violent. Everything was fine.*

Which, in one perspective, is true. You may have been protected from more intense forms of pain, loss, or abuse. However, what I did not realize until I had children of my own and began to study child development both in books and through my own 24-hour teachers — my kids — is that children require some essential emotional nutrients in order to thrive. And if we don't get one or more of these nutrients, we can experience intense emotional pain.

The Essential Four

There are four essential things that young children need in order to develop healthy confidence, self-esteem, and emotional awareness:

1. **Physical Safety:** Children need consistent access to food, shelter, and a stable living environment. Receiving this creates a sense of predictability and control that allows

children to relax and feel safe in the world.

2.   **Witnessed and Known:** Children need at least one adult
     who is able to be present with them, observing them as
     they cry, crawl, walk, and eventually talk, dance, and play
     games. Through this witnessing, the parent deeply knows
     the child, including their personality style, preferences,
     fears, strengths, and quirks. This allows the child to
     feel deeply seen, preventing loneliness, and providing
     a sense of belonging and worthiness of connection and
     love. This "being seen" also creates safety and relaxes the
     nervous system.

3.   **Seen as Significant:** Children need to feel like their
     thoughts, desires, perceptions, and feelings matter and
     that they matter. They need a parent who relates to them
     in a way that communicates that their effort, struggle,
     accomplishments, failures, interests, thoughts, feelings,
     and desires are worthy of attention. Getting this need
     met allows the child to see themselves and their life as
     meaningful and worthwhile.

4.   **Loved for Who You Are:** Children need to feel
     loved and accepted for who they are. This requires
     maturity and growth of the parent's capacity to love
     with fewer conditions and demands, not just when
     the child conforms to their preferences. This leads to
     looser control of the child and a greater respect for
     their individuality and sovereignty. Through this, the
     child learns that they, in all their colors, are worthy of
     belonging, connection, and love. This leads to a capacity
     to take risks, be authentic, share openly, and create
     mutually rewarding relationships based on honesty and
     respect of other people's individuality.

Which of these needs were consistently met in your family growing up? And which ones weren't? Did one parent more fully meet some of these needs than another? I suggest you take some time to reflect on this over the next few weeks. You can journal about it for twenty minutes, several times per week. You can go for a long walk or jog with no headphones and think back to when you were young. Pick different ages or time periods, such as when you first went to school, moved to a new house, or other events from your past.

At first, you may experience some resistance to doing this. For me personally, my inner critic was very dismissive of reflecting on my childhood, often saying things like: *Oh, boohoo. So your dad didn't give you the attention you wanted. You got lots of attention from your mom, and your dad was working hard to support you and give you all the opportunities you've had in life.*

Watch out for this kind of dismissive thinking. It might sound like a mature perspective of acknowledgment of my parents and gratitude for what they gave me, but it's not that at all. It's me blocking the pain of what I'd find when I go a bit deeper. It's about dismissing my own emotional experience and trying to get me to think or feel the "right way." It's me enforcing the same patterns that I learned from my parents growing up!

There is no objective measurement here of what you should or shouldn't feel. This is about discovering what your experience was and how you felt and feel about it. For years after my two sons' births, as we raised them through their infancy and early childhood years, I often felt a profound sense of ache, sadness, longing, and loneliness in my heart. I will share more about this later, but what I discovered was raising my two boys made me acutely aware of the lack of deep emotional connection I had with my dad growing up. I didn't feel witnessed and known or seen as significant by him. My mind would attempt to interrupt the feelings by saying: *But you had that from your mom. That should be enough. Stop moping about it!*

More noise. More resistance. More avoidance. Who's to say what's enough? Who's to say the right amount from one person or another? Let go of these ideas; they are just arbitrary decisions about what you should or shouldn't feel. Instead, let yourself explore and feel freely and fully. Become curious about the little boy or girl inside and listen closely to what he or she is saying to you. You don't need to come to some conclusion or fixed perspective about whether what happened was right or wrong, good or bad. All you're doing is uncovering underlying feelings and bringing your conscious awareness to them, which will help them move and dissolve.

You don't have to run out and talk with your parents about any of this. In fact, I'd encourage you not to do that until you've finished this book. Because while your relationship with them may have been part of the origin of your critic, now the monster is in your head. It's not "out there" or "them," it's in you! And that is where we must face it, deal with it, and overthrow it. Once you've become much more on your own side and have a much greater capacity to neutralize your own inner critic, you can explore the option of having a heart to heart with one or both of your parents. They may have matured greatly since you were young and be able to talk openly with you and fully hear about your experience. Or maybe they are still incapable of this. For now, stay focused on doing your own inner work and give yourself the freedom to fully explore and feel anything and everything.

Super Better

It hurts to be ignored or repeatedly chastised and criticized or forced to be different than who you are because a parent or authority told you to. We might think that food and shelter give us a sense of safety, and they do. But being seen, known, and accepted for who you are by a present adult is also required to create this sense of safety. Without that, we feel uneasy. We feel lonely, even if we're around family and friends. When a parent yells at us or treats us poorly as young children, it shocks our nervous systems and breaks our hearts inside. And we don't like it, so we find a way out.

Enter the fantasy self. This is the version of you that can magically end all the pain by just being exactly right in all the right ways. More of this, less of that, whatever you learned in your environment that would bring less judgment and more attention and love.

Based on my experiences in sports growing up, my fantasy self was faster, stronger, scored goals, and was a star player. But I didn't stop there. If I did better at everything, got better grades, won at all games, and was the best, then...

Then, what? We unconsciously hope we'll get the love, attention, and approval that we so desperately crave inside, especially from the parent where it seemed the least forthcoming. This is the birthplace of your inner critic.

We now start striving to become this fantasy version of ourselves. We feel pressure to be a certain way and fear about not being that way. We fear that if we aren't that way, then we won't get love and approval, that we'll be, and feel, unworthy.

It's all a setup, however, because we aren't unlovable or unworthy. Our parents' inability to meet certain needs was not due to some fundamental flaw in us. It was simply due to a lack of capacity on their part. Due to their own upbringing, fears, pride, and the armoring around their own hearts, they were unable to give more than they did.

But that's a complex concept for a young kid to get, so instead, we make it about us. In response to intense pain that we have no control over, we create the fantasy that we do indeed have control. If I could just do things better and right, be stronger, nicer, less selfish, smarter, less of a bother, more interesting, or whatever else dad or mom wants, then I'll finally feel the relief of getting the love I want.

What are some of the ways you learned you needed to be? Let's start a little list right now. We'll be adding to it more in just a minute because, while this started with your family growing up, it definitely did not stop there.

Open your O.M.O.S. journal and write out the ways you thought you needed to be in order to get love, attention, and approval. When they were upset, how did you need to be to stay safe or make things better? What could you never do because it would instantly make them mad or rejecting? Make a list for your mom and your dad. If you had a different situation growing up and were raised by a single parent, grandparents, or others, simply use these major parental figures in your early life. Got it? Okay, let's do that right now.

So, what did you come up with? Here is what came to me:

Dad:
Better athlete - stronger and faster.
Try harder; show more effort.
Learn faster, and don't make mistakes
Stay quiet and out of the way.
Excel in academics
Never confront or challenge him.

Mom:
Feel happy or neutral, not sad or upset.
Don't cry over things.
Don't do anything "gross."

The list for one parent might come easier for another. This is because, for many people, they felt more seen, known, and loved by one parent than the other. Don't worry about the length of your list or if you're doing it "right" or not. If more ideas come to you later, you can add them. But now, I have to tell you about Bobo.

Bobo, The Clown

When we are young children, we learn how things should be treated. If you see your dad carefully washing and waxing his car every Saturday and notice how stern he gets about never spilling anything in the backseat, you learn that cars are meant to be treated with care, respect, and above all, cleanliness. They must never be treated harshly, carelessly, or damaged.

If your mom loves to paint, has turned one of the rooms in the house into a painting studio, and often talks about artists and galleries and paintings she loves, then you learn that painting is important. Artistic expression, creativity, and perhaps how well-recognized as an artist you are all matter. Why? Because mom shows you, that's what is important.

This communication passed down from our parents stays with us for many years, and we may pass it on to our own children. When my boys do some damage to our house, as young children are known to do, my wife gets very upset. She is an extremely patient woman, but as soon as someone makes a dent in the wall, she goes from zero to 60 in three seconds flat.

She got the message growing up that causing damage in a house is unacceptable. While I'm obviously not pro-damage, I also know that some amount of that is inevitable with small kids. I'm not a zen master; I just didn't get the same training during my upbringing as she did. Her family moved a lot, and her parents struggled financially. Hence, damaging the house was a big deal. My family lived in the same place for a long time, and we didn't struggle financially in the same way.

Well-known psychologist Albert Bandura studied this phe-nomenon in young children in his now-famous Bobo, The Clown experiments. In these experiments, he had a big clown doll that stayed upright, even after you pushed it. It would bend down, then rise back up to standing. Little kids would observe an adult either walking toward the clown and beating it senseless or ignor-ing it. Later, when the children who watched the aggressive adult had access to the clown, guess what they did to Bobo? Not only did they beat him up in the same way as an adult would, but they found new creative ways, such as throwing darts at him. They learned Bobo was bad and worthy of poor treatment, so they were free to come up with all kinds of ways to hurt him.

Bandura called this Social Learning Theory, and it's a big part of how we learn as children and adults. We look at others to learn how to behave toward something, how to treat something, and what to do.

Guess what? The same is true for how you learned how to treat you. When your parents ignored you or gave you minimal attention, you learned that you are supposed to be ignored or only receive minimal attention. When your parents criticized or yelled at you for making a mistake, you learned that that's what you're supposed to do to yourself when you make a mistake. You repeat-edly witnessed how you were supposed to be treated, and so you copied that.

This becomes how you treat yourself and how you talk to yourself in your own mind. Feeling judgment, aversion, or dislike toward parts of yourself can all come from simply learning that's how you're supposed to react to those parts of yourself. For exam-ple, you may hate it when you feel anxious. You judge the anxiety as unwarranted or foolish, judge yourself as weak for feeling that way, and loathe how timidly you act. It turns out that your mom or dad also hates anxiety and judged themselves and you and anyone else for feeling that way. And perhaps their mom or dad also hated anxiety and judged themselves and others for feeling it, and so on up the chain.

Even if your parents tried to shield you from this judgment so they didn't overtly express criticism when you were anxious, the message can still be transmitted. Judgmental thoughts and attitudes they hold, even if unexpressed verbally, can be transmitted and picked up by children.[6] Furthermore, when a parent is judging themselves for their own anxiety, the child can sense this constriction and start to learn through more subtle means that anxiety (or other emotions) are shameful.

If all this sounds complex or overwhelming, don't worry. You don't have to identify every single thing you learned or consciously undo all the programming. All of this is good news. It's all learning. And anything learned can be unlearned, changed, or updated. You can simply learn new ways of being with yourself that are more consciously chosen, rather than unconscious programs passed down from one generation to the next. And the great news is you can learn this stuff way faster than you may think.

The Invisible Obvious

One other way our families install our inner critic machinery when we're young is in the way they dealt with emotions. Each family has an attitude toward emotions that has a major impact on the children. In many families, one or both parents are emotionally immature and have not learned to identify feelings, manage and contain them, or express them in a skillful way.

---

6   For a mindblowing exploration of the scientific research on how consciousness, attitude, and intent can impact other people and the world around us, I recommend Lynne McTaggart's work, including *The Field and The Intention Experiment.*

Think back to your childhood. Did you see your dad walk into the kitchen, looking upset, and your mom moved toward him and said, "What's going on, honey?"

Then, he paused, reflecting for a moment, and said, "I'm feeling anxious about my project at work. There are so many moving parts, and I want to control everything, which is impossible. The uncertainty of it all is making me uncomfortable."

"Yeah, it's so much! It's a big deal for you to be taking this on, and it's so different than what you've done in the past. I'd be anxious too."

And then they talked about it for a few more minutes, her listening, being empathetic, and sharing ways he can relax, let go, and trust more. He is open, vulnerable, and taking responsibility for his own feelings. Even though dad is struggling, there is open communication, respect, love, and connection happening.

Sound familiar?

Certainly not for most people!

In my house growing up, dad wouldn't say any of that. He'd be carrying all of it on his own shoulders and be in his head and feeling stressed out while at home, trying to figure out his next move at work. Mom would ask him how he's doing, and he'd vent about someone who tried to "nickel and dime him on some B.S." Or maybe he wouldn't even share that much. He'd hold it all inside, trying to talk about something else. He'd be tense and distracted. Then, later, he might blow up about something small, like the kitchen sink not working right. He'd yell and bang things around, ranting about how he had to do everything around here. Mom would be quiet and small as if she were trying to make herself invisible.

In my household growing up, and perhaps in yours too, feelings were the invisible obvious. They are arguably the most important aspect of the human experience, driving us to do everything we do, and determining the quality of our lives. If you "have it all" in terms of external success, power, achievements, and accolades, but you feel depressed, empty, or are hurting inside, then you are miserable. How you feel is what matters most to you. Emotions are primary and influence everything in our lives, yet they are invisible, like gravity. And in some strange feat of denial, many people act as if feelings are not there, not happening, or otherwise not that important.

That was the message I got growing up—don't focus on your feelings that much, just focus on doing stuff. In fact, try not to feel so much in the first place. And of course, don't talk about what you're feeling; what's the point of that? So we didn't. We talked about what we did and what other people did. We talked about what happened and what needed to happen. "How was your day?" was answered with a list of where we went and what we did.

If someone was mad or sad or anxious, they didn't tell anyone that. Their feelings and mood may have been visible or apparent in the way they were acting, but nothing was revealed or spoken out loud. As a result, I learned that speaking directly about feelings in the moment was somehow taboo.

Always Be Green Zone

In an attempt to create a home environment that fosters much more confidence and O.M.O.S. in our children, my wife and I have a vastly different approach to emotions. We openly talk about them and help our children learn how to identify, work with, and communicate what they are feeling.

One of my favorite tools to teach kids about emotions is the color zones. There are four zones—green, red, yellow, and blue. Green zone is when you are feeling relaxed, calm, at ease, or happy. Blue zone is feeling tired in your body, or sad or down in your heart. Yellow is when you're energized or agitated inside.

It can be pleasant feelings like excitement or an uncomfortable feeling like irritability. And red zone is when you're feeling angry, enraged, and a strong urge to act out that anger through words, or in the case of my boys, hitting, pulling hair, or throwing the hardest object you can find at your brother.

We used the zones to express how we're feeling inside, and our boys witnessed how my wife and I shared what zone we were in with each other and them. We also asked them what zone they were in. As we did this, however, I discovered that my upbringing taught me one message loud and clear: always be in the green zone.

When my son would ask me, "Daddy, what zone are you in? You seem like you're in the yellow zone," I would feel an instant urge to deny it, even if I knew it was true! I'd feel this sense of shame for being a bad person who didn't have control over my emotions, even though I was just mildly agitated and not acting harshly or cold in any way. I also felt an instant pressure to get back into the green zone now, even though no one was demanding that of me.

As this happened more and more, I became fascinated at how much pressure I put on myself to always be calm, relaxed, and happy. Blue zone was okay sometimes, but only for a short period of time, like maybe an hour. Extended blue zone, yellow zone, and certainly red zone were totally off-limits.

Can you relate? Do you feel a constant pressure inside to be upbeat, happy, and "on"? Do you irrationally fear that your boyfriend, girlfriend, spouse, or friends will suddenly turn on you and leave you for being anything other than green zone? That's a lot of pressure that you may not even be fully aware that you're putting on yourself.

After having children, I had the unique opportunity to observe my own early emotional training in action as I watched my parents interact with their grandchildren. One time, when my younger son was about one year old, he was crying intensely. My mom was there to comfort him, as she's always been a wonderfully present and attentive mother, and now, a grandmother. She feels the emotion and responds to it because she's loving and caring. But remember the family rules! Emotions must not be expressed, so they must be packed up and put away as soon as possible. So as she's providing warmth and physical reassurance, holding and rocking this crying baby, she gently says, "Oh, you're not crying. I don't believe you."

What an odd thing to say, I thought to myself as I watched. He is crying. What does belief have to do with it? But what she's saying is not literal, and I bet she doesn't know exactly what she's saying or why. It's just coming out of her. What's she's communicating is: *your emotions are making me uncomfortable, and I want that feeling to stop. Put your emotions away now.*

This is why I feel pressure to go green zone all the way. And perhaps why you feel pressure to be a certain way emotionally. Maybe your parents taught you that anger was completely unacceptable, and you should never show it, let alone feel it.

One of the head coaches on my team shared a story of crying when he was a young child at McDonald's. His hamburger bun had sesame seeds on it, and he didn't want sesame seeds. His dad said to him, "Stop crying, or I'll give you something to cry about." A client in my mastermind program shared that, when she was a young girl when she walked into the kitchen and said, "Mom, I'm bored!" her mom would reply, "Only boring people get bored. Why don't you go bang your head against the wall."

These are just the moments they remember. I was only able to observe the conditioning in action because of my parents interacting with their grandkids. There are hundreds of thousands of moments that convey to you how you should feel and how you should express yourself. You learn what emotions are okay and which ones are bad, wrong, or shameful. And then you pack all that into your fantasy self and try to make yourself that way in order to be worthy of love and belonging.

PEERS

While the birth of your inner critic began in your family, that is not the end of the story. As you grew out of infancy and into childhood, you began to spend time around other children. There is a strong push in many western countries for kids to spend large amounts of time with their peers. This is seen as healthy, natural, and right, and to do otherwise will lead to maladjusted, socially awkward weirdos (or so the story goes).

But more people are starting to question this concept. In their insightful book, *Hold On to Your Kids*, child psychologist, Dr. Gordon Neufeld, and childhood development expert, Dr. Gabor Maté explore the impact of encouraging kids to spend more time with each other and less and less time with parents and family. One potential pitfall is that kids become "peer-oriented." This means they switch their primary attachment from their parents to other kids. Now, the ones they want love, connection, and approval from are their peers.

What's wrong with that? I used to think. *That's natural and normal. Besides, remember the maladjusted weirdo thing?* But here's the problem. Other kids don't have the capacity to love with the same depth and maturity that parents have toward their children. Parents, even if they are far from perfect, will do so much for their children than other children will. They will give their time, energy, attention, and hard-earned money to help their children in any way they can. They will tolerate them even when they're tantruming, unreasonable, or freaking out. They are deeply bonded to their children by biology, emotion, and purpose.

Peers, on the other hand, have no such inner compulsion to take care of each other. Their relationships are inherently insecure, hence the extreme focus on conformity and being seen as popular. Every single one of us has done dozens of things to fit in, in order to maintain connection and significance, including changing our clothes, our preferences, or our way of talking. Fit in or die.

This has a cumulative effect of making us less and less connected with our actual selves and more focused on being, however we need to be in order to maintain the approval of our peers. We add all these new requirements to our list of attributes for our fantasy self. There's how you need to be for your parents, and now there's how you need to be for your peers.

Around the ages of 11-12, which is described as "middle school" in the United States, is when we start to turn on ourselves. If we don't have a strong foundation of love and communication with our families and enter into a peer-oriented environment, we are highly susceptible to turn on ourselves completely. We are left to navigate this terrain on our own.

I learned within the first few days of starting middle school that there was a clear social hierarchy based on confidence, coolness, and popularity. I also learned that you did not want to be at the bottom of this hierarchy. If you were, you were screwed.

Two kids in my class held this unfortunate position—Matt and Gabe. Both were constantly picked on, criticized, mocked, talked down to, or excluded throughout the school day. Each dealt with it differently. Matt decided to be a loner and kept to himself. Incidentally, I didn't know any of this when I attended an orientation for new students and their families a week before school started. The only other kid from my class at the orientation was Matt. He was friendly and soft-spoken. He seemed nice enough to me, and I liked him. We walked around the soccer field and talked while the parents got oriented. I'm sure they didn't mention brutal social isolation and torment as a feature of their school.

After my first day at school, I realized that Matt was an outcast. And so, I turned my back on him. I felt so insecure and afraid of going down with him to the bottom of that hierarchy, so terrified of being the target, that I quickly recoiled from any contact with him.

I couldn't imagine two years of "Aziz the disease" and other taunts. Looking back, it's shocking how emotionally intense that kind of social ostracization must have been for him. But it gets worse.

About two weeks into the school year, I'd gotten the lay of the land. One way to establish your place in the social pecking order was to tease or mock other boys. I saw this happening a lot but didn't participate. I'd never done this in my life, and it seemed so mean. But then one day in art class, as Matt was painting who knows what, I walked over to him and loudly said, "What's that? Some crap painted on top of some other crap?"

I know, it's a lame insult. But the words were not what mattered; it was the act of attacking that was noticed. My energy and attitude toward him were dismissive, mocking, and condescending. *You are not one of us*, my tone clearly communicated. I could hear Tim and Mark snicker in the background, which was a signal that I had done well. But I'll never forget the look on Matt's face as he gazed at me. I could see the pain in his eyes, the disappointment at how quickly I had turned from friendly and humane into a jerk like the rest. As I think about this, I feel pain in my heart and a love for Matt. I hope his life is amazing.

Gabe, the second outcast, had a different approach than Matt. He tried to fit in. He sat with us at lunch, played sports with the guys during recess, and did everything else to stay close and connected. But we regularly made it clear that he wasn't fully part of the pack. We constantly mocked everything about him, the way he talked, his mannerisms, and even his involuntary physical and verbal tics.

At the time, it was normal. Everyone was doing it. But looking back, it's brutal. What an intense form of psychological and emotional torment to be seen daily as less-than, ugly, and worthy of derisive mockery.

If you were ever in the position of Matt or Gabe, I am so sorry. You did not deserve that. If reading these stories is stirring up pain, this is a good thing. We often try to bury our pain from the past, hoping it will go away for good. But that deep sense of inadequacy, unlovability, and unworthiness does not disappear and does not die. It does not heal unless we go back in there and heal it, giving our younger selves the attention, support, love, and wise perspective we needed at that time. That is exactly what you'll be learning how to do later in this book.

Could you talk in-depth about whatever you were going through in school as a kid with your parents? For most clients I ask, the answer is no. This can be due to your parents' lack of knowledge or ability to be with you through challenging emotions and experiences. Often times, parents unknowingly shut their children down by giving them hasty advice, lovingly dismissing the problem, or getting upset and wanting to get involved.

As a result, kids stop sharing and keep all their experiences inside. Their relationship with their peers rests in their ability to fit in, but vulnerability is generally absent in these relationships because they're not based on mature connection or real intimacy. Could you imagine approaching a peer when you were twelve or fifteen years old and telling them your deepest insecurities and challenges? I don't mean surface level insecurities around your crush or worries about who likes who. I'm referring to how you feel about yourself, your appearance, your relationship with your parents, or struggles at home. None of us were doing that when I was young. Vulnerability and tender emotions would bring on ridicule and vicious attack.

Maybe your experience was different, and you could speak openly with your parents or close friends. If so, that may have lessened the self-judgments you accumulated at school. Of course, you're still reading this book, so you must've picked up a jerky inner critic somewhere. Where else could it come from?

CULTURE

> "A human being is not an organism in an environment,
> but is an organism-environment, that is to say, a unified
> field of behavior. If you describe carefully the behavior of
> any organism, you cannot do so without at the same time
> describing the behavior of the environment."
>
> - Alan Watts

Lousy parents, lousy other kids, making you turn on yourself
and feel crummy inside. Who else can we blame? Those ad men
and women on Madison Avenue with their fancy suits and $300
haircuts? While I'm joking about blame, I am serious about the
massive impact culture and media has had on you from even
before you were born.

Your culture refers to the collective beliefs, customs, values,
and traditions of the groups that you belong to. Your family growing up has its own culture. That family exists in a larger culture,
perhaps of race, ethnicity, religion, or language that is spoken
(i.e., "We are Mexican-American" or "We are Catholic"). This
larger culture impacts your parents and their beliefs and actions,
which in turn, impacts you.

Any tribe has messages that are supportive and life-affirming,
mixed with distortions that are toxic and interfere with growth,
personal evolution, and expansion of our capacity to love and
contribute. For example, a particular religious upbringing might
create a sense of connection with God and provide a deep sense
of faith in life. This can be highly supportive. At the same time,
it might convey messages about right and wrong regarding sexuality. Someone might learn that touching their genitals is dirty
and wrong and will lead to punishment by a heavenly authority.
As you might guess, this message from the culture is not about
expansion and growth but about fear and control.

Then, no matter what groups or tribes you belong to, there is the culture that is disseminated through mass media, including television shows, advertisements, movies, social media, online video streaming, internet ads, and news organizations. While this churning mass of information that is flowing into our minds seems to be coming from a wide variety of sources, there are three major players vying to influence you through this dominant culture.

1. Large corporations with astronomical budgets for advertising.

2. Governing bodies focused on maintaining order and control.

3. Special interest groups that have accumulated a large amount of power and control over a particular industry (i.e., medicine or telecommunications) that want to preserve and expand their power.

From the moment we are born, we are blanketed in airwaves influencing our thoughts, focus, beliefs, and consciousness. By the age of three years old, children in the United States can recognize over 100 corporate brand logos. We reside in a soup of media that mentions millions of products, services, and programs but has just one core message that can be summarized in one sentence: Something is wrong—with you or your life—and this product or service will fix it.

Are you making the terrible mistake of aging? We can fix that. Do you need to be more productive? We have a pill for that. Are you feeling empty inside, lacking a sense of meaning in your work and life? We have pills for that too. And gadgets and cookies and toys and TVs and 10,000 things will distract you from that empty feeling. And so we shop and search and shop and search. Maybe the next purchase will provide the fulfillment I seek. Maybe the next upgrade to my house, my wardrobe, my car, my phone, or myself will provide the lasting happiness I seek. Maybe that next pill, that next wonder drug will provide lasting fulfillment.[7]

The messages from government authorities and special interest groups are only slightly different: Something is wrong, and you are not safe...unless you do what we say to do. This is an ancient tactic of persuasion and control that has been used throughout recorded history.

It gets even more sticky when large corporations influence special interest groups to begin controlling what they do. For example, one powerful group in the United States is made up of medical doctors trained in allopathic medicine. Over the last fifty years, this group has been heavily influenced by corporations that produce chemical drugs to suppress symptoms manifesting as physical, mental, and emotional problems.

Flash forward to the present day, and most everyone I speak with believes depression is a problem with your brain due to a "chemical imbalance" that is "fixed" with a drug produced by a publicly traded, for-profit company. Going to the doctor has become synonymous with getting prescription pills.

In my training in clinical psychology at the department of psychiatry at Stanford University, to suggest that an antidepressant might be a bad idea for a client and potentially even counterproductive and harmful was met with such intense hostility that no one dared to even speak about it. We all learned that the correct thing to say was, "Antidepressants can be a part of an effective

---

7   To more deeply understand exactly what forces are vying for control of your perception, actions, and body, I recommend you read Michael Moss' *Salt Sugar Fat: How the Food Giants Hooked Us* and by Martin Lindstrom, *Brandwashed: Tricks Companies Use to Manipulate Our Minds and Persuade Us to Buy*. They will expose you to the insane extent companies go to control our behavior and will help liberate you from being unconsciously influenced.

treatment plan, which is best when combined with psychotherapy using an approach validated with empirical evidence."

Nevermind the massive amount of research that shows that this might not be the case at all. Nevermind the minimal amount of human research needed to get a psychotropic drug approved for market and the permeability of the governing body designed to monitor what's available to the public (Food and Drug Administration). Nevermind all that. Follow the program and keep your mouth shut.[8]

The key takeaway here is that we are all awash in this culture that directly influences our ideas and perspectives. We have absorbed thousands of toxic messages:

- Don't age.
- Don't get fat (skinny is good, fat is bad).
- Earn more money to be more worthy.
- Be rich, not poor (but not too rich because that's bad too).
- Don't be scared or you're a "coward" (which is bad).
- Have hair that looks like this, not that.

This list could fill an entire book, and we'd just scratch the surface of how we're conditioned to think. Are you seeing how much of this we've taken in? These ideas of right and wrong, good and bad are not your own. They were taught to you, fed to you, installed inside of you. This problem is not just you and your inner critic. This is a formulaic result of exposing the human-animal to this kind of information throughout development. This is the result of being immersed in this environment.

But, as always, do not lose hope. No matter how long you've been absorbing these toxic cultural messages or how much your

---

8   To liberate yourself from the idea that your brain is broken due to a chemical imbalance and learn more about the influence of the pharmacological corporations in medicine, you can read: *The Emperor's New Drugs* by Irving Kirsch and *Lost Connections* by Johann Hari.

critic uses them to make you feel bad, you can break free because conscious awareness is more powerful than any marketing tool or message of influence. Once you become wise to the game, it no longer impacts you in the same way.

Culture controls our perception, what we see as good or bad, healthy or unhealthy, smart or dumb. It controls what we see and what we ignore, deny, or dismiss. Ultimately, the dominant culture merges with your fantasy self to fill in all the gaps. It shows you all the ways you need to be in order to be that perfect person who will finally get the love, respect, and attention that you crave.

What has culture taught you to want? How to be? What to be like?

Let's explore that for a minute. What do you want? Today, this month, this year, for your life? What do you *really* want? What's your gut response? Your inner craving and impulse?

If you could wave a magic wand and transform anything in your world, what would it be? What you want to change that would create an instant sense of relief, satisfaction, excitement, or fulfillment?

While altruistic goals that involve contributing to others and making a difference in the world may come to your mind, most likely, you also have another part of you that wants the following.

If you're a woman, there's a part of you that answers: I want to be thin, pretty, famous, and rich. Or, if you're a man, your version is: muscular, handsome, famous, and rich.

Let's not quibble over terminology. You may not say "thin," but instead talk about reaching your "ideal weight" (which happens to be thinner than you are now). You might not want to be "famous" in a movie star kind of way (even though you secretly might, but think it's impossible so say you don't want that), but instead, you do want more friends on social media, recognition in your career, or to be acknowledged and admired for your creations.

So perhaps it's to be "more well-known," "have a bigger impact," or just be more popular (a.k.a. famous). And maybe "rich" sounds like a dirty word for you, so you'd rather just be "really well-off financially." There, that sounds better now, doesn't it?

Don't believe me? Well then, I'd like to present to you exhibit A: Science. It turns out this exact topic has been researched quite thoroughly by the Higher Education Research Institute.[9] Their insanely detailed 50+ year longitudinal study of Harvard and San Diego State college students records that in 1966, about 45% of college freshmen believed "being very well off financially" was essential or very important. Since 1989, that goal was consistently ranked first *among all other potential life goals.* Most recently, being rich is ranked as essential or very important by 75% of college freshmen.[10]

What about being thinner, fitter, or more shredded? Research suggests that the majority of women and men are dissatisfied with their appearance and habitually focus on their perceived physical flaws and shortcomings. Body dissatisfaction in the western world is rampant. At age thirteen, 53% of American girls are "unhappy with their bodies." This grows to 78% by the time girls reach seventeen.[11] Here are more generally disheartening statistics about how much we hate our bodies:

- Currently, 80% of the women in the United States are dissatisfied with their bodies.

- According to the National Eating Disorders Association, 42% of girls between grades 1-3 want to lose weight, and 81% of 10-year-olds are afraid of being fat.

---

9   To learn more, you can visit the website for the Higher Education Research Institute here: https://heri.ucla.edu/publications-tfs/

10 https://www.consumerismcommentary.com/millennials-want-to-be-rich-more-than-anything/

11 https://now.org/now-foundation/love-your-body/love-your-body-whats-it-all-about/get-the-facts/

- According to a study in pediatrics, over 60% of girls in the 5th to 12th grades said that magazine images influence their vision of an ideal body, and about half of the girls said the images made them want to lose weight.

- By adolescence, studies show that young people are receiving an estimated 5,260 "attractiveness messages" per year from network television commercials alone.

- According to Teen magazine, 35% of girls ages 6 to 12 have been on at least one diet, and 50 to 70% of normal-weight girls think they are overweight.[12]

And it's not just women. Research conducted by Phillippa Diedrichs[13] on men has found that:

- 80% of men talked about their own or others' appearance in ways that draw attention to weight, lack of hair, or slim frame.

- 63% thought their arms or chests were not muscular enough.

- 29% thought about their appearance at least five times a day.

- 23% said concerns about their appearance had deterred them from going to the gym.

So here we are with massive exposure to media on a daily basis (don't even get me started on the statistics about how much time we spend watching TV, streaming video, or browsing the internet each day—as of 2018 it was a whopping 11 hours per day in America[14]), with that exposure making us feel terrible about how we look.

---

12   https://psychcentral.com/blog/why-do-women-hate-their-bodies/
13   https://www.phillippadiedrichs.com/publications-1
14   https://www.nielsen.com/us/en/insights/article/2018/time-flies-us-adults-now-spend-nearly-half-a-day-interacting-with-media/

Yikes. What a complex, interconnected stew of confusion and suffering. How do we get out of this mess? Should we naturally hate ourselves for being overweight, which will motivate us to be thin? If we're an average, healthy weight, should we hate ourselves into becoming model-thin or weird-diet our way into being six-pack abs ripped? Does that even work? No, no, and no. There is a better way. And that's exactly what we're here to discover together.

First, we have to become aware of the omnipresent, pervasive nature of self-rejection that we're dealing with here. It's not just inside of your mind and all in your head. It's in our entire culture. It's in the minds and mouths of everyone around you. It's in the media, movies, books, magazines, and plastered on the windows of the storefronts you walk by on your way to work.

It's like an invisible, odorless gas that we're all breathing in each day that is slowly making us sick with self-hatred and anxiety about our self-worth. And everyone else is breathing it too, so it creates this bizarre sense of normalcy to the point that no one reacts when your friend mentions she hates her face when she sees a photo of herself, or your brother won't go with the family to the pool because he doesn't want to be seen shirtless. Of course, we hate ourselves; why shouldn't we? We're insufficient, lacking, and not something-or-other enough. We're fat and gross and need to get thinner, leaner, stronger, better, prettier, and rich and famous too.

YOUR CRITIC'S MISSION

Let's put it all together so you can get a crystal clear sense of why you have an inner critic and what it's doing in there. Let's look at all the clues you've learned so far.

Early in your life, you experienced emotional pain. This could have come from intense interactions with your parents involving yelling, threats, physical violence, or neglect. It could also have been pain induced by the more subtle, yet still extremely painful, injuries that come from not having your basic emotional needs met. Perhaps your parents were very busy and didn't have much space to pay attention to you, or they were emotionally immature and couldn't tolerate you having feelings, so they threatened you and withdrew until you put those feelings away. Or perhaps they had many expectations of you, constantly putting pressure on you to conform to how they wanted you to be—quieter, more polite, more social, getting better grades, achieving more, outdoing other kids so they could feel adequate, and on and on.

Whatever the reason, and whether you can pinpoint it or not, there is a reservoir of pain there. From that pain, your critic was born. As a child, your little mind came up with an idea of exactly how you needed to be in order for your parents and others to turn toward you with more attention, love, patience, and acceptance. You created your Fantasy Self and strove to be more like this perfect version of you. Your critic was right there by your side, pushing you to get closer to that version and harshly berating you when you fell short.

Then, as you went to school and spent time with peers, your Fantasy Self requirements expanded. You learned new ways of being that were required to fit in, be accepted, and be liked by others. Fitting in feels like survival when we're young, and so you did whatever it took to fit in, regardless of how much it felt like the real you or not. Authenticity took a backseat to survival. Your critic began to constantly survey the scene, making sure you didn't make a mistake, make a fool of yourself, or otherwise draw negative attention to yourself.

All the while, you grew up in a culture that is saturated by intense messages of how you need to be in order to be worthy, liked, admired, and successful. You learned how you were supposed to look, talk, dress, eat, and act. Your critic absorbed even more rules and criteria for you to follow in order to become that Fantasy Self that will be finally accepted, loved, respected, and adored by all.

So what is your critic, and what's it doing for you?

Your critic is an outdated protection strategy, trying to protect you from all emotional pain and discomfort.

It views risks, vulnerability, honesty, and authenticity as dangerous. Any attempt to be the real you is risky because what if it reveals something that is not the Fantasy Self? What if people see that you feel anxious, sad, scared, or down sometimes? What if others knew that you felt insecure, or greedy, or judgmental of others sometimes?

What if you try something and you fail? What if you put yourself out there and get rejected? What if people don't like what you create, offer, and do? Nope, not worth it. Stay safe; stay inside the box. Sure it's cramped, but at least it's safe, dammit!

Your critic is the force that's designed to keep you in that box. It views its job as absolutely essential, as a matter of life and death. It views the emotional pain you felt as a child as life-threatening and is determined to make sure you never feel that, or anything like it, again. So it will say and do whatever it needs to in order to keep you from being bigger, more visible, more transparent, more connected, and more alive.

That is your critic's mission.

Okay, pause. Take a deep breath in and out. And... smile! I mean it. Take a moment and put a big grin on your face, even if it feels silly to do so. Smile because you now know one of the most liberating secrets that lead to permanently being on your own side and a lifetime of confidence. That critical voice in your head is not right. What it's saying is not true. Everything it's saying is part of an elaborate propaganda campaign to make you fear risks, vulnerability, and authentically being yourself. You can smile because you're onto its game.

If you want to get just a little more wild with me, you can even say that out loud right now. "I'm onto you critic. I see what you're up to." Yep, now I got you talking to yourself. Seems crazy, right? Well, it's a lot more sane than the craziness of living under the tyrannical rule of your critic's propaganda machine.

In fact, let's take this knowledge one step further and use it to begin the liberation process now.

PART II:
DECISION

Chapter 4:
A New Way

"So, let's say I have a conversation that goes really awkwardly. Am I supposed to tell myself that it went great?"

"What if I eat the whole bag of cookies? Am I supposed to tell myself that it's no big deal?"

"What if I'm avoiding tasks at work and procrastinating like crazy? Am I supposed to tell myself not to worry about it?"

These are common questions people have when they are introduced to O.M.O.S. Perhaps questions like these are going through your mind as well. You may see that treating yourself so poorly for so long is not helpful and does not feel good. But you might not have ideas on what to do instead, at least, not initially.

It might not be you that's asking those questions; it's more likely that it's your critic. It asks these questions in an incredulous tone, implying that the situation is all-or-nothing. Either you are brutally berating yourself for every little mistake, or you live in a self-delusional fog of "I'm the greatest" while ignoring all feed-back from the outside world. Your critic makes the alternative to self-abuse seem ridiculous, so you dismiss the idea and go back to the old patterns where the critic is firmly in control.

But there is a better way, and the good news is, you already know it! Or you at least have a good sense of what it might be. Let's develop it more now.

O.M.O.S. DEFINED

What does it mean to be "on my own side," no matter what? First off, there is no single definition for this, and, at the end of the day, your own personal meaning is what matters most. In just a few minutes, you'll be creating your own definition, but, to start, I'd like to share some ideas with you.

The simplest way to describe being on your own side is that you treat yourself like you treat those you love. Think for a moment about someone you love dearly—a spouse, child, parent, sibling, or close friend—not someone you're "supposed" to love, but someone you deeply, naturally, fully love. Think of that person now and bring them into your awareness. Imagine their face, smile, and mannerisms. Think of things they say or do that make you smile. Can you feel that sense of love and appreciation in your heart?

That, right there, is a part of O.M.O.S. It's a feeling of positive affinity, of liking yourself, not because you did something amazing to earn it, but simply for existing and being you. Does your child or niece or nephew have to earn your love? Does your best friend have to prove themselves every time you hang out? Or do you just like them, for who they are? Sure, sometimes you might get annoyed, and occasionally, you might have a fight. But through it all, there is a deep bond of mutual appreciation, trust, respect, and love.

The more you are on your own side, the more you feel this way toward yourself. You stop constantly evaluating your performance and your self-worth, and you simply like yourself. You love *your* face, smile, and mannerisms.

Have you ever spent time with someone you deeply loved, be it a friend, lover, or family member, and had a moment where you just loved looking at them? Perhaps it was when they were sharing something that lit them up, or when the sunlight hit their eyes and made them glimmer, or when they lay in bed sleeping next to you. You looked at that face, and the love you felt for them moved you and maybe even brought you to tears. The feeling of warmth in your heart and positive affinity was profound.

What if you could feel this way for yourself?

As you feel a deep sense of love for someone, you naturally start to respect them and care about their well-being. It feels good to treat them with care, kindness, love, and respect. You easily see their positive qualities and are able to highlight these. When you are hurt or angry, you attempt to express yourself in a mature way that cares for the other's feelings. Hence, if you're enraged and want to lash out at them, you might bite your tongue and wait to have a discussion when you've calmed down a bit.

When you are on your own side, you treat yourself with this same level of care and respect. Even if you make a mistake or do something outside your values, you find a way to communicate your frustration or upset in a respectful manner.

Are you getting a sense of what O.M.O.S. is? It's not terribly complex. You already know how to do this when it comes to others. The biggest obstacle is not in figuring out what to do. It's simply being able to direct this love and care toward ourselves.

The Four Elements of O.M.O.S.

There are four key ways of treating yourself when you are on your own side. These are:

1. **Kindness:** You treat yourself with warmth, tenderness, and care. You are concerned about your own well-being, and you actively seek to take care of yourself, give yourself what you need, and respond to your own feelings.

2. **Respect:** You treat yourself with thoughtfulness, consideration, and common courtesy. No matter what happens, you refrain from verbal attacks, name-calling, or other forms of abuse.

3. **Patience:** You realize that life is complex, and the path is not straight. It takes time for growth and change to occur and for us to reach our goals. You are reasonable in what you expect of yourself and leave plenty of space for setbacks, pauses, and other occurrences.

4. **Accountability:** You are skilled at bringing the best out in yourself. If you are not progressing toward goals you truly desire or are not living in alignment with your values, you call yourself out. You are fully honest with yourself and use this awareness to get back on track.

How are you doing with these four elements of O.M.O.S.? If you gave yourself a number between 1-10 for each one based on how you've been treating yourself these last few weeks, what would it be for Kindness, Respect, Patience, and Accountability?

For so many people, the biggest challenge with O.M.O.S. is not knowing how to do it. They already do it with their friends, colleagues, partner, kids, and family. But they don't do it with themselves. They have all kinds of objections to treating themselves this way. They fear it will make them soft, lazy, indulgent, unproductive, or otherwise "weak," and fear what others will think of them. They fear becoming narcissistic or arrogant. Fears upon fears. We'll dispel those myths in just a minute, but first, let's look at one other essential component of O.M.O.S.

HONORING YOURSELF

All of the elements of O.M.O.S. combine in a way that fundamentally changes how you relate to yourself. In a sense, it's a stance of honoring who you are. So many of us grew up in an environment where love and acceptance were not guaranteed. In order for your mom, dad, grandparents, siblings, teachers, and others to accept you, you had to be a certain way. If you acted differently than this expectation, love was withdrawn, punishments were delivered, or worse. This process continues outside of the home as you get older and attempt to fit in with peer groups at different ages.

From these experiences, you learned how you are supposed to be in order to be acceptable, lovable, and worthy. You need to be louder, funnier, cooler, thinner, taller, or smarter. You need to be nicer, more giving, and less selfish. You need to never make mistakes, learn things extremely quickly, push harder, get there faster, and do everything perfectly. These inner dictates become the common refrains of your critic, the incessant reminders that pressure you to be more of this or less of that.

The more you live from your "supposed to" list, the further and further alienated you become from your actual self. It's hard to know who you really are anymore because when you check inside to see what you think, feel, or desire, there's too much noise to hear it, too many layers of judgment and demand about how a good person is *supposed* to think and what you *should* feel.

As you'll see more in the next part of this book, we are not just single-minded people with one set of thoughts and feelings.

We are a collection of many different parts. We can have a wide range of feelings, thoughts, and desires about one topic, and they conflict often.

Have you ever been both excited and nervous about something? Or have you wanted to see someone but also wanted to stay in and not talk to anybody? Perhaps there's something you felt dread about doing, so you decided to avoid it. But then instead of feeling happy about it, you felt sad and disappointed. This is completely normal and part of everyone's experience. We all have different parts of us that want different things.

The skill of O.M.O.S. requires that we learn to listen to all these parts and treat them with respect. We honor our feelings and desires, even though we may choose to not act on them. This might sound reasonable until you try to do it. It turns out that there is quite a bit of momentum to the discounting and dismissing energy of our inner critics.

Later this morning, I'm going to be getting on a plane with my wife and children to fly down to Santa Cruz, California, to visit my parents. I am excited to go on a family trip. I love Santa Cruz as I grew up there and have so many fond memories. The smell of the earth and the trees combine in the air to create a deep sense of home, no matter how long I've lived elsewhere. I love my mom and dad. They have been so generous and devoted to my brother and me throughout our lives. I have countless memories of being with each of them, picking berries with my mom, playing basketball with my dad, and so much more. They love spending time with their grandkids, and it's sweet to watch them play doctor with grandma or 'Chutes and Ladders' with "Gumpie" (as they call my dad).

And, at the same time, I don't want to go. We're leaving on a Wednesday, which means I had a two-day workweek. I'm feeling stressed about all that I didn't get to this week. It's supposed to be intensely raining all four days we are there.

I am anxious about interacting with my parents. Being with them tends to stir up feelings of loneliness, heartache, nostalgia from my own childhood, which are often complex and uncomfortable.

My dad doesn't hear very well, so it's hard to communicate with him. He likes to talk about politics, the news, business, yet I feel most connected when I'm talking with people about our personal lives, things we're passionate about, current struggles, our feelings, and other, more vulnerable aspects of our lives.

Mom was in the hospital twice within the last year. She seems to be doing better now, but I am aware of her mortality, and I feel pangs of sadness in my heart as I see she won't always be here. I love her so much. This desperate energy arises that tells me I need to do something. I need to go on a long walk with her during the visit and have some profound conversation to get the most out of our time together while we have it.

And this is just the "shortlist" of what I'm experiencing. Being on your own side means you allow and honor all of these different parts and their desires, thoughts, and feelings. This is something I've had to train myself how to do. It was quite difficult as my standard approach for many years was to only acknowledge the "positive" feelings to myself and others and deny the "negative."

Hence, if I had mixed feelings about visiting parents, seeing a friend, or going on a second date with someone, I'd tell myself: *Oh, come on now. Don't think that. Don't feel that. Stop it.* Then, this would be followed up by more reasons why I shouldn't be having that experience.

Mom and dad love you so much and have done so much for you. It's not that bad. You're exaggerating those challenging moments from your childhood. If you want something different with dad, then make it happen. Stop moping about it.

If part of me had an aversion to seeing a friend or going on a second date, that voice in my head would say: *You're too judgmen-*

tal. Why don't you like them? You shouldn't dislike someone; they're doing the best they can. Come on.

The exact reasons my critic gives me as to why I shouldn't feel the way I do are not too important. Often, they don't make much sense. They're just fluff to support the major claim of "Don't feel the way you do; don't want what you want; don't think what you think."

This is madness — this is a way of not honoring yourself. And in order to be truly on your own side, it must end. Instead, we need to be real, starting with ourselves. How do I truly feel about this? What do the different parts of me say about this?

The truth is we are all a ball of mixed feelings. Every experience in your life is a mixture of pleasure and pain, likes and dislikes. And yet, we have this expectation that it should be simple and just one way. We talk with others as if this was so all the time.

After attending a concert over the weekend, some work colleagues might ask:

"How was the concert?"

"Oh, it was amazing! It took two hours, but we worked our way to the front. The music was amazing, and they played (insert hit singles here)!"

"Wow, that sounds awesome."

(end of discussion)

While the above recounting of the concert is not false, it's most certainly not complete. Perhaps she left out that she had a fight with her boyfriend on the way to the concert, which lingered in her mind throughout the show. Perhaps there was a guy next to her who kept bumping into her, which was irritating. Perhaps, during some of the songs, she felt a deep sadness that she couldn't explain as if she were missing her sister, or family, or a life she'd never live.

Now, is she going to tell her colleague at work all this when he asks her how the concert was? No, probably not. And I'm not saying she should. What I'm saying is that we humans are complex, and so are our feelings. We need to honor this about ourselves and start acknowledging the truth to *ourselves*.

We can then selectively choose who in our lives we want to be more open with. So while she may not tell her coworker all these details, she can talk more with her boyfriend or a close friend about her experience. She can share with her sister about the feelings of sadness she experienced at the concert.

But only if she's practicing being on her own side! Otherwise, that critic inside will stop her dead in her tracks if she isn't. It will tell her not to talk about this stuff with anyone because it's "weird" or "complaining" or "a downer." *I'm supposed to feel happy at concerts. I'm supposed to be excited and upbeat. I feel too much, anyway. No one else is having this experience; they all seem to be fully happy and having nothing but pure fun.*

Which, in case you don't know it yet, is complete B.S. Everyone is having all kinds of feelings, all of the time. They just don't share them openly. They might be actively holding them back to not look like a weirdo who has feelings. Or they might be so good at stuffing their feelings down that the process is now entirely habitual and unconscious; they don't even know they're feeling something, and they honestly think they're not.

Although, whenever they're at a concert, they have an overwhelming urge to get a few drinks, even though it's a weeknight, and they told themselves they weren't going to drink. And during that sad song, they feel a compulsion to pull out their phone and check their email and social media, without knowing why. Or their back feels tight, their knees start to ache, and they tell themselves it's just from standing too long.

As you read this, it may seem obvious that being more accepting of all your feelings and more expressive with people close to you is beneficial for your health, relationships, and confidence. And yet, right now in your life, where are you not listening to yourself? Where are you ignoring the whispers, or shouts, of your inner self?

O.M.O.S. is about ending this neglect. It's about turning toward yourself with true curiosity and a desire to get to know yourself. Who are you? What makes you tick? What drives you? What do you like? What do you love? What do you dislike?

Like getting to know a partner more and more deeply over the years, you become curious about who you truly are, not who you're supposed to be. Maybe you don't like engineering or medicine even though you're an engineer or a nurse. Maybe you don't like going out to bars or drinking, but you've spent time with people there because that's what "normal" people do.

Forget normal. Normal is a soul-crushing synonym of conformity. Normal is disowning who you are to pick the safe road that will avoid possible rejection. While you may have needed to do that to survive when you were younger, you don't need to keep doing that to yourself.

Let's discover who you are. The more you uncover this and have the courage to act on what you learn by making changes in your life, the better you'll feel.

O.M.O.S. AND YOU

How do you like the sound of treating yourself this way? Does it seem relieving? Exciting? Would it be completely life-changing to stop being so hard on yourself and start enjoying who you are right now?

If you have some reservations about this, don't worry. Many people are concerned about the imagined downsides of being too kind, too loving, or too "soft" with themselves. We'll address that in just a few minutes at the beginning of the next chapter. But for now, let's talk about how to make O.M.O.S. fully your own.

O.M.O.S. is a simple acronym that I started using to capture this idea of being on our own sides, and it stuck. People started using the phrase O.M.O.S. when talking about their goals in my group coaching program. They started defining what O.M.O.S. meant for them in their dating life, at work, with their family, and more.

That's what I want for you as well. I want you to start with my ideas about O.M.O.S. and build on them. What does O.M.O.S. mean for you? What would it mean for you to be on your own side, no matter what, in all the different areas of your life—socially, in dating and intimate relationships, in your workplace and career, in your physical health and fitness, your finances, and everywhere else?

To thoroughly flush these ideas out, I suggest you write your own O.M.O.S. essay. Be sure to address all the key areas of life I mentioned above. Don't overthink it, and don't worry about getting it completely comprehensive or perfect. As one of my mentors always told me: Version one and done is better than perfect. So let's make version one now. Yes, right now.

Here are some sentence stems you can experiment with. Simply choose the ones you like, write or type out the beginning of the sentences, and then let it fly. Write directly from your heart. Bypass all ideas of what is possible, right, reasonable, proper, or nice. Let all that go, and just write freely from a place of possibility.

For me, O.M.O.S. means...
O.M.O.S. is when...
Being on my own side means...
When I'm on my own side at work, I...
When I'm on my own side in dating, I...
Being O.M.O.S. with family means I...

For me, O.M.O.S. is being completely, 100% my own ally, my own advocate, my own best friend. I deeply love myself, care about myself, and treat me with respect and kindness. I listen to all the parts of me and have endless space and patience for all my different feelings and desires. I don't attack myself for feeling anything—sadness, anger, anxiety, grief, a depressed mood, negativity. It's okay for me to feel anything, and there's nothing wrong with me for being human and having emotions.

O.M.O.S. not only means allowing these feelings inside of me without judging or dismissing myself; it also includes sharing them with others. I don't hide my authentic experience out of fear of others' judgment. Being on my own side means I know my feelings and experiences are okay, even if someone else doesn't like it. Their perception is not stronger, more real, or more valid than my own. I own my reality, and in my reality, it's okay to be human and vulnerable. So as an act of O.M.O.S., I regularly choose to flex my vulnerability muscle and share openly with others.

I go easy on myself, especially at work and in sports. I catch myself when I'm demanding perfection, stressing myself with unrelenting demands to go faster and do more. I slow down and acknowledge what I've done and take in the wins and successes as they occur. I regularly remind myself that there is no final endpoint and that I want to enjoy the process. I relax my body and find a way to move toward my big goals in a guided state of flow.

I regularly speak well to myself before tasks, meetings, speaking engagements, sessions, and any other thing that might make me feel nervous. I am a master coach and mentor to myself. I skillfully coach myself through scary or challenging situations with empathy, love, encouragement, and support. When I notice self-attack occurring, I actively stop it, reminding myself that "I don't attack myself. That's not helpful."

Being on my own side as a husband, father, brother, son, and friend means letting me be me. Sometimes, I'm abundantly loving and generous, and sometimes, I just want a break. Sometimes, I'm a super dad who can handle eight things at once while being playful and patient, and sometimes, I get irritated, impatient, or short with my kids. I am a good enough husband, son, brother, and friend.

O.M.O.S. means I don't pressure myself to get back to people instantly. I check inside to see what kind of resources I have in the moment and then give accordingly. I honor that inner signal of what I want to give and what I want to do, and I listen to it before acting out of obligation. If I start worrying about what people will think of me, I short-circuit that loop of social anxiety and come back into myself. I push back against that inner cowering, telling myself, "What matters is what I think. If they don't like it, that's fine. I'm not for everybody."

If I notice ongoing anxiety, stress, or my lizard-brain firing off with threat signals all day long, I receive the message and slow down. I stop ceaseless doing and pause. I breathe and feel my body. I take time in the morning to wake up early, so I have space just to breathe and feel or journal. I uncover what demands I'm putting on myself, and I see if I can let them go. I find ways to soothe myself and calm my nervous system.

I only speak kindly to myself about my body. I interrupt any negative chatter about my appearance. I consciously say positive things to myself and express deep gratitude for my healthy body every day. I choose to eat the world's healthiest vegetables, fruits, and plants to fuel my body. I avoid all substances that create dependency and addiction in order to minimize emotional eating and the suffering of craving things that ultimately make me feel worse.

I take a little time each day to celebrate how amazing my life is, focusing on what's going well and what I'm grateful for.

Above all else, I repeatedly, actively, and frequently through-out every day, consciously speak well to myself. I narrate my story as it's happening in a way that is affirming, supportive, honest, and empowering. Before doing something challenging, I tell myself, "Aziz, you got this." I make a study of how to most effectively motivate myself to do the uncomfortable or difficult things that serve me in my life. I motivate myself with love, respect, kindness, and praise.

When I make a mistake, let someone down, or act in a way that is less mature or loving than I aspire to be, I brutally attack myself and make myself feel like dirt to ensure I never do that again — just kidding. I wanted to make sure you were still with me and paying attention. No! I treat myself with patience and empathy. I explore what I was feeling in the moment and what ideas may have led me to do what I did. I know that shame and blame don't make me learn anything, and that loving inquiry is what creates positive changes over time.

Keep this essay somewhere accessible. How would your life change if you read it once per day? How about if you recorded yourself reading it and listened to it once per day? How much more quickly would being on your own side become your new normal?

You do not have to be good.
You do not have to walk on your knees
for a hundred miles through the desert repenting.
You only have to let the soft animal of your body
love what it loves.
Tell me about despair, yours, and I will tell you mine.
Meanwhile the world goes on.
Meanwhile the sun and the clear pebbles of the rain
are moving across the landscapes,
over the prairies and the deep trees,
the mountains and the rivers.
Meanwhile the wild geese, high in the clean blue air,
are heading home again.
Whoever you are, no matter how lonely,
the world offers itself to your imagination,
calls to you like the wild geese, harsh and exciting -
over and over announcing your place
in the family of things.

- "Wild Geese" by Mary Oliver

Chapter 5:
The Decision of a Lifetime

By now, you may be sold on the idea of O.M.O.S. It may sound appealing, exciting, or relieving to imagine a life where you feel good about yourself, your accomplishments, your appearance, and generally in who you are, right now as you are.

And yet, you may have some doubts. Many people do. If you had a magic button you could push right now that would make you instantly O.M.O.S. forever, would you press it? Or would you have concerns or hesitations about doing so?

When I ask clients this question, most instantly reply that they would press the button without hesitation. Others have concerns that we need to discuss first. But even those who say they'd press the button right away still have objections lurking in the shadows of their minds; they just aren't aware of them yet. These objections to being O.M.O.S. emerge as subtle resistances to being on their own side, an inability to stop their critic, or anxiety about not being so hard on themselves.

In order to fully choose being on your own side from a place of power, integrity, and feeling good about the process, we must first address some of your biggest concerns about living this way.

O.M.O.S. OBJECTIONS

It's time for me to test out my sales skills. But I'm not here to sell you on one of my products or services. I'm interested in selling you on you.

As with any sales process, we have objections about buying, taking the leap, or signing up. We might really want the product or service, but we have fears, concerns, or doubts that need to be addressed first. Next, we will cover the top six most common objections people have to being on their own sides.

Objection #1: Self-Indulgent Waste Of Time

Focusing on loving myself is a selfish, unnecessary thing that only weak people do.

Not too long ago, I met an intelligent, successful, driven attorney in his mid-thirties. I was at a gathering hosted by a friend and was meeting a variety of people in that new environment. Many years ago, this kind of socializing used to terrify me, flooding me with social anxiety and shame. I used to turn on myself harshly and imagine others were judging me ruthlessly (aka not O.M.O.S.). Now, I ask myself what I want. I share what I want to share and feel okay with people liking me or not liking me. I'm okay either way. In other words, O.M.O.S.

I was talking about this exact thing with a woman from New York. She asked me what I did, and I told her I was an author, teacher, and coach. She questioned me further about what I wrote and taught about, and I began telling her about this book.

"So many people are so hard on themselves," I said. "My goal is to help people end the insanity, stop beating themselves up, and get on their own side, no matter what."

She smiled, seemingly inspired by the concept. Just as she opened her mouth to speak, a new voice cut into the scene:

"But don't you think that's part of the problem these days?" I turned to my right to see a clean-shaven, handsome man with dark curly hair and a well-fitted suit. "So many people can't take criticism, can't handle it when things don't go their way. People just want to whine and complain and have things handed to them," he said emphatically, gesturing with the cocktail he held in his hand.

During my social anxiety years, this would have completely derailed me. Heck, I probably wouldn't have even opened up in the first place with the woman to avoid this sort of push-back. But now I relish it. I find it fascinating.

"You think people are too soft, basically. Like they need to go after what they want, handle setbacks, and toughen up," I said.

"Yes!" he agreed emphatically.

"What do you think about this," I began. "What if someone goes after what they want, but when they fail, they brutally attack themselves in their own minds, so much so that they are terrified of trying and failing again?"

"Well, they need to stop crying about it and get over it," he said.

"Sure. How do you imagine they might do that?" I asked.

"I don't know," he said, seemingly irritated by my attempt to explore his perceptions at a deeper level. "The whole self-esteem thing, gold stars and participation trophies for everybody, I don't know. It all strikes me as a self-indulgent waste of time."

Thank you, abrasive lawyer guy. I loved talking with him and appreciated his directness. He voiced one of the most common initial kinds of resistance people can have to examining being kinder to themselves.

Check with yourself right now. Is there a voice inside that is dismissing this whole process of developing more self-love? Is it saying that trying to get on your own side, reading about it, taking time to focus on it is stupid, bad, silly, pointless, selfish, or wrong? Is it a "self-indulgent waste of time"?

Or perhaps your mind is not judging this process that harshly, but you *are* really busy and need to focus on other more important tasks for a while first, and you'll get to this "non-essential" thing later.

Notice whatever resistance might be arising in you. Let's flush it out of the shadows and shine the light of your awareness on it. Take just a moment to slow down, reflect inward, and notice what's happening in your mind and body. Take two slow, deep breaths right now. Do you feel any tension in your body? Are you squeezing, tightening, or grasping in your chest, stomach, throat, face, back, or shoulders?

Take a moment to listen to your thoughts of resistance or judgment. Notice what this voice is saying, but also notice its tone, attitude, and energy. Does it seem wise, grounded, and non-judgmental? Or does it sound angry, scared, dismissive, or impatient?

Do you believe what the voice is saying? Or is it the voice of the critic, trying to undermine the process before you start?

Even if you aren't sure, just asking these questions is important. Right now, most likely, all your thoughts are jumbled together, and the critic's voice is blended seamlessly into your normal thought stream. But as you read this book, you'll become highly skilled at listening to your own mind and identifying when it's your critic talking versus the real you.

Despite what your critic might be saying now, the truth is that developing the skill of being on your own side is quite possibly one of the most valuable things you can do in your entire life. The more you're on your own side, the higher your quality of life will be. You will be able to enjoy being you and feel happy as you achieve and succeed, rather than living in a perpetual sense of striving and inadequacy. You'll handle setbacks, failures, and criticism with so much more ease, openness, and freedom. You won't have to live in fear of other's passing opinions, judgments, and ideas.

The truth is, life is good when you're on your own side, and it's bad when you're not, no matter how many good things you have going on in your world. In a moment, all of that can be wiped away by your mind, leaving you with the twisting disappointment of being an unworthy failure. This is why we see so many amazing people who seemingly have everything, including money, fame, fans, creative expression, and love, yet they still feel depressed or even take their own lives.

Self-indulgent? Hardly! The more you take your own side, the more confident, capable, and grounded you become. You have less need to defend and prove yourself, and you become a much more curious person and a better listener. You become a better spouse, parent, colleague, and friend. You start to care more deeply about other individuals, groups, societies, animals, and the planet. Your heart becomes more awake, alive, connected, and aware. The full, most powerful version of you comes online and starts making life happen faster and faster in the world around you. You become a force for good and unleash your gifts to live out whatever your purpose is here on earth.

Remember, the critic is a malfunctioning attempt to protect you from past and future emotional pain. And one way it does that is by maintaining control over you, steering you away from opening up, sharing, living fully, and taking healthy risks. The last thing it wants is you poking around under the hood and getting closer to the feelings it's trying to avoid. So it will tell you this whole idea of becoming O.M.O.S. is stupid, silly, selfish, and wrong.

It will go on to tell you these objections. But remember, these predictions aren't true; they're just fearful stories used to keep you scared of making positive changes. The critic is trying to stop you from challenging its authority and breaking free.

Blech. No, thank you. Let's question it. Let's challenge it. Let's sweep its legs and topple it to the ground so we can get free now.

Objection #2: Undeserving

I am not good enough yet to deserve to treat myself with love, kindness, and respect.

This objection involves a story that to be ⸱. our own ⸱   ⸱, we have to deserve it. And unfortunately, we don't. We haven't earned it yet. We're not successful enough, beautiful enough, or smart enough yet. We haven't achieved enough, earned enough, or performed well enough. We haven't been the perfect mother, father, son, or daughter. And so, until further notice, we don't deserve to be on our own side. Not yet, at any rate. Sooner or later, or perhaps much, much later, we'll have ticked enough of the worthiness boxes to bask in that glow of self-acceptance.

But not yet. Not now. Not today. Not while I still weigh fourteen more pounds than I "should." Not until I get all these projects done at work. Not until I stop making mistakes and looking like a fool in front of my boss. Not while I drink too much or eat unhealthy food. Besides, I was cranky last night with my spouse and kids. I can't possibly be on my own side while I'm still doing stuff like that. It's totally unacceptable, and I'm a jerk who needs to do better. Come on!

And off we go, back into the river of thoughts that is heavily populated by our inner critic's perspective. Can you relate to this? Would it feel strange or bad or wrong to simply accept yourself and choose to be on your own side right now, just as you are?

The truth is, most of us have such a small capacity to love

ourselves. Listen to the logic of this scenario: I'm not good enough yet, so I can't love myself, like myself, or stop bullying myself until I'm better. Imagine you had a young child or a nephew or niece who you treated that way? You're not smart enough, so I'm going to withdraw love, be cold and impatient, and demand for you to do more and better until you get there. How would that feel?

Unfortunately, this is a parenting style that you may have known. It's still employed by millions of parents all over the world, and it produces a reservoir of insecurity, low self-worth, excessive niceness, and perfectionism in their children. It teaches the child they have to earn their parents' love, that they are worthless unless they achieve or outperform others.

Even well-intentioned and self-aware parents find themselves resorting to this approach sometimes. It takes a great deal of self-awareness, patience, and love to find a way to be with your kids when they're doing something annoying, frustrating, or different than how you'd like. So no matter who you are, that message—*you must earn my love by being worthy* (aka how I want you to be)—will be transmitted to your children. Fortunately, perfection isn't required.

If you're a parent and are curious about how to be more relaxed, confident, and loving with your own children, or want to learn how to "parent" yourself in a much healthier way, then you'll love the appendix later in this book called O.M.O.S. Parenting. In the meantime, let me tell you this. If you are a parent and you're cold with your child, withholding love and internally demanding that they be different than how they are, this feels awful.

Yet, this is what we do to ourselves all the time. This is how we habitually parent ourselves internally. Worse still, part of us feels like this is how it's supposed to be. That to do otherwise is weak, foolish, spoiling, or going to bring about much worse results. So we stick with this mostly ineffective approach, telling ourselves it's the best way to be. It's not. We can do better, way better.

But in order to see this, we have to see through objection number three.

Objection #3: It Keeps Me Good and Safe

Being hard on myself makes me a better, more compassionate, and caring person. Otherwise, I'd be a selfish, bad, mean jerk (and then everyone would eventually leave me).

Let's take a step back and look at this one. You want to be a compassionate, caring, loving person. And to do this, you'll berate and harshly criticize yourself in your head. You'll hate yourself into being a "good person."

What a strange idea. Where did we get that?

This one goes back a long, long time to your earliest days on this planet. Most of us learned to be hard on ourselves because that's how our parents guided us to be "good" people. Despite deeply loving their children, parents can easily fall into a habit of being impatient, irritable, judgmental, or frustrated with their children. They want them to be a certain way; and doggone it, they just aren't!

In order to gain control, parents might yell, criticize, threaten, withdraw love, or otherwise scare their child into being the way they want. They fear that if they don't do something right now to fix their child, they'll end up "bad" in some way. And if they're bad, then they will experience problems later in life, and the parent will have failed at raising their child into a good, proper, successful, well-adjusted member of society. Their child won't be accepted in business or social worlds, and they will live penniless and alone until they die from an overdose on a mattress on the floor in a leaky, abandoned squatter house. Or worse, people will see this poorly-behaved child getting bad grades, and losing at life. What would they think about you as a parent? Even scarier!

When my five-year-old son pushes his three-year-old brother down to the ground, I feel pain in my heart. It hurts to see the young one fall down and start crying. I feel angry at the seeming injustice oft this misuse of the older boy's strength. I also feel fear of him doing this again and again. In addition to this, I fear what others would think of me if they saw that my children are not perfectly-behaved little angels. So, I feel a strong urge to chastise my older son, to yell at him, scare him, bribe him, punish him, *something* to make sure he *never* does that again.

Enter behavioral conditioning and hundreds of books about parenting that teach you how to control the situation to make sure little Johnny never pushes little Susie again. But does punishing Johnny solve the problem? If he gets a punishment, like a time-out or no TV later that day, does he all of a sudden develop a moral compass that tells him not to hurt others? Does it make him develop empathy and compassion? Or does he learn that pushing others makes him not get what he wants, and so he restrains himself to get what he wants? Or does he learn to get his aggression at Susie out in a sneakier way that his parents don't know about?

If you combine the punishment with emotional pain as well by calling him "bad" or "mean," it may make him recoil in shame. He may stop the unpleasant behavior out of fear of losing his connection with you. But again, does this foster empathy and values of kindness and respect? Or does it make him simply afraid of emotional pain? Do we control the behavior, achieving "success" in the short term only to create guilt, shame, and inadequacy in the long term?

If we take a step back and look at what's more effective in life, it's almost always the long game, not the quick fix. Our impulse is to act now to end this forever! The more effective approach is to slowly guide and teach over months and years.

If Zaim pushes Arman down, my wife and I have a policy of moving toward both children. I learned an awesome phrase from my wife, which I use all the time. She swoops in and says, "Boys! I'm here to help." She tries to figure out what's going on like a detective on the case. What was happening that Zaim pushed his brother? Did Arman hit him or scare him?

We try to help him discover what he was feeling that made him want to push his brother. And we explore how he can deal with that feeling in a different way. Sometimes, we have that conversation then, in the moment, or sometimes we create some space, let them cool down, and talk about it later.

But the overall goal is to teach both of them how to identify their feelings, validate their feelings, and then express their feelings in an effective way that doesn't involve punching someone in the face (although that sure seems like a gratifying way to express your feelings of rage towards that annoying coworker, doesn't it? Ahh, to be five years old again).

So what does all this have to do with you? Well, let's find out. How did your parents deal with you when you were young? Did they have an ultra-long game approach focused on fostering your emotional intelligence? If so, that's a fortunate yet all too rare experience. If not, then what did you experience? Were you punished, criticized, intimidated, or shamed? Were you hit, yelled at, or told you were bad, lazy, too needy, too loud, too shy, too whatever?

However you were treated, you tend to adopt this style of relating to yourself. Your parents or other caregivers were the templates for how to do things. If they told you were bad and demanded you act better, then most likely, you regularly tell yourself that you're bad and demand that you act better. Your critic is running ineffective parenting scripts from thirty, forty, or fifty years ago. Like old DOS commands typed on your keyboard, they don't do much on your present computer. Yet you keep typing away, imagining they're working.

The story behind all of this mess is that we have to be hard on ourselves, punish ourselves, and withhold love in order to manipulate ourselves into being good. It's the only way we'll do the "right" thing. Otherwise, we'd be selfish, hurtful, aggressive monsters who just stomped on anyone in our path.

But what if this whole approach to children and yourself is misguided? What if you are inherently a loving human who wants to connect with others, be kind, and treat others and animals with respect and dignity? What if the only problem here is the way in which we are attempting to unlock these natural qualities? What if what you need is *more* love, empathy, and support, not *less*?

Objection #4: Self-Love Makes Me Lazy

If I love myself now, I'll stop striving to get better, and I'll become lazy, self-indulgent, undisciplined, and unsuccessful.

"But Aziz," my client said to me in a slow and measured tone, as if he was trying to communicate something important that I'd missed, "If I love myself more, just as I am, then I won't be driven to achieve so much. I'll lose my motivation and feel good without needing to do more. I'll lose my edge."

"Yep." I said, smiling.

He shook his head in confusion and frustration.

"But that's not acceptable to me," he said, his voice straining to hold back strong emotions.

"I know. You need that edge." I said.

"Yes!" he exclaimed, relieved that I was finally getting him and how important it was for him not to love himself quite yet.

"So here's your plan," I said. "Withhold love from yourself and feel unworthy most of the time. This will make you feel empty and dissatisfied, which will provide you with the rocket fuel you need to achieve your dreams."

"Yes…" he said, hesitating. It sure didn't sound good the way I was describing it, but that was the gist of his plan.

"How long have you been operating with this plan?" I asked.

He paused for a moment to reflect on the answer. "I think mostly my whole life, at least since I was a teenager."

"So what do you think? Are you almost there?" I asked.

"Where?"

"To that place you need to get to. When will you arrive? When will you get to relax, feel worthy, know you're enough, and feel love and pride?"

He stared at me, blankly. There was no place. There was no end.

This client earned a six-figure salary from a prestigious company, had a family, and lived in a nice house in a nice neighborhood. He was healthy and fit and had a thriving social network. He was living the dream, but he felt like a failure.

He came to me because he was feeling anxiety before work meetings. He couldn't manage his stress and fear before big meetings, especially when powerful people were present. And if he wanted to get to that next level of leadership, success, income, and prestige, then he needed to bring his A-game to these meetings.

And here we were, talking about self-love and being on our own sides. What a waste of time. Or, so he thought. We stopped working together after he realized I didn't have some magic confidence pill to allow him to keep doing everything as usual but also give him "that edge."

Are you running that same life formula? The "withhold love from myself, diminish my worth, and invalidate my accomplishments, so I'll be driven to do even more" plan? It's a tried and true method used by millions before you. And it's one of the biggest obstacles to O.M.O.S.

Let's take a step back and see what's most effective. Does it work? Is it driving you ahead further and faster? Maybe it is, I don't know. I've seen many people get burned up by that fuel and burn out, producing even less in the long run. I've also seen people get burned up internally by that fuel so that they achieve everything they've dreamed of but feel empty and sad on the inside. They have no idea what to do with that confusing twist, so they just double down on what they know and create an even bigger set of goals to strive relentlessly toward, treating themselves with ruthless demands for more, faster, better, now.

Is it possible to switch fuel? Is there a different way to motivate ourselves so that we can achieve big things and enjoy the process, or better yet, love ourselves along the way? Can we feel a sense of excitement and enjoyment as we do, act, and create whatever it is we're working toward? Can we feel a sense of pride, accomplishment, and satisfaction with each small milestone along the way?

I believe we can. If you relate to this difficulty of high demands, perfectionism, and a fear that being on your own side means you'll stop growing in life, then you're in the right place. I get it. I lived for 20+ years as a raging closet perfectionist. I didn't know I was a perfectionist; I just thought I was a high-achiever. Nevermind my body pain, stomach issues, or deep sense of sadness, emptiness, or agitation I'd feel when I slowed down and stopped working. Who's got time to worry about that noise? I've got stuff to do!

Fortunately, there's a much better fuel. And yes, you can still achieve like crazy, although it might be slightly less than what you expect of yourself right now. We'll cover that in more detail in Chapter 11: Optimal Motivation & the Art of Relaxed Discipline.

For now, let me ask you this. Are you willing to test out your theory that you need to be driving yourself by depriving yourself of self-love and satisfaction in your achievements? Are you open to testing out a new way of being? Are you willing to give O.M.O.S. a try for 30 or 60 days to see what happens? If it doesn't work out how you want, you can always go back to the adrenaline and drama of the self-worth hustle.

Objection #5: I'm a Realist, Okay?

Being kind to myself no matter what is living in delusion and disconnected from the cold, hard truth of reality that I suck, and I need to know it.

Another common story is that actively being on your own side, focusing on your strengths, and believing in yourself is somehow a distorted view of the world. Your critic can dismiss having a more optimistic or positive viewpoint as pollyannaish or foolish, claiming that it's not grounded in reality.

Like all the objections to O.M.O.S., we often hear this thought and instantly begin to dismiss or doubt ourselves, without checking to see if it's true. Which it's not.

It's operating within the bizarre circular trap of the world of your inner critic. Your critic wants to keep you safe from all risk, protected from others by not really opening up and connecting with them, protected from failure by not risking anything in life. So it repeatedly tells you that you'll fail, and no one will like you anyway, so don't put yourself out there. It tells you this frequently enough that you start to believe it and form a false identity in which you see yourself as an incapable, unlovable, unsuccessful person (regardless of how much love, success, or capability you currently experience).

Then, when you try to see yourself in a different, more balanced, more accurate way by focusing on your strengths and the value you bring to others and the world, your critic says that you're deluded. *Because look,* it says, *you're not any of those positive things, remember? You're that loser that I've always been telling you that you are.*

What's deluded is the small, helpless, incapable story you have about who you are. No matter how many times you've heard it or how certain your critic is that it's true, it's not. It's just an old familiar story that's keeping you stuck.

Let's expand that story and upgrade your identity. Let's get curious about who you truly are, how you impact others, and what you can do in the world in your lifetime. You will be amazed when you see how powerful you already are, how much you've already done, even before you take any new actions, just by taking off the critic's negative filters and starting to see yourself more clearly.

Objection #6: It's Too Late for Me

I've been this way for so long; there's nothing I can do to change it. I'm doomed.

The final objection is your critic's last-ditch effort to keep you stuck in your old ways. It throws out the fixed mindset perspective that once we've been a certain way for a while, then change isn't possible.

Of course, you and I know this isn't true. It's just learned helplessness. It's just fear, masking as hopelessness to stop you from trying. The truth is that you are changing, growing, and evolving all the time. You can't stop changing.

Change is inevitable. And as long as you are willing to take action outside of your comfort zone, then growth is inevitable too. O.M.O.S. is a skill, just like confidence, or starting conversations, or archery, or the guitar, or chess. If you practice, over time, you will change and grow and get better at that skill.

The next part of this book is full of specific tools and strategies you can use immediately to challenge your inner critic and talk to yourself differently than you ever have in your life. It will help you regain control inside your own mind so that you are steering the ship, not this terrified tyrant that you've given the wheel to for way too long. Practice these tools, and you will change. I promise.

THE CORE DECISION

Here's the best news of all. No matter how many years you've been treating yourself poorly, it is possible to radically change that in a short period of time. In the upcoming chapters of this book, you are going to learn the exact tools and techniques I've used to help clients and students from all different cultures, backgrounds, and countries neutralize their critics and live with greater self-esteem and fulfillment.

While I've been obsessed with personal growth and confidence for the last sixteen years, I've been particularly obsessed with this topic of self-criticism. I remember being in seminars or reading books and looking for the tools to turn off my raging critic. I often felt disappointed with what I was learning, as many teachers and authors would only speak to the topic briefly with simple platitudes like, "You have to accept yourself," and "Love yourself first."

But how?? I would think to myself. *How do I do this?* Eventually, I came across some books written by cognitive-behavioral therapists that suggested writing out the critical thoughts and challenging them. This made sense logically; however, it seemed like no matter what I wrote, my critic would get the upper hand. Even if I could logically tell myself that what it was saying wasn't true, I would still be emotionally impacted and feel inferior and insecure.

Fortunately, all my obsessive searching paid off. Over the years, I discovered some incredible teachers and resources who taught me how to truly love myself.[15]

---

15   Several fantastic authors include Theodore Rubin, Tara Brach, and Kristin Neff, in case you want to do some further studies.

The Benefits of Self-Attack

Before I share these tools with you, there is one thing we have to do first. Early on in my training as a psychologist and coach, I discovered this fascinating and strange phenomenon. Part of us doesn't want to stop the criticism. The pattern of self-loathing is somehow meeting our needs, albeit in a limited and unfulfilling way. But it's what we know, and it's familiar and easy. This is true for any destructive behavior or mental pattern. On some level, it's giving us something, and we want to keep it.

The same is true for self-criticism. So my question for you is this: If you could press a button that would permanently turn off your critic, why might you *not* want to press that button? I know it sounds crazy, but take a moment to think about it. What are the hidden benefits of turning on yourself, as bad as it feels?

I will suggest a few possibilities in just a moment, but I encourage you to pause and write out a shortlist. Doing so will actively engage your self-awareness in the process and produce a greater ability to change.

Here are some ways we benefit from attacking ourselves. First and foremost, if you believe the critic, then you tend to avoid risks. When you tell yourself you're incapable or ugly, for example, the critic is ultimately urging you not to take on that new opportunity at work or ask that person out. As long as you're cozy with your critic, you're avoiding risks, which means your avoiding discomfort. **Every positive risk that will make your life better is going to involve some level of discomfort.** Your critic is a warm, heavy blanket to hide under, where you can stay safe and stay small.

Secondly, your critic can provide you with a consistent sense of certainty in an uncertain world. This one blew my mind when I discovered it. For years, I had this awful pattern of predicting failure with total certainty, especially in business ventures. Before

I'd offer a new coaching program or live event, my critic would inform me, with total and complete certainty, that it would not work out. No one would buy it; no one would come to the event (or worse, only two people would come, and they would see how pathetic I was).

Even as you step out into the unknown and take those healthy risks, your critic is there, trying to help in its own messed up sort of way. The truth is, I didn't know how these new ventures would turn out. A new program or event might flop and have poor sales or attendance. That is a natural risk and a healthy part of business growth. And in that uncertainty vacuum, your critic can rush in to meet your need for certainty, albeit in a demoralizing and anxiety-producing kind of way. But remember, happiness, positive growth, connection, and contribution are not the primary goals of your critic! It's focused on keeping you safe and alive by avoiding all potential sources of pain.

This certainty goes beyond specific predictions about the future. It can encompass your whole identity. You have an idea about who you are, a way of seeing yourself, that is very grounding and comforting. I am ugly. I am awkward. As bad as these sound, they help you understand yourself and make sense of the world. I know who I am. I know how people will respond to me. Hence, if you tell someone who thinks they're ugly that you find them beautiful, they will usually find a way to dismiss your perception. Your identity provides you with a great sense of certainty, especially fixed, negative identities that you've carried for many years.

Another interesting hidden benefit of the critic is a limited form of connection. When you are criticizing yourself, who are you focusing on? That's right, yourself! When in the throws of a self-attack episode, we become incredibly self-focused. One colleague of mine put it brilliantly when he said, "I'm a piece of shit at the center of the universe." While this focus is painful and often a harsh litany of our shortcomings and failures, it is still a strange way of relating to ourselves. Thus, self-attack becomes a pattern we turn to when we're feeling lonely or longing for connection. We turn inward and connect with ourselves in a way that feels safer than connecting with others. After all, others might leave or otherwise hurt us. But this critic is never going anywhere.

What are you learning about yourself as you read this? What stands out to you? Take a moment to actively engage with the material and reflect on your own experience. What are the hidden benefits of your critic?

The Cost

This one will be much easier. What is your critic costing you? What negative impact is listening to your critic having on your life? Take several minutes to slow down and really reflect as you read the following questions. Let yourself feel the answers more than just thinking about it mentally. Let yourself be moved, be upset, frustrated, or dismayed. Even though it may not feel good in the moment, this emotional charge is important in making a change.

How is this toxic stream of abuse impacting your energy, mood, and self-esteem? How do you feel about yourself when you look in the mirror? Do you like who you are? Do you love who you are? How demoralizing is it to pick at yourself, criticize yourself, and disparage yourself every day?

What does it feel like to incessantly compare yourself to others and feel inferior and incapable? What's it like to feel like you've never done enough or that you are not enough? How long has it been since you just felt happy and proud to be you? Or is that something you've never felt?

How much has your critic cost you in your love life? What relationships have you lost because you couldn't receive love and didn't feel fully worthy of it? What amazing opportunities have you missed out on because your critic said it wouldn't work out, so you didn't even try? How many years have you been lonely because you bought your critic's story that you didn't deserve a lasting, loving relationship? What does that loneliness feel like?

How has listening to your critic stifled your career? How has having your critic as your trusted advisor limited your opportunities, kept you stuck and stagnant, and wasted years upon years of growth potential in your work? Does it make you feel like an imposter, no matter how much experience and success you accumulate? Does it keep you perpetually stressed and afraid of losing it all, being found out, or failing? Is it sucking the joy out of work that could feel meaningful and fulfilling?

And what is it doing to your health? How is it affecting your organs and cells to be blanketed in fear, frustration, and self-directed anger? What breakdown, damage, or aging is that cost to your body? What diseases may be brewing slowly beneath the surface in that breeding ground of stress and self-hatred?

I know it's not pretty to look at, but let's face it. Don't shy away from, ignore, or sugar-coat the truth. What horrible effects does engaging in this abusive relationship have on your life? How has it limited you? How has it hurt you? What has it damaged or destroyed?

Notice what you are feeling right now as you reflect on this impact your critic has had on you over the years. What's it like to see just how much it has cost you and is currently costing you?

If you are feeling pain right now, good! Perhaps you are upset, angry, shocked, horrified, or outraged. That is a sign of health. Anger and outrage are healthy responses to abuse. Complacency and cold indifference are warning signs that you are believing the abuse and becoming numb to it.

Do you want to live your life this way? Do you want to live another ten or twenty years with your critic harassing and denigrating you each day? Can you imagine this being with you for another decade, following you around, sucking the joy out of your life?

Is this the life you want for yourself?

You may already be subtly shaking your head "NO" right now as you read. To make this even more clear for yourself, answer that last question out loud—is this the life you want for yourself? Is this the life you deserve?

The Decision

Getting on your own side no matter what begins with a core decision. After you see how painful it is to turn on yourself and feel the negative impact, you are ready to take a stand and clearly and firmly declare that you are done. This is your threshold moment.

We all have threshold moments where we reach a clear and dramatic end to something. Perhaps you've been in a romantic relationship that was distant, full of conflict, or otherwise unfulfilling. And yet you stayed, and stayed, perhaps months or even years longer than you knew was optimal. And then, one day, you were done. This day was different than other times when you said you were done, but then you quickly changed your mind and went back. No, this time you clearly and simply decided—that's it, I'm done. Maybe it took some months to have all the conversations and carry out the process, but the end was set in motion the moment you made that clear, powerful decision.

Maybe you've done that with smoking, drinking, or junk food. You made a firm decision that you were done, and you were not turning back. Perhaps you didn't know exactly how you were going to do it, and you didn't have all the strategies and tools yet, but you knew one thing for certain—you were *not* going to live that way anymore.

This, right now, is another threshold moment. You can decide right now, as you read these words, that you are done criticizing yourself. You're done turning on yourself, picking on yourself, dismissing your feelings, abusing yourself, pressuring yourself. You're done with criticizing your appearance, done with the permanent sense that you haven't done enough, done with the constant predictions of failure, done with seeing yourself as small, incapable, and less than others. Done with all of it.

You may not know how to stop your critic, and you may feel a little uncertain that you can. You may doubt that you can ever win and fear that your critic's words will always have power over you. Don't worry about that. Doubt is part of any core decision. Doubt is always there and will always be there. **Doubt doesn't mean you can't make a decision; rather, doubt is a sign that you *must* make a decision.** You must find your inner power and declare your decision with firmness and clarity. You must strengthen your resolve, your grit, your will, your determination, and your faith. You must find that stubborn will inside of you that says: *I don't know how I'm going to do it, but I'm going to do this. I am going to do whatever it takes to change this, to reclaim my life.*

Are you ready to make this choice with me, here and now? A choice that will change the rest of your life? Yes, I know this sounds dramatic because it is. This is you taking your life back; this is you liberating yourself. This is you returning to your own side, which is what you have unknowingly been longing for your whole adult life.

Are you ready?

If so, say the word "YES" out loud. I know it might seem crazy but no crazier than letting a self-hating, scared part of you run your entire life!

If you aren't ready to make this decision, why not? What voice in your head is telling you not to? And what is it saying? Is it saying this is silly, stupid, or ridiculous? Does it have a dismissive, condescending tone? Is it the voice of your critic even now sabotaging your initial attempts at liberation? Perhaps it's telling you that there's no point in making the decision because you'll never be free of the critic's power anyway.

If you are feeling resistant to making this core decision, that's important to notice. Slow down and pay attention. Open up a journal and write for a few minutes about why you would *not* want to decide to be on your own side no matter what. Reflect on why you would want to stay enmeshed with a voice that is so limiting and toxic. How does it allow you to avoid certain challenges and meet your basic needs? If needed, take a few days or weeks to reflect on how much your critic is harming you in your life. In time, once you get a sense of the scope of the damage, you will reach your threshold moment, and you'll be ready.

If you have decided you're ready, then stand up! Yes, as you hold this book or whatever digital device you're viewing. Stand up, full, tall, and upright. Stand with strength. Stand with dignity. You are done being oppressed, done being kicked around, and abused. Find that place inside of you that is sick and tired of this, that refuses to subjugate to the critic, the part of you that resists the critic, that defies the critic.

Breathe fully and deeply into your body. As you do, think back to a time in your life when you felt strong. When was there a moment when you felt powerful in your body and mind? Stand how you were standing then. Breathe how you were breathing then. Imagine being right back in that moment now—what was happening around you? What kind of expression did you have on your face? What were you saying to yourself in your head? Say that in your head now. Purposefully intensify the feeling of strength and power inside of you. You are always this powerful, even if sometimes you forget.

What was your life like when you let this powerful part inside you run the show? How does that part of you face challenges, handle problems, or do what needs to be done? What can the powerful part inside of you make happen? Anything? Anything it puts it's mind to?

From this place of power, of you remembering your strength, make the decision. Decide in this moment that you are going to be on your own side, no matter what, for the rest of your life.

Can you feel that? What happens inside of you as you do this?

Forget about what's happened in the past, even just days or hours ago. Focus on this moment right now. That's all that exists anyway. Right here and now, strengthen that decision, intensify your resolve. Say it out loud: "From now on, I am on my own side."

Good. How does that feel? Say it again, with more clarity and conviction. Say it one more time as if it were completely matter-of-fact, a statement of the obvious.

Great! Now say each one of these sentences out loud, one at a time, as you read them:

I am always on my own side.
No matter what.
I don't turn on myself.
I don't attack myself.
Because I am always on my own side.

Take another full, deep breath in. And smile. You are on the path to victory. How do you feel inside? Relieved? Excited? Nervous? Neutral? It's okay to have any reaction to this exercise. Some people feel that connection to themselves and feel a profound sense of relief as if they are returning home after being gone for decades. Others feel a sense of tenderness, love, and sadness as they feel the impact of how they've treated themselves all these years. Still, others experience tension or anxiety as their critic immediately ramps up the noise factor in their heads, telling them this is never possible and to stop right now!

That last one can be a good sign. When your critic feels that it's power is threatened, it will often change tactics or intensify its approach. As you notice this happening, smile. That means you got him on the run.

If you'd like to experience a process of me guiding you through this decision, visit the book website (www.omosbook.com).

Now What?

So you've made this emphatic declaration to be on your own side. Now what? Well, my friend, now you sail off into the sunset, kicking back on a lounge chair while sipping a margarita. No, I'm kidding. While that vacation can be a part of your future self-care plan, your work is not done yet. Because if you don't get a handle on this critic, it will rob you of your happiness and enjoyment, even while you are on that cruise ship. You could be floating through paradise without a care in the world, and your critic will be right there, picking at your thighs or comparing you to the people on the boat who are prettier, richer, more confident, or having more fun than you.

Deciding to be on your own side no matter what is an essential and powerful first step. It gives you focus, energy, and resolve to change the mental patterns of self-talk and self-treatment you've developed over the years.

Our next step is to train together in the ways of self-talk judo. You are well aware of positive self-talk, I'm sure, where you say pleasant and affirming things to yourself through the day. You know, affirmations. Let me ask you—how well did they work? In my experience, not very well, and not for very long. And I'm guessing your experience is similar to mine; or why would you be reading this book?

Your critic is much smarter than that. It has been creating a subversive, mind-controlling propaganda campaign for decades, shaping your complete and total perception of yourself. The affirmation is a clunky counter-message that does not jive at all with what you've been telling yourself for years. As perfect as it sounds, it just doesn't land. It doesn't sink in.

That, of course, is why you must say them to yourself 4,000 times per day, right when you wake up, as you brush your teeth, in your head while your wife is talking to you, on your way to work, while you're at your desk, before your meeting with your boss, during your meeting with your boss. Oh, and you should listen to them all night long while you sleep too. Yep, that's how it will sink into your subconscious.

But does it really work? Have you tried it? Have you been disciplined and motivated about it? Maybe it had a temporary effect, but did it last? Did it stick? Did it fundamentally, at your core, change your identity, beliefs, actions, and choices? Perhaps it did for you. For almost everyone I've spoken with about the topic, it has not.

Why not? Why doesn't it work? Because it's a symptomatic solution to the problem. It's trying to stop the self-criticism with a pill of self-affirmation. But this pill doesn't address why you have the self-criticism in the first place. People are often drawn to affirmations and positive self-talk for this very reason. It promises a simple fix to resolve deep self-hatred without having to address any of the scary stuff in the closet. You can just slather on a nice new coat of paint, and the room will look as good as new.

You need more than a new technique or tactic; you need a fundamentally different approach. You need to address the problem at its root, thereby healing the source. As you do this, you will then be able to build a more natural, healthy form of self-talk, one that is reasonable and sustainable, and one that feels natural and true.

Think about it for a second. Imagine you are with a child or spouse, and you applied the affirmation-style form of communication out loud with them. You told them hundreds of times per day they were beautiful, they were great, they were intelligent. How absurd would that be? After a day or two, how tiresome would that be?

What about this instead: Imagine you are sitting in your cozy living room with your beloved and your small child. It's a cold, crisp autumn day, and the sun is shining through the windows, lighting up the eyes of each person in the room. As you look at your spouse, you feel a powerful surge of love in your heart, and you say to him or her, "Sweetheart, I love you so much. I am so grateful to share this life with you." You share a sweet moment of love and connection that lasts a moment but creates a beautiful memory for a lifetime.

That is what happens when you resolve your self-hatred at its root. You truly do love and appreciate yourself. You generally feel love, compassion, empathy, and appreciation of yourself. You say sweet, loving, encouraging, or supportive things to yourself, as is needed. You have a deep, solid, respectful relationship with yourself. This is what we are going to work together to create right now. And this, my friend, requires some self-talk judo.

PART III:
HOW TO BE ON
YOUR OWN SIDE
(NO MATTER WHAT)

The time will come
when, with elation
you will greet yourself arriving
at your own door, in your own mirror
and each will smile at the other's welcome,

and say, sit here. Eat.
You will love again the stranger who was your self.
Give wine. Give bread. Give back your heart
to itself, to the stranger who has loved you

all your life, whom you ignored
for another, who knows you by heart.
Take down the love letters from the bookshelf,

the photographs, the desperate notes,
peel your own image from the mirror.
Sit. Feast on your life.

- "Love After Love" by Derek Walcott

Chapter 6:
Regain Control

Yes! Here we go. If you made it this far, then I know that you are motivated and determined to make a big shift inside of your mind and heart. You are fed up with treating yourself poorly and ready to experience a life of more self-compassion, enjoyment, and O.M.O.S. I want to give you a map of the terrain ahead, including the stages you will go through on your journey to being more and more on your own side.

THE FOUR LEVELS OF O.M.O.S.

While a powerful decision is the first step to being on your own side, it does not mean that your work is done. That decision is the springboard to changing your long-standing negative habits of relating to yourself poorly. Here is what the path of changing that habit looks like:

Level Zero: Swimming in Self-Attack

Even before level one of O.M.O.S., there is, unfortunately, a level zero. This is where I spent many years, where you may have been before reading this book, and sadly, where a large number of people live their lives.

They are generally unaware of their inner critic, responding to its claims as if they are accurate reflections of their worth and ability. When the critic says they are an idiot for making a mistake, they think they're an idiot and feel ashamed and embarrassed. When their critic says not to try because they could never achieve something, they refuse to take the risk.

They feel like their self-hatred is justified—*Of course, I should be disgusted by myself; look at those thighs. Of course, I should feel inferior; look at my apartment and how small and unglamorous it is.*

In response to all this inner self-hatred, they may be living in a constant quest for glory, trying to become their fantasy self. They may be working themselves ragged, driven forward relentlessly by perfectionism and the promise of one day being worthy, or rich enough, or successful enough to finally be respected and admired by others.

As you may guess, living in level 0 is deeply unsatisfying. It doesn't end well.

Level One: Catch and Interrupt Direct Self-Attack

In level one of being on your own side, you are able to catch yourself when you fall into a spiral of direct self-attack. You notice it when you are saying mean, harsh, or critical things to yourself.

For example, after you get rejected by someone, and you think—*I am such a loser. How embarrassing for me to have even asked*—you don't automatically agree with that criticism. Instead, an alarm bell goes off inside of you, alerting you that you are now in self-attack mode, which is not helpful.

You then employ the tools you'll learn in this chapter to interrupt that criticism and stop it in its tracks before it grows into a 40-story monster that's destroying the city.

And, if that is already happening, and you've fallen into a pit of self-hatred and perceived unworthiness, you are equipped with a tool belt that helps you get out faster than ever before.

Level Two: Catch-All Forms of Self-Undermining and Return to O.M.O.S.

In this level, your alert radar goes off whenever you turn on yourself, in any way, no matter how subtle. Direct self-attack is a more rare occurrence and is surprising and jarring when it occurs. You ask yourself, *How did I tolerate that kind of treatment?*

As you catch and eliminate this direct self-attack, your critic turns to more sneaky methods of undermining your sense of confidence and worth. In this level of O.M.O.S., you get better and better at seeing those sneaky methods in action and finding your way back to being more compassionate and loving with yourself.

You regularly ask yourself, *Am I being on my own side right now?* When you're struggling, you get curious about how you're turning on yourself and what you can do to take care of yourself. You are actively curious about your own well-being and committed to quickly offering yourself the love and support you need.

The more you practice this, the better you get at it, and the better you feel. Turning on yourself in any way starts to feel unacceptable. It's almost like you have an O.M.O.S. immune system that mobilizes a quick response to combat any form of self-attack and return you to optimal health.

Level Three: Mostly O.M.O.S.

You reside mostly on your own side. This is your center of gravity and what you keep coming back to naturally. This results in a radical reduction of social anxiety, self-judgment, and all other forms of self-doubt. You like who you are, and you are less obsessively focused on how you come across and whether people will like you or not. You are okay with you.

You rarely engage in direct self-attack anymore. If it does start to happen, you are surprised and maybe even slightly amused. You think to yourself, *Wow, something must've gotten my critic really fired up!*

You approach your critic and all the parts of you with curiosity and acceptance. When you are suffering emotionally, you are truly empathic and looking to see what you need and what will help you.

You take more healthy risks because you are not afraid of the horrible berating that used to follow failure or rejection. You are more open to and engaged with life.

You sometimes catch ways you turn subtly on yourself. You are curious about the roots of these patterns and plant your focus on healing them at their core. You are uncovering and letting go of long-standing beliefs about who you should be and how you should operate to be lovable and worthy. You are becoming more and more you.

Level Four: Permanent O.M.O.S.

You are truly accepting of who you are in the world, including all of your past mistakes and painful moments. You see the magic and beauty in who you are and how your life is unfolding.

It goes way beyond begrudgingly accepting yourself in spite of your shortcomings. Rather, it's deeply falling in love with yourself, loving all of who you are, including the way your left eye gets smaller than your right when you smile, and the way you get secretly irritated when someone starts playing a Michael Jackson song because you never really liked his music, but everyone else seems to think it's amazing and you never saw what all the fuss was about (that's just hypothetical of course).

You are doing you. Life is moving through you, and you're letting it. You relish who you are. You love being in your body and are so grateful to have this incredible vehicle to move through the world.

At this level, you only want the best for yourself. You don't tolerate poor treatment. Instead, you cultivate a relationship that's affirming, inspiring, and loving. You are doing work that feels meaningful and fulfilling for you. In short, your life is awesome.

When there is pain, loss, heartache, or other inevitable challenges that arise in your life, you are on your side throughout. You hold yourself with tenderness and patience as you feel the inevitable pains that this human life brings.

Does that sound good to you? Do you want less of level zero and more of level four? Me too. And we start by mastering level one. Like any good video game, we gotta level our way up! Let's get started.

I AM THE CAPTAIN

You are clear, determined, and motivated. And your critic is not happy about any of this. The first key skill you must develop to truly stay on your own side is to become the head of your household, the captain of your ship, the master of your domain—your inner domain.

Up until now, your critic has been running amok in your inner household. It has often been in charge, giving orders, yelling and screaming at other family members, and causing dysfunction. This must change, and you are the one to change it.

You are a collection of parts. There is the critical part of you, and there is the part of you that wants to love yourself more. You have a scared part that acts up at different times in your life, and you have a courageous part that takes bold action in the world. You have a generous part that gives freely and a selfish part that wants to horde everything for you and yours. This is natural and universally the case for all humans.

But we don't talk about this much. We say, "I decided to do this," or, "I told him that," as if there was just one "I" in there. But, what you decided to do was based on the input of various parts of you and on which parts are loudest and most dominant. For example, did you decide to eat a healthy dinner yesterday? Or did you just grab some fast food or eat some processed food from your cupboard? If you ate the healthy meal, then the health-oriented part of you was dominant last night. If you ate fast food or junk food, then the lazy or comfort-seeking part of you was in charge at that moment.

That's a simple example with just two basic parts. But what about something like this. Imagine you are at work, and you have an unpleasant encounter with a colleague in which he disparages your work in front of several other team members. He is condescending and dismissive, and you feel embarrassed and don't say much in your defense. After the meeting, there is a storm going on inside of you. You feel embarrassed, humiliated, angry, hurt, upset, and inferior. Your mind is abuzz with thoughts:

Oh my God, that was terrible! He called my work uninspired and unclear. He even said it was sloppy. So bad. So awful. And Jared and Carol were watching the whole thing, and I didn't even do anything. I just sat there taking it like the pathetic doormat that I always am. What the hell is wrong with me? Anyone else would have said something, at least. So weak. How dare he say that? What a jerk. As if his work is so great; he is so full of himself.

Can you relate? Whether it's a tough work meeting, an awkward first date, or a difficult conversation with a loved one, we can leave experiencing a flurry of emotions and thoughts. We often think of this as "me" having "my" thoughts. But, what if it's a collection of different parts in there? Can you pick up a few different parts in this hypothetical work scenario? What are they?

There's the part of you that is hurt and embarrassed by your colleague's treatment. His criticisms stung, and the fact they were delivered publicly was even more painful. This part might feel like a small child who was criticized by the teacher and feels ashamed, inferior, and worthless. Then, there's another part of you that is enraged at your colleague, that wants to tear him down, get revenge, or give him a piece of your mind.

And finally, there's also your critic in there. Of course it's there because, remember, your critic is there to protect you from painful emotional experiences like this one. So whenever you are hurting inside, guess who's going to be in the mix, throwing out a handful of spiked barbs at you? That's right, your critic! In this case, it's picking on you about your history with a lack of assertiveness and what this says about your character.

Instead of a singular entity, this is more like a bunch of family members all talking at once around the kitchen table. Each part is inserting its perspective, speaking loudly, and cutting off other parts. This creates a cacophony of noise and adds to the sense of tension and upset you are feeling after a difficult encounter. It's hard to know what's going on. In fact, after a difficult experience, you may feel overwhelmed and confused and have a sense of "I don't even know what I think about it."

Discovering that you are a collection of parts might be a big revelation or something you already knew. My question for you is, how do these parts inside of you relate to each other? If you imagine all these parts are like a family inside of you, how does the family operate? Is it harmonious and respectful? Or is it chaotic, disruptive, harsh, or even violent? Who's in charge? Who's the loudest and most dominant one? How does it ensure its voice is the loudest, and how does it silence other parts?

A Dysfunctional Household

What is the nature of your "inner household"? We will do an exercise in just a little bit that will help illuminate this even more, but for now, what's your initial sense? How do the different parts inside of you relate?

Certain parts, such as your inner critic, a judgmental part, or a fearful part that is terrified of failing, looking bad, or being hurt, may be a dominant voice inside of you. You may be living from this part for large periods of the day, thinking thoughts from this place of fear or judgment, and feeling the associated feelings.

How do these dominant parts relate to other parts of you? Are they dismissive, intimidating, or condescending? Are other parts of you being pushed out and now resigned to a subordinate role in which they are submissive and meek?

And then, there are the parts that have been so habitually ignored and denied that they are pushed out of conscious awareness and seemingly gone. However, you can't get rid of parts in this internal household, so instead, they are down in the basement, out of sight, out of mind. However, these can manifest as anxiety symptoms, immune system problems, stomach issues, and chronic muscle, tendon, or joint pains.

Of course, most of this occurs outside of people's conscious awareness. They're focused on the external world—work duties, family responsibilities, desires, cravings, and making life go how they want it to go. If they pay attention to their inner world, they are aware of feelings, which are often jumbled, conflicted, and confusing or uncomfortable. If they slow down even further to notice thoughts, they often witness a fast, random thought stream that bounces from one thing to the next.

However, when you start to pay attention to your inner world as an internal family, as a collection of parts, everything makes more sense. You have conflicting feelings because you have two or more parts that feel very differently about an issue, and they're arguing inside of you. Your mind is bouncing all over the place because you have three parts that are all highly active in the moment, each loudly expressing their viewpoints without pausing to listen to the others. You feel depressed because there is a part inside of you that deeply wants to pursue something meaningful, but a dominant rational part has smashed it out of awareness, which takes tremendous energy each day.

One of the biggest problems that leads to social anxiety, low self-esteem, and insufficient confidence is having an overactive critical part that is running your inner household. Take a moment right now to see if this is the case for you. At certain times, does your critic kick in the door and start running the show? Is it acting like an angry, abusive, or alcoholic parent who is terrorizing the household? How do you relate to this critical part when it barges in and starts disparaging other members of the household? Do you stand by and watch in fear? Do you cower in terror? Do you submit and glumly nod, agreeing to its attacks? What do you typically do when your critic gets active?

This reflection will tell you a great deal about the current state of affairs in your household. When I was under the thumb of my critic, it would totally run the show. When it arrived to dispense a verbal beatdown, I would cower and submit to the onslaught. In some ways, I would agree with whatever it was saying as if it was laying down an awful and brutal truth about me.

I would spend a great evening with close friends enjoying myself and their company. And then, on the drive home, instead of enjoying the residual afterglow of love and connection, my critic would begin to pick at me. He would tell me I talked too much, that others were secretly annoyed with me, that they were just humoring me when I shared stories about myself. The moment my critic said these things, I would contract inside, feeling embarrassed or ashamed for how I acted, and for who I was.

It's like my inner family was having this sweet party with a cake and shiny plastic party hats, and everyone was smiling and laughing and loving each other. And then the scary patriarch bursts in the door, drunk and looking for trouble. He tears everyone down, shouting, disparaging, and telling them how nobody could actually love them.

And in that moment, I would take it in entirely like the child who takes in the poisonous venom of a verbally abusive parent. *I guess I did talk too much. Why did I do that? Oh, and then I told that story, which was so stupid. I was too excited, just going on and on.*

In a way, I would actually get on board with the critic. I didn't even stop to ask, "Is this true? Did I talk too much? How do I know that? Didn't they seem to be engaged and enjoying my company as much as I was theirs?"

But that would have involved questioning and challenging the critic. And it's hard to question someone who's screaming at you and slapping you in the face. It's much more familiar to cower and take it. Especially if that's the boss, the head of the house, the alpha, which your critic might have been…until now.

Forget that noise. Forget that loud, obnoxious, mean, abusive S.O.B. You don't have to take this anymore. You shouldn't take this anymore. You don't deserve it. You never deserve to be treated that way by anyone—inside or outside of you. And it's time to stand up to it. Now.

Reclaiming Your Seat

You might imagine that now we're going to have you go "head-to-head" with the critic and take it down. When he bursts in the door, you stand upright, cock your arm back, and give it a solid punch right in the kisser. It tumbles down in a disoriented jumble of limbs, completely shocked that anyone would dare stand up to it as you have bravely done. And then it slinks back out the door, and your inner family lives in harmony and peace for the rest of your days.

It's tempting. And I wish it were so simple, but it's not. The thing about abusive relationships is that we want to stay in them on some level. Have you ever seen this in yourself or someone you know who's been in a toxic romantic relationship? You know it's not working, and you know it never will, and you know you should end it. But you don't. You find a way to explain or justify their behavior or why it would be too hurtful or dangerous to leave them.

Or, in some cases, you eventually do leave them. But then, one day, or one week later, you feel so awful. You just want that person back. You feel guilty, unsettled, empty, or otherwise lost without them. You feel like you *need* them to be okay. And so you go back, apologize, make up, and get back on for another ride on the merry-go-round.

It's the same with your inner critic. That sucker has been in there guiding you for decades. Your critic's views about you, your worth, your lovability, and your potential are extremely familiar to you. Its view of reality is the dominant view of reality, and you take it as true.

Is this not so?

I've tried this little experiment with dozens of clients. Let's try it together now. Think of one negative, toxic, unhelpful thing that your critic says about you regularly. Perhaps it's that you're not good enough to be in a loving relationship, that you'll never achieve a meaningful goal in your work or other areas of your life, or that you'll never be happy. You got one? Okay, great.

Now, let me ask you this. Are you willing to let that go now? Be totally open to the possibility that later today will not be like right now. And tomorrow doesn't have to be like today. So no matter what happened in your past, it's possible for you to have what you want, experience the love you want, achieve a goal, etc.

What happens inside of you?

For almost everyone, the initial response is: Nope. Sure, that sounds great, but I can't let that old story go. I can't just disbelieve my critic right now, instantly for no reason other than that I choose to!

"Why not?" I would ask my clients.

"Because what my critic is saying is *true.*"

And then our real work would begin the work of unhooking their identity from their critic, the work of decoupling ourselves from this poisonous propaganda that we've taken in for years. Because instantly rejecting that old identity that our critic has created for us and setting a new course sounds fantastic in theory, but often leads to a break up followed by a reconciliation. Before you know it, the critic is back on the scene, louder than ever. What's worse is that now it's ready for you to try to stand up to it, and it's going to do even more to make sure you never try anything like that again.

Instead, we are going to use a much more powerful and effective approach to undermining your critic's dominance, the power of awareness. For when you start to systematically observe your critic and witness what it's doing day after day inside of you, something will naturally start to shift. You will see, *really* see, just how intense and hateful it's comments are. You will feel how much they hurt other parts of you and how much damage they cause. And you will begin to feel repulsed. You may even start to feel outraged at this kind of mistreatment with a growing sense of compassion to put an end to this inner tyranny.

Maybe that's already starting to happen right now. Can you remember the last time you were being hard on yourself? Maybe it was earlier this week, or even earlier today. What was the moment you last turned on yourself? What was that like? What were you saying to yourself? Or, to be more specific, what was your critic saying to you?

Take a moment to imagine it as if it were a family inside of you. How does this critical part relate to the others? How do you feel about that as you witness it? Is it okay? Does it feel right or wrong? What is your natural impulse as you watch?

Whatever you feel is okay—do not fight it, resist it, or judge it. Sometimes when people start to see how they've been treating themselves for years, instead of feeling happy or liberated, they feel pain. They feel the sadness and grief of being so hard on themselves for so long. They feel remorse and heartache for how cruel they've been. Others feel despair or regret about how many opportunities they've missed or how much joy they've sucked from their lives by being so hard on themselves.

Or you may not be feeling much at all, and that's okay too. Sometimes we need more time to witness this treatment of ourselves before it really sinks in. When it does, something will crack open inside of you, and you will open your heart toward yourself, perhaps for the first time in your life.

Naming Your Critic

One simple, highly effective technique to start using immediately is to give your critic a name. Naming your critic instantly enhances the separation, so you are not fused with your critic. When you hear your mind listing that litany of shortcomings, you will be able to quickly see that it is your critic and not you.

So what do you name your critic? Whatever you like! It can be a serious name or a silly name, a descriptive name, or a random name. Clients of mine have used names including Mr. Angry, The Critic, Harold, Rupert, Allison, VOF (which stands for "Voice of Fear"), and many others.

Take a moment now to come up with a name for your critic. Don't overthink it or try to come up with the best name. Whatever first comes to your mind is often perfect. If it makes you smile or laugh, even better. That can be helpful in removing some of the critic's authority and intimidation factor.

Now, whenever you notice that critical voice inside of you acting up, you can smile and acknowledge it. Imagine yourself waving and saying, "Hi, Harold!" You can even imagine a whole character that seems to fit this part of you. What does it look like? What gender does he or she seem to be? How would she sit, stand, and move? How would he talk? The more you can personify this part of you in your mind, the more power you will have in taming it.

If you'd like, you can draw a picture of your critic. Give it the features, body posture, and expressions you imagine it would have. One client I worked with created a stick figure comic strip of her interacting with her critic in different settings. Even if you don't consider yourself an artist, this isn't about creating something aesthetically impressive. It's about increasing your awareness of this part of your psyche so that you can relate to it differently.

As you name and greet your critic, you are creating greater awareness of when this part of you is active. This will reduce the likelihood that it will instantly take over your thoughts, feelings, and actions without you even knowing it. In other words, the more you can consciously relate to this inner critic, the more you will remain in control.

To aid in this, you can practice hearing your critic speak to you as if it were another person talking to you. Let me explain.

When we are mostly unconscious of our critic and its impact on our lives, we often experience ongoing periods of self-critical thoughts and feelings of inadequacy and shame. Our thoughts often come in phrases like:

I'm ugly.
No one will want to be with me.
I'm such a loser.
I can't do that.
I'll mess that up.

Notice how these statements are from the first person ("I"). In this case, you are totally fused with your critic's perspective. It is you, and you are it. As you name your critic and greet it when it shows up, start hearing its words from the second person ("you"). Thus, when it speaks to you, you can hear his criticisms as:

You are ugly.
No one will want to be with you.
You're such a loser.
You can't do that.
You'll mess that up.

I know, this list seems about as depressing as the one before it. But it's very different because now it's your critic talking to you. It is not *you*. This is just something that someone is saying that you can choose to believe or not. And just like when a constricted parent or colleague tells you that you'll never achieve something, you might respond with an internal rejection of their pessimism and a decision that you'll "show them." Or you might just laugh and dismiss their comment entirely, seeing it as nothing more than the voice of their own fear and self-imposed limitations.

Your critic is no different. It's just a part of you that is trying to influence you with these statements. The key is to not believe its words, to see through the entire game, and discover that it's not there to support or guide you. Rather, it's there to keep you safe by avoiding all healthy risks and will say and do whatever it needs to in order to carry out that mission.

So the next time you hear Harold, or Allison, or Mr. Angry, say "hi" to him or her for me.

The Dojo

Naming your critic and seeing it as a part of you, rather than all of you, is an important step in liberating yourself. However, this in itself is usually insufficient because your critic has been operating for years, even decades, and has established itself quite firmly in your psychology.

In other words, your critic has been running the show for a long time. He or she is head of that household and wants to keep it that way. Like a tyrannical patriarch or matriarch, they rule with an iron fist, and any opposition is quickly met with brute force and then promptly crushed.

Have you ever tried to talk back to your critic? Tried to challenge its claims and think more positively about yourself or a situation? What has happened? Did it work? This is one of the major tools of cognitive therapy. To uncover the distorted, self-critical thought, write it down on paper, and challenge it with a more rational thought.

For example, after making a mistake at work, your critic is telling you that you are an idiot, so you write down: "I am an idiot." You then challenge that thought, and you write down: "This is labeling; I am not an idiot. It's okay to make mistakes; that is part of learning." Sounds good, appears more reasonable, and makes sense on paper. Challenge your critic enough times, and eventually, you'll stop calling yourself an idiot, right?

In my experience, and in my work with many clients over the years, there seems to be a fault in this system. The main problem is that when we write down the positive statement, it often falls flat. It sounds good, and it's the "right" thing to say because it's reasonable, compassionate, and true. And yet, it doesn't *feel* true at all. What feels true is: "I'm a freaking idiot, and I can't believe I made that mistake! How awful!"

What's missing from this sterile approach is the emotion. In an attempt to become Vulcan-like rational beings, we lose sight of the fact that we are emotionally driven animals. Our feelings are a dominant force in our lives and drive us more than anything else. It's like trying to have a conversation with a four-year-old child who's having a meltdown—it just doesn't work. They can't hear you. No matter how solid your points are, they just don't land.

And while it has the emotional energy of a tantruming child, your inner critic has the power and stature of a ten-foot-tall wild beast. You're going up against this raging, intense, brutal force inside of you and trying to calmly put up your hand and say, "Now, now... let's all calm down and be rational here." But your critic has none of that. It chooses to kick aside your rational statements and squashes you like a bug with an onslaught of vitriol.

There must be a better way. Fortunately, there is. Enter the dojo.

Out of the night that covers me,
Black as the pit from pole to pole,
I thank whatever gods may be
For my unconquerable soul.

In the fell clutch of circumstance
I have not winced nor cried aloud.
Under the bludgeonings of chance
My head is bloody, but unbowed.

Beyond this place of wrath and tears
Looms but the Horror of the shade,
And yet the menace of the years
Finds and shall find me unafraid.

It matters not how strait the gate,
How charged with punishments the scroll,
I am the master of my fate,
I am the captain of my soul.

- "Invictus" by William Ernest Henley

Chapter 7:
Tame Your Critic

How is all this landing? Are you a little confused? Don't worry; this all becomes clear as you practice it over time. Of course, you may be wondering, "Well, if I'm a collection of parts, then who am I really? Which part is the real me?"

That question is surprisingly deep and has been the focus of inquiry for much of human history. Buddhists say that there is no clear "self" running the show in there at all, and it's just an illusion. In fact, neuroscientists studying the brain have not been able to find any specific region that is responsible for our capacity for self-awareness and consciousness.

While these inquiries are fascinating from a philosophical perspective, we need something practical we can work with in our day-to-day lives. Enter the concept of your core self. Your core self is the part of you that is able to sit back and observe all the other parts of you. Some people call this "the witness" or "the watcher." This core self is able to hear the words and observe the feelings of the other parts of you, but is not swept up by them, nor does the core self feel overwhelmed. It is centered, present, curious, and grounded. Think of it as a loving parent, or a good friend, or a skilled counselor.

To become more aware of your core self, let's do this quick exercise together. As you read, bring your attention to your breath. Feel the air as it goes into your nose or mouth, fills your lungs, and then flows out of your body. Notice the sensations of your body as your lungs fill and release. Can you feel your body against the chair or bed?

Now slow down for just a moment and tune into the sounds you are currently hearing. Can you sit in silence and become very still, listening for the next five distinct sounds you hear?

Now bring your attention to your chest and the area around your heart. Notice any sensations of feelings or emotions you're experiencing. Without needing to label, judge, or fix anything, just feel what's happening there in the body. Remember to keep breathing as you do this, softening your belly and letting the air move freely.

Notice what thoughts are passing through your mind. Imagine you are standing next to a gently flowing stream. Each thought is like a leaf floating on the top of that water. If you notice yourself getting sucked into a certain thought, and adding to it, fighting with it, debating something, and so forth, simply imagine placing that thought on a leaf and watching it float down the river. Surrender each thought as it arises. Return your attention to your breath, to your heart, to your body.

Here you are. Centered in yourself, present in this moment. This is you residing in your core self. From here, you can relate to all the other parts of you without getting completely sucked into the drama or taken over by another part, especially your critic. Now you are ready for some sparring.

SPARRING

In order to tame your critic, you must develop your skill of relating to this part inside of you. Much like a martial art, you must learn to dodge, counter, and strike. In order to be most effective, however, it's essential to remember that your critic is a part of you and is therefore indestructible. No matter how much you don't like a part of you—whether it's your critic, or the scared part of you, or the part of you that's sensitive to criticism—you can't get rid of it. You can't oust any family members, even if you sometimes wish you could.

So in this metaphor of sparring in a dojo, keep in mind that you are not trying to beat your opponent violently into submission or destroy them. Rather, you must develop your skills to dodge your critic's attacks, and then subdue it. Your ultimate goal is to have it tire itself out, lose its raging fire, and then bring it back into the fold. You are restoring a natural order in your inner household in which your core self is in charge.

But, currently, you might not feel like you have many judo skills. Your critic just walks all over you. If so, that's okay; that's exactly what you're here to learn. And, the good news is, you already have a secret move that is incredibly powerful at subduing your critic. In fact, you already learned it in the first two chapters of this book. Much like Daniel-san painting fences for Mr. Miage in the original Karate Kid, you were learning essential moves to tame your critic.

For you see, the most powerful move is to know your critic's motive. Once you know this, you can dodge all of its barbs, cut straight to the heart of it, and give it what it needs to calm down. As any engaging martial arts instructor does, let me demonstrate first, then teach you exactly how to do it.

Demo

About thirty minutes ago, I was struggling in my writing for today. Each line felt hard to craft as if I were trying to run into a twenty-miles-per-hour headwind. I slowed down to listen, and sure enough, my critic was there. Here is a written dialogue between me (aka my core self) and my critic. As you read, pay close attention to how I respond to the critic.

Critic: Dude, this book sucks. It's awful! So dry and boring. It's not flowing at all. No one is going to like reading it. There are so many better books already out there on the subject. Every freaking psychologist has a book on this subject. Yours is nothing new. So far, it's confusing, disjointed, and meandering all over the place. No one wants to hear your stories. Your stories aren't good enough. No one wants to hear about your damn kids. Shut the f--k up! Shut up; I hate you. Shut up!

Me: Yikes! You are scared and pissed. Tell me more. I'm here, and I'm listening. You have my full attention.

Critic: Grrrggghhh! F--k you. I hate you. This book sucks. No one is going to like it. It's not going to do as well as your last book. It's not good. What the hell are you writing? This sucks. This topic is no good; no one really wants to read about this self-esteem stuff. I hate you.

Me: It sounds like people not liking this book is something you really don't want. It seems like those negative reviews where people criticize us for telling personal stories about our life really sting and you are unwilling to experience any more of those negative reviews.

Critic: Yes! I don't want any more of those. And you've been holding back on those personal stories, which is making the book more dry and boring and disjointed. You should delete the entire thing and start again. Or better yet, write something else, or stop writing entirely.

Me: Yeah, those critical reviews can be harsh. I don't like reading them either. They can hurt my heart too. People can get cruel and forget that we're just putting our heart out there in the world and doing what we can to help people.

Critic: I don't like it. I don't want it.

Me: Ha, me neither! I want only positive reviews and loving comments forever. Wouldn't that be nice!

Critic: Ha, yeah.

Me: Sweetie, I love you. Thank you for your input. I can see you're scared. I'm here to take care of you. I will protect you from that negative energy. I will always be here for you. When people criticize us, I'll be there to support and guide you through it. Trust me; I got you. I can handle some whiny, upset people. Stick with me. I got you. You're safe.

I could go on, but this is just a demo, so we'll stop here. What did you notice? What stood out to you most as you read this? Is this how you relate to your critic, or is it quite different? Let's highlight the key elements of how to respond to your critic, so you start to gain a sense of inner mastery and control.

Always Remember This

First things first, the critic is attacking me for writing a poor quality book. The tone is frustrated, outraged, and angry. The critic often comes out swinging like this, regardless of the topic.

In the past, what has been your most common way of dealing with the critic when it comes at you like this? Do you try to ignore it? Or do you agree with it and think you or your performance are subpar? Or are you beaten down into submission and cease whatever activity your critic is attacking you about? Or perhaps you've attempted to speak back to your critic, defend yourself, and challenge its claims. While the latter is certainly better than the rest of these responses, it still is often ineffective.

To become a master at maneuvering around your critic, you must remember its motivation. Pop quiz! Why is your critic attacking you in the first place? It always has one primary motivation, regardless of the million scenarios in which it can pick on you. No matter what, your critic is always focused on avoiding emotional pain.

So what is my critic afraid of in the demo above? Reading negative reviews of my book can create emotional pain. Secondarily, it's afraid of the book not doing well, lower sales, and whatever emotional pain might come with that—feelings of inadequacy or failure, lower income, and more financial fears.

Take a moment to reflect on your own critic's last few attacks. What emotional pain was it trying to avoid by attacking you? I strongly encourage you to take a moment to think about this. Seeing this pattern gives you Neo-like superpowers when sparring with your critic because you no longer get caught in the content of what it's saying, and you can respond directly to the fear underneath.

In every scenario, if you listen to your critic, it's telling you to do something or not do something. It often does this with heavy-handed "shoulds" or "should haves." *You should ask her out. You should call him. You should've spoken up for yourself there. You shouldn't record this video. You shouldn't speak up; you shouldn't bring attention to yourself. You should say hi. You should never do that again.*

Each of these directives is accompanied by a hefty dose of berating comments and condemnation, conveying the sense that you should not only do what the critic wants, but that you should already know this, and the critic shouldn't even have to tell you. What is wrong with you for not already having done it?

And, if you follow the logic of the critic's directives, you will see exactly what it is trying to protect you from. Let's practice a few together. Below you'll read commands from the critic, and you will determine what it is trying to protect you from. Come up with answers for all three examples before reading the answers below. Ready?

1. **You should go ask her out.** What is this trying to protect you from?

2. **You shouldn't speak up.** How about this one?

3. **You should've spoken up for yourself there.** And this one?

Ok, I'll share my answers below. These are not the "right" answers as there are many ways to interpret this. The key here is to start to look for the underlying pain. That, in itself, is the transforming factor in dealing with your critic.

1. **You should go ask her out.**
Trying to protect from: *Loneliness, isolation, heartache.*

2. **You shouldn't speak up.**
Trying to protect from: *Embarrassment, conflict, disapproval, rejection, the end of a relationship.*

3. **You should've spoken up for yourself there.**
Trying to protect from: *Pain of being passive, pent up resentment, feeling inferior or powerless, doing unpleasant tasks you don't want to do.*

Do you see the pattern here? This is true for every criticism coming from this part of you. Its purpose is to protect you from these emotional pains. So any time there is a potential threat of emotional pain, it will do what it can to try to make you stop what you're doing. For example, it will tell you that you are an ugly loser, and no one would want to go out with you, so you lose your mojo and don't ask that person out.

When you are feeling bad and thus already exposed to emotional pain, then your critic attacks you for having done whatever you did to bring that on. Even if you're not entirely sure why you're feeling bad, your critic will make something up and blame it on that. So if you did already ask that person out, and he or she said, "No," then your critic will pounce on you with something like, *Of course, they said no! You are pathetic. You did it wrong. You are an idiot. You'll never find anybody who'll want to be with you.*

When that onslaught of gut punches are coming your way, it's hard not to believe the critic's truth. You might instantly start to feel inferior, ashamed, and highly pessimistic about your future love-life and happiness. In other words, it's easy to believe the critic. After all, you just got rejected, which creates emotional pain for almost every human out there. Your critic does *not* want emotional pain. So now, it must do what it can to teach you a lesson and make sure you never do anything like that again.

That's your critic's main goal—to make sure you never ask anyone out again, thereby protecting you from emotional pain. Of course, it exposes you to much more emotional pain in the long run through isolation and a lack of love and connection, but your critic is not forward-thinking and proactive. It is a limited, reactive, defensive pattern designed to keep you safe in the moment. And it's not as scary as you think.

What Not to Do

Now that you are completely clear on why the critic is coming at you, you are almost ready for your training in basic maneuvers. First off, here's what *not* to do:

Critic: Your presentation sucks, and so do you.

You: Sigh. Yeah. You're right. Who am I kidding to try this? It's terrible.

(You can replace "your presentation" with any other challenge you are currently facing in your life.)

This might seem obvious when you see it on the page, but it is hands down the most common response most people have to their critic! This extremely negative, pessimistic, toxic voice is treated like a trusted advisor who has a good grip on the situation and a sound perspective on life. Would you respond to another person that way if they spoke like that? Imagine being in a company meeting and listening to various leaders speak up. One of them clears her throat and says, "We're doomed. Our core product is completely ineffective, and we're relying on expensive marketing that is just a gimmick. Of course, this is the case, because our design team is utterly incompetent, and our marketing team is full of talentless idiots."

Or what if you were having a hard time in your relationship and you consulted a friend who said, "Well, you're doomed. I mean, you are shy and awkward. You've never been good around men. Your smile looks so bad with your tooth like that. And you're fat and gross, so even if a man was interested in you at first, as soon as he saw you with your shirt off, it would all be over."

In these scenarios, would you be slowly nodding your head, thinking to yourself, *Yes! This is exactly the kind of guidance I need in my life right now. I like your ideas, and I want to have you as my personal, in-house counsel to guide me through all my daily decisions in life.*

As absurd as this sounds, this is exactly what most of us do. We submit to this terrified inner tyrant and treat it as an absolute authority who speaks the truth. Any attempts to challenge or question these statements are met with dismissive ridicule and a feeling that we're deluding ourselves because we know the real, brutal truth. This keeps us bound and subdued, living life with our heads down, avoiding risk, and playing small, which, by now, I'm sure you're sick and tired of. So, let's not do that anymore.

Once people decide they're done agreeing with their critic, they often make the second mistake, which looks like the following:

Critic: Your presentation sucks, and so do you.

You: Hey, now, that's not true. I am intelligent and articulate, and my presentation is clear and effective. It's going to go great.

What's wrong with this? Isn't this how you're supposed to talk with yourself? Isn't that "positive self-talk" and a "rational response" that would make a CBT therapist salivate? Yes, it does look good on paper, and it sounds good too. And it seems like it should work. But does it? I'm sure you tried something like this in the past, and what has happened? Usually, the dialogue continues:

Critic: Your presentation sucks, and so do you.

You: Hey, now, that's not true. I am intelligent and articulate, and my presentation is clear and effective. It's going to go great.

Critic: How do you know that? Are you sure? All those people are going to be watching you. Remember the last presentation you gave? You prepared even more for that one, and it went so badly. You were halting, trembling, and clearly nervous. You are going to do that again tomorrow.

At which point, you counter with another rational response, and then your critic says something else, to which you respond, and so forth. At least you're not instantly agreeing with your critic's toxic claims and are instead attempting to defend yourself. And yet, it doesn't quite land, does it? Deep down, you often don't believe those rational claims. Or, you know that they're true; you are articulate and well prepared, and yet, you still don't *feel* confident. You still feel nervous, anxious, and unsafe inside. The critic's words are still influencing your self-esteem, beliefs, and behaviors. It's still winning, no matter what you say.

There is a time and place to challenge the critic and defend yourself; it just can't be your only technique. Something else is much more effective and produces a much bigger shift in your emotional state. Let's learn that now.

FIVE STEPS TO TAME YOUR CRITIC

Here is a proven five-step process that will help you tame your critic, no matter how long it feels like it's been running the show. Practice these steps consistently, and you will completely shift the way you relate to yourself, creating much more self-love, patience, compassion, and enjoyment of your day-to-day life.

Here is an overview of the five steps. We will then discuss each one in more detail.

Step One: Identify When You Are Being Self-Critical
Step Two: Move Toward Your Critic
Step Three: Explore the Root Fears and Empathize
Step Four: Regroup and Problem-Solve
Step Five: Into the Roar

Step One: Identify When You Are Being Self-Critical

More good news! You've already been building your skill with the first step throughout this book. The O.M.O.S. assessment, the exercise counting your self-criticisms, and naming your critic are all methods of helping you catch when your critic is acting up.

To further strengthen this awareness, it's helpful to create a simple phrase to use internally when you notice it's the critic speaking, such as "this is criticism" or "inner critic" or saying the name of your critic.

Step Two: Move Toward Your Critic

The second step in taming your critic is to turn toward it. You must face it head-on with openness, curiosity, and warmth. Yes, I know this is vastly different than what you've done in the past and may seem difficult to do, yet it is the path to liberation. It's okay if you're not good at it at first and if it takes some time to learn. Any skill worth learning in life takes some time.

In the demonstration above, my critic came at me with several attacks at once. Each one is like a hook that is designed to make me bite. If I swallow the hook, then I'm either demoralized and follow the critic's directives, or I fight it and thrash around for who knows how long. Either way, I'm worse off than if I didn't bite the hook.

Here's a recap of that first exchange:

Critic: Dude, this book sucks. It's awful! So dry and boring. It's not flowing at all. No one is going to like reading it. There are so many better books already out there on the subject. Every freaking psychologist has a book on this subject. Yours is nothing new. So far, it's confusing, disjointed, and meandering all over the place. No one wants to hear your stories. Your stories aren't good enough. No one wants to hear about your damn kids. Shut the f--k up! Shut up. I hate you. Shut up!

Me: Yikes! You are scared and pissed. Tell me more. I'm here, and I'm listening. You have my full attention.

Notice how I don't agree with the critic that my book is bad, and no one is going to like it. I also don't go into the topic of how good my stories are either (which we all know are objectively awesome). I don't bite any of the hooks. Instead, I turn toward the critic and acknowledge the feelings underneath his attacks. He's angry and scared.

I also let him know that he has my full attention, and I'm listening. Your critical part, much like another person outside of you, wants to be seen, heard, and acknowledged. When someone in your life is angry with you, what they want first and foremost is to feel heard. Only then are you able to work together to solve the underlying problem or issue.

My question for you is: Are you willing to try approaching your critic this way? Some people resist doing this for several reasons. For one, they have spent so many years living under their critic's tyrannical abuse that they feel completely done with it. They are angry at their critic, and the last thing they want to do is slow down and listen to it. They want to tell it to get the hell out of here, to shut up, or worse. One client told me he wanted my help so he could "murder his critic." When I heard that, I laughed a little, only to find he was completely serious.

Other people are afraid to acknowledge their critic and turn toward it because they are afraid of what it's saying. The content is so intense and so loaded with hooks that they can't imagine listening to it without feeling completely demoralized or overwhelmed. The main problem here is not what your critic is saying; it's that you're believing what it's saying. The best way to untangle from that web is to do the following.

Instead of being an intimidating authority, start to imagine your critic as an enraged four-year-old child. Have you ever spent time with a little kid who is losing it? It's typically a dramatic, expressive, emotional experience that is unfiltered and not self-conscious in the least. For example, my three-year-old son, Arman, will wail at the top of his lungs after his brother breaks his Magna-Tiles House. Of course, his older brother is taking unfair advantage of his size and stature while he can, and his house-smashing was unprovoked and undoubtedly upsetting to Arman. He will then collapse to the ground, face first, in a position that looks similar to child's pose in yoga. There, he cries into the ground as his face turns a bright crimson red. Any attempt to soothe him or entice him to build something else with you is met with an increased volume of wail or some other sort of scream. After several minutes of this, he will emerge from his child's pose and begin his proclamations.

"I don't ever want to play with bro-bro again!" is a common refrain. If we happen to be going somewhere later that morning, or have recently been somewhere, his proclamations will include that as well. "I don't want to go to the store!" or "I never want to go to Grandma's house again!"

This is how you want to see your critic. It's not the adult of your inner household; it's the child. It's not an intimidating adult male with a beer in his hand threatening to hit you. It's a scared child who is afraid of being hurt and yelling things at you. It desperately wants your attention, and beyond that, wants reassurance that it will be safe, that you will keep it safe, that it won't experience more pain than it can handle.

If you are truly committed to being on your own side, no matter what, then you must learn how to give your critic that reassurance. We'll get more into the specifics of how to do that in a bit, but this second step is to move toward it with curiosity, warmth, and love (even if you're scared or resistant at first.)

Let's have you try it. Yes, right now. A dojo is not worth its salt if it doesn't have its members practice the moves as they learn them! Take a moment now to recall a recent criticism your critic launched at you. Perhaps it was from earlier today or is even happening right now. Then, write what the critic is saying down somewhere. As I mentioned earlier, I highly recommend creating a file on your phone or computer for ongoing practice with this. A journal is great as well; however, it's even better to be able to practice these maneuvers in real-time. And in this day in age, most of us have our cell phones glued to our hands, so it will always be right there to jot it down.

Write down the specific criticism. You can use "Critic:" at the beginning or the name you've given your critic. This simple distinction helps your subconscious see that this is a part of you and not all of you. Be as direct, real, specific, and raw as possible. Do not filter anything in your dialogues with your critic. I password protect these kinds of note files on my phone because it allows for a sense of complete privacy.

Go ahead and do that now, and then resume reading.

Okay, so now you have captured your critic's statement. What is it like to read it? Is it upsetting? Do you feel sad, hurt, angry, pessimistic, or scared? Bring your attention to your breath and your body. Notice where you feel these uncomfortable emotions. Do you feel a squeezing in your chest, stomach, or throat or tightness, burning, or contraction somewhere in your body? Just bring your attention to it now, without needing to fix it, change it, or make it go away. Surrender to it being there and allow it.

This is you residing in your core self. Your core self can handle any experience in this life because you can handle any emotion, no matter how intense it may be. Your mind may protest, resist, writhe around, or try to flee. But your heart is vast, and its capacity to feel is infinite.

Re-read your critic's statement out loud now. Read it slowly and deliberately. As you read, imagine who is saying this? If you close your eyes, do you see a specific person? Is it your mom or dad? Does this voice remind you of somebody? Is it perhaps the voice of a critical friend from when you were young or an angry teacher you had in school? Or maybe it's not a specific person, but you still have a sense of whether it's a male or female and about how old. Take your time and become more familiar with who this part of you is.

Now imagine that person, as intimidating as they might be, getting younger as if they drank some strange potion from a 1960's sci-fi movie that made them reverse age. In moments, they are no longer a fully grown adult but rather a small child. And if you didn't have a clear visual sense of your critic to begin with, start by imagining a young child. See if it's a boy or girl. How upset does it seem?

Reread your critic's statement one more time, but this time imagine the child saying this, red-faced, crying, enraged, and hurting. "I don't ever want to go to the zoo again!" Is what it's saying true? Does it truly think you're terrible or that no one likes you? Does it genuinely hate you, or is that just what little kids say sometimes when they're upset and expressing their emotions?

Can you feel that urge inside to take care of this scared little kid, a desire to move toward her, hold her, and tell her she's going to be okay? Tell her that you got her, and it's okay to be upset with you, and that you're not going anywhere no matter how upset she gets and no matter what she says. Imagine yourself doing that now in whatever way feels right for you.

Last night, my son Zaim was out of resources before bed-time. Arman had just hit him in the back of the head with a Magna-Tile — no doubt, retaliation for some past injustice. This threw Zaim over the deep end into a crying, enraged, thrashing kick machine, with an overwhelming desire for revenge. My wife Candace moved toward Zaim to intervene and prevent him from kicking his brother.

"I want to kick him!" He yelled in a hoarse voice as he sobbed. His face was red with sadness, anger, and pain.

"I know, sweetie," Candace replied soothingly. "I can't let you hurt your brother."

"I want to kick you then! I don't like you!" He yelled.

"You're angry at me right now," she said. "I know you're hurting inside a lot."

I watched in a mild state of awe, as I often do when I see Candace skillfully handling all sorts of mini-crises and meltdowns. Her demonstrations of exactly what to say and how to be deeply loving, patient, and compassionate are continual lessons for me, not only in how to relate to my children but to parts of myself as well.

Take a moment now to write out a response to your critic in your note file. Create a new line and start it with "me:" or "core self:" and then write a response. It's not a rebuttal, or a pep talk, or a list of logical reasons why your critic shouldn't be scared, angry, or have any feelings whatsoever. Instead, respond with patience and compassion. Respond with love. Turn toward your critic. Do that now; then resume reading.

What was that like? How did it feel? Was it different than how you typically relate to your critic and perhaps different than anything you've ever said to your inner critic?

Keep practicing this maneuver over the next few weeks. Whenever you are out and about in the world, and you notice your critic acting up, take a moment to pull out your phone and jot down what it's saying. You don't have to get all perfectionistic or neurotic about this and do it 80 times per day; just a few times is sufficient. It may take a moment or two to slow down and listen to what your critic is saying to you. Then, write it down and take another moment to breathe and center yourself. See it as an upset child, and then write a loving response, one of acknowledgment, validation, and inquiry. "Tell me more" is your general attitude and stance toward your critic.

You will learn more maneuvers in this chapter as well, so if you want to combine this first one with other ways of relating, by all means, do so. But be sure to start with this one, because it is required for all the others to be effective.

You may be thinking, *But, wait! What if I don't feel like being all warm and fuzzy with my critic? What if I don't want to be loving and patient? What if I want to tell him to buzz off and get the hell out of my head? What if I feel like gritting my teeth and fighting back, are you saying I can't do that?*

Don't worry. You get to learn some pretty sweet judo chop moves in a moment to deal with your critic. It's not like it comes in kicking, and you go to hug it out, and it's all over Kumbaya style. You will need to use specific, strategic maneuvers to handle your critic's attacks, so they don't derail you. And you can and will fight back. But, it looks different than you might think.

However, if you want to experiment on your own, I recommend it. Try writing out a dialogue where you don't move toward your critic. Write down what it's saying and then respond however you want. Maybe you tell it to shut up, grow up, or get out of here. Maybe you tell it you're done with its nonsense and that you're not going to listen to it anymore or whatever else you are drawn to write.

And then notice what happens as you do this. Over several days of relating to your critic this way, what is the effect? Does it diminish and become less dominant in your mind? Do you feel more confident and less afraid? If so, good! That is probably a sign that you are no longer letting it be the head of the household. And sometimes, this "tough love" approach can work.

O.M.O.S. is an art form. There is no one single way to be on your own side. Things that worked in the past for you will need to be updated and changed as you mature and experience different and new life circumstances. The key is to pay attention to what is working and consistently do it.

For many of my clients and me, pushing the critic away doesn't fully work. It may have some modest effect, but if the issue is big enough, the critic entrenches in, and I get into an all-out battle in my head. Or, I banish the critic and have rebuttals to all his statements, but I don't feel confident, liberated, and happy. I still feel anxious, tense, or inferior. So even though what I'm saying sounds good, it isn't working.

Above all else, test things out. You learn the set moves in the dojo, then you go out into the real world and see what works for you in the moment. Speaking of the dojo, let's get back in there and learn a few more key moves.

Step Three: Explore the Root Fears and Empathize

Let's recap the first two steps of the Five-Step Critic Taming Process. Step one is to simply become aware when your critic is speaking to you so that you can identify it as a distinct voice in your head that is *not* you. Step two is to consciously move toward your critic with curiosity and openness. You realize it is a part of you that you can't get rid of, and that you must find a way to work with it to regain an inner sense of harmony. In addition, you can see that it's not as terrifying as you might have thought. Rather, it is like a scared child that needs attention, support, reassurance, and love.

Let's move on to step three now, which is: Explore the Root Fears and Empathize. If you truly are willing to listen and be curious, then your critic will share more of its upset with you. This will often come in the form of anger and judgment toward you. Your task in step three is to listen to these attacks without getting hooked into the surface level of criticisms. Rather, your goal is to focus on the fears underneath the attacks.

In the previous demo, after I told my critic I was listening and he had my full attention, it went on to say:

> Critic: Grrrggghhh! F–k you. I hate you. This book sucks. No one is going to like it. It's not going to do as well as your last book. It's not good. What the hell are you writing? This sucks. This topic is no good; no one really wants to read about this self-esteem stuff. I hate you.

As you can see, my critic is thrashing around, expressing anger toward me and dislike of the quality of my writing. When your critic launches a list of specific issues with you, your performance, or your behavior, the natural impulse is to cower or challenge it. But remember this—there is always fear underneath, even if it only looks like anger, even if your critic denies it's afraid (which mine has done many times). The secret to regaining control in this relationship with your critic is to remember that the critic equals fear. When the critic is speaking, that is a form of fear manifesting itself as self-judgment, pessimism, anger, and so forth.

Here's how I responded to my critic:

> Me: It sounds like people not liking this book is something you don't want. Those negative reviews where people criticize us for telling personal stories about our life really sting. It seems like you are unwilling to experience any more of those negative reviews.

As I tune into the critic and look for what it's afraid of, it's obvious that it's afraid of writing this book. It's afraid of potential exposure to emotional pain. Whenever you put any form of creative expression out there in the world—a book, music, your art, a business idea—others can, and will, judge it. This is an inevitable fact of life, and yet, my critic does not want this to be so.

How did I know his fear was specifically about the negative reviews from my previous books? I scanned back through my memory to see where I had felt the greatest emotional pain around my books in the past. Sure enough, it was when I read negative reviews that were not just critical of the material in the book but harshly critical of me as an author and a human. As I read them, I worked with my internal reaction to become more resilient and, I thought, not be impacted by them. While some part of me was able to have the right perspective and not take it personally, there was another part of me that remembered—my critic.

Remember, your critic's primary job is to keep you safe. Judgment, rejection of you as a person, loss of connection, people being upset with you—all of these are threatening. In a bygone era, if you were wholeheartedly rejected enough by the tribe, you may be ousted. On a biological level, if you lost connection with your parents at a young age and they weren't there to take care of you, you would die. So deep down in your brain, beyond rational awareness and logic, there is a primal part of you that is terrified of these emotional hurts and views them as completely unacceptable risks.

When seeking the root fears that underlie your critic's attacks, remember to look beyond the rational. Your critic is a young, primal part of you that does not think in linear or logical terms. To my critic, someone saying they highly dislike me because of what I wrote in a book is a dangerous event that must never occur.

Once you've discovered your best guess as to what the fear underneath is, reflect that back to your critic, as I did in the demo. When you do this, your critic often responds just like an upset person would when they feel like they're being heard. They emphatically agree and keep telling you more. "Yes! You're finally hearing me!"

Below you can see how my critic responded. Notice how it agrees and then wants to share more. Also, pay attention to how I respond to the critic over the next several exchanges. See if you can identify what I am doing:

> Critic: Yes! I don't want any more of those. And you've been holding back on those personal stories, which is making the book more dry and boring and disjointed. You should delete the entire thing and start again. Or better yet, write something else, or stop writing entirely.

> Me: Yeah, those critical reviews can be harsh. I don't like reading them either. They can hurt my heart too. People can be cruel and forget that we're just putting our heart out there in the world and doing what we can to help people.

> Critic: I don't like it. I don't want it.

> Me: Ha, me neither! I only want positive reviews and loving comments forever. Wouldn't that be nice!

> Critic: Ha, yeah.

What did you notice?

This is the empathize part of step three. When a friend, lover, spouse, or child is upset with you, the most powerful and effective way to deal with that situation is to truly hear them and respond with empathy, to "get" them and their experience. Of course, we all know that in the moment of conflict, this is easier said than done!

When someone close to us feels upset, we often imagine it's

our fault and feel blamed or criticized, even if the other person is not doing that. We react with defensiveness, hardness, counter-attack, withdrawal, or self-pity. We focus more on protecting and repairing our own ego rather than being with the other person, who is hurting.

And yet, when you can listen to them, reflect back what you hear, and empathize, something magical happens—they soften. The anger melts away; they become less afraid, hurt, and constricted. Harmony and love are restored. Of course, this is a summary of the process. It often can take some time or multiple conversations, and the moment-to-moment process is messier. But overall, empathy is the essential ingredient in the process.

That is how I responded to my critic in the previous demo. I agreed that critical reviews can be painful and that I didn't like them either, instead of telling the critic to "Be rational" and, "Don't let it get to you." I acknowledged that I get my feelings hurt, too, that I had a silly fantasy that we'd only have people love us and our books. It was such a sweet little exchange that was so simple, yet so powerful. Relating to your critic with empathy can make all the difference in turning the corner with your critic in a combative conversation that could last literally for years. It's that important.

Empathy 101

Empathy is one of the master skills that allows all our relationships to flourish. However, many of us are not consistent in regularly practicing empathy in our daily lives—with others or with ourselves.

This doesn't mean we are heartless sociopaths who care nothing for the people around us or narcissists who laugh inappropriately when our friend tells us about a woman who was beaten up so badly that she ended up in a hospital on Guerrero street[16]. It just means we are out of the habit of offering empathy.

In fact, the more self-critical we are, the more difficulty we have in regulating empathy with others. We are dealing with so much ongoing emotional pain due to the conflict within ourselves, that we don't have that much room to be with someone else's emotional pain. As a result, we lovingly attempt to cheer them up or dismiss their fears, doubts, and hurts.

A friend tells you about a conflict in their relationship, and you give them advice on what to say and do to fix it. Your brother gets dumped after three dates and is crestfallen. You tell him he's awesome, that she is a fool for dumping him, and that he will find someone perfect for him. Your spouse had a hard day at work, and you are full of ideas on how she can improve her mindset so that tomorrow will be better.

This is normal. This is extremely common. It's happening all day long. Others are doing it to you, and you're doing it to others. This is how we treat the people we love because we don't want them to hurt, and we want them to feel better. We are all doing this all of the time, but it doesn't work very well. To be fair, the "future will be brighter" pep-talk or the "how to improve your mindset" strategy conversations have their places. They can be extremely helpful but only when used at the right time, which is almost always after empathy.

Listen to these two scenarios, and put yourself in Rick's shoes.

Rick: Man, what a rough day. I woke up at 4 a.m. again, super anxious. I couldn't get back to sleep. I was stressing about the mistakes I made yesterday and all the work I am behind on.

---

16   For further demonstrations of bizarrely ineffective empathy, check out the movie, *The Disaster Artist*.

Aziz: Aww man, I bet you did fine yesterday. You do such great work. Have you tried herbal tea before bed? That can help you sleep better. Also, if you wake up early, it's best to hop right out of bed. Laying there can make you feel more anxious and overwhelmed.

Okay, that was scenario number one. Remember, you're Rick. How do you feel now? Perhaps you feel reassured by my confidence that you did well yesterday. But perhaps not, since I wasn't there, so how would I know? Did you enjoy my great tips about sleep hygiene?

The act of sharing and getting some response can be relieving and connecting. However, most likely, you felt a mixture of relief and also something else a little unpleasant. You may not let yourself fully acknowledge it because, hey, you're complaining here, so you should take whatever response you get. You're lucky that someone is even listening to you. But if you were to slow down and feel inside, it's most likely some element of not being fully seen or understood. You are not being fully met, fully known. And with that comes feelings of isolation, sadness, pain, irritation, or frustration, a sense of, "He doesn't really get it or get me."

Contrast that with this scenario:

Rick: Man, what a rough day. I woke up at 4 a.m. again, super anxious. I couldn't get back to sleep. I was stressing about the mistakes I made yesterday and all the work I am behind on.

Aziz: I'm sorry bro, getting short sleep is rough. I've had the same thing, where I wake up with a storm of anxious thoughts, focusing on everything I need to get done with a sense of pressure and urgency. What kind of mistakes are you stressing about?

Once again, you are Rick. How do you feel with this response? Does it feel better? Do you feel more connected, more understood than with the first scenario? Also, notice how ending with a question opens up the door for you to share more. Part of empathy is curiosity. Empathy is communicating this: *I hear you, and I see you. I get what you are feeling and why you'd be feeling that way. I'm curious about you and your experience. Tell me more.*

Empathy training is a key component of the group programs I run. People get a lot of practice viewing how other group members and I respond to people with empathy. Sometimes, there will be silence after someone shares. As the group facilitator, I will sometimes model empathy and speak first. Other times, I will ask the group, "What's up? I am curious about what's happening for people who are being silent."

When people were being quiet, they were not checked out or bored. It's quite the opposite. They were impacted by what the person was sharing, and they didn't know how to respond. The most common reason is, "I've never been in that scenario, so I don't know what to say or have a solution."

Aha! That's when I get excited because I get to teach them something extremely empowering about empathy. First off, you don't need a solution to their situation. In fact, as demonstrated above, coming in with a quick solution is often much *less* helpful. Instead, you simply need to acknowledge them and their feelings, and that's the biggest secret for being skilled in empathy. You don't have to have first-hand experience. You just have to guess the emotions they might feel. You do this by listening to what they're saying and what emotions they're expressing. You can also imagine what you might feel in a similar situation.

So if you're speaking with a friend who's getting divorced, you don't have to have gone through a divorce to be empathic. You can listen to what she is feeling and acknowledge it. Perhaps she is saying or showing she feels sad, lonely, hurt, or angry. You can acknowledge this by naming it: "Wow, that sounds really painful. That would be hard to have a conversation like that and hear him say all those things. Ugh. I'd feel so hurt and angry after that."

Empathy and this way of responding is a skill that you can develop. It's extremely valuable and will greatly enhance the quality of all your relationships, including the one with yourself. Over the next few days or weeks, notice how you respond to people when they share with you. Do you jump to pep talks, solutions, or advice? If so, experiment with empathy first. Ask yourself, "What is this person feeling right now?" Then, ask yourself if you can allow them to be feeling that without needing to fix it, be different, or otherwise "get over it." What if it makes sense that they'd be feeling that way, that it is okay for them to feel that way? How would you be with them then? What would you say?

Of Course

As you dialogue with your critic, you will have many opportunities to practice empathy. If your default instinct is to quickly challenge or dismiss what the critic says, that's okay. Simply acknowledge that, and call it out when it happens. You can even have "re-dos" with your critic (and other people in your life). You can say, "Wait, I think I jumped to a quick solution there without listening to you fully. Let's try that again."

One powerful technique to increase empathy for your critic is to use this simple but profoundly healing phrase: *of course*. This embodies deep empathy and validation, which is something we rarely give ourselves, our feelings, or our experience.

This lack of empathy with ourselves is partly due to a lack of receiving this regularly as children. When a small child is scared of the dark, of monsters, or to go upstairs by themselves, many well-meaning parents will reassure their child. "There's nothing in your closet. There's nothing upstairs." This might reassure the child, but usually not.

As our son Zaim grew beyond his toddler years, he started to gain more independence and began going into the bathroom by himself. This was in contrast to when he wanted an adult in there with him for support with both the mechanics and company. Now, he was enjoying the time alone in there and just needing some help at the end. Exciting times in the Gazipura household!

But then, all of a sudden, with no clear reason as to why, he reverted to needing someone in the bathroom with him at all times. He also became reluctant to go upstairs by himself, even to quickly retrieve a toy. He'd make demands for us to get him something from upstairs or stop eating and come into the bathroom with him.

As I sat on the edge of the tub, watching my four-year-old son sit on the toilet, I felt frustration and impatience. I didn't want to be in the bathroom. I wanted to be back at the dinner table, eating my meal. While I could've refused to go in with him and demanded he go by himself, I knew that probably would not have ended well. So I tried a different approach.

I paused for a moment, closed my eyes, and took a deep, slow breath. Yes, in the bathroom; parenting is a level 5 commitment baby—whatever it takes! I reminded myself that I am at choice and choosing to be here with him. I also imagined about ten years from now, he'll be driving a car, off with friends, and I'll probably be missing moments just like this.

From this place of empathy and curiosity, I said, "I noticed you don't want to go to the bathroom by yourself. You were doing that before, and then you stopped. What happened?"

"I don't know," he replied. "I just like being with someone in here."

"I see," I said, pausing for a moment. "Did something happen? Are you afraid to be in here by yourself?"

"Yeah."

"I see. I used to be afraid to go to certain parts of my house when I was a kid, too."

He looked up as I said this, clearly interested. "Like where? Where were you scared of?"

"Hmm, let me remember. I was scared of downstairs, especially the garage. I was afraid of the spiders in the garage and the dark. One time, I found a huge spider tucked right against the bottom step, and then I was scared to go downstairs at all for a while." I laughed as I remembered these moments for the first time in years.

"I'm scared in the bathroom," he said.

"Ahh. What are you scared of?" I asked.

"A lion." He said immediately.

"A lion?" I asked with genuine surprise. I would not have guessed that one in a million years. "Like a lion in the bathroom?"

"Yeah!" he exclaimed.

"Would it jump through the window?" I asked.

"I guess."

"If it jumped through the window, it would get cut pretty badly," I pointed out.

"Yeah, and start bleeding all over the place!" he added, sounding pleased at this treacherous lion's fate.

We went on to have an extended conversation about the lion, where it would come from, and what its motive would be for jumping through our bathroom window. He went on to tell me about certain parts in children's movies he'd seen during which he'd felt scared, even moments that I would not have thought of as scary.

It's unclear if he literally was afraid of a lion or if that is merely something tangible his mind came up with the try to explain the underlying sense of fear he felt about being alone. My goal was not to pinpoint the irrational thought and eradicate it (although eating an uninterrupted meal sure would've been nice). My main goal was to create an experience of empathy and curiosity, an attitude of "of course."

Of course, you're feeling scared; let's find out why. Of course, you don't want to be alone in the bathroom; there must be a good reason for it.

This is the exact attitude you can take with yourself and your own fears, hurts, and frustrations. Of course, you're feeling anxious about your upcoming meeting. Of course, you're dreading that tense conversation you've been avoiding. Of course, you don't feel like going to the gym this morning. Whatever the feeling is, you meet it with "of course."

That doesn't mean that you have to act on the feeling. You can still go to the meeting, have the difficult conversation, and get your butt into the gym. But you meet yourself and the different parts of you with empathy and love, rather than dismissal, frustration, or impatience.

Step Four: Regroup and Problem-Solve

When I was early in my training as a clinical psychologist, one of the first courses we had was on listening, empathy, and supportive therapy. We practiced all kinds of listening skills and empathy-building exercises. We were taught that all we needed to do was witness our clients, hold them in unconditional positive regard, and ask them questions, and they would find solutions to all their own problems. We didn't have solutions or need to have solutions, for they were the experts in their own lives. We just needed to listen, support, and love.

Sounds great, doesn't it? It's especially great sounding to a brand new graduate student who is flooded with doubt about his ability to help anyone. The only problem was when I went into the field to apply it.

I remember sitting there across the table from a fourteen-year-old girl named Veronica. She had long black curly hair, a thick coat of makeup on her face, and always wore a black hoodie sweatshirt. She shared about her father and his alcohol use. She shared about her hatred of her body. She shared about her boyfriend, who seemed to oscillate each week between being awesome and a total jerk. She shared, and I listened. I nodded and empathized and asked her questions. Working with her throughout the year, I noticed that not much had changed in her life.

I do think having someone to talk to was helpful and relieving for her. And yet, there was so much more we could have done. Looking back years later, I see all the things I could have taught her, how we could have tackled each of her problems one by one, and explored specific solutions. Even if she couldn't change her living situation, we could've strategized over ways to deal with her father and had her test these approaches out in her life, reporting back to me each week so we could refine our solutions. But I was following the rules of how I was trained and didn't yet trust my own natural approach to helping.

It's the same with your inner critic. Empathy and inquiry are extremely important and helpful ways to connect and relate to this part of you. Yet, doing this and only this can often be insufficient to produce a major sense of relief and liberation. More is needed. This is where step four comes in—Regroup and Problem-Solve.

Regrouping is about getting everyone on the same team. You may have been at odds with yourself for quite some time, with the critic screaming and pounding the table while other members cowered or shouted back. Your scared part may be sitting in the corner, covering its ears and crying, upset by all the noise and lack of attention for it. In other words, it might be a mess in there! We need to regroup.

With this step, you are interacting with your critic as if you are the loving father or mother, the older sibling, or the wise counselor. You care about all the different parts inside of you. You care about your own pain and are there to help the situation in any way you can. At the same time, you're not overwhelmed or intimidated by the blustering of this critic. It may have been in charge of the house before, but now you're here. And you can hold your own against it.

There are many ways to regroup, and the more you practice doing this, the better you'll become at figuring out what is needed. Like a masterful family therapist, you can walk into the situation, read the patterns, and see what needs to happen to turn this thing around. For now, here are a few key ways you can practice regrouping.

First is by listening to and reassuring the different parts of you, especially the parts of you that are scared. This may be your critic or another more vulnerable part that is terrified of judgment, failure, mistakes, loss, or pain.

To calm and reassure this part, you can take several minutes to slow down, turn off distractions, and bring your attention inward. Notice what emotions you are feeling and what the physical sensations of those emotions are. Bring your awareness to the squeezing sensations, the tightness, or the constriction you feel in your body. Breathe slowly and fully, and notice if you're clenching against the feeling or fighting it in some way. Remember, this is just fear. It's just a scared part of you that needs love, attention, and reassurance. Bracing against it and mentally telling it to "hurry up and get out of here" doesn't work and makes that part get much louder and more difficult to work with.

Instead, simply allow the feeling to be there. Notice the mental judgment and the emotional resistance inside of you. Can you let go of needing it to be the way you want? Can you let go of fighting what's already happening?

Can you surrender to the fact that you have a part of you that gets scared of other people at work, or your boss, or that beautiful stranger? It's okay. That's allowed. There's nothing wrong with you or that part of you. The problem is in the way you relate to that part — by denying it, criticizing it, shouting at it, berating it, shoving it in the closet while you focus on video games, beer, pizza, and so forth.

Open to that part now. Allow yourself to feel the sensations. Breathe and soften. As you do this, notice if that part has anything to say to you. Does it tell you what it's afraid of? Does it tell you what it wants or doesn't want?

Whatever it shares, be patient and nonreactive as you listen to it. Meet it as a deeply loving parent or grandparent would with a small child who's scared and hurting. Imagine this wiser part of you saying calming and soothing things, such as:

I know you're scared. It's okay; I love you no matter what.
No matter what happens in this meeting, I love you.
You're safe.
Even if they are upset with you, you're safe.
I'm here for you.
I'm not going anywhere.

These are not meant to be mindlessly repeated hundreds of times per day. Rather, imagine a solid, present father getting down to one knee to be on eye level with his five-year-old son. He brings his little boy in for a big, firm embrace, then leans back so he can look his son right in the eyes. As he looks directly into his soul, he says, "I know you're scared, son. And that's okay. I get scared too sometimes. And, I got you. No matter what you feel, and no matter what happens, I'm always here. I'm not going anywhere. I love you so much."

Meet it like that, only this happens within you, from one part of you to another part. It's steady, centered, and grounded. It's reminding you of the truth — that you are safe, and that you can handle whatever life brings.

In other instances, your critic can be so noisy and disruptive that it's hard to reassure it or any other part of you. In that case, you need to tap into the power of this fatherly or motherly part of you to step up to meet the critic and gain control of the situation. This is less of a soft, warm, reassuring vibe and more of a referee getting in there and breaking up a fight.

It looks very similar to when I intervene with my two small boys when things get out of hand. I'll be nearby, washing dishes, keeping one ear open to see what's happening between the two of them. Then, what my wife calls 'The Circle of Pain' begins. One boy does something that upsets the other, so one retaliates, then the other is enraged and wants revenge and must retaliate even more forcefully. You know, basically what humans (and nations) seem to do with each other all the time.

At some point, the circle of pain gets out of hand, and my older son Zaim is coming at his little bro Arman with a clear intent to injure. This is kind of like your critic viciously berating some other part of you, and then, when you come in to intervene, your critic turns toward you and tells you to shut up. Not in my house! This is where you have to step up and claim your inner authority. You are the boss of you. You are the head of the household, remember!

In this case, I will swoop in and physically block or restrain Zaim, so he can't hurt Arman. He is enraged by having his retaliation attempt thwarted, overcome by a feeling of injustice at Arman having the last strike in the circle of pain. In this case, I keep holding him and say, "I know, you're so angry at him! He hit you, and you want to hit him back. I know. I can't let you hurt him, buddy."

When I say those first lines, I am allowing my voice to be louder and full of more intensity, so he can see that I get how upsetting it is. I'm matching the energy inside of him, so he feels more seen and heard, which typically helps him calm down much faster.

This is often what is needed with your critic, especially earlier in this process, when you are first experimenting with becoming the head of your household. If you try to come in all warm and fuzzy, your critic might rip your head off. Instead, you need to step into your full power, own the room, and do what is needed to take control of the situation.

If you'd like to go through a fun and engaging process to activate this inner power and authority, go to www.omosbook.com, and I'll guide you through it.

As you get everyone's attention and things have calmed down a bit, then you can begin to problem-solve. You can listen to the different parts of you and see if there is a valid fear based on an actual threat, and whether action is required or not, or if it's just the scared part thrashing around, being afraid of all change, uncertainty, and unknowns. You can see if the critic that is telling you that you're a terrible employee, spouse, or parent is highlighting some internal rule that you did not live up to, but you actually believe in. Perhaps you see some place you want to apologize for behaving out of alignment with your values.

If your critic is attacking you for not being more bold and outgoing in your dating or social life, you can explore ways you might increase your romantic and social connection. If your critic is harshly judging you for not being assertive in a particular situation, you can brainstorm ways to take care of yourself and meet your needs.

These solutions can be very helpful and relieve some of the angst and frustration. The key is to lead with empathy, connection, and reassurance first, and then explore solutions. Otherwise, the critic will still feel unsafe and will generally be unwilling to test out any solutions, regardless of how effective they might be.

Step Five: Into the Roar

A classic tale at the Training for Warriors gym I frequent in Portland goes as follows:

> In the savannah of Africa, female lions are the primary hunters of the pride. They have a special method of hunting gazelles, which involves chasing them until they are all packed together in a tight herd. They then run the herd toward several male lions hiding in the grass. As the herd of frightened gazelles approaches the hidden lions, these males let out an ear-splitting, guttural roar. This startles the gazelles who then instinctively make a choice. Most immediately retreat from the shocking sound, running away in the opposite direction, right into the pack of lionesses. However, some gazelles run toward the sound of the roar, despite their fear. Those gazelles, the ones who run into the roar, survive.

Ultimately, to be truly liberated from your critic and the voices of fear, self-doubt, and self-criticism, you must go into the roar in your own life, not just once, but again and again and again.

You must do the things that your critic says you cannot do. You must challenge the completely false and limiting stories of your safety police. Your critic says you can't take on that project at work because you're not smart enough, and you'll fail and publicly humiliate yourself in the company and end up jobless, homeless, penniless, and friendless in a flophouse under a bridge.

That is the terrifying sound of a 400-pound lion roaring in front of you. That is the oh-so-convincing claims of your critic that stun you into inaction or life-diminishing retreat. That is the roar into which you must run to be free. And so you deal with all these parts inside, love the heck out of all of them, regroup your insane internal family (don't worry, we all have one), and take on that freakin' project. You step up and say yes, even when you're scared. You approach that person who's out of your league. You offer that new product or service in your business that your critic says no one would ever want. You share your opinion in the group. You speak up. You step up. You take bold action. That is the only way to be truly free of your critic and to diminish its power over you.

As you take bold action, not everything will go according to your plan. You won't get all the outcomes you want immediately, with no rejection, setback, or discomfort. But through the action, you will realize this: In the vast majority of cases, the fears are not based on actual dangers. The fear is based on believing that scared, inaccurate, critical voice in your head that tells you that you can't do things. That voice is not interested in what is true, or what could be amazing for your life or the lives of others, but what is safe and sure to be devoid of risk, pain, and discomfort. That is the voice most of us are listening to all the time, and that is the voice that kills your passion, soul, power, purpose, and drive. Fuck that voice. It does not own you. It will not defeat you.

I am the captain of my ship
I am the master of my destiny
I defy doubt
I defeat doubt
I destroy doubt.

PUTTING IT ALL TOGETHER

Now you have a clear, step-by-step framework to neutralize your critic in the moment. You know the basic moves of the sequence, the core steps of the dance. And yet, you can know these moves intellectually and verbally and even be able to recite them on a test, but that doesn't mean anything about a feeling of liberation and self-love in your daily life.

To create this, you must practice these moves. You must consciously engage with your critic in dialogues, again and again, on paper, in your head, and even with another person who you rope into role-playing with you (this last one is extremely powerful for rapidly building your skills if you have the courage to find someone who will do it with you!).

In my group program, The Unstoppable Confidence Mastermind, we meet regularly in small group calls to master confidence and our lives. While we focus on all key areas of confidence, including dating and relationships, career, social life, and more, a common topic of conversation is O.M.O.S. Being on your own side (or being at odds with yourself) heavily impacts your confidence and your success in every area of life.

In the calls, I regularly lead people through role-plays and dialogue exercises where they can practice responding to their inner critic. We take the intellectual learning and turn it into repetitions and drills so that responding to their critic in a loving, centered way becomes their natural response.

Below are some excerpts from a Mastermind call. I will describe what is happening before each section, so it will be like you're there in the room. Pay close attention to how you would respond to your critic if you were in the same situation.

Here's the setup. Charles is a skilled, highly effective, and successful developer in the tech industry. He's worked for several major companies and has always done well at his work. In spite of this, he is plagued by feelings of inferiority, a sense that he should do more and know more, and a fear of speaking up and being seen as incompetent or unintelligent in meetings. This chronic inadequacy and fear are leading to perpetual neck and shoulder pain, periods of high anxiety, irritability around his family, and feelings of depression and hopelessness.

In this section, one group member plays Charles' critic, so we can all see how Charles responds. As I set up the role-play, I help Charles center himself. He is a devout Christian, and I remind him of his connection with God as a source of unconditional love and power.

--

Aziz: So, David, you're going to play the critic, and Charles, you are going to play you. The bigger you, the wiser you, the parent in you who is going to intervene and support this little angry, scared part of you. This is the part of you that remembers who you really are, which is a child of God. You up for that, Charles?

Charles: Yes.

Aziz: Okay, let's begin.

Critic (played by David): These projects you are working on always get messed up. What's the deal with that? It's always been this way. Do you even know what you're doing?

Charles: Hold on, critical part. I think this project is going okay. It's not as messed up as you said. This project involves a lot of communication between so many teams and team members; it's not possible for anyone to understand everything.

Critic: I agree that it's not possible for everyone to understand everything, but you don't seem to get anything on this team. I mean, when we're talking apples, you're thinking oranges. It's like you speak a different language.

Charles: Well, that's too extreme. I do understand the part I am supposed to understand, and obviously, there are

some things I don't understand, but that's why we're in the
meetings, right? I mean, the meetings are to learn things,
to get better communication about the real concerns,
so that we understand the project as a team in a better
way. That's why we need the meetings. If you understand
everything, why do we need a meeting?

Aziz: Okay, pause. Great job. People witnessing the role-
play, what did you notice?

--

I will ask you the same question. What did you notice about
Charles' response? What did he do well? What did he miss or
forget to do? Take a moment now to imagine how you'd respond
to this kind of internal criticism. Mentally putting yourself on the
mat will help you get much more out of these dojo training sessions!

When I asked the group this, one person pointed out that he
seemed less comforting and more combative, that he was pushing
back on his critic. Charles agreed. He said he didn't know what
else to do.

Surprisingly, this is a great situation because pushing back
and disagreeing with your critic is way better than rolling over
and taking its abuse. Even if it doesn't neutralize the situation, at
least you are fighting for some semblance of self-esteem and inner
self-respect, instead of submitting to the inner tyranny of toxic
abuse. Forget that noise.

And we can do even better.

There was one group member—Jonathan—who seemed to
understand the process well. I asked if he wanted to play Charles
in the next role play. We'd have Charles play his own critic, and
Jonathan could demonstrate how to respond in a more receptive
manner. Here's what happened:

--

Critic: What the f— is wrong with you? You don't even know what they are talking about, and you are sitting here pretending you know something.

Jonathan: Hey, hey, buddy, it sounds like you're upset. What do you mean? I'm confused when you say, "I don't know anything." Talk to me a little more about that.

Critic: Well, the thing people were just talking about with the data package. You've never even heard of this! Why don't you know about this thing?

Jonathan: Yeah, I noticed when he talked about the package, I tensed up. You're right; you're absolutely right. I didn't know what they were talking about. I'm not sure why I didn't know that. But that's why we are in this meeting. If we just take a moment to breathe for a little bit and collect our thoughts, I'm pretty sure I'll be able to get that package info down, and I'll know exactly what we're talking about. But it sounds like we're scared of something here, and I want to connect with you about that.

Critic: Don't you think it's too late? The other people know about it, you are quite behind, dude. You're quite behind.

Jonathan: Well, I don't think it's ever too late. And, if those people know about it, then I think it would be easier for me to figure it out. Don't you think?

Critic: Well, obviously, you're not good enough. You're supposed to know everything in a meeting.

Jonathan: Yeah, you're right. It's challenging to go into this meeting, not feeling fully prepared. Maybe the next time we go into a meeting, we can talk to our colleagues and see what we want to know before we go in. But, we're not going to be able to know everything at all times. And, so, *of course*, you're upset with me not knowing what I'm supposed to know right now.

Critic: Wow, you don't know it because you don't work hard enough. You are not smart enough. You need to do better.

Jonathan: Yeah, yeah, I see where you're coming from. Aziz, I need your help!

--

What did you notice there? What was Jonathan doing right? So many things! How warm and loving did he feel? Could you tell how much he was on his own side, how much he was treating the critic like an upset family member rather than an enemy? Also, notice the subtle maneuvers, like deepening empathy by saying, "of course…" to the critic's feelings and experience.

It primarily was a demonstration of step two: Move Toward Your Critic. There were also some attempts at empathy and problem-solving, as well.

However, it did not fully accomplish step three: Explore the Root Fears and Empathize. Empathy is more than just being sweet and nurturing and saying, "I'm sorry you're hurting." That's compassion, and it's important. But we also need to be fully seen, heard, and understood. We (and our critics) need someone to listen and fully get us, to understand what's bothering us, what we're afraid of, and to know where we are coming from.

To demonstrate this, I jumped into the role play. My goal was to fully do step three, so the critic felt completely seen, heard, and understood. I also wanted to get clarity on what the root fears were because I couldn't quite tell so far.

Then, I could move on to step four: Regroup and Problem-Solve. Observe.

--

Aziz: You guys are both doing awesome. And, I want everyone listening to notice what Jonathan was doing. And, what I'm going to do is very similar but with a slight tweak. But, Jonathan, you were super on track. Charles, say the last thing you just said as your critic.

Critic: Here's the truth. You're not smart enough. You don't work hard enough, and that's why you don't know things.

Aziz: Whoa, that one's got some heat on it. You're pissed. You are so pissed at me right now, aren't you?

Critic: Yes, yes.

Aziz: Yeah, you're pissed. You wanted me to know stuff in that meeting that I didn't know.

Critic: That's right.

Aziz: Yeah. You're angry at me for not knowing it, and so now you're yelling at me, telling me I should have known it.

Critic: Yes.

Aziz: Yeah. Okay, so it sounds like it was extremely important for you to know that stuff in the meeting, and my guess is that, because I didn't, you're angry and probably feeling uncomfortable or something?

Critic: Yes, you make me lose face in the meeting.

--

Okay, pause. Did you see what just happened here? First off, as part of feeling empathy, I acknowledged that the critic was angry. When someone is angry, it's helpful to acknowledge that they're angry. Typically, out of a fear of conflict, we attempt to address the issue and solve the problem without mentioning this, but that actually makes things worse. Because it's a form of missing empathy—the person does not feel fully seen.

We attempt to respond with warmth, love, and an almost too-patient sounding calmness, which often enrages someone further when they're angry. Instead, it is hugely effective to match their intensity, minus the anger. So, in this conversation, my voice got louder when I said, "You're pissed!"

Notice how I kept saying that and acknowledging that the critic was angry and the reasons why he was angry (without challenging them). This allowed me to take more control of the conversation. As the critic felt more seen and understood, out of nowhere, it added this key piece of information: "You'll make me lose face in the meeting."

Part of the root fear is now revealed. Like a paleontologist slowly and patiently moving aside dirt with a small brush, we uncover something special. Once I see this fear, I explore that more, which is also part of step three: Explore the Root Fears and Empathize.

Okay, let's resume.

--

Aziz: Okay, tell me more about that. You're pissed at me because you felt you lost face in the meeting?

Critic: Yeah, sometimes when you're talking to people, and they ask you a question you don't know, don't you think it's embarrassing?

Aziz: Right, I see. So the real issue is that someone asked us a question, and we didn't know the answer.

Critic: Well, that's part of it. Sometimes when people ask a question, you don't understand, and then you're just sitting there like an idiot. And why do you sit there? Why don't you know what's going on??

Aziz: Yeah, okay, so you hate feeling like we're looking foolish, or like an idiot, or we're losing face, like people in the meeting aren't respecting us?

Critic: That's right.

Aziz: Yeah, okay, so that's what's going on here. It felt like we lost face in the meeting, and you f---ing hate losing face in the meeting.

Critic: Of course.

Aziz: That enrages you.

Critic: Right.

Aziz: Yeah, that's intense. I don't like it either.

--

Now that I've empathized and explored the root fear more, I can move on to step four: Regroup and Problem-Solve. For this step, we need to get on the same page with the critic. As I described earlier, there are many ways to do this—gentle reassurance, visualization, humor, being direct, making requests, and many more. Regrouping is always different, depending on the situation in that moment. Here's how I proceeded in this instance.

--

Aziz: Yeah, that's intense, man. I don't like it either.

Critic: Then do something if you don't like it.

Aziz: Why don't you do something?

Critic: Well, that's what I'm doing. I'm criticizing you so that you improve.

Aziz: This? Your plan is to beat me up, and somehow, it's going to make it all go away? Dude, I don't think that's going to work, teammate.

Critic: Well, that's the only thing I know.

Aziz: Look, I don't think crapping on me is going to help us get any better. Let's get one thing straight—I'm with you, I don't want to lose face in meetings. I don't like it either! But, you attacking me afterward, man, I don't know. Does this feel like it's working? Does it make me perform any better? Does it make us do better in the next meeting?

Critic: Well, sadly, it's getting worse with this technique.

Aziz: Yeah, I've noticed that too. You're stressing me out, dude. I'm all stressed out in the meeting, not because I'm not going to know something, but because you're going to harshly attack me afterward. We gotta work together on this; this is not working.

Critic: Yeah, I agree.

Aziz: But, check this out. We're on the same page. I don't want to lose face, and you don't want to lose face. And, you're blaming me like it's my fault. We need all of our brainpower to solve this.

Critic: Yeah.

Aziz: Okay, pause. People observing—what did you notice?

--

What stands out to you as you read this dialogue? What do you notice about how I relate to the critic? What might be helpful for you to use when you work with your critic?

Some members from the group contributed some of the following insightful observations:

"It felt like the way I talk to my brother. He and I are always on the same page, but sometimes we have different energy. You were less soft and nurturing and more like the friendly pushback I give my brother when we're disagreeing. I love imagining being with my critic that way."

"You were assertive with your critic. You bluntly pointed out his approach wasn't working. You stood up to him and reasoned with him."

"You kept drilling into the critic, trying to see what was happening underneath. That gave you much more power to relate to him and diffuse the situation."

"You calibrated your style to the intensity of the critic's. Jonathan was reassuring and warm, but that wasn't fully landing. So you parried and put the critic in the hot seat, right? You put some back on him, telling him, 'Hey, we're on the same page, but also, I'm not going to take your sh-t, so, how are you going to help me? Because this ain't working.'"

How can you take what you are learning now and practice it in your dialogues with your critic? What techniques are you going to experiment with? It's essential to ask yourself these questions because the liberation you seek does not lie in simply reading

my dialogue with someone else's critic. Even if you heavily identify with Charles and have a similar challenge in your workplace,
reading his dialogue will only partially help.

The key to success in taming your critic is practice. I recommend setting aside some time—about 20 minutes, several times
per week—to practice dialoguing with your critic on paper. You
can do this more often if you'd like, and the more you practice,
the more adept you'll become at relating to this part of you.

The next time you are having a challenging moment or a
rough day that you just want to be over, take a few minutes to jot
down some notes in your phone. What is the critic saying about
you, your abilities, your intelligence, or your future? Even if you
don't have time to fully dive in and respond to everything, just
capturing the critic's comments is helpful. Then, later that day or
the next, you can revisit those criticisms and practice dialoguing
with your critic using the five-step process you learned above.

The Triangle

The Triangle is a powerful exercise that can accelerate your
capacity to get a handle on your critic and strengthen your
self-compassion at the same time. To do this exercise, find a place
where you can feel total privacy and know that you will not be
heard or disturbed, such as your bedroom. You will be voicing the
different parts of you out loud from different places in your room.

There are three characters in this exercise, hence the name.
First, you have your critic (insert boxing match entrance theme
music here). You also have the wise, compassionate, loving part
of you that is here to treat you with kindness and respect. And
finally, you have a part of you that is struggling in some way; perhaps it is scared, sad, lonely, needy, hurting, or discouraged.

What often happens when we're feeling bad is this: The hurting part is hurting and feeling anxious, sad, or other painful emotions. The critic enters to put a stop to all this nonsense. It will usually berate the hurting part, pointing out its flaws, and having zero empathy for its feelings. The hurting part either shrivels into a ball and takes the abuse, or gets more anxious, tense, or distressed. It may argue with the critic or try meekly to defend itself, but it is no match for the authority and intensity the critic has. This battle rages on inside your mind and heart, causing tension, stress, anxiety, and general emotional distress. It might also lead to compulsive behaviors, repetitive checking of texts or social media, emotional eating, or drug and alcohol use, which, of course, your critic berates you for doing as well. Ah, what a chap, that critic!

The Triangle is a way to train yourself to do something different. What's often missing in the scenario above is a third part of you—the wise, compassionate part. This is the part we want to strengthen to defend all the parts of you and to help regain control of the situation. So, here's what you do.

Start by having whichever part feels the most active in your mind, usually the critic or the hurting part. Have that part sit in a specific place in the room that is it's designated spot. For example, the critic sits at the foot of your bed or in a desk chair. Let that part speak out loud, as if it were talking directly to the part it's upset with.

Then, switch chairs to the hurting part. How does it feel when the critic berates it? What does it say in response? Usually, it's an ineffective attempt to defend itself, a weak counter-attack, or most often, quiet acquiescence.

Then, practice stepping into the third part of you—your compassionate, wise self. This is the part of you that knows that setbacks are inevitable, that perfection is impossible, and that life and relationships are messy. It's the part of you that is committed to O.M.O.S. and treating you with love and patience, no matter what. It knows that not only does this feel better, but it's the most effective way to work with feelings, overcome fears, and get results in life.

Have this part speak out loud as well. What would it say to the hurting part? What would it say to the critic? Then, see where the conversation goes. In many ways, it's like the dialogues on paper, only acted out in real life. Speaking these things out loud, moving to different places in your room, and embodying these characters makes the exercise even more impactful.

When you hear the way a part of you speaks to you, it can be jarring. *Do I really say that to myself?* You will also hear the voice tone of your critic and your compassionate side. For many clients I've guided through this process, their compassionate side often starts by sounding hesitant, unsure, or forced. It's as if it's out of practice. They've heavily exercised the critic, but their self-compassion muscle has atrophied from underuse.

It's time to hit the gym. Start practicing speaking to yourself from this compassionate voice in The Triangle exercise. Repeat the exercise many times over the course of the next few weeks. Get to the point where your compassionate side is strong, firm, and an inner authority. Practice having this part interrupt the critic when it's viciously attacking the hurting part.

Eventually, your compassionate side will say things like this to your inner critic: "Hang on a second. Don't talk to her like that. I hear that you're upset, and I want to talk with you about it. I want to hear more about what you're scared of or upset about. But I'm not going to let you talk to her that way. That doesn't help any of us."

That's when you know you're on the right track. And that's when you know you need to add even more fuel to the fire.

Chapter 8:
Show Me Everything You Got

Living on your own side is not an all-or-nothing way of being, where you are either fully on your own side or totally against yourself. Most people live somewhere between these two extremes. They are sort of on their own side throughout much of the day, but when they experience a setback, imagine someone is disapproving of them, or feel anxious, they immediately and habitually turn on themselves without even knowing it.

With the self-reflection and exercises you've been doing as you read this book, you are becoming much more aware than most people. You are seeing your critic in action and short-circuiting that unhelpful process of self-attack. This is an essential skill to develop; however, it is not the complete path to being fully on your own side, no matter what.

To reach higher and higher levels of O.M.O.S., you must go beyond catching your critic and taming it in the moment. There is another required skill to reach the next level of self-love and freedom that you must cultivate to feel that deep sense of peace and ease that comes with being on your own side. This skill is a complete willingness to go anywhere inside of your own mind and heart, a willingness to face any feelings and be with any emo-

223

tional pain, no matter how intense, how ancient, or how confusing it may be and to truly be with all the parts of yourself without retreating, fleeing, dismissing, or letting your critic attack them. I am continually amazed at our mind's endless tactics to avoid emotional discomfort and keep parts of ourselves out of our full awareness.

THE HABIT OF INVALIDATION

What is your default stance toward your feelings? Are you aware of them as you're feeling them? Or do they take a back seat to taking action and getting through the day? Do you operate on top of your feelings, finding a way to push through any internal discomfort? Do you feel like you don't have time for them, that they are a bother or insignificant?

Perhaps you treat your feelings as if they are dangerous or threatening. They wield a power over you that makes you uneasy, and so you try not to "go there" for fear of being taken over. If you let yourself truly feel how you're feeling, you'll be lost in a sea of emotion from which you'll never emerge.

A large number of people in our world today have a default stance of invalidation toward their own feelings. To make something invalid means you perceive it as untrue, not real, or otherwise unjustified. In essence, it's an attitude of, "I shouldn't be feeling this." The feelings seem wrong, inappropriate, irrational, or otherwise incorrect.

In many cultures throughout the world, feelings are disregarded as a nuisance that must be dealt with on the side. Life is about performance, achievement, success, and getting what you want in the world "out there." We don't talk much with others about what's going on "in here," and when we do, we feel vulnerable or exposed. Expressions of feelings are often met with overt or subtle messages to stop feeling, to hurry up and put those feelings away, and "get over it."

As a society, our capacity to feel feelings and be with natural human emotions like anger, fear, or grief is greatly atrophied. Parents are often stunted in their own emotional development and maturity and are unable to teach their children how to identify feelings and work skillfully with them. Instead, kids receive the message that their feelings are either dangerous or unacceptable and must be hidden away and replaced with nice and polite behavior.

This might seem normal because most people are living this way today, but it's actually quite bizarre. We are extremely emotional creatures. Emotion is at the root of everything we do. We have strong emotional needs from birth until death, and much, if not all, of our actions, are designed to constantly meet our needs so we feel safe, connected, loved, and worthwhile.

But when our emotions are not acknowledged, and we're actively taught to ignore our feelings and "just get things done," we don't learn how to navigate our emotional world. It's like trying to operate in the world without being taught language or how to walk or move your body. It's an absolutely essential element to healthy relationships, happiness, and a sense of security and safety in the world.

While this originates with your family growing up and the culture in which you live, the biggest problem is not what parents say or have said to you or how your coworker would react if you were emotionally authentic with them. The biggest problem is inside your own mind. It's your own pattern of chronically invalidating your own feelings, discounting and dismissing what you think, feel, and want in a variety of situations.

When we habitually dismiss our own feelings, we lose access to an incredibly valuable feedback mechanism within our nervous system. If we feel aversion toward somebody and want to get away, we don't act on that feeling and end up staying way longer than we should. If we feel fear about something, we dismiss the fear and try to push through it, which creates tension and mixed results. Sometimes, we can make ourselves do it but are unable to sustain this forced action. Then, our critic berates us for being weak, lazy, or undisciplined. Just as often, trying to push through the fear doesn't work at all, and we are just paralyzed and avoid the stuff that scares us. Then our critic berates us for being weak, lazy, wimpy, and undisciplined. Delightful.

The strange thing about emotional invalidation is we may have done it for so long that we don't even realize we're doing it. It feels normal and natural to relate to our feelings the way we always have. It's familiar and feels "right." To do otherwise can feel foreign, forced, or almost inappropriate. And our critic is just waiting for the opportunity to jump out of the bushes to judge our attempts to empathize with ourselves as self-indulgent, pathetic, sappy, or otherwise shameful.

Watch out for this! And don't buy into this voice of invalidation. Instead, take a moment to get outside of yourself and run it through the five-year-old test. If you were spending time with a five-year-old child that you loved, how would you be? If you have children of your own, or a niece or nephew, you can imagine them when they were around this age. If not, imagine how you'd like to be or what you think would be the most loving and effective way to be.

If they were scared to go to school or to go to a friend's house, what would you do? What would you say to them? Take a moment to imagine this scenario. See this five-year-old boy or girl as they fight back tears, telling you they don't want to go. What do you think is the most skillful way to handle this?

Let's make it a game. Games are fun. We'll turn it into a multiple-choice question. Which answer seems best to you?

In this scenario, it seems most loving and effective to say:

a.   There's nothing to be scared of. It's just your friend Johnny's house. Let's go. We're going to be late.

b.   Fine, if you don't want to go, we don't have to go.

c.   Why are you always like this? Why are you so scared of everything? You never want to leave the house. What's wrong with you?

d.   You have three seconds to get in the car, or I'm leaving you. Move. Now.

e.   You're scared to go to Johnny's house, huh? That's okay to be scared. I get scared sometimes too. Do you know what you're scared of? Is there something you don't like about going to Johnny's house?

Which one sounds best to you?
Which ones would your parents have used with you?

No Permission

The habitual pattern of emotional invalidation that you experienced growing up and now regularly use with yourself leads to a variety of challenges. One of the biggest problems is a chronic sense of shame about how you are feeling.

You learned growing up that having certain feelings or expressing your feelings leads to a host of unpleasant results. Perhaps you were ignored, mocked, or chastised. Your parents had enough difficulty tolerating their own emotions, let alone yours. So they told you, directly or indirectly, to put those emotions away, to keep that stuff hidden.

Whenever we're taught as children that something must be hidden, we automatically assume that it is somehow shameful or bad. We may not even know why it's bad, but we know that it must be kept to ourselves. This secrecy is a breeding ground for shame and creates a chronic sense of shame around your feelings.

You might experience this shame as intense feelings of badness or inferiority when you feel a particular emotion, such as anxiety, anger, or sexual desire. You have a strong urge to control or hide the feeling, hoping no one will notice you are feeling that way. Imagining revealing what you're feeling to others seems horrifying, as you are convinced they would judge you as weak, bad, or wrong.

Even basic, natural, everyday emotions can be relegated to the category of shameful or wrong. I bet you have certain basic human emotions that you don't let yourself feel, emotions that you label as bad and wrong every time you experience them, such as anxiety, inferiority, or lust.

What emotions are not okay for you to experience? What emotions are okay to experience, but not okay to express? How often do you feel a background sense that something is wrong, simply because you are experiencing normal human emotions?

Breakdown

"Sometimes, you just do things."

- Scott Jurek

So here's the major dilemma. First, the setup. You are a collection of different parts that make up your "internal family." Each part has its own desires, feelings, and agenda, and sometimes, these may conflict with each other. The challenge occurs when you want to set your course and take consistent action in the world. You pick your path and set off down the road...or maybe not. What if all family members are not on board? What if some want to go and some want to stay? And still others want to go but in a completely different direction?

Imagine a little team of people at a fork in the road on a trail. Some want to go to the left, some to the right, and one guy wants to turn around and head back the way you came. Everyone has a different opinion and is talking at once. What do you do? Oh, before you answer that, let me throw in one more condition. The team cannot split up. Now, what do you do?

This, my friend, is your life. And yet, no one in your upbringing ever talked with you about it. No one ever sat you down and helped you learn how to listen to and navigate your own inner world. For the most part, your parents probably didn't have a clear strategy of how to work with their own inner families and perhaps didn't even have an awareness that they had one.

Most likely, each parent (or whoever raised you) had a dominant strategy that they used all the time. They had a part inside of them that took control and got everyone else on their inner team to follow by using whatever means possible, usually brute force. There's no time for whiners, worriers, or complainers. Just shut up and get in line. That's how they treated their inner team, and that's maybe how they treated you as a child as well.

There was no time for crying or protesting, no time to hear your perspective, your wants, or your desires. Stop feeling and do what's needed. Get in the car. Get your schoolwork done. We're moving now. You're changing schools. You have feelings about things? Why? Stop that. Put those away.

And so you did. And you do. Only now, most likely, your mom or dad is not there to regularly tell you not to feel. You've taken that inside and have an internal family member that is doing that all day, all night. Most likely, it's one of your critic's jobs.

Here's the thing—this invalidating way of relating to yourself kind of works. Let's call this way of being 'Strategy A.' Operating from 'Strategy A' can help you get by, meet people, make friends, hold a job or run a business, and have a family. You can go through all the normal motions of life and be and seem totally "normal," just like your parents, or other family members, or people you see at the mall or the bank.

It kinda works, but it also kinda doesn't. Because what happens when one part of you railroads its agenda and rolls right over the other parts of you? What happens when other parts and their feelings are a nuisance that you don't have time to deal with, so you push them down and keep going?

At first, you can do this, and you can keep going. You keep getting work done, progressing in your projects, work, finances, and life. Everything is fine. You're not one of those snowflakes that sits around feeling their feelings and crying all day. You get stuff done. You've got it all handled. You're tough.

But then, it comes. Sometimes, it's subtle at first. You have a hard time falling asleep, or you wake up at 3 a.m. with a jolt of anxiety. Or, you have strange and disturbing dreams that repeat. Or you wake up feeling tired and physically drained even after a full night of sleep. No matter. You got stuff to do. You drink extra coffee in the morning, take sleeping pills in the evening, and get back on track. There's a race to win here, and we don't have time to be held up by something as pointless as feelings.

Then, symptoms might come on more severely. Here are just a few of the many strange things that might start happening.

> You experience an extremely intense period of anxiety before a work meeting. It's so strong that you have no idea what's happening, and you wonder if you're losing your mind.

> You start to feel more negative, dissatisfied, and empty inside, despite all the good things you have going in your life. You wonder if you're depressed, so you talk to your

doctor. After a ten-minute assessment, he agrees you are depressed and prescribes antidepressant pills. You start taking them, but they don't seem to do much.

You wake up with a back so stiff you can barely move your neck or shoulder, or bend over. You worry you have a "bad back" and start seeing specialist after specialist, without relief.

You are agitated and irritable at work or at home. You do your best to contain it inside, but it explodes outward here and there, like steam shooting out of a geyser.

You get a cold, and then, as you're getting better, you get a cold again. You seem to get sick a lot. Or you have lots of allergies that are always acting up. Or your stomach seems to get upset all the time.

What's happening with all these weird symptoms in your body? Who cares? Get over it. Take some pills, work through it, and tough it out. You're getting old, you know; that's what happens. Plus, you have bad genes in your family, so it's probably just those coming to get you anyway. Just shut up and keep going.

What's happening here is you're bumping up against the limits of what 'Strategy A' can do for you. While you may be able to function in the world for a time and appear fine, it's unsustainable because you are ignoring a fundamental aspect of yourself—your feelings.

It's like your critic, or other dominant parts, decided to walk down one fork of the trail. When other parts of you hesitated, your critic forcefully grabbed them, yelling at them to shut up and get moving. It then dragged this part by the arm as it cried. When this scared part tried to speak up, protest, or make any sort of claim, your critic met it with fierce and aggressive attacks, so that part went silent.

But here's a fundamental property of being a human that you must understand if you want to thrive in this life. You cannot kill, or amputate, or get rid of any part of yourself. You can't ignore it until it disappears or criticize it away. You can't vote it off the island. Each part inside of you is here to stay, even the anxious, scared, or timid parts.

When you oppress them for too long, these parts start to wreak havoc inside your mind, emotions, and physical body in strange and alarming ways. They start to rattle the cage so intensely that you have to slow down and pay attention to them.

Unfortunately, we currently live in a culture of feeling-denial and suppression, so often, these signals are not heard. People have the symptoms I described, and they go to trained professionals who tell them to solve the problem with medical interventions that in no way address underlying emotions or the fundamental way the person is treating themselves. As a result, the symptoms continue, often for months, years, or decades, switching from one thing to the next.

Before I realized this, I experienced and was diagnosed with the following conditions over a ten-year period:

Osgood-Schlatter disease
Piriformis syndrome
Ankylosing spondylitis
Irritable bowel syndrome
Repetitive strain injury
Carpal tunnel syndrome
Temporomandibular joint disorder
Plantar fasciitis
Chronic neck and upper back pain

In addition to these conditions, when I exercised, I would inevitably get pain somewhere in my body—in my groin, my knee, my ankle, my Achilles tendon, or somewhere else. I was always going to see some doctor, chiropractor, acupuncturist, Chinese medicine doctor, naturopath, surgeon, or somebody who was going to help me fix the problem and solve the pain.

But nothing ever worked. Because the problem was not in my knee, or the alignment of my hips, or my intestinal flora balance, or my computer work station ergonomics, or my shoes. The problem was not mechanical or structural. The problem was in my own mind. It was the way I related to the parts of myself. It was due to my denial of my own feelings and my inability to even hear the parts of me I'd shut out for so many years, the parts I'd learned to shut down and suppress as a young child, that I kept running 'Strategy A' with for years.

Sooner or later, 'Strategy A' leads to a breakdown. Regardless of what you were taught about feelings, they are an important and absolutely essential part of being a human. In order to live with mental and emotional health and be free from ongoing physical problems and pains, we must adopt an entirely new strategy, a new way of being with all these parts ourselves. We must learn how to listen to these different parts and work with them in a way that creates inner harmony and unified action in the world. We must learn 'Strategy B.'

Unanimous

U·nan·i·mous - held or carried by everyone involved; united; congruent; undivided.

Here's 'Strategy B' in a nutshell:

Everyone on this team matters. Everyone here is valuable and has a purpose in being here. Each member has a right to be heard, have their feelings be acknowledged, and their desires considered.

How does that sound to you? Does it sound pretty reasonable? Perhaps this is how a healthy workplace or family operates? Like many things with O.M.O.S., our challenge is not often in knowing what to do; it's doing what we know and applying this basic level of respect and maturity to ourselves.

To truly be on your own side, you must upgrade from 'Strategy A' to 'Strategy B.' That means meeting every part of you, every emotion you feel with an attitude of curiosity, empathy, acceptance, and respect.

At first, this may be challenging or downright impossible for you. You may have run 'Strategy A' for so long that you don't know how to relate to yourself with more patience and empathy. But, through practice, you will learn how to transform the way you treat yourself. You will find a new way to relate to these parts of you that are begging for your attention and love.

Let's practice right now.

Where is there a situation in your life that you could focus on right now, where you feel some tension, stress, or angst? Perhaps it's something in your workplace, business, or finances. Maybe it's in a personal relationship, your romantic life, or a friendship. Whatever pops into your mind first is perfect; use that.

As you focus on this situation, take a moment to slow down. Stop whatever else you're doing and bring your full attention inward as you think about this area of your life. Feel your breath go in and out of your body for the next three breaths.

What do you feel inside? Where do you feel tension, stress, or angst in your body? Slow down even more and move toward those feelings of discomfort. Notice your internal attitude or stance toward these feelings. Are you resisting them? Are you bracing yourself physically or mentally?

Take another full deep breath in, and as you exhale, let go of the fight. Allow these feelings to be there, just as they are, without needing to change or fix anything right now. Surrender to the feelings being here as they are in this moment.

If you notice some part of you is still fighting the feelings, that's okay. You can bring your attention to this resistance, this fighting part. Where do you feel that? Where are you tensing up to protect yourself from feeling so much? What is the voice of the resistance? What is it saying in your mind?

Some of the most common voices of resistance are variations of these:

> *I don't want to feel this.*
> *I don't have time to feel this. I've got stuff to do!*
> *This feeling is too strong; it's too much to feel.*
> *If I stop fighting this feeling, it will keep getting stronger.*
> *This feeling will last forever.*
> *This feeling will overtake me and make me do something.*
> *I'll get lost in the feeling and become overwhelmed or depressed.*
> *I'm bad for feeling this way.*
> *Other people would think I'm pathetic for feeling this way.*
> *I don't have a reason to feel this way.*
> *This feeling has lasted too long already. I'm tired of feeling this.*
> *I've dealt with this feeling before; it should be gone by now.*

This is just the shortlist. I bet you could add a few forms of resistance of your own. What do you say to yourself when feelings arise that you don't want to feel? How do you fight them?

Of course, running from them by turning to alcohol, drugs, television, or our phones is always an option. Or there's good old-fashioned "powering through" and operating on top of the feelings as we get absorbed in compulsive busyness at work, moving from one task to the next with frantic urgency and stress. Oh, and refined sugar, rich, and chemically-laden flavor "enhanced" processed foods work great too for a few minutes while you're eating them. And then, whether it's five minutes, five hours, or five days later when whatever method you're using stops, guess what's waiting there for you? Those darn feelings!

Trust me, the best way out is through. The only way out is through. As a child, your parents may have taught you that feelings were mysterious, unpredictable, and dangerous. They were not to be trusted. And so, when you had a feeling, they did whatever they could to help you stop feeling instantly. They told you not to be scared when you were scared. They told you not to cry when you were sad. They tried to hurry along those feelings so that you could get back to "normal," to Green Zone—the only acceptable zone.

As a result, you did not learn about the natural arc of human emotion. All emotions begin, increase in intensity, and eventually peak like a wave. After the peak, the intensity recedes, and the emotion passes. Without experiencing this many times ourselves, we don't believe that will happen. When we sense a strong emotion coming on, we start to feel a panicky, unsettled, "I gotta get out of here!" feeling. The only problem is, "here" is inside of you and your own body. That's a problem if you're trying to escape.

But if you can stay with it and remain centered in your body and your breath, the emotion will pass no matter what emotion and no matter how intense. It will pass. Unless, ironically enough, we fight it. When we resist the feeling, we lock it in place, and it gets frozen or otherwise diverted. It starts to spill all over the place, wreaking havoc in our thoughts, creating intense mood swings, physical symptoms, or other internal messes.

Instead, drop the resistance. Cease the fight, and allow your feelings, fully and openly. Experiment with internally saying "yes" to everything you notice, everything that is happening. Say yes to the feeling, yes to part of you wanting the feeling to stop, yes to that situation in your life, and yes to any resistance you have to say yes.

What are you experiencing as you read this? Are you feeling more? Sometimes when we stop fighting the feeling, it increases in intensity. This is good. We're allowing the natural arc to continue.

As you focus on the sensations in your body and your breathing, become even more curious about your experience. These feelings are coming from a part of you—perhaps it's scared, hurt, sad, or angry. What is it afraid of? What is it hurting about?

The more you slow down and become fully present with these feelings, the more you can hear the message from that part of you. What does it want? What message does it have for you?

SHOW ME EVERYTHING YOU GOT

As you grow in your skill of O.M.O.S., you will be able to relate to yourself with more and more patience and compassion. This creates more space to have feelings and more permission to be you. And yet, even though we want to be completely ourselves, we usually find a way to halt this process at a certain point. Each of us has a few parts of ourselves that we find very challenging to face, make space for, or treat with patience. We abhor these parts, detest the emotions they feel, and do our best to get away from them or make them go away (albeit ineffectively).

We may have buried these parts so deeply, and at such a young age, that we don't even consciously feel them. But on some level, part of us knows they are there and is running a constant campaign to keep us protected from them. We often have many strategies of distraction and avoidance that we use consciously and unconsciously to stay away from these vulnerable feelings.

As you turn toward yourself more and more with love and self-compassion, you will get closer and closer to these vulnerable parts that you've been pushing down. It's like these parts have been kept locked in a basement, and the door has been covered with a painting. As you gain control over your inner critic and begin to meet all your feelings with love and patience, you start to hear the faint sounds coming from down below.

You move toward the painting, hearing the sounds behind the wall grow louder. These parts can feel you moving toward them, and they are desperate for your attention. They need you. And even though you may not realize it yet, you need them. Because keeping parts of yourself buried takes a great deal of mental and emotional energy and can be quite draining. In addition, it can create a chronic background sense of unease because you are scared of these feelings that are inside of you. At any moment, they can escape, like runaway lions from the zoo. Perceiving these feelings as threatening makes you uneasy without even knowing why. You're afraid of your own feelings, even though they don't have the power to harm you.

I spent many years fully absorbed at the top levels of my house, completely unaware of that painting in the basement. I had layers upon layers of distraction keeping me from becoming aware of those feelings, let alone feeling them. I swirled in a sea of perfectionistic demands and incessant attempts to prove myself through my achievements and finally be enough. All the while, I was constantly absorbed in thoughts about my body, fearing ongoing chronic pain or new injuries, getting physical treatments, or researching new solutions to my unending pain. In between all that, I would "relax" with countless hours of video games and TV, often while using cannabis. Yes, there was much too much going on upstairs for me to hear the sounds from behind the basement door.

Step by step, I followed the path you are on now back to being on my own side. I discovered how to relate to my chronic pain by thinking psychologically instead of structurally or physically. I began to inquire more about what feelings I might be avoiding, what this physical pain might be distracting me from. I deeply examined the roots of my perfectionism, seeing it as yet another addiction I used to avoid uncomfortable feelings, including inferiority, conflict, or uncertainty (more on this in Chapter 10 - Letting Go Of Perfectionism). I stopped using cannabis, tobacco, alcohol, and rich foods, which I thought were just "fun," but were really things I did habitually to keep unwanted feelings out of my awareness. All this didn't happen all at once but rather as a progression over many years. That's how becoming more O.M.O.S. works, one step at a time, one choice at a time.

Eventually, as I let go of all these forms of distraction and escape, I began to hear the sounds from down in the basement. I thought I had already learned to be with my feelings with love and curiosity and go deeper. But there's always another level to that basement, isn't there? There's always another level of O.M.O.S. So, I went further down, and I discovered one feeling down there that was absolutely intolerable to be with. This feeling was so unpleasant that it seemed like everything I had been doing—drugs, body pain, perfectionistic striving—all were designed to avoid this one feeling.

I've seen that in many clients over the years. There seems to be one or two major feelings that people can spend their entire lives running from, without even knowing it. Frankly, most people don't want to know it. They want to keep that sucker locked away for life, too terrified to face what's within. But you and me, my friend, we're warriors of the heart, so we can't run forever. We are compelled to confront our fears to see what's on the other side, which is exactly what I did.

Without all those distractions, when I would slow down and be by myself, I would feel this strong, aching pain in my heart. The best words I had for it at the time were heartache, sadness, or grief. I had no idea what I was grieving, what I was missing, or what I could be sad about.

Despite my years of O.M.O.S. practice, I approached this feeling with my old standard approach of confusion, impatience, and invalidation. *Why am I feeling this? I have no idea what I'm sad about.* My mind would offer potential sources of what I might be missing, or what might be happening, but these mental attempts to interpret the feeling fell flat. They were about quickly identifying the problem and solving it in my head, so I wouldn't have to feel these messy, uncomfortable feelings, the standard intellectual approach to feeling avoidance, and one that I am quite practiced at.

Sometimes, I would slow down and be with the feeling, meditating on the sensations in my heart. But this would bring little relief, and no matter what I did, the feeling would be there again, morning after morning, day after day. I began meditating more, hoping that slowing down and looking inward would somehow help me unlock this mystery grief.

What I didn't realize at the time was this: While I thought I was feeling my feelings with openness and curiosity, in reality, I was spending 95% of my time in subtle resistance to the feeling. Even though I was meditating and feeling it directly, my underlying attitude was one of waiting it out until it would go away. The message I was sending the feeling was: *I know I'm supposed to accept you, but I don't like you, and I want you to go away now so I can get on with my life.*

The feeling persisted for months. It was exhausting. My inquiries didn't seem to lead anywhere helpful. Until one evening, as I lay in bed before falling asleep, focusing on the pain in my heart, I began to experience vivid memories of the outside of my childhood home, the dirt in our yard, the strong oak trees, and the white stucco on the outside of the house. The images were so clear; it felt like I could reach out and touch them as if I was right there.

As I saw these images, I felt a deep, intensely painful feeling of loneliness. My mind kicked in immediately—what's this all about? *Why are you feeling lonely? What's there to feel lonely about here?* This part of me was running one of its favorite strategies to try to reduce or stop painful emotions. Its approach is simple. To have a feeling, you must have a valid enough reason to have that feeling. If your reason isn't deemed valid, then you should no longer have the feeling. Of course, this part was the judge, and it generally found feelings to be unjustified, especially ones that are painful.

This whole experience persisted for the better part of a year. At times, I would feel a sense of despair, wondering if I would carry this heaviness in my heart forever, despite having so many things to feel joyful about in my life. I was able to connect deeply with others, laugh, enjoy my wife and children, and feel engaged at work. But there in the background, whenever I stopped focusing outward, was that painful heartache.

Until one day, something profound changed.

I went for an early morning run, heading toward Mt. Tabor. Mountain is a generous title, as its peak is only about 700 feet above the rest of the city, but it's a good climb, and it's the closest place I can run to that has a big patch of tall trees. I ran in the predawn darkness, feeling the pain in my heart. It was so intense. It seemed like it hadn't gotten any less intense even after almost a year of working with it. I was constantly doing things like this — rating how intense it was, comparing it to other times to see if it was getting better or worse, and other forms of mental obsession and subtle resistance.

And then something broke. My will to resist snapped, and I couldn't fight it anymore. *Okay, okay,* I thought. *I'm done resisting you; I'm done fighting with you. Show me anything you want. Feel as intensely as you want, for as long as you want. Show me everything you got.*

One moment later, I felt an incredible wave of intense feelings wash over me. The best words I can use to describe it are utter aloneness, isolation, and unworthiness of love. Even though

I was a grown man running down the middle of the vacant city streets, I felt like a scared, lonely child. I felt intense aching, grasping, longing. I wanted love and attention so badly. I wanted to be seen, to have my emotions and feelings seen, known, and understood, but all that was there was a void.

As the feelings became more intense, I did not lose my nerve or pull away. Instead, I leaned in. *Show me everything you got*, I thought again. *Show me everything you're feeling. Yes, I can feel that loneliness you experienced. Show me more. Show me what it felt like, what it feels like. I'm here, and I'm not going anywhere.*

Hundreds of images, moments, memories, and feelings flooded my heart, mind, and body, things from my childhood that I had not thought about in years, and some that I'd never reflected on. I felt all the ways this younger version of myself longed to be seen and met emotionally by my dad and how I ached for him to slow down and be present with me, to truly be with me and know me deeply, and how much pain I felt about being in a house where none of us knew how to talk about what we were feeling or experiencing inside. How isolating it was to be so close together but emotionally miles apart, each alone in our internal worlds. I ran and felt, ran, and felt. Show me everything you got.

This moment was a significant turning point in my life. I began a new way of being with myself, committing to a new level of O.M.O.S. While there was still so much more to uncover, feel, and heal, I had surrendered more deeply than ever before. With this willingness came a major shift in the feelings in my heart. They were no longer stuck in there; I had moved the painting aside and opened that door. I began a new phase of listening to these exiled parts of myself, hearing their stories, and connected with their ignored feelings.

I wonder what parts are down in your basement, and what would happen if you turned toward them, seeking them out, inviting them to show you everything they got? What major feelings might you have spent the last fifteen or thirty-five years running from?

Thunderstorm

"But I can't stand this feeling," Feizel said emphatically. "That's why I'm working with you to get rid of this or over it, or whatever."

Feizel was always direct and to the point. He was an intelligent businessman in his forties who had built several successful companies, yet perpetually struggled with confidence beneath the surface. He felt a constant background tension of anxiety, worried about money despite having more than enough, and felt nervous and insecure when talking with anyone outside of a business context. He was working with me to "get rid of the anxiety."

Can you relate to this? When you slow down to be with the parts of you that are uncomfortable to be with, how do you react to them? Do you find them intolerable and attempt to make them go away? Which feelings are unacceptable to you? Is it anxiety, sadness, grief, neediness? Is it the part of you that feels scared before going into a meeting where you'll need to be the center of attention? Or is it the part that hungers for more attention and praise from your partner? What parts of yourself do you habitually reject?

For Feizel, it was the anxious part of him that was nervous around others, the part that wanted everyone to like him and felt unsettled and unsafe if they might not. He had spent years suppressing this part with alcohol, trying to blast through it with sheer will and more achievements, and other strategies to ignore or amputate this "weakness" in him, as he called it.

"You hate that anxious feeling," I said.

"Yes," he replied.

"And you want it to go away."

"Yes."

"And you've read dozens of books to figure it out, done therapy, tried hundreds of techniques, and yet here we are."

"Yeah. That's why I'm talking to you," he said.

I paused for a moment, thinking about what to say next. He could see the futility in fighting that feeling, but he was so scared of it. He feared fear, something we all can relate to.

"How old are your kids now?" I asked. I knew he had three children of different ages.

"Sixteen, thirteen, and nine," he replied.

"What's your nine-year-old's name?"

"Shareen," he said.

"Do you remember when Shareen was four or five years old?"

"Of course," he said.

"Was there anything she was scared of back then? " I asked.

He paused for a moment, reflecting on my question. "She used to be scared of thunderstorms." I was surprised to hear how different his voice sounded when he said this. The hard edge was gone, and there was a softness in his voice. He had a hint of a smile forming on his face.

"Thunderstorms?" I said.

"Yeah," he laughed now. "She used to be terrified of thunderstorms."

"Would she cry?" I asked.

"Oh yeah. She'd cry and shake the whole time it was happening. She couldn't sleep or relax or anything."

"What did you do?" I asked.

"I held her," he replied instantly.

"For how long?"

He paused for a long moment before responding, seeing what I was guiding him toward in the conversation.

"I held her the whole time," he said quietly.

I could tell he was back in that moment now, holding his sweet, scared daughter as the storm raged outside, gently rocking her, whispering reassuring things to her, kissing her on the top of her head.

"What did you say to her when she was scared like that?" I asked.

"It's okay, sweetie. You're okay. Daddy's here with you." He said, his eyes welling up with tears. "I repeated that to her, over and over and over again. Sometimes, she'd fall asleep, but then wake back up again if there was a loud wind or thunderclap."

I knew he was getting my point, but I wanted to make the connection even more clear, the path to being on his own side even more obvious. I wanted to activate his own natural self-compassion mechanisms that had gone dormant so that he would feel aversion at treating himself harshly. I wanted to awaken his heart.

"How would it have been to tell her to get over her stupid fears, that there was nothing to be scared of, and to stop crying?"

He grimaced involuntarily. "Bad." He said.

"Or what about being with her for a few minutes, telling her she would be okay, and waiting out the clock until she'd calm down and get over it?"

He sighed. Good enough.

"You deserve this, Feizel, this kind of treatment. That little boy in you needs the exact same care and love that you gave Shareen. He needs it even more because he didn't grow up with a loving, present father. He grew up in a much harsher, scarier environment. He needs so much of your love and attention."

"Anything else is madness," I continued. "Criticizing that little boy, berating him, ignoring him, or telling him he shouldn't exist is all insanity. It doesn't work. It hasn't worked for you for decades. It can't ever work because that's not how we heal. It's like trying to correct a vitamin or mineral deficiency by drinking poison. You need the missing vitamin to correct the deficiency. You need an excess of that vitamin to rebuild your body's reserves."

--

What happens when you turn toward the scared, upset, hurting, tender parts of you with this kind of openness and love? Take a moment to try it with me right now. Let yourself fully, feel whatever feelings are there, letting that part of you know that it's okay to share more with you.

If you notice you are experiencing resistance or judgment or a hardening inside, that's okay. That's just fear. You're just scared to feel feelings; that's all. And that's okay. Everyone is scared to feel some of their feelings some of the time. You may want to do some more work with your critic who's judging this process or judging the hurting parts of you. See if you can tame it and regain control enough to go deeper into the pain and discomfort beneath. Because whether it's now or later, that's where the healing takes place. That's where the liberation is.

See if you can relax even more and surrender to that part of you. Allow yourself to be seen fully with yourself. Show anything and everything to yourself. Just keep breathing and feeling, opening, and allowing it all, holding it like a child who's crying at night, scared, overwhelmed, or lonely.

You don't need to solve the feelings, make them go away, or reason with this part of you. You don't need to tell it there's nothing to be scared of, and to get over this feeling now. Just be with it. All you need to do is to keep letting go of needing this feeling, and this part of you, to be different in any way. Surrender the need to control or manipulate it. Fully submit to the feelings.

Stay connected with your awareness to your body and your breath. If you find yourself getting lost in the feelings, remember, *You Are the Center*. You are the inner parent and authority who is relating with these parts. You can observe them, hold them, and be with them with love, without getting swallowed or lost in them. Of course, if that happens sometimes, that's okay too. Don't worry or stress about it. You'll find your way back soon enough.

Something profound and magical happens when we can turn to any part inside of us and say, "Show me everything you got. I'm not going anywhere," and really mean it. Something inside of us relaxes in a deep and powerful way. The first time I said this to myself, the scared part of me was dismissive and mistrustful. "Yeah, right," it replied.

I get it, though. Of course, it didn't believe me. Because truth be told, I hadn't been there for it for much of my life. And my recent attempts at developing self-compassion had been intermittent at best. Sometimes, I was there for myself, being on my own side, and sometimes, the critic was running amok, knocking down chairs, and flipping over tables.

I needed to rebuild trust with these tender parts of myself. I needed to prove over a period of months that something big had changed, that I was going to be there in a new and different way. As I demonstrated this and kept holding these scared, hurting, lonely, and other vulnerable parts in love, they began to relax more, to trust more.

This is becoming right with yourself. This is being on your own side. This is O.M.O.S.

LOVE THE UNLOVABLE

"Salvation is communal."

- Elliot Geller

So how do we do it? How do we love these feelings inside, these parts of us that feel so unpleasant, so bad or wrong, so unlovable? So far in this book, we have been focused on what you can do internally to make this shift—seeing the pain you cause yourself from continual self-rejection, making a powerful decision to change this and be on your own side, transforming the way you relate to your critic, and moving toward all parts of you with more love and openness. While all of this is essential, I have never found it to be enough for any of my clients or for myself because it's missing one key ingredient—other people.

So far, you can do all of the work in private, in the safety of your own room, within the confines of your own walls, both literal and metaphorical. We can retreat to our cave and lick our wounds, perfecting self-love until we emerge as invincible, flawless beings, or so the fantasy goes. But the truth is, these pains came about in response to the thoughts, feelings, and actions of other people. You learned that there was something wrong with you, which made you not good enough for other people, that you would not be liked or loved for who you are by other people. Thus, the only true way out is to involve other people.

Not only do we have to face the most uncomfortable, disowned parts of ourselves and hold them with love and tenderness, we must share these parts with other people. When we do this, and we see that we are not brutally rejected, shamed, or ostracized, something profoundly healing occurs within us, which allows us to relax into being ourselves in an entirely new way.

Into the Cringe

Into the roar sounds much more cool, powerful, and exciting. But often, the fear we face of sharing ourselves with other people is more like running into the cringe, or the wince, than anything else. Do you know what I'm talking about here? Those parts of you—feelings, thoughts, desires, or actions—make you cringe when you imagine other people knowing that about you.

You know, it's that stuff you've done that makes you grimace when you think back on it. Yeah, *that* stuff.

That cringe is a sign that you are not okay with who you are, not at peace with yourself. It shows that you still have a grudge you're holding against yourself, some rejection of a shameful or "bad" part of you that must be kept down and hidden from yourself and others.

The path to fully being on your own side requires you to share the things you'd rather keep hidden. Don't worry; it doesn't have to be with everybody via a loudspeaker at your workplace or over social media. You don't have to tell your spouse's parents about your reckless days of drug binges before you married their son or daughter.

But you will need to find some people close to you and make those relationships even closer by revealing yourself to the other person. You can share something that you've never told anyone with a close friend. You can talk with your spouse about your reckless days of drug use, sharing some of the stories that you feel most ashamed of.

There will be a part inside of you that is cringing and wincing. Your critic will most likely freak out, insisting that sharing is a horrible idea and will certainly lead to harsh rejection and the end of the relationship. But, like all of your critic's blusterings, this is just another false prediction designed to keep you safe from any risk of rejection or disapproval, safe from difficult conversations, even those that are extremely growthful and ultimately end well. They're simply uncomfortable along the way, and your critic hates that.

On the other side of your critic's predictions, past that wall of fear and mistrust, is a deep and profound level of self-acceptance. Because in almost all cases, what happens is incredibly healing. Rather than harshly rejecting you, your friend or spouse remains open, curious, and attentive. They don't see your behaviors or "unacceptable" feelings as so unacceptable. They might not hold it with nearly the same amount of judgment and emotional charge that you've been imbuing it with for years.

And then there's the relief, **the sweet relief of being able to fully rest and let go of any need to be anyone other than who you are.** That's when you get to feel the sweet bliss of true safety, the safety we feel when we are fully open and connected with another human, cared for, loved, and appreciated just for being ourselves with no pressure or need to be someone else, no fear about hiding something or tension about deciding which parts of ourselves we're allowed to reveal. You're just you, delightfully you.

Have you experienced this before? Do you know what I'm talking about? If so, awesome! Do more of it. It's a big piece of the puzzle when it comes to raising your level of O.M.O.S. in your daily life. If you have not experienced what I'm talking about, perhaps you've felt it from the other side. Have you ever had someone open up with you? It could have been a friend, or colleague, or someone you're dating. They take down the walls and reveal that they're struggling with something, anxious at work, or that they have a crush on you but were nervous that you wouldn't like them back. What did that feel like? Did it repel you, or actually bring you closer to them?

Let's find out.

Bitter Medicine

Here's a story that I've never told anyone, not even my closest friends, not even my wife. Shame can run deep sometimes. I've never shared it because I still reject the me that did this. When I think of the story, my nose crinkles, and my lips squeeze together as if I just tasted something bitter and smelled something bad at the same time.

Regardless, it's a sign that there is something here that I am judging as not okay, a reason why my critic says I'm not lovable as I am. And I've been through this process enough times to know that on the other side of sharing, it is a new level of self-love and inner freedom. So, here we go, into the cringe.

When I was in high school, I experienced intense social anxiety. I viewed myself as inferior to other boys and unattractive to women. I had a recurring case of acne, which I imagined made me even more undesirable. I didn't approach women, or hang out with the cool kids, or meet new people. I spent time with several close friends while trying to maintain my place in the pecking order so that I wouldn't plummet to the bottom of the pit.

It was quite rare for me to go to parties during these years, primarily because I was rarely invited. I went to a small school, so I was used to hearing about parties and activities the cooler kids did after the fact when they'd mention them at school. But once in a while, when someone was having a BIG party and wanted to invite a lot of people from all different classes and even different schools, then guess who'd get the invite? That's right, me! Everything's coming up Milhouse!

On one such occasion, I was invited to Kelly's house. Her parents owned a large house in the town of Scotts Valley, just outside of Santa Cruz, California. They lived out in the woods and had a large open patio area, a pool, and a big space indoors to host gatherings. Of course, they didn't know they would be hosting a gathering because Kelly waited until her parents were out of town to throw the mega-bash of the year.

So I'm at this party, stoned and drinking. That's how I dealt with social anxiety at that time, trying to numb out my inner critic enough to let me talk with others. Oh boy, here comes the cringey part. I can feel my chest tightening and my heart beating faster.

In the middle of one of the large rooms near a black piano, I saw six or seven guys standing in a circle, facing inward. As I moved closer, I could see many of them bobbing their heads, and then I heard the sound of someone beatboxing. I paused about ten feet away, watching as different guys would take a turn free-style rapping.

It was badass, impressive, and inspiring. I wanted to be able to do that. I wanted that kind of confidence to not only speak up in a group but just start flowing, trusting that whatever you were going to say was going to be good enough. They seemed so mature, so cool. I stood still, listening from afar. It felt like the story of my life—ten feet away from where life was happening, frozen in a wide orbit.

But tonight, I had liquid courage in me, and I was going in. I saw a number of kids I didn't recognize who must have been from other schools. Adam, the coolest kid in my class, was in the circle too. I walked right up and joined in, standing there and bobbing my head like the rest. It was way cooler close up. The guy beatboxing was awesome. The guy rapping was incredible. The energy was crackling, fast-paced, and exciting. I felt alive.

And then, without any warning, one of the guys in the group pointed to me, indicating it was my turn to rap. I stopped bobbing my head and froze. In retrospect, I think he was being inclusive and trying to help me feel welcome to join in with the group. Or maybe it was a test to see if I would dive in and be one of them. But in that moment, I felt utterly terrified. I had never freestyled before. I didn't know what to do or how to begin.

The beat kept coming. Everyone was looking at me. What now?

I did what I'd been trained to do—guard myself from shame and fear with mockery. I made a joke of it. I bobbed my head in an exaggerated manner and said to the beat, "Ugh, yeah, wassup nigga." I was mimicking some of the intro words a rapper might use on a track before he started his rap. I was also attempting to make fun of everyone there in some strange, weak way.

The beat kept coming. Everyone kept staring. So I did it again. I said the same thing again. It was a train wreck unfolding before me, and I was the engineer driving it to destruction, but I didn't know how to stop it or what else to do. About a third of the guys in the group were black. Here's some awkward brown kid throwing the n-word around.

One of the most dominant and charismatic of the freestyle rappers took a step toward me and said, "Yeah, man. Say it one more time."

The whole thing was out of control now. I imagined he was going to hit me at any moment, and the rest would either jump in or stand by and watch me get what I deserved.

With no plan or ability to do anything else, I repeated it one more time, just as awkward, offensive, and not funny as the first time. Then, I slowly backed out of the group as a hot feeling of shame flushed from my stomach, through my chest, down my arms, up my neck, and into my cheeks.

They filled in their circle, and someone else stepped forward to start rapping again. It was like I was never even there. They might not have thought much of some dumb kid saying some stupid stuff for a minute. But I sure didn't forget it. I felt utter embarrassment and shame. I was awkward, anxious, unlovable, and pathetic. When I tried to go into the center and join life, I made a fool of myself. And so I decided, or rather my critic decided for me, that we were going to spend the next seven years as far on the outside as possible, never experiencing that kind of humiliation again.

--

What was it like to read that story? How do you feel toward me in this moment? Do you feel judgment, aversion, or dislike? Do you think I'm a rotten racist and want to stop reading this book?

Perhaps. But my guess is that it's quite the opposite. You probably felt the tension building as you read the story. Maybe you were rooting for me to do well. As it all fell apart, perhaps you cringed with me, feeling the pain and awkwardness of this scared, shy teenage boy who desperately wanted to fit in but hated himself so. Most likely, reading this story made you feel closer to me.

And writing it made me feel closer to you. That is how connection works. There is a tremendous healing force in the power of sharing and being seen. Salvation is communal. And through the sharing, as I work with the heat of embarrassment and shame that arise even as I write about this, I can feel something lifting. I feel any residual judgment or shame I felt about this moment of my life evaporate, like morning dew turning to white vapor wisping toward the bright morning sun.

That happened, and it's okay. I feel a deep sense of love and compassion for the younger version of me. I wish my adult self could be with him that night and help him through that experience, help him navigate it without turning on himself even more, burying his heart and light ever deeper, to talk it through, help him see his value, and be able to share who he is with the world.

I wonder if you are moved to do the same with the younger versions of you?

Chapter 9:
My Own Best Friend

Originally, I was going to call this chapter Optimal Self-Talk, but as I started writing, I realized being on your own side goes way beyond the exact right words to say to yourself.

Because we've all been there. You have an affirmation or empowering phrase that you heard and liked. And so you started saying it to yourself out loud when you were alone and in your head when you were around others. At first, it felt exciting and empowering. Maybe I can feel this way; maybe this can be true; maybe I am whatever I'm telling myself I am!

But then, one day or one week later, something starts to go amiss. You forget to keep saying the empowering phrases to yourself. When you do remember, instead of feeling excited, you feel exhausted. It seems so effortful to keep running the new words through your mind, and instead of resounding with bright promise and optimism, they seem hollow and flat. Your critic smells blood and pounces, denying the new empowering phrases, discounting your dreams, and reminding you of what you truly are and always have been—doomed to be small, inadequate, and never quite enough. Ugh.

So we need to do something different than just "improve our self-talk." Instead of more techniques and strategies, we need to fundamentally change where we are coming from when we relate to ourselves, hence, the new title of this chapter—My Own Best Friend.

Are you your own best friend? What's your immediate gut response to that question? Yes? No? Maybe, kind of, sorta? Sometimes but not others? What does that mean to be your own best friend? How do you feel when you imagine being that way in everyday life? Is it exciting, relieving, liberating?

Or does your critic squash the idea immediately, filling you with resistance, judgment, or cynicism? Does your critic judge it as "corny" or "cheesy" and therefore deem it as unworthy of examination? Or does your critic use projected dislike and imagine how other people would think of you if they knew that you were trying to be your own best friend? Perhaps it conjures up imagined judgments from those cool, successful, confident people who would never have to do such a thing and would just mock you mercilessly if they only knew.

Regardless of what initially happens, let's not dismiss the subject or avoid it. Let's stay in this together for a bit, exploring this beautiful idea of truly treating yourself with the love, care, and respect you would someone that you would call your best friend.

BESTIES

Do you have an official "best friend"? I don't think I do at this point. Back when I was a kid, I certainly did. There was Jeff, then Nick, then Tim, then Chris, then Brian. Usually, their reign as king would last for many years as we played, explored, and grew together. At some point, I stopped using the designator "best" because I imagined how my other close friends would feel if they knew that they didn't make the cut for the first draft spot. Also, I got close with so many amazing people, and I love each of them in a slightly different way, that it seems kind of arbitrary to label one as "best."

So do you have a best friend right now? Maybe you don't officially use that term or introduce people to them with that title at a dinner party ("Hi, there. This is my BEST friend, Sue. We're besties for life") but you still deeply love and care about this person. You love spending time with them, talking with them, being with them, and sharing life together. Perhaps you've known them since you were a kid, or maybe it's someone who's relatively recent in your life, but regardless, you can't imagine life without them now. They are awesome. And when you're together, you are awesome too. Life is awesome. Can you think of that person?

If your social life is in flux due to a move or changes in friendships, or any other reason, and you don't feel like you currently have any close friends, not to worry. Just think back to the last time you did have a close friend.

Okay, so now you have that person in your mind, right? Take a few moments to focus on them right now. Imagine their face, their smile, their eyes. Can you hear the sound of their voice, their laugh? How do you feel when you think of them? Do you feel loving? Do you feel a warmth in your heart, or an open feeling in your chest? Does thinking of them automatically make you feel grateful? Does it make you want to smile?

That's it, right there! That's the feeling we're going for, only toward yourself, too, not just toward your super awesome bestie. Take a moment to think of you. Imagine your face, your smile, your eyes. Can you hear the sound of your voice, your laugh? Can you feel the same loving energy toward yourself?

If so, how does it feel? Can you let it in fully, without having to earn it, strive for it, or prove anything to get it? Can you let yourself be worthy of your love, right now? If so, enjoy it!

If you can't, what's getting in the way? What self-imposed, arbitrary demands are you holding yourself for ransom with right now? What grudges are you still holding onto? What are you stubbornly refusing to forgive yourself for?

The Ideal Ratio

First and foremost, when determining the best way to relate to yourself, you will want to raise your standard. Being able to stop harshly attacking yourself is an essential first step, but it sure is a low bar for a loving relationship, isn't it? Imagine if that was your standard for your close friendships or romantic relationship. As long as they're not verbally abusing me, that's good enough for me! Yikes. No, we can shoot for much more than that. You deserve much more than that.

Dr. John Gottman, one of the world's leading researchers in the field of romantic relationships, has an uncanny ability to tell whether couples are going to divorce, long before they do. He's so good at it that he could predict with a high degree of accuracy whether a couple was going to break up based on watching a few minutes of a video recording of them having a discussion over a "challenging" issue in their relationship.

People were amazed at his apparent superpowers, so they asked him how he could predict these couples' futures. He said he looked for two things: their ratio of positive to negative statements to each other, and the four horsemen of the apocalypse. The four horsemen are his slightly dramatic term for the four kinds of negative statements that tended to be the most corrosive to relationships. These include:

- Defensiveness (unwillingness to even hear the other person's hurts, challenges, or frustrations about the relationship)

- Criticism (attacking the partner's appearance, intelligence, character, or other attributes)

- Contempt (condescending, acidic, derisive mockery of the other person's words or feelings, as best epitomized in the gesture of eye-rolling and scoffing)

- Stonewalling (good old-fashioned silent treatment, withdrawal, and "you're dead to me" nonverbal messages sent to your enemy… I mean your beloved)

If Gottman saw one of the partners doing these moves in a conversation, he could predict certain doom. Further still, though, he said he was looking for the ratio between positive and negative statements. While discussing a challenging issue, couples might be less patient, spacious, and loving with each other. But even still, the ones that thrive have an average ratio of at least five positive interactions for every one negative interaction. Positive interactions include listening closely, empathy, understanding, compassion, curiosity, playfulness, problem-solving, touch, and more.

For a relationship to truly thrive, the ratio is often much higher than five to one and is more in the range of 10 to 15 positive interactions for each negative one. And the negative is often not one of the four horsemen but rather a milder form of conflict, misunderstanding, impatience, or pushing the other person away temporarily.

So what does that have to do with your relationship with yourself? Everything! What's your ratio of positive to negative statements toward yourself? If your O.M.O.S. score is low, it's probably less than five to one. It might be as low as one to one, or even worse, maybe it's the other way around - being one positive for multiple negative statements.

Now, wait a minute! You might be thinking. *It's not that bad all the time. Sometimes I treat myself quite well. It's only once in a while that things get that bad.* If so, that's good news, I suppose. But remember, our goal here is to raise your standard of what you will tolerate in both external relationships and your relationship with yourself. What if your spouse was generally loving with you, but whenever issue X or Y came up, he became intensely critical, defensive, unreasonable, and contemptuous. How would that impact the entire relationship?

That's why Dr. Gottman was so good at predicting divorce — because those four horsemen are like acid to a relationship. When someone behaves that way frequently or very intensely, it tends to burn the love and connection that is there. Sure, the bond can handle a certain amount of that, but eventually, the acid eats right through it, and there's nothing strong enough left to hold it together.

The same is true for you. When you harshly attack yourself or treat your feelings with contempt, you are pouring acid on your relationship with yourself. It's toxic not only to your mood, happiness, life satisfaction, and ability to focus but also to your physical energy level and overall health as well. Because here's the scary thing about this relationship — there's no way out. There's no separation, no divorce, or no taking "some" space. You can't move away and never see that person again because that critic is inside of you. It is a part of you, and you can't escape by moving somewhere else, changing your job, changing your relationship, or changing anything else "out there."

So let's re-up on your commitment to O.M.O.S. and find a better way. Let's stop the insanity and start treating ourselves with love, compassion, and kindness, just like we would a lover, a partner, or a best friend.

The Bestie Test

I adore this technique, and I'm so excited to share it with you. It goes like this. Whenever you tune into your self-talk, ask yourself this question: "Is this how I would talk to my best friend?"

You can also think of this as the "lover test" or "five-year-old test", where you ask the same basic question, only with a lover or young child as the criteria. "Is this how I would talk to my lover?" "Is this how I would talk with a five-year-old child?"

One client in my Mastermind program found a website online where you could order a bracelet with a custom image on it, sort of like a small watch face without the clock on it. She uploaded a picture of herself when she was four years old. Now, she wears this bracelet everywhere she goes, and when she starts being critical of herself, she looks down at her wrist. "Is this how I'd speak to this little girl?" she asks herself.

Many times per day, you'll want to ask yourself questions just like this. When you look in the mirror and start nitpicking yourself (or worse), slow down and ask if this is how you'd talk with a lover when you saw their naked body. When you start grinding away on all your list of mistakes and shortcomings on your commute home from work, ask yourself if you'd be speaking like this with your best friend after he or she had a hard day at work.

In other words, you are catching your habits of how you treat yourself and consciously upgrading them. You are breaking the default treatment of self-abuse and consciously reminding yourself of how you would treat someone you love so that you may treat yourself like someone that you actually love.

Hype (Wo)Man

The other day I was driving to the movie theater alone. While I enjoy watching movies with my wife or friends, I must admit, there's something I greatly enjoy about going to the movies by myself.

On this particular car ride, I had an impulse to choose some music that I rarely listen to—instrumental beats. So, god bless

YouTube; I typed that into the search bar, and within seconds, I have dozens of compilation tracks of amazing instrumental beats. I choose one and start listening. Damn, it's good. I start bobbing my head involuntarily. And then I feel it coming. I'm alone and inspired, and so I let it fly. I start rapping.

Yep, my miserable first attempt at freestyling from Kelly's party notwithstanding, I love testing my mind in this way to see how quickly it can work to create compelling strings of rhyme to the rhythm. When I'm doing it right, freestyling is like flying down-hill on a bike or skis, going a bit faster than you think you can, forcing your body to figure it out unconsciously to keep you going and upright.

So there I go, rapping about whatever comes to mind—thoughts, ideas, feelings, experiences, challenges, dreams. It all comes pouring out. Some days, it flows and comes easily, and today was one of those days. I was coming up with such great stuff I was starting to impress myself.

My mind was working so quickly that I would say a line and immediately know how the next line was going to end. It was almost like I had an audience inside of me that was watching the performance unfold, ready to burst into uproarious noise each time I hit a line.

Have you ever watched any freestyle rap? Guess where you can go to see tons of it? That's right, good old YouTube. Here's how it always works. Unless the rapper is alone, there will always be at least one hype man or woman in his or her crew, standing nearby. They are deeply into it, feeling the beat, bobbing their head, and generally in awe of the main rapper. When the rapper drops a dope rhyme or strings together a particularly clever set of words or makes an incisive or cutting jab at someone, the hype man goes off. He shouts, exclaims, or otherwise indicates that what just happened was badass.

Well that day, as I drove to the movie theater, freestyling for an audience of no one, I had my own internal hype man. He was right there with me, bobbing his head, waiting on my every word, and shouting in celebration whenever I dropped my next unthinkably awesome line.

I laughed. The whole thing was so absurd, yet so fun. I was being light, silly, and free. Then I had a more serious thought— what if we all had an internal hype man or woman inside of us? What if instead of our critic waiting to pounce on our every misstep, we had a supportive, admiring fan who absolutely adored us, and was waiting on our every move to celebrate us?

OPTIMAL SELF-TALK

(Aha! I knew I'd find a place for that title.)

To truly be on our own sides, we need to go beyond refraining from self-attack. Instead, we must consciously speak with ourselves in a much more inspiring, loving, respectful manner. Rather than relentlessly tearing ourselves down, we must consistently build ourselves up.

What's your experience with this? Have you tried this before, perhaps through affirmations or picking a phrase or two that sounded good, and then repeating it to yourself again and again? What happened?

For many people, changing self-talk is like changing any habit. There can be a flurry of energy and enthusiasm at the beginning of the change plan, typically the first 3-5 days. Sometimes, this initial motivation can last up to two weeks. But usually, by then, we bump up against the reality that changing habits takes work. Training new pathways in our brains requires sustained effort over time. And so we give up on that unpleasant pursuit and look for the next silver bullet that will cure all our woes with minimal effort and maximum ease.

But let's not give up so easily. Let's not dismiss saying affirming things to ourselves as ineffective because we tried, and "It didn't work." Or because you read an article about a research study that finally proved once and for all that "Affirmations don't work!" Now your critic has 'All Mighty Science' on your side to never experiment with speaking more lovingly with yourself ever again.

So, then, what is optimal self-talk? Is it to say great things to ourselves, like "I am beautiful," "I am lovable," and "Everyone wants to be my friend." Is it to affirm how we want to be by saying things like, "I am confident," "I am relaxed," "I easily make jokes around others." Or perhaps it's saying how we want to feel by repeating phrases like, "I am happy," "I am grateful," or "I am bold"?

Do we need to deliver it in just the right way? Do we need to look into our own eyes in the mirror as we say these things? Do we need to yell them out with passion and intensity? Do we need to record them and listen to them four thousand times while we're asleep so they penetrate deep into the caverns of our subconscious mind?

What's the answer? What's the universally best way to do it so that we feel amazing all the time without another moment of insecurity, doubt, or fear ever again?

I don't know.

I don't think there is one perfect method that works for everybody. But I do believe this—there are better ways for you to speak to yourself than you are doing. I would also suggest that finding our way to better self-talk is less of a mechanical application of a sterile strategy and more a process of self-discovery.

It's much like the optimal diet must be discovered through a process of study, testing, application, exploration, and adaptation over a long period of time. And then, just when you think you've nailed the perfect diet, your lifestyle might change, or a health issue arises, or you have kids and can't spend the same amount of time you did preparing meals. In other words, your optimal diet is a work in progress. And so is your optimal self-talk.

And so, like O.M.O.S., your own optimal self-talk is something that you get to decide on, that you get to discover. What do you think works best for you? What helps you cut out the criticism and enjoy being you in the key areas of your life, such as work, relationships, family, and health? What helps you quickly let go of unreasonable demands, harsh judgments, and expectations, and return to forgiveness, compassion, and unconditional self-love?

I will share a few of the key strategies that I have found work for my clients and me. You can build on these, add to them, or adapt them to make them work for you. Instead of this being a list of "The Way" and something you should implement to the letter, they are simply pointers on your path and methods that you can test out to see how they work for you.

Some will work splendidly for the first few weeks that you try them, then become less impactful. Others will work in one area of life, such as your workplace, but do nothing when it comes to your body image. And still others will be seemingly worthless to you but might become extremely valuable months or even years down the line.

Six Strategies of Skillful Self-Talk

When testing out any of these methods, notice what happens in your mind, heart, and body as you practice them. Sometimes, a method could be extremely effective at helping you get on your own side, relax, and feel a deep sense of peace and love. However, the only thing stopping this is the big stink your critic is making in your head. It's terrified of letting love in, relaxing, and letting go of control. So it's up there banging pots and pans, yelling threats, and otherwise trying to prevent you from receiving the healing benefits of a more positive message. In these cases, you can use the strategies from earlier in this book to tame your critic. Or, you can move to a different self-talk strategy that seems to bypass your critic and not stir up so much turmoil. Either way is fine.

1. Self-Soothing

This method of self-talk involves saying soothing and calming things to yourself when you're anxious, upset, panicked, scared, hurt, angry, overwhelmed, or feeling out of control. This was one of the primary approaches you learned earlier in this book to deal with your critic and the scared or hurting parts inside of you.

In this approach, you meet the pain with curiosity, openness, and deep empathy. You validate the parts that are hurting and don't dismiss them as bad or wrong.

Since we've already covered it thoroughly, I will not go more into it here. But I wanted to remind you of this strategy and let you know how powerful it can be to simply say gentle, soothing, loving things to yourself when you're hurting.

To strengthen the effect, place your palm on the center of your chest, over your heart center. Focus your attention on your heart as you say soothing things to yourself.

Examples:

"It's okay, sweetie. I'm sorry you're hurting right now."

"Wow, what a rough day! I can see why you're so upset."

"Yeah, it is challenging to be around him. Of course, you feel sadness right now."

2. Encouragement

Our critic spends so much time telling us what we can't do, how we're going to mess things up, and how it won't go the way we want. It predicts doom, failure, and misfortune at every step. Man, forget that noise. Why not blanket yourself with encouragement throughout the day?

When my son Zaim was two and a half years old, I took him on a bike ride. He sat in a kids bike seat that was mounted to a rack on the back of my bike, so he was able to sit nestled right behind me. He had his jumbo helmet on with his poofy brown hair smashing out the sides. We set off and went further than we'd ever gone. I asked him, "Do you want to go down the big hill I go on sometimes?"

"Yeah!" he exclaimed.

Once we got to the big hill and started going down, he exclaimed, "Wheee!" with the utter glee and excitement that only a two-year-old can channel.

About halfway down the hill, we hit a small bump, and the bike bounced slightly. His delight turned to terror as he fiercely grabbed hold of the sides of my body, instantly becoming silent until we reached the bottom. After a brief discussion, it was decided that he didn't like that hill, and we'd never go near it again.

However, there was one small problem. We needed to get back up somehow. So we went down to a parallel street and began the slow climb back up to the top. Whew, pedaling with a toddler was no joke. Not only was he heavy, but I couldn't use my signature power move that helped me get up hills—standing up as I pedaled. I began struggling.

"I'm not sure I can make it up without walking the bike," I said between gasps.

"You can do it, Daddy!" he shouted.

I was startled by the force and enthusiasm of his voice. Before I could react, he exclaimed, "You can do it!"

His words instantly put a smile on my face, and it felt like I had a hot air balloon inflating in my chest, filling me with love and expansive energy. By golly, he was right! I *could* do it!

I pedaled harder with renewed vigor. Sensing the positive effect of his words, Zaim continued his chant: "You can do it! You can do it! You can do it!"

He repeated this mantra all the way up the hill, not stopping until we crested the top and were on flat ground. Perhaps he wanted to make sure that we made it to the top, and he knew his daddy needed the encouragement. Or perhaps he was delighting in the act of encouraging someone you love to be more of their true selves. In either case, he was right. I could do it.

What if you actively encouraged yourself each day? What would that look like? What would it sound like? What would you say? What's an area in your life where you *need* encouragement right now? Where are you huffing up a steep hill, unsure if you'll make it?

Encouragement involves trying different things until you find the right combination of words and energy that activate something deep within you. No one can tell you what to say, because no one knows what encourages you more than you do.

To discover what might work best, try this little game. Imagine your favorite mentor, author, coach, teacher, or friend is by your side, helping you face whatever challenges are on your plate. Maybe it's a tough situation at work or with your kids or partner. Maybe you're in a dark place financially or emotionally, and your critic is telling you that there's no way out.

Whatever the situation, think about your mentor, friend, or teacher, and ask yourself, "What would I most want to hear from this person?" Whatever came to your mind right now is a great place to start when finding your voice of encouragement for yourself. You can build on this by noticing how you naturally encourage others around you. Pay close attention to the attitude you take with them, the words you use, and how you deal with their discouragement or pessimism. We typically encourage others in the way that we would like to be encouraged.

Experiment with different ways of encouraging yourself until you find methods that resonate with you. Then do them regularly. Encouragement, when we're facing something hard, scary, or bigger than we've done before is essential, but don't forget about daily encouragement. Build the habit of encouraging yourself before and during meetings, exercise sessions, or social engagements. Get on your own side, and be your own best friend.

Examples:

"I got this."

"You'll find your way through this."

"You are holding so much right now. And handling it all so well. I'm so proud of you!"

"This too, shall pass. You won't be feeling this forever."

NOTE: You may notice the language of self-talk shifts from "you" to "I." This is another personal adjustment you can make to determine what works best for you. I've also found that using your own name in these strategies can be extremely helpful, such as, "Aziz, you got this."

3. Praise

How often are we pushing ourselves to do more, overextending, overreaching, and overcommitting so others will like us, not be disappointed, and hopefully be impressed? We are secretly hoping for that little morsel of congratulations in the form of a compliment or a "Wow," or something from the outside that shows us we are finally worthy.

But praise from the outside is, unfortunately, few and far between. Even if you're amazing, and people see this and think you're amazing, it's rare for people to say it out loud. Meanwhile, even if some people praise you for being great, there are inevitably going to be people who blame you for not being good enough or doing it the way they wanted you to.

The venture of striving for external praise is destined to fail. Instead, what if you gave yourself that acknowledgment that you hunger for?

The biggest obstacle to this and many of these other self-talk strategies is the dismissive thought of your critic that says that somehow, your own praise, encouragement, or love "doesn't count."

Let's take a second to examine this. Why wouldn't your perspective count? And why would other people's perspectives somehow be more valuable or valid? If a random stranger thinks you're cute, does that carry more weight than you thinking you look cute? Is what your boss or an accomplished colleague thinks about your work somehow more real or meaningful than what you think about your own work? Why?

The only reason it feels more meaningful is because we give it that meaning. We decide that somehow, other people's perspectives are more valid than our own. But part of becoming more on your own side is taking that power back inside of you. To do this, you must stop giving other people's perspectives more weight or validity than your own and stop seeing them as more *real*.

If anything, we have it all backward. You are the one who spends 24 hours per day with yourself. You are the one who feels the emotional effect of judgment or praise. If anything, your perspective holds much greater significance than anyone else's.

This is especially true for praise. How often do you praise yourself? Do you find the good in yourself, your actions, and your choices? Do you habitually seek out and appreciate the ways you're showing up and how things are going well as a result of your efforts?

I start all of my coaching sessions, group Mastermind calls, and any other form of working with someone with a ritual of sharing wins. I believe in this so much that I have trained every coach on my team to do the same. I do this because most people are woefully underdeveloped in their capacity to identify their own wins and to acknowledge themselves for them.

Instead, they habitually discount their wins, dismissing them as insignificant or not big enough to acknowledge. Or, worse still, they have such a habit of dismissal that they've developed a huge blind spot and cannot even see any wins from their day or week. When they are initially asked this question, they simply stare at me with a confused, searching look. After a moment, their brain returns with the message: *No results found.*

Let me ask you—what are three wins from this week? They could be little or big, in any area of life. They could be insights or internal shifts. They could be actions you've taken, even if the results didn't go the way you anticipated or wanted. In other words, what's going right? What are you doing well? What could you feel good about?

Your ability to come up with an answer to these questions reveals a lot about your confidence and what you tend to focus on. Many people with lower confidence tend to focus on what's not going well, what they're doing wrong, and what won't work. As a result, they don't believe in themselves, predict negative outcomes, hesitate, and avoid risk. This reinforces their story that they can't do things, and nothing will work out (because they're the problem), and the cycle continues.

People with higher confidence tend to focus on what's going well, their little wins, and the progress they're making. This focus inspires them to keep going and reinforces the possibility that they can change, grow, and move their lives in the direction they aspire. They live in possibility, yes, and "I can."

I see our ability to come up with wins as a muscle that is worth strengthening. If we can do this quickly and easily, it demonstrates that we have been practicing this regularly, and our capacity to focus in this way is strong, which is a reflection of confidence and positive results in life. That is why I am a fan of a practice I call the "Eight Great," which I will share with you in a moment. But first, I have to address the elephant in the room — narcissism.

Many people fear praising themselves because they imagine it will make them arrogant, egotistical, and narcissistic. As a precaution against this unwanted effect, my parents had a strict "no praise" policy. They rarely commented on anything I did well, praised me, or told me I did a great job. When I asked my mom about this many years later as an adult, she said, "We didn't want you to get a big head."

This is what so many of us do with ourselves. We imagine that acknowledging ourselves will lead to an inflated, artificial, and unfounded sense of self-esteem and unhealthy pride. And there is some merit to this fear that makes it worth addressing.

In the attempt to help their children have high self-esteem, some parents jump on board the praise train and crank that sucker up to full speed. They praise their children for everything. Every action warrants a "Great Job!" including crawling, walking, opening a jar, wiping their own butts, and smiling for a photo. They then slam that train into hyperdrive by piling on positive character labels and traits, such as, "You're brilliant!", "You're so good at math!" and "You are awesome at baseball."

What's the problem with all this? Doesn't it help the kid know their strengths and value and approach life with total confidence? Surprisingly, it might not. Eye-opening research by child psychologist, Dr. Carol Dweck, demonstrates a tricky aspect of human nature — fear of loss mucks everything up. In her seminal research, kids were told that they were great at spelling or math, for example, before they were given a spelling or math test. When the test was easy, they smoked that sucker. I mean, they're good at math after all, so of course, they would. But then when they gave those kids a test that was more challenging, one they were meant to struggle with, guess what they did? Gave up! Why?

Because they didn't want to lose the identity of being "good at math." When they realized that they were going to lose that perception of themselves, they withdrew and didn't even try. Meanwhile, kids who were not given that priming before the test kept at it during the hard questions. In fact, when they were instead praised for their effort with statements like, "You kept sticking with it on those tough problems!" they ended up doing even better.

Before I read this research, I was all aboard the praise train. I was "good jobbing" all over the place with my kids. My wife Candace was pointing out ways this might bring about the sense of conditional worth that I was trying to protect my kids from, but I was hearing none of it. "My parents didn't praise me enough, so by golly, I'm going to praise my kids whenever I want!" I think many parents are trying to support their children in ways they felt unsupported as children but sometimes overdo it as a result.

After reading Dr. Dweck's research and understanding the psychology behind it, I've become much more skillful in my praise delivery. Instead of telling them how brilliant they are, I point out the things they are choosing to do that are in their control. So if my son Zaim is doing well in math, I'll say, "You can add up those numbers quickly," or "I like watching how your mind solves those problems." These statements allow him to see his own capabilities and what he's doing, rather than me assigning a label to him that he then feels like he must live up to, such as "You're awesome at math."

Of course, at the same time, I want to help him see his strengths, so I will occasionally highlight what I see in him by saying something like, "You are picking up this game quickly, even though it's pretty complex. You seem to be quite good at learning games." And sometimes, when he does something that I delight in, I express that delight through praise. So is that contradicting myself, setting him up with an identity that he now fears to lose?

Who knows? Welcome to the confusing world of parenting.

What does all of this have to do with how we praise ourselves? Focus on little moments, actions, and effort rather than sweeping claims about your brilliance. Many of those statements, which are often the bread and butter of affirmations, create a lot of internal tension anyway. When you tell yourself, "I'm brilliant," or "I'm beautiful," but your critic has been telling you for years that you're not smart enough and ugly, the internal war begins.

But instead, what if you tell yourself, "I stayed with it in that challenging project today, even when I wanted to quit. And two hours in, I had a big breakthrough! Now, I'm really flowing, and it feels great." It's much harder to argue with that one. It's more of a narration of what just happened.

Instead of telling yourself, "I'm beautiful," you can say, "My entire face lights up when I smile," or "This shirt fits me well and shows the contours of my body in a way that I like." Notice how these are harder to contest.

Of course, as with anything in this book, try it out yourself! If looking in the mirror and praising your beauty, telling yourself that you look fantastic, sexy, strong, and beautiful lights you up, then, by all means, do it! If telling yourself that you're a math genius, a negotiation wizard, a badass presenter, or a skillful speaker helps you feel confident and empowered to do those things more fully and boldly in the world, then use it! Find your own way with praising yourself, like anything along this O.M.O.S. journey.

Examples of praise:

"Nice work, Aziz!"

"I love the way you handled that upset client—that was so skillful."

"You crushed it in that meeting today. Well done!"

"I was scared to face that conversation, so I took a few minutes to prepare and then walked in the room and immediately brought it up. I faced my fear. I am courageous."

Oh, and I bet you're wondering about the "Eight Great." This is a practice I came up with recently when one of my coaches asked me to share some wins from my business and life. I sat in silence for a good minute before I could come up with some wins. All that went through my mind at first were challenges, ways I was falling short, and frustrations. Yikes.

I realized I needed some reconditioning of my focus on wins, so I came up with the 'Eight Great.' Each day, I would write down eight things that are going well. These are a combination of wins that I had something to do with that I could praise myself for, and things that I could be grateful for, whether I had a hand in their unfolding or not. So basically, it's a list of wins and gratitude.

You can add to this list in several sessions throughout the day or do it all at once before bed or right when you wake up in the morning. Once I started practicing this, my ability to fire off wins and gratitude quickly came back, and, as you might expect, I started to feel happier and more confident. So give it a shot— each day, capture your eight great things on paper or in a note file on your phone or computer.

4. Inquiry

Sometimes our critic is so active or strong that it blocks all attempts at positive self-talk. When you point out wins, it immediately highlights what you didn't do. When you acknowledge something that you could feel good about, your critic slams you with three things that aren't going well and half a dozen mistakes you've made in the last week, month, or decade.

If you're struggling to say something encouraging or loving to yourself, using the method of inquiry can be one way to bypass your critic. In this method, you don't declare something positive as much as ask questions to discover what might be true.

You allow yourself to wonder and become curious about who you are, what you're capable of, and how things might go. For example, before a big meeting at work where you may feel nervous and a desire to appear smart to avoid being judged, you can use inquiry to help you.

Perhaps saying, "I got this!" is falling flat. Maybe this stirs up your critic, who launches into a tirade about how you don't "got this," and in reality, you are going to humiliate yourself, and everyone will see what an imposter/failure/loser you are. Yikes.

When that happens, you can use the five-step process to tame your critic to wrangle that sucker down. Or you can use inquiry. You can ask yourself questions like:

What if I can pull this off?

I wonder how this will go.

Will I be okay if I make a mistake and don't look perfect in there? How could I handle that?

What is a scary meeting that I've been to in the past and performed well in? How did I feel after that meeting?

Do you see how these questions guide your focus toward something more empowering? They are not emphatic declarations of your ability or inevitable success or even statements at all. They are simply questions guided to help you see more of your strengths, capability, and inherent self-worth.

5. Gratitude

One of my favorite ways to strongly feel on my own side is through simple use of my gratitude muscle. This approach, much like inquiry, allows you to bypass the immediate pushback of your critic, which wants to deny any claims of self-love, affirmation, or encouragement.

Let me demonstrate. Read the following statements, out loud if possible. After each one, notice how it lands for you—how you feel as you read it.

I am intelligent.
I am good looking.
I am beautiful and sexy.
I am wealthy.

Undoubtedly, it's a great list of affirmations, right? But what's the impact of saying those phrases? Do you feel like a good looking, smart, sexy, rich superstud? If so, awesome! Use it. This might mean that your level of O.M.O.S. is high enough that you can easily receive loving praise and affirmation and let it in.

However, if you experienced something other than that, then trying to force these with more repetition is probably not the answer. Instead, you can bypass all this by simply using gratitude instead. Watch. Read this list below, and notice how you feel as you read each of these:

Thank you for my intelligence.
Thank you for my good looks.
Thank you for my beautiful, sexy body.
Thank you for my wealth and abundance.

How does that feel? Are you able to let it in more? In my experience using this with many clients, people often report that the first list creates a conflict inside, while the second list doesn't. When they read the second list, they feel more soft, relaxed, and open.

Giving thanks for our strengths, abilities, gifts, and talents allows us to more fully own them. It bypasses the fear of egotism and arrogance and allows us to see our own greatness. We also are inherently acknowledging that something bigger than ourselves has bestowed us with these gifts, and it puts us in right relation with these greater forces.

What could your list look like? What are five things you are grateful for about yourself and your strengths and abilities? Perhaps it's your sense of humor, your nourishing friendships, your natural gifts with music, public speaking, or technology. For each one, start with "Thank you for my..." and then finish the sentence either verbally or on paper.

Feels good, doesn't it? You just might make a habit of it.

6. Unconditional Love

Hands down, my favorite form of optimal self-talk is to treat myself with unconditional love. Unconditional love is perhaps the most healing force in the universe and something we all desperately want and need. Unfortunately, we learn early on that love from those close to us can be quite conditional, and we quickly learn how we should be to be worthy of receiving it. In the next chapter, you will be going through an incredibly liberating process that will help you shed that conditional sense of worthiness. For now, let's focus on just giving yourself the gift of unconditional love.

There's a game that new lovers sometimes play. Perhaps you played it recently, or long ago, but it goes something like this. When you are snuggled up close to each other in bed, awash in the warmth and glow of love flowing between you, you ask each other questions that begin with, "Would you still love me if..."

"Would you still love me if I went blind?"
"Would you still love me if I couldn't speak?"
"Would you still love me if I gained 50 pounds?"

Of course, in that field of love, each lover reassures the other that they would love no matter what. Through these playful proclamations, trust deepens, the bond grows stronger, and both people feel emboldened to be even more fully themselves, knowing they will be loved no matter what.

What if you played that game with yourself? What if you decided to give yourself unconditional love no matter what? The other day I was visiting Southern California, and I went for a long run along the coastline. As I looked out over the vast expanse of water, smelled the fresh ocean air, and watched all the people around me carrying out their lives, I felt tight inside. Instead of being open, joyful, and energized, I felt constricted and upset. I was stuck in some pattern of mental grinding—solving different problems in my professional and personal life with grim determination. I was trying to manipulate all the pieces of the chess game around in my mind, getting the board just right, getting all the outcomes I wanted so that I would feel good. You know that game? Isn't it a delight to play?

Then, all of a sudden, I exclaimed out loud, "Aziz, I love you no matter what!"

> I love you if you earn a lot of money or not very much.
> I love you when you are lean as can be or when you weigh an extra five pounds, or 15.
> I love you when you look tired and when you slouch.
> I love you with long hair, short hair, or no hair.
> I love you when you're cranky and short with your kids.
> I love you when you avoid something you're scared of.
> I love you no matter what, Aziz.

I said these phrases so myself, using them as a beacon to return back to self-acceptance, unconditional self-love, and sanity. Isn't it crazy to only love ourselves when we achieve certain outcomes? To only feel love in our hearts when we earn a certain amount or have a certain amount of fans or followers, or accolades or a professional position?

I wanted to take back my power to love. It's loving myself now, no matter what, and not just if now is a perfect moment where I lived up to all my unconscious expectations for myself. And I'll especially love myself when I fall short, don't hit my targets, and make mistakes.

As I did this, my inner tension melted away, and all of a sudden, the present moment sparkled with beauty. The deep blue ocean and the bright sky felt utterly immense. The air smelled fresh, clear, and sweet. I felt so alive as I breathed it in. All the people bustling about struck me as beautiful, and I felt a sense of love for all of them.

There I was, thinking about everything I needed to happen in my life, but all I needed was love. All I was wanting and craving in that moment was love. And I was the one holding the keys to the vault!

What would happen in your life if you made it a habit to tell yourself regularly that you loved yourself no matter what? What could unconditional love bring to your life?

Before we conclude this chapter on being your own best friend, there is one more key role your critic can play that we must address: nay-saying. This pattern of instantly saying no to yourself, your dreams, and your goals is most certainly not what a best friend would do.

HOW TO DEAL WITH YOUR INNER NAYSAYER

Do you remember when you were a young kid, and you had ideas about what you wanted to do when you grew up? What did you want to do? What ideas did you have?

The other day, my son Zaim said to me, "Daddy, when I grow up, I want to make Magic cards."

He is referring to the fantasy and strategy card game, "Magic: The Gathering," that has 12 million active players all over the world and is Hasbro's biggest card gaming brand in its $1.2 billion games portfolio.

He wants to be a card designer and create the content for the new cards that are created every year, a position that is undoubtedly limited and highly sought after.

So I knelt and put my arm around his shoulder, looked him in the eye, and said, "Son, you? No, I'm afraid not. That's not possible for you. Too many people want that job, and your ideas and skills are not good enough. *You* are not good enough, and you never will be, so don't even try."

Father of the year!

Sounds pretty dismal, doesn't it? And it's especially disheartening to imagine shutting down a five-year-old from even having the fantasy of a future dream.

Yet this is what we're doing to ourselves all the time. Our inner critics consistently shut the doors of possibility by naysaying our goals and dreams, both big and little. We've allowed this process to happen for so long that it may not even be noticeable. You may think of yourself as "realistic" or "reasonable." But the truth is there are so many things you want to do, create, achieve, and experience in this life, so many things that you've shied away from or completely shut down because that voice in your head said "No, you can't," and then you believed it.

Perhaps you believed it because one of your parents said the same thing. Maybe others in your life told you directly that some desire you had was foolish or impossible. Or maybe you observed the culture around you, saw the collective shut down, the fear of failure, and decided on your own to give it up and settle.

To be clear, I'm not saying that every desire we have, every dream or fantasy we create is our destiny. In fact, sometimes letting go of a dream or goal and deciding to focus on something else is an act of O.M.O.S. and something we must do.

What I'm talking about here is the habitual pattern of your critic telling you that you can't have what you want and you buying into it. Instead, we want to cultivate an attitude of curiosity and encouragement to explore possibilities. Is this desire a clear outcome that you will achieve or a temporary expression of interest, passion, and life moving through you? This can only be determined when the desire is met with openness, rather than immediately being discounted by your critic. In either case, it will serve you best to feed this energy, to give fuel to this fire.

Who knows whether Zaim is going to design Magic cards? Maybe it's a passing fantasy emerging from this period in his life when he's obsessively in love with this game. Hence, his statement, his vision for himself, is an expression of that passion, enjoyment, and love he feels for the experience of learning about and playing Magic with his dad.

Who knows? Maybe he does have this inner calling to create in this way. Maybe he keeps playing and becomes one of those brilliant, nerdy genius kids at the game shop who beats the adults in the "Friday Night Magic" tournaments. Maybe he goes down this path, and twenty years from now, he's part of the design team at the Magic The Gathering division of Hasbro, sharing his ideas for cards for the new set. Why not? Why not him?

I don't know about the outcome, but I do know this: feeding the flame is what matters. Because even if it's not a long-term destiny and just a passing fancy, that is still as important to nourish. When you say yes to what you want to do, yes to your goals, yes to possibility, how does that feel?

Take a moment right now to imagine something you would love to experience or achieve in your life. It could be a small desire or something big that you've never done before. Maybe it's something you've been thinking about for a long time or something that is coming to you now as you're reading this section.

Now imagine yourself saying "Yes" to this desire, goal, or dream being possible and you being able to get it, do it, or experience it. Say yes to the whole thing. How does that feel? Exciting? Liberating? Satisfying? Perhaps you feel lighter and more expansive in your chest. Tune in even more closely. What does it feel like to *really* say yes to yourself? Stay with this for just a moment if you'd like, then keep reading.

Now, just for comparison sake, what does the opposite feel like? Take that same desire, dream, or goal and tell yourself, "No." No, you can't. It's not possible. You'll never be able to do that, never get there, never have that. You could never have that exciting and fulfilling job that feels deeply meaningful and provides you a great income. You can never date the people you want. You can't be in a deep, loving relationship that gets better year after year. You can never be truly happy or joyful in your life.

How does this feel? Further still, what if you make yourself wrong for wanting it in the first place? Isn't this what we do? We say it's not possible, and then we become suspicious of our motives. We treat ourselves like a cold attorney cross-examining a witness that she thinks is clearly untrustworthy. Are you sure you even want it? You better be sure. And besides, why do you want that anyway? You shouldn't want that. You shouldn't need that. That's _____ (insert your preferred judgment here: needy, greedy, superficial, selfish, bad).

Is this O.M.O.S.? Forget about the specifics of any particular desire or dream for a moment, and just examine the treatment. Is this how you'd want to speak to your own child or a niece or nephew that you love? Is this how you'd want to talk to your own best friend?

This is another form of insanity. It's yet another subtle way we turn on ourselves, doing something that might seem so small and trivial as to not even matter. But, like taking a small dose of arsenic each day, after a long enough period of time, we become sick. We become sick in our hearts, foggy in our minds, and depleted in our bodies. This is a depressing way to live, and something we must change if we are to truly be on our own sides. So let's do that right now.

The Cozy "I Can't"

The reason we buy into this naysaying nonsense is the same reason we listen to our critic in any other situation—survival. Remember, what is your critic's primary objective? What's its main focus, its main purpose?

That's right; it's to keep you alive! And it does this by avoiding all risk, all unknowns, and therefore, staying safe. At least, so the theory goes, despite the reality that this still does not protect us from all pain, loss, or hardship as these are inevitable human experiences. Nevertheless, our critic persists in its mission! Perhaps it can't avoid all pain, but it sure is going to do what it can to try to minimize it all. Enter the naysayer.

The story of "I can" is dangerous. Desire is fraught with peril. Just the act of wanting something can feel uncomfortable or even downright painful. That ache, hunger, or longing can be intense. And then there's all the stuff we need to do along the path of achieving this dream, all these things we have to learn and perhaps not be that good at to begin with. That's embarrassing to be a beginner, making lots of mistakes. And then there's rejection along the way, people saying "No" to you, and sometimes not getting the outcomes you hope for. And then there are failures and people seeing you not get it right away, people seeing you falter, have setbacks, waver. And then, what if you put all this effort in, experience all this pain and setback, and *still* don't get what you want in the timeframe you imagine?

Nope. That's too much. Forget that noise. I can't deal with all that pain. I'm unwilling to be judged, disliked, or embarrassed. I'm unwilling to be seen as anything less than polished and perfect, and so I will abstain. I will crawl into my cozy blanket of "I Can't" where I sing myself this sweet lullaby:

No, you can't,
No, you can't,
And you never will be able.
You aren't worthy.
You're not good enough.
And everybody knows.

Barf. Enough of this! You know this drill. You've seen this again and again in all the many manifestations of your inner critic, which is good news! Your inner naysayer is not something different; it's just your critic doing the same old thing. And that, you know how to handle.

Three Ways to Neutralize Your Naysayer

So what do we do in the moment to work with that voice of doubt that says we can't do something? That voice often gets louder just as we attempt to make positive change or are in the midst of taking bold action to enhance our lives. Here are three specific strategies you can use in your life right now. Test each one out to see which one is most helpful at different times.

Escort

This approach is similar to what you were practicing earlier in your judo moves with your critic. You are going to become the champion or defender of your critic. Instead of fighting it and having it delay or derail you, you are going to become its protector as you pursue your dreams. First things first, you need to reclaim the authority and remember that you are driving the car, and your critic is in the backseat. It might be making all kinds of noise back there—screaming, kicking, threatening, or throwing things—but it's not in control of the vehicle.

Just remember, your critic is a survival program rooted in fear. It's terrified of failure, loss of love, and what it imagines will be overwhelming pain, death, and ruin.

Just putting on headphones, gripping the steering wheel tightly, and jamming your foot down on the gas pedal doesn't typically work well in the long run. You might be able to power through for a bit, but eventually, all that noise from the back seat and internal tension burns out your motivation and stamina.

Instead, empathy works much better with your critic. Acknowledge what it's saying, and be truly curious about what it's afraid of.

So when it says, "You can't do that," or "You'll never have that," you can tell it: "I know you're scared right now. I'm listening. Tell me more. What are you afraid of, sweetie? I got you. I'm not going anywhere."

And then, really listen. Don't listen for a second and then pounce on your critic, pointing out all the ways it's being irrational. This breaks down the communication, and your critic resorts to the scream and kick method described earlier.

Listening can be challenging because your critic may throw a lot of doubt, fear, negative predictions, stories of unworthiness, and anything else toward you all at once. But you don't need to have answers for all of this. You don't need to figure it all out with your head. You just need to be in your heart, breathe, reside in your body, and love this little scared part of you.

As your critic rants, keep acknowledging its basic core fears.

Keep reminding it that it's okay to feel afraid, that you're here with it, that you aren't going anywhere.

Here's a quick example to demonstrate what this sounds like:

Critic: You're never going to reach all the people you want to reach. Your idea to bring hundreds of people together in a room at a live event or reach hundreds of thousands or even millions through your books is not gonna happen. No way.

Me: Haha, you seem so certain. How are you so sure?

Critic: Come on, Aziz. It's obvious, isn't it? Not enough people want what you can provide. And besides, wanting to reach more people is bad anyway; it's all about you and your ego.

Let's pause before I dialogue further. Notice what's happening here. Some part of me feels excited, expansive, and alive when I imagine reaching even more people, touching people all over the world, helping to inspire and liberate them. When I imagine hundreds of these people joining me for a live event, my energy increases even more. What we could do together! With our collective focus on liberation and my experience leading groups and knowledge on this topic, it all feels so good, so right, like I'm meant to do this, like I am called to make it happen.

The same is true for you. Whatever your goal, dream, or vision is, when you imagine it, part of you feels expansive, excited, and alive. Energy starts to flow through you, your chest and heart open up, and your body naturally becomes more upright and alert.

But then, enters the naysayer. Notice how mine is first saying it's not possible in a dismissive, condescending tone. It's attempting to generate an aura of authority by playing the role of a wise parent or mentor who knows what it's like and is going to talk you down to the "real world." Then it hits me with a quick one-two punch: It says what I have to offer isn't that helpful or desirable (aka I'm not good enough) and then says that it's bad for me to even want to reach more people.

I want to slow down this process and show you what's happening step by step because you would not believe how many people are completely stopped in their tracks right here in this first exchange. They spend their entire lives under the iron heel of their inner critic, afraid to even question its authority, unaware that they are suffering deeply from squashing their dreams, desires, and essential aliveness.

What does your naysayer hit you with? The same "Come on now, that's unreasonable and impossible" speech? Does it shame you for wanting whatever it is you want? Let's take this further.

In response to my critic's maneuver, I decide to poke the bear and see if I can access the fear underneath. Remember, there's always fear underneath your naysayer, as there's always fear underneath your critic. You might not be feeling it consciously because your critic is keeping your awareness locked up in your head or making you feel depressed and down with all its dismal stories of lack and incapacity. One way to access this fear is to take bold action in the face of what your critic is saying, which I'll get to in a moment. But first, I decided to take a moment to visualize what I want and proclaim it out loud in the present tense.

> Me: I am a New York Times bestselling author. My books reach millions of people all over the world and provide healing, love, and support for them to be their most liberated, confident, authentic selves. I bring together hundreds of people in large, exciting events where we collectively supercharge our confidence and lives.

> Critic: Noooooo!

Haha, I can't help but be amused by this process. I can hear my critic in my head shouting its dissent as I proclaim my vision. I can feel it squeezing my throat and creating tightness and heat in my upper chest.

Let's see what happens for you. Take a moment now to recall that goal, dream, or vision you were thinking about earlier. Take a moment to focus on that again in vivid detail, and then proclaim out loud in the present tense what you want to be. Do this now.

How do you feel? What is happening in your mind and, more importantly, your body? What is your critic saying? Is it active? Do you feel any constriction, tightness, squeezing, or other tension in your body? Check the central channel of your body; perhaps your jaw, throat, chest, or stomach feels tight. When you take a full, deep breath in all the way down to your belly, do you notice any place where it feels constricted or hard for the breath to pass through?

How do you relate to this fear or inner tension? What do you say to your critic?

Me: My darling, I love you. I can feel that fear, squeezing in my throat. What's up? What are you afraid of?

Critic: I hate being exposed. I hate being so open and vulnerable with so many people. So many angry people out there can judge me, hate me. And the more you put us out there, especially being all open and vulnerable as you do it, the more we can be attacked, and the more exposed we are. I hate that feeling. I *hate* it.

Me: You hate feeling exposed and open to attack.

Critic: Yeah. You seem to handle it fine, but when someone sends us a hateful message, it hurts me. I hate that feeling. I don't want to feel more of that, which we will if we reach even more people. We'll be so exposed!

Me: I'm right here with you, buddy. I hear you. You hate
feeling exposed, and you never want to feel that way.

As I say this, I open even more to that discomfort of "exposed."
I turn toward that part that feels hatred, dislike, and pain about
feeling exposed and breathe deeply into my body. Instead of
clamping down and not trying to feel it, I do the opposite. I
welcome it in. *Show me everything you got.* Anything and everything you feel about being exposed, I want to see, feel, and know.
That's what I mean when I say *I'm right here, and I'm not going
anywhere. I'm going to hold you all night long, through the entire
thunderstorm.*
   As I sit with that feeling for a few minutes, truly being with it
without making it hurry up, go away, or otherwise get rid of it, I
feel relaxing happening inside of me. That's the signal that I can
start to offer reassurance that will be received by the scared or
hurting part of me.

Me: My darling, I love you so much. I got you no matter
what. No matter what anyone says to you or does to you,
I will be right here. You can always count on me for the
rest of your life. I will protect you. We will expel out their
hatred and negative energy and help you feel light, happy,
and free. We are safe, no matter what happens. I got you.

What happens when you speak to yourself in this way? If your
critic was becoming active as you imagined pursuing or achieving
your goal, how is it now after you cut through to the underlying
fear and empathize with it?
   You'll notice these are a different application of the same skills
you learned earlier in this part of the book. That repetition is by
design. Working with your inner critic is truly like learning a martial art, and massive repetition is the key to becoming proficient
or even a master at it. I suggest you take it one step further—don't

just read about my dialogues here; have them yourself, with yourself, with your critic and any other parts of you.

The more you practice, the better you become at this skill, which improves every moment of your life.

Watch Me

Do you want to know the best part of any movie, the moment that gratifies the audience more than anything in the world? Is it when the guy gets the girl in the rom-com? That's certainly heartwarming, but no. Is it when the hero defeats the villain in the final battle scene? Eh, that is necessary for the movie to end but often can feel sort of anticlimactic and unfulfilling, can't it? No, hands down, the most enjoyable part of the movie is when someone who deeply deserves it gets what's coming to them. They get their "comeuppance." In fact, when you leave a movie and the bad guy loses, and the heroine wins and finds true love, you can still be slightly dissatisfied because justice was not served.

But now, picture this. There's a movie where the villain is the cold, harsh, rejecting baseball coach. Earlier in the movie, he rejected our hero, telling him he wasn't good enough and could never even play baseball, let alone on his team. But through determination, grit, and grace, our hero faces his demons and earns his way onto another baseball team. Now, in the final scenes of the movie, it's the championship game, and our hero's team is playing none other than coach poopy pants' team. It's the final inning, and our hero is up to bat.

The nasty coach hisses criticisms from his dugout, words that used to cut our hero to the core. He tells him he's not worthy to swing a bat, that all his good fortune is just luck, that soon he'll fail, and it will all fall apart. He tells him that he'll never be able to hit that ball.

Then our hero sets up his stance, strong, taught, and powerful in his body and focused and clear in his mind. He turns toward the coach and says, "Oh yeah? Watch me."

Then, there's the pitch, and there's a split second where it's unclear what's going to happen. He swings hard, fast, and true. He strikes the ball square in the center of the bat, smashing it high into the air, soaring over everyone's heads, out past right field, and over the fence for a home run.

The audience in the baseball stands erupts! The audience in the theater cheers! Our hero bounds toward first base, and that mean old coach stares out onto the field, dumbfounded. Boy, was he wrong. He sure got his.

Now *that* is a movie we leave feeling fully satisfied.

Well, my friend, the same applies to you as the hero of your own life. When that voice pops up proclaiming that you can't do something, that you're not good enough to ever pull it off, turn toward it, smile, and say, "Watch me."

And then, take bold action. Take the next step on the path toward your goal. If your critic tells you that you can't be in a leadership position at work, that you can't speak up in meetings, that you don't have what it takes to be a powerful player in your career, smile at it and say, "Watch me." Then, walk into your next meeting and intentionally speak up more. Share your ideas. Approach colleagues, enhance communication, proactively solve problems, and start carrying yourself like a leader, even before you are officially given that designation.

If that voice says you can't experience a deeply loving relationship, that you'll never be able to date who you want, and that you're doomed to either be alone or settle for something unfulfilling, smile, and say, "Oh, yeah? Watch me." Then, approach five people you find attractive and start conversations with them. Reach out to a dozen people on dating apps. Tell your close friends you're looking to meet someone amazing, and see who they know.

Do the very thing your critic says you cannot. Do the very things your critic dismisses as "pointless" because "they won't work anyway." Stop listening to this nonsense! Remember, your critic is not a wise, trusted advisor with accurate predictions based on experience and a neutral stance. It's a terrified, frantic part that is willing to dismiss reality, lie, or make up whatever absurd things it must to keep you safe.

So the next time it makes up an absurd story, telling you that you can't do something, what are you going to say to it?

Maybe, Maybe Not

So, you have this goal or dream that excites and inspires you… and terrifies your critic. You can soothe that sucker, or smile and walk right past it. But all the while, it keeps the doubt going, doesn't it?

I can't do that. It won't ever happen.
What if I get it but then can't sustain it?
Will this next step work? What if it doesn't?
What if I try and fail?
What if I try twenty things, and all of them fail?
What if I try everything, and nothing works?
What if, no matter what I did, I'd never be able to achieve it?

Once you start indulging these thoughts and questions, before you know it, you're deep down Doubt Alley, all turned around. Doubt is yet another tool used by your critic to trip you up, slow you down, and hopefully even make you stop entirely.

It can lead to half-hearted attempts or a limited willingness to try only a certain number of approaches to reach our goal. Or it can lead to this strange mental trap I see in clients all the time: *I am willing to do _____ (insert bold action here), but only if I can get total certainty that it will bring me closer to the result I want quickly.*

For example, I'm willing to go on some dates if I can know for certain that I will meet someone amazing who I want to spend the rest of my life with on these dates. Otherwise, it's a waste of time, and I don't want to put myself out there at all.

This need for total certainty before we take action or rigidity to only try a few approaches to reach our goals leads us down an inevitable path of failure to achieve what we most desire. It's only a matter of time before we find ourselves back under that cozy *I can't* blanket, singing that sweet lullaby.

One way out of this trap is to open to the truth of "I don't know." Sometimes, in an attempt to alleviate doubt, people try to activate total certainty in their achievement of their dream, as in, "I will do this, and nothing will stop me. Warrior battle charge—Grraaggg-hhh!" This is certainly a helpful energy to activate when needed, but as a permanent way of being, it's hard to sustain. Hence, even after a day of successful warrioring and dragon slaying, when you're resting on the couch, doubt can still creep in. *Am I doing enough? Is it going to work? What if it doesn't?* And off we go again.

Instead of trying to cling to certainty—be it positive or negative in terms of achieving our desires—what if we surrender to the fact that just don't know. Hence, when your mind says something is impossible, you say, "Maybe, maybe not."

Will I become a New York Times bestselling author? I don't know. Maybe, maybe not.

Will you find that amazing life partner? Maybe, maybe not.

Will you be able to have another child? Will you grow your own successful business? Will you save a certain amount of money? Will you completely free yourself from chronic pain? Will you heal yourself of cancer?

I don't know. Maybe, maybe not.

How do you feel when you hold your dream in that space of uncertainty, of openness? For many of my clients, this can feel surprisingly relieving. They can let go of some of that inner tension they're constantly holding in the form of pressure to "make it happen." Often, this doesn't even mean taking a specific action in the moment. It's just a background clenching—a sense that they have to do something to the world to push things into the right place…or else.

Letting go in this way creates a space where you can allow life to unfold. It's certainly not a resignation, where you put down your oars and let the current of the ocean carry you toward whatever. But rather, it's a more Taoist approach of being present in this moment, surrendering to the greater forces at work, tuning in to what is the right action in this moment, and then taking it without much drama or fuss.

So, the complete statement you can say to your naysayer when using this approach can be summed up like this: "I don't know. Maybe, maybe not. Let's take one more step along the path and see where we end up, friend."

Take that step and see what happens. Let yourself be aware to what feedback you're receiving from life and the world around you. Then, take another step.

Will all these steps certainly bring the outcome you want? Are they the right ones? Are they the best ones? Is it all going to work? I don't know. Maybe, maybe not. Let's take another step.

Beyond Damage Control

You now have a powerful set of tools that you can use to rapidly change the way you talk to yourself, treat yourself, and ultimately feel each day of your life. Like any other skill, improving your self-talk and being on your own side develop through practice. The more you set aside time and focus on doing what you are learning here, the faster you'll make the changes you seek.

While the abilities you're developing now to regain control inside and stop the self-abuse are essential, the whole process is still quite effortful. It's like borax. Let me explain.

Seemingly all the time, regardless of the season, our house

is under attack by ants. They pour in through the kitchen window seal, the walls, and even through the basement door. They descend upon any fruit or food left out for a few hours.

Our solution? Borax. We don't want to use harsh, poisonous ant traps in our kitchen, so we have a home-remedy solution that works quite well. We mix some borax, which is a mild household chemical used for a variety of things, including laundry and killing ants. We mix it with some white sugar in water and pour the mixture on little squares of paper towel in small bowls. The ants are drawn to the sugar, eat it (and the hidden borax within), and die a terrible death. Silly ants, don't they know we humans own the planet and everything on it? (And we'll never get our comeuppance. Never, I say!).

This solution works great, sort of, except when we don't put out the borax. Then, within a day or two, the ants get wind of our failing perimeter and are back at it, demolishing bits of peach and strawberry left out on the counter overnight.

This is similar to the skills you are mastering in this part of the book. You need to learn them to work with your critic and learn how to treat yourself with love and kindness. But we're not necessarily solving the problem at the root. Why do the ants keep coming? Why do you keep attacking yourself and need to use these tools to calm your critic? Is there a way to go deeper to heal the underlying patterns that create all this self-hatred in the first place?

Is there a way to make some fundamental shifts in the way you relate to yourself so that your overall level of self-criticism radically decreases? You bet! That's what Part IV of this book focuses on. Let's explore that now.

PART IV: PERMANENT O.M.O.S.

Chapter 10:
Unconditional Self-Worth

Is your sense of self-worth unconditional? Do you feel worthy of love, belonging, and respectful treatment, no matter what? Or is your sense of self-worth conditional? Perhaps *very* conditional indeed.

Earlier parts of this book were about helping you shift your relationship with your inner critic to start treating yourself with much more love, compassion, and respect. This is an essential skill set that you must have to wrestle control from your inner critic and return to being on your own side. However, to reach higher levels of O.M.O.S., you will need to stop all that self-hatred from forming in the first place.

Much like mold growing in a basement, it's important to have the appropriate cleaner and tools to remove it after it forms. But then, you want to figure out why you keep getting mold down there in the first place. Similarly, what patterns do you have that continually generate self-judgment, dislike, and hatred? The chapters in this section of the book are focused on helping you do just that—solving self-criticism at its root, so you don't have to battle your critic so much, and you can just live with more natural self-love, ease, and freedom. Sound good? Let's do it.

NOT ENOUGH

"I need blue eyes," I declared toward the ceiling.

"What?" Arash asked.

"I need blue eyes," I repeated, as I propped myself up on my elbow and looked at him.

I was lounging on the bed in his college dorm room as he attempted to do some homework at his desk.

"What do you mean?" he said, putting his book down.

"Guys with darker skin and hair look especially attractive with bright green or blue eyes," I explained.

"Yeah. They do," he agreed.

He was an easy sell. The next week, we went together to the campus vision center to explore the option of blue or green contact lenses. I tried to test out a pair of blue contact lenses, only to find that I had great difficulty in touching my own eyeball without becoming a flinching, eye-watering mess.

Arash, on the other hand, had no difficulty inserting the contacts as he wore prescription contacts for vision purposes. I looked at him with his brown skin, five-o'clock shadow, and two blue eyes. But he didn't look quite right. Instead of being clear, as blue eyes are, they had a thick, opaque quality to them like a blue shell on top of a brown eye. He looked in the mirror and grunted in disapproval, apparently agreeing with my assessment. So, we left the vision center empty-handed.

Arash was mostly there to be with his friend and try out some novelty that was mildly interesting. I, however, was there to save my life.

For years, I had experienced a chronic sense of being inadequate, inferior, and less-than. When I compared myself to other men, which was all of the time, I found myself lacking. I generally focused on physical appearance comparisons—height, eye and skin color, muscle size, leanness, etc. In addition, I would assess how confident, funny, outgoing, and popular someone seemed to be. If they were confident in groups, with strangers, or with women, I'd feel a sinking, crushing feeling in my chest, as if I wanted to lower my head and curl up my spine like a roly-poly bug.

Interestingly enough, I never compared my intelligence with others'. Over time, I discovered we all do this. We have areas we use for comparison, markers to measure our worth, value, and lovability.

The Inferiority Trap

> "And then I'll go down to the Wilds of Nantucket
> And capture a family of Lunks in a bucket.
> Then people will say, "Now I like that boy heaps.
> His New Zoo, McGrew Zoo, is growing by leaps."
> - *"If I Ran the Zoo"* by Dr. Seuss

Remember way back when I asked you why you were so hard on yourself? One of the most common reasons people give is to "make myself better in some way." This begs the question — where are you lacking? Why do you need to be better?

It's worth slowing down and examining this question. You may have been steeped in the personal development world for so long that you take it as a fundamental truth that you must identify all your shortcomings and fix them, thus making yourself a superior human being.

Perhaps improvement and getting better are pathways to success and having more of what you want in life. If you get more physically fit, maybe you'll feel better about yourself, and you'll be more desirable in the dating world. If you improve your speaking skills, you may gain opportunities for advancement in your career and earn more money.

But let's take a moment and see what happens. Think of something about yourself that is not how you want it and what you'd like to be different. Can you feel a sense of needing to improve? Take a moment to pause and reflect on that. What does it feel like? What is the experience of wanting to be different or better?

Typically, it's a combination of disliking who you are right now and wanting something that you don't have, in other words, a combo of aversion and craving. For example, you might not like your appearance or personality, and you want to be in a relationship or to have more friends. You may be single or often find yourself alone, which you do not like, and want to be different. You then tell yourself, "If only I were more beautiful or handsome, then I wouldn't be single." Or, "If only I were funnier and more outgoing, then I'd have lots of friends and never feel lonely."

As you read this, you may be subtly nodding your head in agreement. *That's right! I do need to be more outgoing and funnier. Then I would have more friends!* And, you're right. On the surface, that story checks out. If someone is beautiful by societal standards, they may have an easier time getting dates. If someone is funny and outgoing, they may have an easier time meeting people and making friends. The problem is not in you wanting those things or in having goals to move toward. The problem is the underlying dislike of yourself, the underlying sense of low worth or value. The problem is where you're coming from.

Because while being funnier and more outgoing might land you more friends, it does not automatically turn off that inner dislike. If being more beautiful or handsome only turned off that internal dislike and increased our sense of self-worth automatically, then plastic surgery would be our golden ticket to permanent self-esteem. Alas, a change in our physical appearance does not necessarily mean we feel any different about our self-worth or sense of value. And there are millions of people who look outstanding, who have faces and bodies others would trade anything for, who are dissatisfied with their appearance and hate themselves. This is not the way out.

The way out of this trap of feeling inferior, inadequate, not quite there yet, not enough yet, is to do the inner work to unhook yourself. There's no quick fix in a pill, a magic spray, a needle, or a knife. The problem is not "out there." It's "in here," in our own minds and hearts. Let's solve it now, together.

What Would It Take?

Do you relate to my story about the blue contact lenses above? Do you know the feeling of being inferior or not enough in some way? Where and when does that feeling show up for you? Where do you feel inadequate right now in your life?

Perhaps you feel inferior about some aspect of your appearance, your physical abilities, your knowledge or education, your status at work, or your income. These are just a few of the areas on which we can compare ourselves to others. Here is a quick list of some of the big ones:

- Career accomplishment/status
- Body appearance (weight, body fat, muscle size, strength, waist size, etc.)
- Facial appearance (facial shape and features, eye color, hair color, hair amount, etc.)
- Current salary or income
- Total net worth
- Social confidence
- Success in dating (dates, opportunities, being sought after)

- Popularity (both in real life and as measured by followers or fans on social media)
- Humor
- Intelligence
- Education

Take several minutes to make your own list right now. You can write down anything from the above list that you feel insecure or inadequate about. Also, reflect on any other things you rate your self-worth on and often find yourself lacking.

Keep in mind that to put something on your list doesn't mean you have to be lacking in this area. We often compare ourselves to others or an imaginary standard in our minds and feel inadequate in the areas where we are already highly successful.

For example, I have an internal image of the "ideal man" when it comes to body shape and size. He is extremely lean and also strong and muscular at the same time, you know, the typical men's fitness magazine cover image.

Thanks to amazing, beautiful, and exciting liberation in my health, I've gone from seeing myself as broken and incapable of regular exercise to being able to do all kinds of activities. I love running and lifting weights and have gotten stronger and fitter over the years. In other words, this area of my life is great, and yet, in an instant, I compare myself to that *Men's Health* magazine cover in my head and feel that swirling mixture of inadequacy and craving.

In your list, include any area you feel inadequate in, even if you're already awesome in that area from an outside perspective, and even if you only intermittently feel insecure in this area.

Okay, go ahead and make that list now.

Do you have your list? Great.

Okay, now pick one area of your list that you often feel inadequate in, and let me ask you this: **What would you need to be**

like, look like, have, or do to be enough in this area? Be as specific as possible. Take the time to get clear on what it would take to feel totally adequate, complete, and worthwhile in this area, to feel enough.

When I did this exercise recently with a client, his answer was "a million." He ran a small business, and if he got his total sales to over one million USD per year, then he'd feel accomplished and adequate in his career.

Another client told me that in order to be an adequate, "good" mother, she needed to never get angry with her children and always respond with warmth, playfulness, and patience, no matter what the circumstances.

What is it for you in the area you chose?

Now, I'd like to ask you a follow-up question. If you had that, or did that, or accomplished that, or looked the way you wanted, would you feel a sense of self-worth and being "enough" as you are?

Take a moment to imagine it. For just a moment, set aside any claims your critic makes "impossible" and let yourself step into your vision of this ideal self.

Now, let me ask you this: Would that sense of worth be a permanent state? Or would it evaporate if you stopped doing or being that certain way? In other words, is your sense of self-worth solid or fragile? Would your standards or expectations change to be higher in the future? Or would that target provide you with an indefinite sense of self-worth?

Has this ever happened to you before?

When I ask this last question to my small business owner client, he laughed. "Yep," he said, as he shook his head from side to side in amusement at himself. "When I was first starting my business, I wanted to make enough to replace my salary, which was about $80,000. I thought if I could just do that, I'd feel amazing. I'd be a true business owner and wouldn't have to work for anyone else ever again."

"And you did that," I said. "What was it like?"

"Yes, I did." He replied. "And the moment I realized I was going to exceed that amount, I felt elated, but also like it wasn't enough. I realized that 80K in revenue was not 80K in profit. So my next goal was to make 80K in personal profit."

"And you did that too," I said.

"Ha, yes, I did," he smiled.

"What happened then?" I asked.

"I needed more. My target went up to $250,000, then $500,000." He said.

"Now, it's a million," I added.

"Yeah."

"And there's nothing wrong with that," I said. "Of course, you want your business to grow and thrive; who wouldn't? The point here is that you have your self-worth hitched to that revenue or profit number in your business. Not only that, you have it hitched to some future target number so that you don't even feel the self-worth you seek now, despite having a flourishing, amazing business."

"Yeah, it's crazy," he said.

"Indeed," I agreed. "Insanity." I paused to let him reflect on that. I know that when people see clearly what they have been doing and how it truly does not serve them, this is a powerful motivating force for lasting change.

"But so good to see!" I said enthusiastically. "When you see the game you're playing, and you get how unwinnable it is, then it becomes much more possible to change the game."

VALUE EQUIVALENTS

So, what's on your list? In your mind, what currently equals your worth? These are your value equivalents—the metrics you use to measure your sense of self-worth, your value as a human, and ultimately, your worthiness for acceptance, love, belonging, and happiness.

As I was writing this book, I made a study of my value equivalents. When I noticed myself feeling scared, hurt, reactive, or down, I asked myself what was challenging my self-worth? What was I hitching to worth? Here are a few I discovered:

Client Results = Worth

When clients make big changes, significant shifts, and achieve inner and outer goals, that means I'm a good coach. I helped them and am therefore valuable. If they seem stuck, refuse to take risks, and don't make major progress, then I have failed in some way. My worth goes down.

Yes = Worth

If someone says yes to working with me, partnering with me, or promoting me, then I'm the man. If they say no, then I must be inadequate, unworthy, and not enough in some way.

Professional Success = Worth

This can be measured in impact or income. If I can reach more people, grow a larger following, have more book reviews and sales, etc., then I'm worthwhile. If fewer people come to an event, or if I start comparing my impact to someone else's, I can feel a sinking feeling of worthlessness.

As far as income, if mine is strong (and ideally increasing), then I'm all good. I'm safe, smart, and capable. If it's less for a period of time, or I have a down year, then I'm not a smart-enough businessman. Teachers, mentors, and others would look down upon my foolishness and ineptitude.

Body Fat Percentage = Worth

If I am lean, strong, and muscular, then I'm worthy. If I'm

not working out for whatever reason, not progressing toward my next fitness goal or otherwise developing in this area, then I am unworthy and bad.

What about you? What are you making equal to your worth and lovability as a human being? What equals your worth?

Remember the list you just made in the last section—the list of things you can feel insecure about? For each one, underneath, there's a value equivalent that you're linking to your sense of self-worth.

So if you tend to feel insecure around someone you find beautiful, in your mind: Beauty = Worth

Or if you feel inferior or down after looking in the mirror, then: Beauty = Worth.

This one value equivalent can make you feel insecure in a thousand different moments throughout your day.

That is why uncovering your major insecurities is such a valuable activity. What are the top five value equivalents that are impacting you on a regular basis? Take just a few minutes to uncover these now and write them down in your O.M.O.S. journal. Even if you just come up with one or two, that will be of great benefit in liberating yourself. Over this next week, other value equivalents will become clear to you as you pay attention to what's underneath your moments of insecurity.

The Games You Play

Here's a thought-provoking question for you: Why are some things on your list and not others?

How come you feel inferior when you see your colleague confidently speak up in a work meeting, but you don't feel inferior when your muscular friend takes off his shirt at the pool? Or, for you, it might be the other way around, and you don't even notice in the meeting but feel a wave of inferiority and self-loathing about your body wash over you when you see your friend's figure. Or maybe you feel bad in both scenarios, in which case, you're doomed, and there's no hope for you, my friend. No! I'm kidding.

The truth is we all have specific metrics we use for comparison to determine our own value and worth. These value equivalents (VEQ) are the things you make equal to your value. To test your growing abilities to identify these value equivalents, what is the VEQ for the work meeting scenario?

Confidently speaking up in meetings = Valuable/Worthy
Sitting quietly and/or feeling anxious = Not Valuable/Worthy

And what about the pool scenario?

Having visible muscles = Valuable/Worthy
Being skinny, not muscular, or overweight = Not Valuable/Worthy

Valuable here means valued by you and others. If something makes you higher value, that gives you something to feel proud of and hitch your self-esteem to. You also imagine it will make others view you as more valuable as well, thus making them respect you, admire you, be attracted to you, and want to be close to you.

Men! Six-pack abs will get you the ladies. Ladies! Losing those extra pounds of belly or thigh fat will make all the men want you.

You've been bombarded by this and millions of other messages just like it for your entire life, so it starts to seem completely and unsha.k.a.bly true. But here's the thing, the value equivalents are arbitrary. You think it's objective and agreed upon by everyone, AND you find evidence to support this and discount evidence against it. But, actually, it's subjective, and you can change your list!

The value equivalents that you rate your self-worth on are simply chosen (consciously or unconsciously). They are just games that you play and try to win to receive the ultimate reward or tro-phy—a feeling of self-worth and lovability.

One client in my Mastermind program had never been that physically active or in shape in his lifetime. He was in his early forties and was inspired by other people in the group who had taken on physical health as part of their confidence journey. The only problem was that he had a hang-up about going to the gym.

"I hate going into the gym," he said one day during a group call. "I see all these buff guys lifting tons of weight. I can barely lift anything, don't know what I'm doing, and feel self-conscious when I'm there."

And that was that. That self-consciousness (a.k.a. self-judg-ment) had prevented him from consistently going to a gym, work-ing out, doing classes, or any other sort of physical health regimen for his entire life. And he'd never questioned it until now.

So, pop quiz number two, hotshot—What's his value equiva-lent in this scenario? What's your guess? There could be a few in there...

Lifting Heavy Weights = Valuable

Being Big, Muscular, and Strong = Valuable

While this equation is completely true in his mind, perhaps you can see how it's arbitrary. Maybe you have a similar value equivalent, in which case you're nodding your head, exclaiming, "That's right! That's why the gym is terrible!"

Or perhaps you don't share that VEQ, in which case you see the situation completely differently. I don't have the first one about lifting heavy weights, but I did when I was younger. I felt a desire to lift as much as I possibly could to keep up with friends or not appear to be the weakest guy in the gym. As I got into strength training in my thirties, I was much more focused on doing the exercises with proper form, feeling strong in my body, and seeing what my limits were. I feel no need to have a certain size barbell in my hand. If a light weight for a particular exercise is difficult for me, then that's great; it means I am being challenged!

But, alas, I do share his second value equivalent about being muscular being linked to worth. When I was a teenager, I latched onto that one with gusto, imagining that muscles were the path to ladies, popularity, and love. And honestly, I wanted to have completely "gotten over it" by the time I got to this section of the book so that I could write about it fully in the past tense. But, alas, this value equivalent still lurks in the shadows, occasionally being used by my critic to incite fear, grasping, or self-doubt.

Despite not having gotten to the other side on this one, I want to share it with you anyway, for several reasons. First, you can see how we get hooked into our value equivalents and what the process is for freeing ourselves. Secondly, I want to demonstrate how O.M.O.S. is not a state that we achieve once and sustain forever. Instead, it's a practice that we keep coming back to, again and again. And finally, part of being O.M.O.S. for me is not hiding things or pretending to be perfect and neurosis-free. I strengthen being on my own side by sharing my journey, including victories and struggles, each step of the way. I have nothing to hide, and I'm on my own side no matter what. So here we go…

Bigger, Leaner, Stronger

Unbeknownst to me, over twenty years ago, a seed of self-hatred was planted in my brain. There it remained dormant all these years, only to sprout wildly in the last two years, creating an endless stream of weeds in my mind. What was this form of self-hatred, this value equivalent?

My value and worth are equal to me being bigger, leaner, and stronger. Of course, this is not unique to me, hence the massive success of the fitness book targeted toward men titled exactly this. In my case, the significance was in this order: Leaner, then bigger, then stronger. First and foremost, I must be lean, under 12% body fat lean. And once I'm that lean, I must progressively become bigger and more muscular, not too big like a hulking weight-lifter type but more like a shredded, nimble, athlete—the kind you'd see on the cover of *Men's Health* magazine.

This is not a unique goal or desire for a man in our culture. So why was it all of a sudden so strong in me, starting at the age of 34? Well, at this age, the flood gates finally opened. For the last twenty years, I had been extremely limited due to chronic pain, which was diagnosed as an autoimmune condition called Ankylosing Spondylitis. Of course, it turned out to be a mind-body pain that I could completely resolve working with underlying emotional patterns of stress, perfectionism, self-criticism, and too much niceness. As I addressed these and upgraded my mindset and actions in the world, my pain resolved (huzzah!).

So there I was at age 34, free to do anything with my body. All the things I thought I could never consistently do—run, lift weights, play soccer, play the guitar, push-ups, pull-ups, sprints, biking, hiking, dancing, anything. My body was healthy and capable! So I set out to see what my body could do. It was an exciting and liberating experience as I shattered my perceived limitations of having a weak and injury-prone body. I began to lift weights, go on long hikes, and play the guitar again. I started running regularly, which was something I had only dabbled in over the years because my body became injured almost instantly from running. I was so scared of it as so many people are unfortunately conditioned to be. But oh, how I ran. I ran more and more. I ran 10ks, then a half marathon, then a marathon. The feeling of freedom was absolutely beautiful.

But something else emerged in this period of liberation. That seed of self-hatred also exploded forth, without me even knowing it. While my goals started out from a place of pure excitement to see what I could do, they soon would get co-opted by perfectionism, and my agenda boosted all my value equivalents. I became fixated on achieving the next physical target and doing whatever it took to get there. I was going to hit 10% body fat, no matter what! So I studied what to do and took massive action on it. I counted my calories, made meal plans, and did calorie cuts. I worked out hungry, stayed in a caloric deficit, and exerted massive willpower to stay the course.

I made progress, but it wasn't fast enough. I wanted more gains more quickly. I wanted to be leaner faster. And then, when I hit the 10% mark, I wanted to get bigger and stronger, faster. No matter what positive changes I made in the way my body looked, it didn't seem to provide any satisfaction. The hunger for more progress more quickly grew bigger and bigger. So there I was with a body that I would have dreamed of when I was younger, doing things that I only wished I could do in my days of chronic pain, and instead of feeling joy and fulfillment, I felt craving, grasping, and discontent. Sigh.

Running started to take on the same insanity. I decided to sign up for a race longer than a marathon. If I could run 26 miles in the Portland Marathon, then why couldn't I run 31 miles in the woods in an Ultra Marathon? While this goal was exciting and part of my path of liberation to see what my body is capable of, it was also co-opted by this value equivalent. How far and how fast I could run became a new value equivalent, one I didn't even know I had!

I began increasing my training, running further and further. I overrode signals from my body when it was tired or in need of a break. On top of that, I wanted to keep getting leaner and stronger, so I was only eating just enough calories to keep me going for a while.

And then, I hit a wall. I couldn't do it anymore. I couldn't keep undereating. I couldn't keep pushing through my runs, feeling exhausted. What was I doing? What madness had overtaken me?

What's more, this wasn't the first time. About eight months ago, I saw how neurotic I was being about body fat and calories. In response, I made a deep study of perfectionism and how it operated in me. In that process, I decided to let go of being fixated on a certain body fat percentage as a goal. I let go and focused on being healthy and full of energy. In other words, I let go of that value equivalent for a while.

But now, I realized I'd done it again. In a slightly different way, I was playing the same game, striving to get some ideal body image, to run further and faster, to get somewhere. From the outside, the solution is easy enough, isn't it? Just stop playing that game. Just stop putting your self-worth on that target. But that's easier said than done, isn't it? Have you found it hard to let go of one of your value equivalents? I sure have.

I noticed a stubborn part inside of me that refused to give up, refused to surrender. "I will keep going! I will not run a little less or eat a little more! I will not gain any body fat! I will make sure we stay on target to achieve the ultimate glory! Never give up, never surrender! Agghh!"

That all sounds sane and reasonable. We should put that part in charge, don't you think? So I writhed around for a while, hearing this stubborn part and knowing it was being unreasonable, knowing it was unsustainable, but I still was not quite ready to let go yet. Can you relate to this? Where have you held on longer than you needed to out of pride or stubbornness?

The next night, I lay in bed with my wife Candace having a deep conversation in the middle of the night as we snuggled close. I wanted to stop this insanity. I could see that what I was doing didn't serve me. I wanted to let go. But this stubborn part held on tightly!

And then, during our conversation, I was flooded with memories of being at the gym when I was fourteen years old. I would spend hours there working out (but mostly hanging out) with my friend Chris.

Chris was my best friend throughout my teenage years. All throughout high school and college, we were inseparable, sitting together and making offensive jokes in class that no one else found funny, working the same summer jobs, spending weekends together making home movies and prank phone calls, and even living together for three years in college. Chris was like a second brother to me, and I deeply loved and admired him.

There was just one problem. Chris was sought after by the ladies, and I was not. He was tall, an accomplished runner, and a muscular weightlifter. He wasn't that much more outgoing than I was, but young women gravitated toward him. Every month or two, he would somehow be dating a new girl. Each time I felt baffled as to how he made this happen and a crushing sense of longing and inferiority.

As a young teenager, our sexual and romantic systems come online, and we begin looking out into the world to find connections, dates, and love. My systems turned on, but no inputs were received—ghost town. I didn't see it at the time, but I actively kept women away due to my social anxiety. I didn't approach them, actively talk with them, or make any interest of mine known. In fact, in rare instances when a woman was engaging with me and perhaps giving signals of interest, my anxiety would spike, and I would retreat! My mind would convince me that she couldn't possibly be interested in me and that to pursue anything would only end in rejection and humiliation for being such a fool.

But back then, I couldn't see any of this. All I could see was "out there." And no women were coming to me; therefore, I was not worthy of love. But Chris was. And he was lean, muscular, and strong. *Ah-ha!* My mind concluded. *That's why women approached him. That's why he was always dating someone. That's what made him worthy.*

I'd intellectually known where I got this value equivalent for years. But that night, as I laid in bed, I got it emotionally. I felt it all. I felt what it was like to be in that gym or around a woman my own age and feel this deep sense of ache and longing, combined with a crushing feeling of unworthiness and hopelessness. *I am not worthy of that. I will never have that.*

Using the approaches we've talked about in this book, I opened to these feelings. Show me everything you got. I'm not going anywhere. I was right there, parenting my teenage self with love, empathy, and compassion. I see you. I see and feel how painful this is, how much you longed for connection, and the pain of how impossible and out of reach it feels. I feel this unworthiness and the pain of it all.

I could feel the genesis of that deep craving to get that worth, that hunger to become lean and strong like Chris so I too could be desired and enjoy sex and intimacy with women. I went into all of it, surrendering to each feeling as it arose.

And then I said to myself the two most powerful phrases you can ever say to yourself. I gave myself the message that my teenage self desperately needed to hear, to that teenager in me who was still stubbornly trying to earn his worth to this day.

WORTHY NO MATTER WHAT

As I laid there feeling all this pain of inadequacy and unworthiness, I said to this teenager inside of me:

Aziz,
I love you, no matter what.
You are worthy, no matter what.

This, my dear friend, is the way out of self-hatred and to a life of greater self-compassion and living on your own side. These two phrases, these two powerful messages, will set you free.

In that moment, the second statement really landed. I could feel the truth of that statement as I said it. I could see past the value equivalent and let go of needing to become something in order to be worthy.

What value equivalents are you holding onto? What is your version of my story around body image? Perhaps you, too, struggle to love yourself no matter what when it comes to your weight, or your smile, or some aspect of your appearance. Or maybe it's in a different area of life, and part of you is tightly holding onto the need to earn more money, become a confident person, or achieve a certain goal before you will allow yourself to feel worthy and loved.

This is conditional worth, and it creates a tremendous amount of suffering. Worse still, all these conditions on your worth and lovability make it impossible to be on your own side. Because then, you can only feel good about yourself and be on your own side when you are on track to your goals, achieving them, and making rapid and massive progress. (Of course, for my perfectionist friends, even that is not enough! We'll discuss more on that in the next chapter.)

When you experience a setback, fall short of your ideal self, don't live up to your expectations, make a mistake, get rejected, or fail, then all bets are off. O.M.O.S. goes out the window, and you resort to savage devaluing and self-attack.

The way out of this trap is to fully let go of the conditions you've placed on your lovability and worth. The way out is to see that you hold the combination to the safe.

Opening the Safe

Right now, in this moment, as you read these words, you are

whole, complete, lovable, and beautiful. You are worthy and valuable.

How true do my words feel to you? On a scale from 1-10, how much are you letting them in? Are you nodding your head in silent acknowledgment, seeing and feeling the truth of this statement? Or is your mind resisting it, saying: *How can he say that? He doesn't know me.*

Here's the thing, you are lovable and worthy no matter what. You were born that way, you are that way right now, and you will die that way, no matter how much money you have or cool possessions you acquire, or fans or followers you gather, whether you're loved by thousands, and there is a standing crowd at your funeral, or you die alone, and no one even knows you're gone. Your worth as a human is inherent, unchanging, and static. Each person has the same inherent worth, the same right to feel valuable and lovable.

If this is the case, how come we don't all walk around feeling that way all the time? Because we tend to keep this feeling of self-worth locked up in a thick, solid safe. We make it hard to get to, only allowing it out when we've entered the secret combination in the lock. What is this combination? Let's find out.

Can you remember a time when you felt good about yourself when you had high self-esteem, a high sense of self-worth? Take a moment right now to think of a moment in time when you felt great about yourself, how you were showing up, and what you were doing. How old were you? Where were you? What was going on in your life at that time? How did you move, act, think, and feel? How did others respond to you? What did you think of yourself during this time of high confidence?

If you'd like, you can take another minute to close your eyes and imagine this time in your life. Go back to that time right now, as if you're floating up out of your body and back down into that moment, seeing what you saw, hearing what you heard, and feeling just how you were feeling then. Take a moment to enjoy it as you breathe fully and deeply.

So what was creating your sense of high self-esteem and self-worth? What was happening at that time in your life that led to the opening of the safe where you keep your self-worth locked up? The stars aligned and circumstance configured just right to punch in the exact combination on the lock, and the door swung open. Perhaps you looked a certain way or had a certain body weight. Maybe you had a boyfriend or girlfriend or spouse who admired you, loved you, and thought you were sexy. Maybe you were rich, or earning good money, increasing your monetary success in the world. Or were you achieving your goals on your way to somewhere big with a life full of promise?

Take note of the specific factors, for these are your criteria. This is what needs to happen for that safe door to swing open. At least, it did in the past. The good news is, you don't need to keep your self-worth locked up in a safe with a complex combination code! You can just leave that sucker in a box with no lock and no lid. You can even leave it out in the open on a table, freely and easily, and always accessible. Huzzah!

I am worthy, no matter what.

Say it with me. Say it out loud.

How does it feel to say? What happens inside of you when you say these words? Do you smile? Does your heart expand, and your body feel lighter or more energetic? Is there any resistance to this statement? Any, "yeah, but…" or "not until…"

If so, I encourage you to get curious and go into it. Instead of taking it as truth, see it as a chosen criteria that you are imposing on yourself. It's the game you're playing with the rules that you have set for yourself. You can change them at any time! No one knows you're even playing that game. No one cares! You're free to choose differently, right now, in this moment.

But here's the thing. What I've seen in my clients and myself is that choosing something new often involves feeling some uncomfortable feelings that we locked away during those earlier moments when we felt unworthy. As you let go of these criteria for self-worth, you may need to feel some of the pain from the moments when you felt unworthy. For it was in those moments that you came up with your "Fantasy Self" and all the ways you have to be in order to be worthy (a.k.a. the code to your safe.)

I created the requirement of a certain body appearance, body fat, muscle size, and strength in response to the pain of feeling unworthy of love when I was younger. Letting these demands go can allow the buried pain to emerge. But don't run from it or bury it further under more demands that you'll never meet. Don't keep playing this insane game.

How long have you been playing the conditional worth game? How long have you secretly felt unworthy in one or more areas of your life? How long have you been striving to overcompensate and never quite getting there, no matter how much you succeed or achieve? This pursuit is endless and will never give you what you truly seek, which is peace, love, and a deep sense of being okay with who you are. More money, more accolades, more recognition, more power, more followers, more fans, more abs, more sexual partners, more cars…none of it will give you the worth you seek.

Instead, let's turn toward that hurting kid inside who didn't feel worthy around his friend Chris. For you, it might be with your brother or sister, or on the sports field with your dad, or around that group of kids at school, or with your critical mother that you could never satisfy. Go right into that pain and meet that child with open arms, loving her so deeply and fully that it surprises her. Treat that part with empathy, inviting it to share more with you, and then more still. As you listen fully, sweetly remind this part that you love him no matter what. She's worthy, no matter what.

Chapter 11:
Letting Go of Perfectionism

Now you know that you have the code to the safe in which you've hidden your self-worth. You see that you can grant yourself worthiness right now, long before you achieve all your goals, perfect yourself, and become the ideal human specimen.

Of course, you just learned this and may have been operating in a very different way for a long time. You may have been playing the endless game of trying to earn your worth each day, each moment, through each activity, project, or conversation.

You may have been trapped in the self-abusive pattern of perfectionism, which forces you to perpetually strive to do better, perform better, be better, and otherwise prove yourself in every way. If you don't, you plummet into a pit of despair, unworthiness, and self-loathing. Sounds delightful, doesn't it?

Yet despite its insanity, perfectionistic patterns of thought and behavior can be surprisingly subtle and hard to identify and even harder to let go of. In this chapter, we'll explore the relationship between perfectionism and O.M.O.S. and how the former prevents the latter.

You'll discover how to let go of long-standing patterns of self-judgment that drive you toward perfectionism but ultimately do not serve you in being a fully confident, relaxed, happy person.

And don't worry, lest your inner perfectionist is freaking out at the idea of letting go of this or that and being all relaxed, in the next chapter, you will learn about the ancient art of Relaxed Discipline. This method will allow you to still achieve epic things, excel, and generally be awesome without all the tension, fear, and self-hatred running the show. You know, keep the good and get rid of the bad.

THE POISON OF PERFECTIONISM

Perfectionism is the opposite of O.M.O.S. It's keeping your sense of worthiness locked up tightly in a safe that has a freakishly long code to open it. One of my private clients, Roger, was a highly successful CFO in the banking industry. Throughout his career, he had risen through the ranks in each organization he was a part of and achieved high levels of power and influence, despite being ten or twenty years younger than most people at his career level. He was highly fit, muscular, looked good in a suit, and had a nice haircut. After overcoming his social anxiety working with me, he was able to approach women, be charming, and have a bounty of dating options. In short, he was a badass.

But the only problem is Roger didn't feel like a badass. Well, that's not true. He sometimes felt like a badass but only rarely. One day, we broke it down, and I asked him exactly what he had to do in a day in order to feel great about himself. Here's what he came up with:

- Woke up early in the morning and got out of bed without hitting snooze.
- Did his morning routines and ate a healthy breakfast.

- Hit the gym and was able to lift all the weight he decided he should be able to lift.

- Felt clear, positive, and confident on the way to work.

- Was highly productive and focused throughout the day, accomplishing a ton.

- Was confident and assertive in meetings and relaxed and social before and after the meeting.

That might sound like a pretty long list to you, but wait, there's more! In addition to all this, if Roger was dating any woman, he had to feel completely relaxed, confident, and unattached. He couldn't feel any longing, anxiety, or uncertainty about his dating relationships.

If, and only if, he hit every single one of these targets, then Roger could feel good about himself. But if something fell off track, such as sleeping in or not being able to work out as hard as he wanted to, he would spiral into a pattern of internal judgment and self-hatred.

This is the poisonous nature of perfectionism. It sets us up with perpetual reasons for self-hatred, making it difficult to get through the day while feeling good about ourselves. Perhaps you relate to Roger and have your own extensive list. Or maybe you think Roger sounds extreme, and you imagine that you aren't that much of a perfectionist.

I used to think that way too. I never identified with the term "perfectionist." I thought that meant that everything had to be done a certain way, that you re-read your emails ten times, that you procrastinated on starting projects and couldn't stop working on them until they were flawless, and, of course, your desk was spotless. Sure, I like a clean, organized desk, but more often than not, it's got some piles of papers on it. I don't re-read emails and often just want to complete projects sooner, without redoing them a million times to make sure they're perfect. Therefore, I am not a perfectionist. Or so I thought...

Perfectionism is way more varied than what I just described. Perfectionism can apply to any activity, project, behavior, or even your emotions. All perfectionism means is that you have an internal image of how something is supposed to be, and you compare reality to it. When reality falls short of this ideal, you get anxious, angry, demoralized, hopeless, or otherwise upset.

As a result, you can be a perfectionist when it comes to your emails and desk tidiness, but you can also be a perfectionist in how you dress, what you eat, and what your body looks like. You can be a perfectionist in how you approach your fitness, your work tasks, or even how you load the dishwasher in your kitchen. In each of these areas, you can have a specific idea of how it's "supposed" to be, then feel upset if it's not and a compulsive need to make sure it is that way (a.k.a. perfect).

As if this is not stressful enough, it becomes even more consuming when you bring that expectation to your social life, relationships, and emotions. You have an idea of how you're supposed to be socially, such as charming, funny, outgoing, witty, intelligent, or assertive. When you fall short of this, you feel wretched. You've failed, yet again. Even worse, in your mind, you *are* a failure.

Then, there's emotional perfectionism, which I shared about earlier in this book when I talked about my internal pressure to always be in a good mood, always be in the "green zone." We expect ourselves to never feel anger, grief, or anxiety. When we do experience these emotions, we feel a hefty dose of self-criticism and shame.

The worst part about this poison is how subtle it can be. It's like swallowing a subthreshold dose of a toxin. It might not be enough to make you get completely ill instantly, but day after day, it is having a negative effect on your body. This is exactly what perfectionism does—it burns you out emotionally, robs you of enjoyment and satisfaction despite high external achievement, and can be a major source of chronic pain, injury, and other illnesses.

If you want to reach the higher levels of O.M.O.S., there's no doubt about it; perfectionism has got to go. Let's take a deeper look at you and perfectionism now so you can grab it by the roots and pull it out.

Your "Fantasy Self," Revisited

Remember, in Chapter 3, when we talked about the origins of your inner critic, and we touched on the idea of your "Fantasy Self"? This is the imaginary version of you that would magically solve all your problems. For example, if dad seemed frustrated with you for not being good enough at sports, your "Fantasy Self" is an amazing athlete. This would undoubtedly win dad's effusive love and approval, right? If kids made fun of you for being fat, then your "Fantasy Self" might be extremely fit or thin, which would have made them stop mocking you and instead welcome you into the group to be showered with acceptance, love, and approval, right?

This process mostly happens unconsciously as we grow up, yet this "Fantasy Self" can be heavily influencing all the major conscious choices and actions we take in our lives. We unwittingly create an extremely detailed list of all the ways this "Fantasy Self" must be in all the different situations in our life.

The crazy thing is, we're often engaging in this process of building our "Fantasy Self" without being aware of it. It's happening behind the scenes. As a result, you might feel intense pressure to perform a certain way or achieve a certain outcome without knowing why it feels so urgent or intense. Or, you may feel a wave of self-loathing after being at a party or meeting, getting lost in hours of self-judgment for how awkward or meek you seemed.

What's happening here? Let's take a moment to make this whole process conscious, so it becomes crystal clear to you. This will save you years of self-induced suffering and help liberate you to the next level of O.M.O.S.

Your "Fantasy Self" is made up of this big long list of ways you're supposed to be in order to be lovable and awesome, right? In every situation in your life, you have this internal idea of how your "Fantasy Self" would handle things. Imagine, for example, you are at a social mixer of some sort. A lot of people are milling about, many of whom you'd like to get to know for potential benefits to your social, romantic, or business life. How are you "supposed to be" in this situation? Outgoing? Bold and direct? Quick-witted and funny? Charming? Cool and composed? Take a moment to imagine the scene and get a sense of that fantasy version of you.

Okay, great. So far, so good. You're seeing and feeling the most awesome version of you. Now, simply go out there and be just like that. Approach others without hesitation and with total boldness and self-assuredness. Jump right into the conversation with a warm smile and a witty quip as the ladies flutter their fans, and the gentlemen smile with admiration and instant acceptance. Oh, and be sure to get that attractive person's number, make some new friends who can't wait to hang out with you again, and wow some new business contacts that will undoubtedly lead to some huge contracts in the imminent future.

Ready? Okay. Now, go. You know exactly what to do.

Wait, what do you mean? What if you fall short of that? What if you feel nervous or anxious? That's ridiculous. There's no room for anxiety here in this fantasy. And certainly, don't hesitate on the edge of the group, awkwardly waiting for your chance to jump in. No, no, no! You're doing it all wrong!

But sooner or later, this is exactly what happens. We unconsciously expect ourselves to be this Fantasy Self, but then when lousy reality shows up to reveal to us that we're not, a part inside of us gets enraged. The critic smashes through the door, ranting and raving about how bad, wrong, embarrassing, and pathetic we are. It launches a flurry of attacks in a confused attempt to motivate us to do better next time by berating us for falling short. If you punish yourself enough, you'll somehow emerge as that 'Fantasy Self' next time.

Underneath this inner attack, however, is a wave of pain and fear. There is a part of us that is terrified of not living up to these perfectionistic ideals. *If I'm not my Fantasy Self, then I won't be loved. Ahhhh!* We are terrified of feeling this – terrified of those painful moments from our past where we felt unloved– and unwilling to revisit them. Yet, as you learned in Part III of this book, the only way out is through. When you become willing to feel anything and everything, you don't need to feel so afraid of these feelings. You can meet them with curiosity and love, tending to that young part of you that was hurting so much back then. The more you do this, the more brutal pressure to live up to your 'Fantasy Self' subsides, as you no longer need to be that person to be worthy of love.

You have already been engaging in this process throughout this book, but we will take it one step further in this chapter as you fully let go of your inner pressure to be this perfect self. Before we do that, however, we must identify how perfectionism is manifesting in your own life so that you can catch it in action.

PERFECTIONISM PARTY

Worst part ever! There are many ways perfectionism can manifest in your daily life. Some of these might be so common or familiar that you might not even have identified them as a form of perfectionism. See which ones you can relate to:

Anticipatory Anxiety

Before an event, meeting, date, or any number of experiences, you feel anxious. This can start up to a month or more before the event or begin just a few hours prior. You feel nervous, unsettled, agitated. Your mind keeps worrying about the upcoming event, unable to put it down or relax. You may feel an intense need to prepare even more, study, or otherwise figure something out. At the root of it, you are afraid some undesirable outcome will occur, which will lead to failure, rejection, loss, or shame. You know— good old fashioned "death and ruin."

Pressure to Be Perfect

You feel an intense pressure to achieve, excel, and do well. This could be in specific areas of life, such as your career or social life. However, it can often generalize into everything you do. You need to perform well at work, earn more money, be well dressed, make the witty joke at the party, be in great shape, have well-behaved children, be up to date on all the current news stories, always sounds intelligent, and always feel happy regardless of what's happening in your life.

This last pressure is highly ironic because the rest of the pressures you place on yourself make it impossible to stay happy for more than a few moments.

This pressure to be perfect can prevent you from trying new things, being a beginner, admitting you don't know something, being silly and playfully foolish, dancing freely, speaking freely and spontaneously, and otherwise simply enjoying who you are. Instead, it generates a constant state of internal tension, driving you to do more faster while being perpetually dissatisfied with your performance, no matter how much you get done.

Unacceptable Outcomes

Perfectionism creates all-or-nothing ideas about how you should be and how life should go. It puts all this pressure on you to be perfect and all this fear about events because it has a list of outcomes that are totally unacceptable. My not getting the sale in my presentation? Unacceptable! This person not thinking I'm amazing and not wanting to go on further dates with me? Unacceptable! Others seeing that I don't know everything about a certain topic? UNACCEPTABLE!

We have this voice inside our heads loudly proclaiming that all these outcomes are not allowed. We must do everything in our power to ensure they do not happen. We must use all our intelligence, charm, skill, sweat, whatever it takes to make sure that doesn't happen. We link those outcomes with death in our nervous system, and our fight or flight system kicks into high gear.

When we are in the grips of this form of perfectionism, we can overwork, become extremely agitated and irritable, close our hearts to friends and family, and become a frantic mess. If someone tries to reassure us, or we try to talk ourselves into a more reasonable perspective, the voice of perfectionism smashes through the door and pummels us with catastrophic images of pain, loss, and humiliation.

Post-Event Plummet

After the stressful event, be it a big meeting or date, or just a regular thing that you do every week, you might feel some temporary relief, or not. Soon, your mind kicks in with relentless post-game analysis—did they like you? Did you say that right? You should have done this instead of that.

If you perceive the outcome to be negative or potentially heading toward the unacceptable camp, then this rumination takes on a panicky quality. You have a sinking feeling in your chest or squeezing in your stomach as you replay your awkward moments and failures, certain that you ruined everything. You condemn yourself for not doing it right, being smart, motivated, charming, or otherwise good enough to pull it off. Oh, and John or Samantha, or whoever else you compare yourself to, could've pulled it off better than you.

The Perfectionistic Co-Opt

This one is sneaky. You start down a path with expansive motivations—you are inspired, excited, and joyful. It sounds like fun to start that new workout routine or sign up for that half marathon. You'd love to help your parents with their home improvement or take on that new project in your business. It all starts out great.

But then, within a few days or weeks, something shifted. The habit of perfectionism has crept in and taken over. Instead of being fun, you're upset with yourself for being slow to make progress in your workout routine. You aren't running long enough, far enough, or fast enough. You aren't doing enough to help your parents. You have to do way more now on your own project or else!

Back to the familiar inner tension and stress. Back to grinding away, trying to get ahead, prevent unacceptable outcomes, and find some momentary relief for the future.

Do you relate to some or all of these experiences? Isn't it exhausting? Is this a miserable way to live? And yet, even though we can see that, it can be hard to stop because there's this core fear driving us—if I'm not perfect, I won't be loved. I won't be worthy. I won't be safe. So as much as it would be awesome to relax, let go, and enjoy my life and relationships more, I'm afraid that's not an option.

Fortunately, that's all a big misunderstanding and completely false. You are quite free to be you and remain safe, loved, and worthy. Huzzah!

Let's figure out how to get out of this mess right now, so you can enjoy being you in this life, starting right now.

LET'S ALL BE NOT PERFECT

"It's so easy to focus on the moments when we weren't PERFECT, but they don't get perfect parents. If I have to be a perfect dad, and you have to be a perfect mom, then our boys have to be perfect too. Barf. Let's all not be perfect together and just be humans, loving each other, sharing this life together while we have it."

- Me (in a text message to my wife)

It is possible to free yourself from the pain, stress, and pressure of perfectionism. And you can do so while still being successful at the things that matter to you in life. That's the good news! The bad news? It takes effort over time to make this happen. In just a moment, I'm going to share a five-step process to unravel perfectionistic pressure and all the self-judgment and pain it generates. Hundreds of my clients and I have used this exact process to reach higher and higher levels of O.M.O.S., self-love, and enjoyment of life—right here in this present moment (as opposed to some fantasy future when you and your life circumstances have finally become perfect).

First, you must realize that the internal demand to be perfect and the harsh treatment of yourself about being imperfect is just another form of self-attack. And all self-attack is designed to do what? That's right; it's to protect you from uncomfortable or painful feelings. In other words, the pursuit of perfectionism, in any area of life, is a highly absorbing distraction we unconsciously use to try to get away from the natural complexity of life.

Life is everything. In any given moment, we may feel a wide array of shifting feelings, from gratitude to happiness to emptiness to upset to humor to fear, all at once, all swooshing around in there. Nothing has taught me this more than having children and spending lots of time with them as they are young. When a friend asks me how the weekend was after I've spent two full days with my boys, I find it hard to sum up in a few short sentences. Because over the span of even just an hour with my boys, I can feel deep and profound love and gratitude for them, their existence, and my life. I feel deep wonder at how all this life is happening, how humans are born and grow into these amazing, complex, chaotic creatures. But right there, mixed in with that joy, I may feel some aching or yearning that I can't even fully understand intellectu-ally–whispers and shadows of my past, a wistful longing for my own childhood, or who knows what else.

And then, out of nowhere, conflict explodes on the scene—one brother is hitting the other and laughing about it. Grr! The gleeful laughter after as the younger brother is crying is the most enraging part. Then, it's nonstop fighting and demands for the next thirty minutes, and I am draining patience out of my patience tank at an accelerated rate. I have my internal Chief Engineer from the engine bay on the intercom giving me updates: "Captain! We're hemorrhaging patience! The ship can't take much more of this!" I may stay present and centered, or I may get absorbed in the conflict energy and start having dramatic thoughts about how hard this is and how my life is not as fun and easy as it used to be. And that's all in the hour during breakfast.

This is life, yours and mine. Even if you don't have small chil-dren, each moment is a rich tapestry of thoughts, feelings, experi-ences, and meaning. There is no moment that is entirely simple or singularly just "one thing"—a moment where you feel grateful or happy and nothing else. Yet this is what part of us craves and perpetually strives for. We want to escape the messiness of life and the inherent mixed experience of this existence. We want to feel pure joy, perpetual bliss, always "up" and "high."

Consciously, we know this is unrealistic, and intellectually, we can acknowledge that it won't happen. But if we follow the trail left by our cravings and compulsive behaviors, we can see this is exactly what we've been striving for all along. Rationality be damned!

With perfectionism, we pick one area of life and unconsciously decide on some perfect outcome or experience. We imagine that when we achieve this outcome, get this item, get into that relationship, hit that bodyweight, or go on that trip, then we will have finally achieved that state of perpetual bliss we've been seeking. All the messiness of life and complex emotions will melt away, and we'll reside in nirvana forever.

I know this sounds crazy when I'm writing it here, and yes, it is. But that doesn't stop us from getting sucked into it again and again and again. Even well educated and successful people, emotionally aware and intelligent people–no one is immune. In fact, often the smart, successful, emotionally aware people are the most susceptible to getting sucked into the trap of perfectionism because they are highly effective at making things happen in the world, so the attainment of the ideal seems even more possible.

The Insanity Sphere

Here's how it works. We are going about our daily lives, which, as described above, is a mixture of everything—pleasure and pain, fulfillment, and dissatisfaction. We don't like this mixed, messy experience. We want more pleasure and less pain. We want all pleasant feelings and no uncomfortable ones. We want quick and easy success and fewer challenges, obstacles, setbacks, and problems.

And so we embark on a Quest For Glory. In this quest, we pick a certain outcome that will undoubtedly whisk away our problems and pain and give us unending pleasure and joy. All quests for glory can be summed up in the following sentence: When I get X, I'll feel Y.

When I earn $100,000 in a year, I'll feel rich, free, powerful, and worthy.

When I reach my goal weight, I'll feel proud, strong, sexy, and desirable.

When I find my life partner, I'll feel love, fulfillment, sexy, and happy.

When my business generates $1 million in a year, I'll feel relaxed, happy, abundant, accomplished, and valuable.

The fantasy is that, in the attainment of our goal, we will feel all these positive feelings *and* an absence of uncomfortable feelings. Of course, when we achieve one of these goals, we feel a wide variety of feelings. Some might be the desired feelings that we hoped for, but they also might be accompanied by all kinds of others we didn't anticipate.

For example, when you do get that bigger salary and hit $100K, maybe you feel powerful and more free with money. But you also might feel more stressed and anxious due to the increased responsibility of your new position. You may find yourself worrying a lot about work problems, management dilemmas, and other issues. You also might feel more worthy for a bit, or you might not. So, you get the goal, but your emotional experience is mixed, just like it was before the goal. Lousy human experience!

I know what's missing. Your goal wasn't big enough. It wasn't the right one. You need a new one. So then, we pick a new direction and set out on our quest for glory yet again.

In addition, the way this game is set up, you must achieve X in order to feel Y. So now it's rigged so that you can't feel all those good feelings until you achieve your goal. That's kind of sucky, isn't it?

What's that? You want to feel beautiful, sexy, and desirable? Mmm, I'm afraid not, not until you have a life partner. Until then, you are obviously not any of those things. So you better get on it and start questing.

One of the more recent quests I undertook several years ago was optimal health and fitness. That doesn't sound so bad, does it? I decided to eat healthier, exercise more, and get fit. Indeed, this is a worthy area of life to learn and grow in, as are many of the things we turn into a quest for glory. The problem is not in the goal or area we're trying to excel in. The problem is the "Insanity Sphere."

Here's how the Insanity Sphere works. I have a desire to be fit, healthy, and strong. After decades of chronic pain and perceived weakness in my body, this is a beautiful goal of liberation, power, strength, and freedom. There's already a seed of suffering in there as well though, as I'm also hoping to achieve the ideal body image, which will bring me all those amazing feelings I'd longed for since I was a teenager: power, sexiness, and general worthiness of love, admiration, and acceptance.

On our quest for glory, we meet a shriveled old wizard on the path. He tells us of a most mysterious and magical item known as The Orb of Power (stick with me. Yes, I've played a lot of fantasy games, but this metaphor is solid and will help you). Naturally, as a valiant and determined quester, you seek to obtain this item on your path to ultimate victory and glory. Sure enough, you find this orb, deep within a cave in the mountains. There it is –hovering slightly above the ground, glowing a deep, dark purple. As you pick it up, the hairs on your arms stand on end, and you feel the crackle of energy surging through your body.

This is that surge of energy I need to make sure I achieve my goal. I have more energy and motivation than ever! Absolute power! Sure, I'll do a sustained calorie deficit to reduce my body fat percentage. Will I work out harder? Of course! Will I track everything I eat to ensure I'm eating just the right amount of calories? No problem!

But over the next few days and weeks, the orb starts to gain more and more control over its wielder's thoughts and actions.

Calorie counting becomes an obsession, and making food choices and eating become rigid, tense experiences. Fear and neurosis start to become more apparent–fear of eating too much, fear of "getting fat." The orb that promised so much power turns out to be an 'Insanity Sphere.'

And once we're holding that sphere, it can be hard to put down. We get trapped in the thoughts that it's fed us–trapped in our own reality. *Well, I can't eat that because it has this many calories, and this food is better than that food. And I shouldn't eat after this time of day, because that's after this hour and outside my eating window.* When we look in the mirror, our mind goes to the parts that don't look quite right yet, and the insane thoughts flow freely, the sphere having total power over us now: *I need to work out harder. I should eat less today. I need to get rid of that belly fat!*

It all feels so important, so absorbing, so real. We've gotten lost in our endless quest, grasping after shadows. We've gone mad from the sphere, but we can't imagine putting it down. What do you mean, stop tracking my calories? What do you mean, stop trying to become a perfect image that I saw in a magazine? How on earth could I put that down? Besides, if I didn't clutch onto this sphere, I'd have no power at all to exercise, eat healthy, or be fit. All my power is coming from this sphere!

We become like Sméagol from Lord of The Rings with his "precious" ring. Tolkien knew what was up.

I see and hear the 'Insanity Sphere' gripping people around me all the time. My wife was just telling me how she gets obsessed with this clothing company she loves. Each season, they have new dresses, new fashion that comes out. Of course, it's in limited supply, and the good stuff goes fast. So there she is on her phone, trying to figure out what to buy, overbuying to try stuff on at home, then stressing about what to return, then not being satisfied with how it fits, then worrying about the whole thing.

She'll be happy with the items she has, but then sees an ad for the newest item. It's got a beautiful model standing on a beach in an elegant white dress, the wind blowing through her hair. Ahh, the glamour. Don't you want this? Don't you want to feel Y? Well, my friend, all you need is X. And X happens to be this white dress! Ahhh! I have to have it now! And the cycle continues.

My brother is involved in an intense murder trial right now, defending someone who's facing prison for life without parole. He's deep in the grips of the 'Insanity Sphere'—working 100 hours per week, barely sleeping, and spending every moment outside the courtroom in stress about making the right decisions, doing a good enough job, and not failing in the eyes of his client and colleagues.

I need to be more productive.

I need to lose 30 pounds.

I need to go on more dates and find my life partner.

I need to earn more money.

Each of these internal demands has an unspoken word at the end of it: NOW. As in, I need to be more productive NOW. I need to lose 30 pounds NOW. There is an urgency around the entire thing, an obsessive, absorbing intensity that the sphere has infused us with.

The truth is my wife, my brother, all the clients I mentioned, and I only *need* to do one thing: drop the 'Insanity Sphere.' When you do this, all of a sudden, everything calms down. You can breathe more deeply, hear the sounds of the world around you, and return to this moment of your life. You return to yourself, to your center.

You realize the truth that you don't need to do, achieve, or experience any of these things right this instant to be okay. You don't have to accomplish X to feel Y. In fact, the delightful truth is you can experience Y right now, even before you've achieved X. You can feel Y right now, even if you *never* achieve X!

You can feel powerful, strong, healthy, and vibrantly alive right now, at the weight you are or body fat percentage you have. You can feel full of love, connection, and fulfillment right now, even before you've met your partner. And you can feel rich right now, even before you earn any more money.

What?! What kind of blasphemy is this? How dare I say that to you? Even though this perspective is true and accessible right now, we can have the strange reaction of resisting it. *I can't just let these goals go, Aziz. You don't understand. This is real. For reals! People could go to jail for life! My kid has a learning disability, so I can't feel happy and relaxed right now. I gotta get this thing figured out NOW. And how am I supposed to feel sexy and beautiful with this belly? Are you kidding? Stop living in a fantasy world and come back to reality! How dare you?!*

To this, I would respond—I was just upset because of the tile in my bathroom, wasn't I?

(You'll see.)

THE FIVE-STEP PROCESS TO FREE YOURSELF FROM PERFECTIONISM

> "We are rich! We are rich in money, and love, and rhododendron flowers."
>
> - Zaim Gazipura, age five

So how do we end this madness, put down the "Insanity Sphere," and stop our endless quest for glory? How do we let go of our perfectionistic ideals and internal demands and truly appreciate who we are right now and enjoy our lives in this moment?

That's exactly what you'll discover how to do in this process to free yourself from perfectionism. It is not something that you can skim through quickly, implement instantly, and be free once and for all. Oh, how I wish!

Rather this is a process of self-discovery, as is this entire journey of O.M.O.S. You are continuing to learn about who you are and letting go of everything that is false that does not serve you. You are letting go of all the pressures to be somebody that others told you that you had to be in order to be good enough, that you told yourself you had to be in order to be worthy of love.

Perfectionism is simply a way of being with yourself and the world around you. It's a fearful stance that creates enormous amounts of stress, inner tension, and even chronic pain symptoms. But none of that is required. **You are not in that state of stress and tension because of your life circumstances. You are in that state of tension because of the way you are relating to your circumstances.** This insight can be hard to see and believe at first, as we can be so attached to our story that "out there" is causing "in here." But when you get it, you'll experience a huge wave of relief and freedom.

The other night, I was lying in bed with Candace after our boys fell asleep. I was so agitated, uncomfortable, and irritable. My heart was hurting, and negative thoughts were cascading through my mind. I was afraid of unwanted outcomes in my business and resistant to the demands of parenting and all my responsibilities in general. Candace was attempting to support me, but I sure wasn't making it easy. I was trying to hold back my blame from going toward her, but I was so stuck in victim story that I couldn't help it from oozing out.

I was particularly enraged about our broken tiles in our bathroom. They'd been broken for over a month. Water could be getting underneath when we showered, which could cause a bigger problem that I'd have to pay for. We taped the tiles down with painter's tape because our three-year-old wanted to take them and run off with them. Every day, he'd make multiple attempts to peel the tape off to get at the tile treasures.

Candace was lovingly pointing out that the way I was relating to the situation was what was making me so upset. But I was so deep in it; I felt a strong urge to defend my anger. I was justified, dang it! This situation is objectively agitating! Anyone would feel angry about this! I'm allowed to have my feelings!

And then I had a fascinating thought—it's possible for someone to be in this exact scenario and *not* feel upset. I sat with that for a minute, seeing the truth of it. But, I'm angry because of the broken tile and Arman's behavior! Is it possible for the tile to be broken and Arman to be pulling tape off and for me to not feel upset?

And then something magical happened. Right there, in the midst of my intense discomfort and agitation, I realized that I'm not upset because of the tile situation. I'm upset because of the way I'm being with that situation. I'm upset because I'm demanding it be a certain way, which it's not, and fighting against reality.

I'm also upset about it because I'm looking for an outlet to discharge my upset. I'm already agitated in my nervous system from holding a dozen things from that day as if they were life and death. This amped up my body, created tension, and left me looking for an external reason to blame for my upset in the moment.

Then, I started laughing. I felt a wave of relief and joy. I was so amused at myself and my attempts to cling to being upset. In an instant, I let go, and my upset about the tile melted away. I wasn't trying to be more patient; I simply felt neutral about the whole thing. There were some broken tiles, and we were going to get them fixed. We had painter's tape on them, and Arman liked to peel it off.

The shift was so sudden and so effortless that it became an incredibly valuable metaphor for me. When I am upset in other situations, I now consciously draw upon the tile experience. I remind myself that my upset is not in the situation but in how I'm relating to the situation.

The same is true for the upset caused by perfectionism. It's possible for you to be giving a presentation, going on a date, or doing anything else that you used to feel intense pressure about and instead feel relaxed and happy. Yes, even in that high-stakes situation! The stress, pressure, tension, and drama is internal. It's in the way you're holding it. Even if other people are all worked up and stressed about it, even if it involves large amounts of money, people's welfare, or other seemingly significant outcomes, you do not need to be tense inside. Isn't that liberating? When you get it, it's positively delightful.

But perhaps you're not quite on board yet. You doubt that letting go is possible, or you might see it as irresponsible or somehow dangerous to do so. Here's the thing to realize: letting go of your inner freakout doesn't mean you stop taking effective action to bring about your desired results. It doesn't mean I let Arman peel the tape off and bury the tiles in the backyard. It doesn't mean you don't prepare at all for your sales presentation and show up hungover. It just means you are more relaxed inside as you do what's most effective.

And, as counterintuitive as it might seem, when you let go of your upset about the situation, you get way better outcomes. When you don't desperately need them to say yes to your sales offer, you sell more. When you don't need this person to like you or else, they are more attracted to you. As the old saying goes— desperation is not sexy.

Guess what happened the night after I let go of my tile-rage? Arman completely stopped going after the tape and the tiles. I kid you not. He went from trying to peel it off at least four times per day to completely ignoring it. It was a beautiful demonstration of how, when we let go, not only do we instantly feel better inside, but we affect the world around us.

Unwinding perfectionism is an ongoing process. It involves catching that pattern as it is winding up and consciously choosing a different track. Here are the steps in that process that you will repeat many, many times.

Five Steps to Free Yourself From Perfectionism

I suggest you practice this process with all the ways you tend to be perfectionistic, but not all at once as that can be overwhelming and unproductive. You can't perfectly resolve your perfectionism, faster, quicker, better, and more permanently than everyone else! Unless, of course, you find that Orb of Power. Have you heard of it?

The best way to engage with this process is to pick one particular form of perfectionism that you're currently engaging in and go through the process while focusing on that. Let's see what that is right now. In this moment, what pressure are you feeling to make things different or better than they are?

Take a moment to slow down, focusing on your breath for a few moments. Notice if you're squeezing or tensing in your face, jaw, or the area around your eyes. As you breathe in and out, relax these areas, and let more air move into your chest and stomach. What do you feel in your throat, chest, and stomach? Do you feel squeezing, grasping, aching, tension, or pressure? What are you grasping for or resisting right now?

What is your mind telling you that you need to achieve or complete before you can relax and feel at peace? What do you have to change or fix in yourself or the world around you? What is "wrong" with you that you need to resolve?

Another way to uncover what perfectionistic stress is impacting your life is to ask yourself: What's causing me the most suffering in my life right now? Is it your job or work life? Something in your health? A relationship issue with a friend, spouse, partner, or one of your children?

Great, now that you have something, let's work through the process. The good news is you've already done one of the five steps!

Step 1: Feel Bad

The first step in the process is to notice when we're suffering and slow down to acknowledge it. With the demands of day-to-day life combined with our frantic quest for glory, we can barrel through large portions of our day, week, and life. Sure, we don't feel all that great inside, but I gotta get this stuff done and don't have too much time to sit around and feel things.

When we do have downtime, we fill it with TV, games, social media, scrolling, rich foods, drugs and alcohol, and other methods to stay ahead of our feelings.

Step 1 simply requires us to look inward with curiosity and compassion. How am I doing right now? Am I feeling good or hurting inside? Am I suffering right now? Am I having fun?

When in the grips of perfectionism, the answer will be yes, you're suffering and hurting inside, and no, you're not having fun. Once you see that, that's success! You're well on your way to liberation.

Step 2: Identify the Demand

Ask yourself this: What internal demand is creating my upset?

When we're suffering, we want something to be different in our lives. We may want something unpleasant to stop or change, or we may feel desire to achieve or experience something else.

We compare ourselves or our life circumstances to some idea in our minds and then say that we or life should be different. Instead of this being a preference that we hold lightly, we contract inside with an internal demand. We use words like "should" or "must" or "have to." All of these mean the same thing in this case and indicate a sense of pressure, urgency, or necessity.

See if you can identify the real expectation you have for yourself or your life, even if it's unrealistic, absurd, or you'd be embarrassed about other people knowing this. In other words, don't worry about "looking good" as you inquire within. This isn't about anyone else, and you don't even need to share this with anybody. Part of the trap of perfectionism is that we feel we must not only look perfect to others, but we have to look perfect to ourselves as well. This self-delusion keeps us trapped even longer. To break free fast, we have to be totally honest with ourselves.

For example, when I tune into that grasping, craving energy in me that wants to achieve this certain body ideal, it says something like this:

I must have a rock hard, lean stomach with no fat on it.

I must have a narrow waist, wide shoulders, and muscular defined arms.

When you are exploring the inner demand, you'll know you're on the right track when you feel an intensification of your grasping as you name it. It's like the perfectionistic part lights up and says, "Yes, yes! That's right! We do need to achieve that exact thing!"

Let's take a moment now to see what it is for you. What is the inner demand you have for yourself? Here are just a few that I've heard from clients in different areas of life. They may help shed light on what your expectation is for yourself:

I have to be productive every moment of my day.

I should never get upset with my children and never raise my voice.

I should only eat healthy, "clean" foods.

I have to look fashionable, beautiful, sexy, or "just right" for every occasion.

I should be able to approach any woman in any setting and charm her so much that she gives me her phone number and wants to date me.

(That last example is not only one I've heard from numerous clients, but one I experienced during my dating days).

Don't strain too hard to figure it out and get it right. Just get curious and allow whatever comes to you. This process is less left-brain intellectual and much more centered in your heart and intuition. For now, just pick the biggest pressure, demand, or expectation you feel in this area and go with that.

As you do this process more, you'll become better and better at quickly identifying the internal demands. You'll also discover that all of them spring forth from your 'Fantasy Self' and are attempts to push or drive you to become that perfect version of you that will never feel pain and only feel love, acceptance, and all things good.

Step 3: Uncover Your Pride Positions

Underneath your "must," "should," or "have to," there is something called a pride position. This is an incredibly valuable concept that I learned from the brilliant psychoanalyst Theodore Rubin. A pride position is the aspect of our "Fantasy Self" that we reach toward to feel pride in ourselves. It's the way that we want to be that will allow us to feel proud, good enough, and maybe even superior.

For example, my pride position when it comes to fitness is one I call *Ultra Fit Man*. *Ultra Fit Man* is incredibly muscular, has that coveted v-shape with broad shoulders and a narrow waist. He has excellent posture, washboard abs, and zero belly fat, even down at the bottom of his abdomen. He runs incredible distances, further and faster than most. Friends and strangers alike can't match his physique or abilities, and they are both impressed and envious. They feel in awe of him and slightly inferior about themselves.

That one is amusing and slightly embarrassing to write about. But that's how these pride positions are. Here's another one I uncovered a while back. When I first started doing more public speaking, I had the pride position that I call *Speaker Extraordinaire*. *Speaker Extraordinaire* is, as you might guess, an amazing speaker. He is confident, articulate, charming, and funny. He is so compelling and dynamic, so good that people are entranced as he speaks. They can't help but focus on him, and they never feel a moment of boredom, distraction, or desire to be anywhere else other than following along with his every word.

I love writing these out. I am so amused by that one. That's a sign of letting go and liberation—when you are able to articulate these pride positions and feel amusement and love for yourself. But I'm getting ahead of myself here. Let's stay with Step 3.

Let me share one more so you can get a sense of what these look and sound like. Then, we'll help you identify your own. This last one I call *Dr. Aziz, Super-Coach*. This one became strong in me once I started practicing therapy and stayed with me for the first handful of years in my coaching career as well. *Dr. Aziz, Super-Coach*, can transform anyone in one conversation. He is so smart, skilled, and awesome that he can take someone from anxiety, depression, or low confidence and instantly help them feel confident, powerful, optimistic, courageous, and ready for any action, no matter how big or how bold.

These are insane, aren't they? And yet, I held onto that one for years. My goodness, how stressful and impossible it all was. But it can sometimes be hard to see our insanity when we're in it. That's why this exercise can be so liberating—because it makes the entire process conscious so you can see through the futility of these pursuits.

Can you see how each of these examples has me being super-human? That's why Dr. Theodore Rubin called these pride positions because we derive a sense of pride from imagining that we are this way (or someday could be). As crazy as it sounds, we somehow convince ourselves that we are this mega-amazing person, and we derive a pseudo-sense of pride from it. Days or weeks may go by when we perceive ourselves living up to this ideal standard, and feel a sense of accomplishment, pride, and superiority to others.

Of course, when reality shows us that we aren't that person (i.e., my audience isn't completely enraptured when I speak, and there are people in the back looking at their cell phones and yawning—*how dare they?!*); we then feel an onslaught of self-hatred. Our critics pounce on us, cataloging our fall from grace and this pride position.

Then comes the relentless campaign of demands to do better, fix it, try harder, and do whatever it takes to make ourselves become this pride position again. We can also settle into a state of resignation in which we imagine we'll never achieve this pride position. There we reside in a perpetual state of self-rejection, disliking who we are and feeling hopeless about our lives.

My question for you is, what pride position is underneath your inner demand? What is your version of "perfect" in whatever situation you're examining? Take a few moments now to flush that part out and get a sense of it. You'll notice that I named my pride positions, which helps give me a sense of this caricature aspect of my Fantasy Self. Other common pride positions that I've seen in myself, family members, friends, and clients include:

The Saint: Totally loving, giving, and always generous with money, time, and attention. Able to forgive and let go, not be upset or resentful, and otherwise operate with Jesus-like levels of peace and love.

Supermom: Able to do everything and be everything to everyone all at once. Present and loving with her children and family, on it with her career and work responsibilities, and keeping a clean and orderly house as well. Oh, not to mention time for friends, exercise, and whatever else anyone asks of her.

The Perfected Human: Having overcome all past pain, problems, and emotional challenges, this perfect specimen is always highly productive, creative, and successful at any endeavor. Always knows what to say, speaks up with authority, and carries self with total self-assured confidence and poise.

Mr./Ms. Irresistible: So interesting, charming, funny, smart, witty, and socially confident that this person is *never* rejected. Never. Not in love, dating, business, or friendships. Always desired, always sought after, always loved.

This list could go on for pages, but hopefully, these samples give you a general idea of the kinds of pride positions we're talking about here. They can range across any aspect of your life experience, from dating and relationships to career and business, to aging, beauty, and physical health.

Take a few moments now to think about one of your pride positions. What role do you demand yourself to be, and what are the qualities of this character? How do other people respond to him or her? This aspect is part of the pride position, as well. Others usually view this amazing perfected version of ourselves with awe, respect, love, or envy. What would you call this pride position? What name comes to mind for this character?

I was guiding my wife through this process last night after our boys went to sleep. She had a particularly challenging day that required 40,000 acts of patience, surrender, and finding her way back to love despite agitating behaviors, conflict, and whatever else our boys cooked up. As is often the case, from my perspective, she handles things incredibly well and is truly the most loving and patient human I know.

But in her mind, it's different. She catalogs the moments where she fell short, wasn't creative enough, playful enough, patient, or loving enough, how she could have done things better, how she needs to be more unconditionally loving. Whew! Sound exhausting? It sure is. Perfectionism is a heavy burden to bear.

As we explored her underlying pride position, she came up with *The Unconditionally Loving Mother*. This person is completely loving and patient in every moment, no matter what is happening. She handles all problems and conflict with creativity, playful energy, and sweetness. She never gets upset, even if one son pushes the other down and stomps on his back, then runs away laughing about it. Or if one of the boys pokes her in her privates in the kitchen and yells "Boop!" and laughs. She handles these moments with grace and unconditional love. Oh, and she never feels fed up, wants to escape, or uses her phone as a method of distraction or coping.

Sound reasonable? It certainly doesn't.

So what do we do now that you've uncovered this pride position? Before we move on to the next step, I want to ask you, how does it feel to flush this unconscious expectation out a bit more? Do you find it relieving? Does something about the impossibility of its extreme demand help you begin to let go of the insane pressure to be this way?

Step 4: Surrender Your Pride Positions

"Surrender is the ultimate life skill."

- Christian Mickelsen

A most profound and joyous thing happens when you let go of the pressure to become your pride positions. You may experience this right now as you read through this five-step process, or it may happen later as you work with this approach over the next days and weeks to come. All of a sudden, you'll feel free. You'll discover that all this pressure, pain, and suffering is unnecessary. It's completely self-generated and something that you can choose to stop doing. And nothing bad will happen. Your world won't crumble, and everything will be okay. In reality, everything will become magnificently better because not only will you feel the daily joy that comes from truly being on your own side, and bask in a greater sense of shared love for yourself and others, but you'll also notice a significant improvement in all the external circumstances in your life.

To surrender your pride position, start by asking yourself— what would it mean if I wasn't (insert your pride position name here)? If I wasn't this perfected human being, or *Supermom*, or whatever your position is. Who would you be? What would you be like?

For example, what would it mean about me if I wasn't *Ultra Fit Man*? What if I was just Kinda Fit Guy? I like to run, workout, and move my body because it feels good, and I'm naturally drawn to do it. I generally eat healthy because it makes me feel high energy and happy, but I don't eat "perfectly" 100% of the time. I'm pretty muscular and lean because of my lifestyle, but I'm not "rock hard." I have some fat on my belly. I sometimes slump in my posture. I sometimes push through and do hard workouts or long runs. And sometimes I take a break, be lazy, or decide not to run a certain distance or race.

As I write that, it sounds delightful, and I feel a sense of relief, peace, and happiness. But that's because I recently surrendered my pride position of *Ultra Fit Man* (thanks to writing this book! Thanks to you!). But before I'd surrendered this pride position, I felt a lot of resistance to this idea of not being this perfected version of myself when it comes to fitness.

So, who would you be if you weren't your pride position? Just say out loud, or in a journal, what comes to your mind now. What do you feel as you describe this more realistic version of yourself? Relief? Joy? Love? Fear? Resistance? Tension?

If you're feeling mostly positive feelings, that's a sign you're ready to let go. But if you're feeling a lot of tension and resistance, that's a sign that part of you is not quite ready to let go yet. Inside, you may experience a lot of fear about relaxing your death grip on being this amazing person. You might think: *if I don't pressure myself and brutally strive to become this version of me, then that's awful! Something terrible will happen to me or others. I won't be good enough or worthy of love or respect!*

In your mind, it can feel unacceptable to "give up" on this expectation because it is essential that you be this way. To not be that way is bad, wrong, gross, or otherwise unlovable. This grasping attachment is why we have this pride position in the first place.

The way to soften our grip and start to let go is to remember that letting go doesn't mean giving up, not trying, or doing the complete opposite. It doesn't mean you completely unravel, break all your own values and morals, and become an uncontrollable juggernaut of depravity and exploitation who is reviled by all.

Instead, it means you humble yourself and acknowledge the reality of what it means to be a human. You are not superhuman, better than everyone else, or an unflinching machine. You get tired, or upset, or down, or anxious, or reactive, or whatever. Maybe you aren't so much different or better than everyone else, after all. And that's okay! It turns out we're all in this together, and you can relax and just be you–all of you.

Be the you that is brilliant and funny and lights up the room. Be the you that gets so fired up and passionate about things that you can't stop thinking or talking about them. Be the you that wasn't assertive when it would have been optimal to do so, and now you have to go back and clean up that mess. Be the you that crushes it at work sometimes and has a space cadet day other times where you can't seem to get anything done. Be the you that loves generously and is creative, funny, and playful with your kids, family, or other loved ones. And be the you that gets tired, cranky, and sometimes says hurtful things to those you love most. Be that you–all of you.

What's happening for you right now as you read this? Think about your pride position that you're working with. How attached do you feel to *needing* yourself to be this way, to appear this way to yourself and others? On a scale of 0-10, how much are you holding onto this position (10 being grasping that sucker so tight your knuckles are turning white, 0 being you are at peace with just being you, not needing to be anything else, or prove anything at all to anyone, including yourself)?

Whatever your number is, that's okay. Just breathe and relax. You can't force this process. You can't perfectly let go of your perfectionism! Just notice where you feel that tightness or constriction in your body, that resistance to letting go, that internal "noooooo!" to the idea of just dropping the whole mess and not having to worry about it all so much.

It's okay to let go of this pride position. It's safe. You're safe. Underneath all that tension and grasping is a reservoir of feelings that you've been avoiding – the pain or hurt or misunderstanding of that little girl or boy inside, the one who didn't fit in when you were in high school, the one who got mercilessly picked on for being fat or darker-skinned or different, or the one who was repeatedly chastised unfairly by a parent who was not emotionally aware or mature enough to see they were taking out their unresolved feelings on you. Whatever the incidents might have been, it's only feelings there now. And you can feel all your feelings. It's safe to feel your feelings. You can hold that little girl or boy with love and curiosity, saying, "show me everything you got. I'm not going anywhere."

The more willing you are to feel anything and everything, the more swiftly your pressure to uphold your pride position dissolves. All this perfectionism is just a defense against feeling. When you are ready, willing, and able to feel whatever's in your heart and body, then your need for the defense evaporates.

When you've let go of your need to become this pride position, you will feel a shift inside. Instead of the fear, pressure, and frantic energy that usually accompanies these demands, you'll feel a sense of space, peace, and stillness inside. You may still like the outcome or goal that your pride position is demanding you achieve. You may even keep working toward it. But overall, there is a feeling of acceptance—it's okay, and you're okay. You're okay if you are this super version of you at times, and you're okay if you're not. You're okay, no matter what. You're worthy, no matter what.

Step 5: Surrender to All Outcomes

"A person often meets his destiny on the road he took to avoid it."

- Jean de La Fontaine

One of the main reasons we don't want to let go of our pride position is the fear that if we do, we will stop achieving or progressing and become a complete slug. We will not achieve or accomplish anything of merit, lose all motivation and willpower, and settle into a life of listless inadequacy. Worse still, others will see that we're not all that great after all. We're certainly not worthy of all that admiration, respect, or even love. We're just some lazy nobody worth nothin'.

All of this is not true, of course.

But perfectionism is just another form of anxiety. And anxious thoughts are not known to be the most accurate predictors of reality.

As you'll discover in the next chapter, there is a vastly superior way to motivate yourself to achieve all kinds of amazing things in your life, none of which require fear, inner pressure, or self-hatred. But before we get into that, we have to surrender even further.

Swapping our motivation fuel from perfectionism to something else is not the complete solution. Underneath, if we're still striving to achieve our worth and prove something, it doesn't matter what fuel we're using; we're still going down the wrong road.

Instead, we experience the deepest level of freedom from perfectionism and inner criticism when we are willing to surrender to any outcome that life might give us. Here are a few examples:

To surrender the pride position of *Ultra Fit Man*, I need to face the outcome that part of me is the most afraid of. In this case, it's the fear that I'll get soft, my belly will stick out, and I will be seen as lazy, not worthy of respect, not sexy or desirable, and otherwise bad. In this case, the way out is to acknowledge the potential reality of me being pudgy or having more belly fat. I take a moment to focus on that reality and say, "Yes. It's okay if this happens. I'm worthy if I have more fat on my belly or less fat on my belly. I'm worthy, no matter what." If I feel inner resistance or tension when I say this, then I find that part inside of me that is resisting and fighting this outcome, fearing it, clenching against it, and I soften and relax this part. I breathe into the tension and send unconditional love and acceptance to this part of me.

My wife Candace has the *Unconditionally Loving Mother* pride position, remember? In her case, her greatest fear is that if she isn't this way, then she'll be a "bad" mother and her children will be "damaged" by her treatment, struggling in their lives with poor choices, unwise actions, difficulty in relationships, and a deep sense of inadequacy. So in her case, the thing to surrender to is the potential reality in which one or both of her boys struggles with feelings of low self-worth and challenges in their life and relationships.

What is it for you? What is the unacceptable potential reality that you are fighting against? Can you let go and surrender to the simple truth that this could happen and that you would be okay if it did? Could you choose to love yourself even if that were to occur? Do you have the power to acknowledge and know your unconditional worth, no matter what happens?

This doesn't mean that you are hoping for this worst-case scenario and eagerly anticipating it. It just means you relax your terrified (and completely ineffective) attempt to play God and control all outcomes in your life.

Of course, as is often the case in this beautiful and magical life, surrendering to unwanted outcomes is a paradox. When you are internally fighting against a certain outcome, unwilling for it to happen, and slamming yourself with pressure to be perfect to ensure it never, ever happens, guess what? It's more likely to happen!

But when you let go and stop trying to force things to happen "out there" by squeezing your internal organs and hating yourself, something delightful happens. You feel more energy, vitality, creativity, and joy. When I stop trying to be *Ultra Fit Man* and surrender into being Kinda Fit Guy, I find more joy in running and working out. When it's more joyful, guess what I want to do more of?

When Candace stops being so hard on herself, she says to herself, "Whew! These little rascals. Yeah, I get irritated and burnt out sometimes and want to check my phone and get away. Of course, I feel that way!" When she stops hating herself for not being that perfect mother who should always be loving and flexible and creative, guess what happens? She naturally feels better about herself and more self-love. And when she feels more love for herself, she ends up feeling more loving and having more energy to be flexible and creative!

So what outcomes are you resisting, and what will happen in your life if you surrender to the possibility that this might happen, knowing you'll be okay even if they do, that you'll be okay, no matter what?

Two Paths in a Wood

This process of noticing when you are driving yourself with perfectionism, catching it, uncovering the underlying pride positions, and surrendering them is just that—a process. It's not something that you nail on your first attempt, surrendering perfectly once and for all, thus achieving permanent freedom and happiness. That's just perfectionism sneaking in the back door, trying to once again avoid the wholeness and messiness of human life and emotions.

The process is more like walking along a path in the woods. You might have been walking for some time before you notice that something isn't right. The ground is lumpy, brambles are scraping your legs, branches are slapping across your face, and a squirrel has its teeth buried into your ankle. *How long has that thing been there? Why am I on this path? Isn't there a better way?*

No! Your mind replies. *Life isn't all fun, ease, penny cakes, and moon candies. Shut up and keep going. Goggins this sh*t.* And so you keep going, pressing on with your head down, legs bleeding from the bramble scrapes, and dragging that tenacious forest creature with each step.

And then, you remember something. Something that delights you, makes you smile, and you start to laugh out loud. You take ten steps over to your left, and there's another path, going the same way. This path is in the sunshine. It's clear, open, spacious, and bright. There are no brambles, no branches, and no angry forest creatures attacking you. You can move forward with ease and joy.

The first path in this metaphor is the path of perfectionism. It's hard, strenuous, and generally unfun. Yet we persist on this path by telling ourselves that this the only way, that we "must" do it this way. We must live out our pride position and become our superhuman Fantasy Self. It's the only way!

The second path is the path of O.M.O.S. It's open, bright, spacious, and full of love. And it's way more fun. As I've walked this path more and more in the last few years, I've realized that if I'm engaging in any process with a "grit-my-teeth and white-knuckle it for a bit longer" attitude, then I'm on the wrong path. In other words, if it's "awful," you're not doing it right.

This doesn't mean your goals are all wrong, you need to change jobs or careers, or completely reorganize your life. It might just mean that the way you are approaching your life is way more stressful, harsh, and serious than it needs to be. It's possible to be going in the same direction, pursuing the same dreams in a way that is relaxed and joyful.

At first, the idea of getting off the brutal path of perfectionism seems scary, hard, or dangerous. Those first few times off can feel unsettling or risky. But eventually, when you see that life doesn't crumble, loved ones don't leave you, and your career and livelihood don't melt away like sandcastles in the sea, then you become willing to get off that perfectionism path much more readily.

The next level is to see how quickly you can identify when you're on that path and quickly hop over to O.M.O.S. Then, you learn how to sustain walking on that O.M.O.S. path for longer and longer periods of time. This might sound easy, especially if the path is full of spaciousness, love, and fun. But remember, the human experience is the full catastrophe. This path is one of an open heart that feels love, joy, and fun, as well as inevitable hurt, pain, and loss. This is the path of the unguarded heart, and it requires a courageous spirit and a willingness to be a warrior of the heart.

So, my dear friend, when you notice yourself on that path of perfectionism, remember that just a few feet away is another path

This path not only feels way better and allows you to enjoy your life now; it also leads you to all the amazing things you want in your life much faster!

Does that sound far-fetched or too good to be true? I used to think that too until I discovered a method to pursue expansive goals, to move beyond my perceived limits, and do the impossible, and enjoy incredible achievement, all while using self-love and other forms of optimal fuel. This is what I now call "The Art of Relaxed Discipline," and what I'm going to teach you in the next chapter.

Chapter 12:
Optimal Motivation and
the Art of Relaxed Discipline

"The Tao does nothing yet leaves nothing undone."
- *Tao Te Ching* by Lao Tzu

"I like your idea of O.M.O.S., and when I practice it, I definitely feel better," said my client, "but when I look at guys who achieved the highest levels of peak performance like Michael Jordan or David Goggins, I don't think they're doing this. I mean, I don't think they're saying to themselves that it's okay whether they win or lose, and they love themselves no matter what. They're telling themselves it's completely unacceptable to lose and drive themselves hard to make the impossible happen."

I love this question. This client was a high-level athlete, and he desired to be best in his sport. He doubted whether O.M.O.S. and self-love were enough to get him to where he wanted to be. We had quite an interesting discussion about it in a Mastermind call. If you'd like to hear a segment of it, you can find it at www.omosbook.com.

But isn't that the main fear for all of us? Even if we aren't gunning for a number one standing in a sport, we share this concern that easing up on ourselves will lead to a reduction in our drive, motivation, and accomplishment.

We feel confident that we can achieve a certain amount using the methods we've been using, and we fear making a change that might jeopardize this. You might not trust that O.M.O.S. can help you achieve. Perhaps you imagine that you have two choices—to push hard with perfectionism and self-dissatisfaction to achieve the goals and glory you seek or to get on your own side and give up on all those goals, settle into a small, boring, accomplishment-free life.

Fortunately, this is not a choice you have to make! As you'll see in this chapter, pursuing big dreams, creating amazing outcomes, and doing the impossible is all achievable using O.M.O.S. In fact, you'll discover that your critic has tricked you with yet another inversion of the truth. Rather than stopping your progress, being on your own side will help you achieve even more, faster, while enjoying the process.

What? Is this even possible? Now we're just talking fairy tales, aren't we?

No, I assure you; this is possible. I have spent the last several years making a deep study of this new way of being, extensively testing it with my clients and myself. The results have been delightful and inspiring. I can't wait to share more with you now.

DIRTY FUEL

Let's say you were about to start a new job. During your orientation day, your boss is sharing how she plans to teach you the essentials of your role, help you understand how to do the work, and motivate you during long projects or other challenging tasks.

"Okay," she begins. "First, before you do something, I'll tell you that you can't do it well and that you'll probably fail. I'll also tell you that it would be horrible to fail and that something awful will happen if you do. This will jack up your stress hormones and give you a ton of energy. Trust me; this technique is awesome — you won't ever need coffee again."

"Then, I'll regularly point out what you're doing wrong and all the ways you're falling short. Many times per day, I'll swing by your desk to fill you in on how you're not doing enough and remind you how bad and dangerous that is."

"To inspire you, I'll tell you that maybe you can overcome your messed up nature and somehow achieve some greatness in this life. You might be able to make top salesperson or get promoted to the head of this division. To motivate you toward these goals, I'll make you feel awful and incomplete inside, reminding you daily that you're not worth anything until you achieve it. This, you see, will give you a relentless drive to achieve your goal, because you'll feel so terrible until you do. Any questions?"

"No, this all makes great sense to me and sounds healthy and effective. Sign me up!"

It's pretty crazy when you hear it described out loud like this, yet this is the approach most people use inside with themselves. They use fear of loss, pain, or "bad outcomes" to jolt themselves into cortisol-fueled action. They can add even more boost to the fuel by imagining shame or public humiliation on top of those bad outcomes. Friends, family, parents, colleagues, or respected mentors would all think less of you if they found out about your failure, lack of achievement of your goal, and your general ineptitude. Boom! Now you're in motion.

Yes, this does work. In a purely mechanical sense, it gets the engine running and the vehicle moving forward. But what are the costs of this kind of motivation? What impact does it have on the "engine," which in this case is you? How does it impact your mind, body, and heart?

In addition to fear, the other main component of the fuel

most people use is the worthiness carrot. They utilize a conditional sense of self-worth as a form of leverage to get themselves moving. A sense of self-worth and all the good feelings associated with loving yourself get shot out into the future. It's the reward you'll get to feel once you've achieved the goal. Each time you take successful action toward your goal, you dole out a tiny teaser of self-worth, giving you a taste of what it will be like once you hit that amazing target.

Again, this does work, at least sort of. Feeling empty or unworthy of love is extremely painful, and you will often become highly motivated to get out of that state of pain. But what are the costs of this? What is the impact on you to feel unworthy much of the time before you achieve your goal? What happens if you don't make progress that day? Let's say you don't make those sales calls, handle those tasks at work, or make it to the gym? *Then I berate myself for being a pathetic loser and threaten myself until I promise to do it tomorrow, extra hard.*

Of course, the story you tell yourself is that this is all temporary. As soon as you achieve that target, accomplish that goal, become that person, then you'll feel happy forever. Hurray! You'll feel powerful, accomplished, admirable, lovable, worthy, and sexy. You'll be way more relaxed, calm, stress-free, and happy. Soon, but not now. Now, it's back to self-hatred and stress, which is obviously the path to love and happiness.

This is all starting to sound pretty dismal, isn't it? Isn't there a better way? Of course, there is, and not only do you know this, but you already know what it is and how to do it. It's O.M.O.S.! But the main obstacle here is not how to apply the new strategy; it's in your fear of letting your old strategy go. This can create resistance or unwillingness to switch over. To help aid in that transition, let's take a look at what dirty fuel does for you.

Check Engine

What happens if you use dirty fuel in a car? For fun, I decided to do a little online research, and I came across an article called "Symptoms of a Failing Fuel Filter." Bingo. Your fuel filter keeps debris and dirt out of your engine, so everything runs smoothly. If your fuel filter gets all gunked up, then your engine starts running on dirty fuel. Here are some of the symptoms. Check to see if any of them sound familiar for you—not for your car, but for your mind and body.

1. Car Is Hard to Start

Sometimes a spike of cortisol wakes you up or gets you out of bed, charged up, and ready to attack the problems of the day. But eventually, after you've done this long enough, it doesn't work so well. Rather, you can find it hard to get up, waking up tired even after a full night of sleep. You also may find it hard to start the engine when it comes to your work tasks, or workout, or whatever project you've been running dirty fuel on for a while. You try to use fear or self-hatred (a.k.a. jam the gas), but the engine just revs and sputters. You've got nothing left.

2. Misfires or Hesitations

When you press the gas, instead of responding, your mind and body are slower to respond. This can be a literal slowing down of your body and movements or a sense of delay in your thoughts and actions. Instead of hopping on that task and getting it done, there's a lot more inner resistance, fatigue, or other discomfort to push through before you can do it. This leads to delays between the inner command and you getting it done.

3. Stalling

Stalling in a vehicle is when your engine randomly stops. We used to have an old beat-up Chrysler Concorde that would sometimes stall when you were idling at a stoplight. All of a sudden, the wheel would lock up so you couldn't steer, and everything would go dead. As far as your human engine, it's unlikely that your body drops to the floor like a sack of potatoes as you lose consciousness while you're walking down the hall in your office. If that's happening, you may have some bigger fish to fry. In this case, stalling more so refers to sitting at your desk, knowing you have all this work to do, and you just sit there, staring at the papers on your desk, doing nothing. Maybe you try to open something on your computer, but all you're able to do is open a new browser to go to some mindless distraction website. Hours go by. You've stalled out.

4. Decrease in Power and Acceleration

This one is extremely common. After a period of time, you don't have much pep in your step. Even imagining achieving your goal doesn't give you much juice like it used to. You're still making progress, plodding forward, but it's far from energetic or enthusiastic. Even if you needed to jam the gas for a short sprint or burst, it's doubtful you'd even be able to get much more speed out of you right now. You're not totally burnt out, but you're not lit up either. You're in that grey zone. Your job, your relationships, your fitness, your friendships, your hobbies are all sorta grey and meh. Nothing is all that exciting or joyful right now. But you just keep going, staying on track, because what else are you going to do? Stop? That's not an option.

How's your engine doing these days? What symptoms can you relate to? Some or all of them? I know that when I'm running dirty fuel for weeks on end, I'll start to notice these symptoms showing up. Slowly at first, but eventually, they become undeniable and significantly impact my mood, performance, and general enjoyment of life.

So, to summarize, the key kinds of dirty fuel you'll want to watch out for in your life are:

Fear: Using fear of failure, catastrophic outcomes, humiliation, and imagined judgment.

Conditional Worthiness: You don't feel worthy yet, but when you achieve X, you'll finally become good enough, worthy of love and respect, and finally "be somebody."

Future Relief/Happiness: You just have to get through this and get to X. Then everything will be different. You'll be relaxed, spacious, confident, and happy.

Good Ol' Fashioned Self-Hatred: Your critic disparages and berates you, shaming you into action. (i.e., "Your body is disgusting. Get to the gym, you fat slob," or "You're so lazy! What's wrong with you? You have to be way more productive today at work!")

Imagine you had a warning light on your internal dashboard that went off whenever you were using one of these forms of motivation. It was a little orange light that said: DF. This stands for dirty fuel, and it is there to remind you that you're now using an unsustainable form of fuel that will have consequences both sooner and later.

Of course, you may be wondering, *so what do I do instead? I mean, stop using fear, conditional worthiness, and self-hatred? What else is there, man? That's all I got!*

Not to worry, my friend. That's exactly what we will discover in the next section.

Cartoon by Travis Kotzebue 2019

HIGH-QUALITY FUEL

So how do we motivate ourselves in ways that help us stay engaged, enthusiastic, and productive? How do we burn clean fuel so that we can keep going, keep enjoying ourselves, and play whatever games we're playing for the long haul? Let's explore some kinds of high-quality fuel now.

Interest/Fascination

> "Learning is the human activity that least needs manipulation by others. Most learning is not the result of instruction. It is rather the result of unhampered participation in a meaningful activity."
>
> - Ivan Illich

This morning, after I got back from the gym, I crawled into our family bed. The rest of my family had slept in until 6:45 a.m. and was just starting to wake up in the early morning light filtering through the curtains. My son Zaim stretched his body and yawned.

"Daddy," he whispered.

"Yeah?" I said.

"That eight-eight indestructible creature with flying that makes all your other cards indestructible." He whispered.

I laughed. "Yeah?"

"Remember that card?" he said.

"Yeah, I remember that card," I replied.

"Yeah," he said, stretching again.

Magic the Gathering was the first thought in his mind upon waking. The night before, his last thought before he went to sleep was about the magic cards we were reading about in a book. To say he is fascinated by this card game would be an understatement.

He has an insatiable desire to study, learn, explore, imagine, think about, and play Magic. While we walk somewhere, eat, or do chores in the house, he'll say, "Ask me a Magic question." Then, I'll ask him something about the game that gets him to think, learn, do math, or solve strategy questions.

There's no forced "math time" where I try to get him to do his homework. I'm not forcing him to do anything. I'm paying attention to the flame of his interest and nurturing that flame, feeding it as much as I can reasonably tolerate each day.

The same goes for you and me. When you get interested in something, I mean fascinated by it, then the motivation that springs forth is endless. You don't need to force anything, make yourself do something, or push anything. You just want to. Your heart lights up when you think about learning more. You want to study on your lunch breaks. You think about it when you're walking somewhere, eating, or doing chores around the house.

The challenge for many people is their fascination is being misspent on things that don't serve them. They are letting their minds get filled with random inputs dozens or hundreds of times per day—random news stories from their phones, computers, TV, or the radio. The ongoing drama of who said what about who in the political, arts and entertainment, or business sectors. The tragedies and calamities of the hour from across the globe. And that's just on the way to work!

Then, throughout the day, we continuously ingest thousands of ideas, messages, and images from the internet, scrolling social media, listening to this, watching that. We do this all day long. We hunger for it and get addicted to consumption. When we first wake up, we grab our phones and start ingesting this morning's random information. While on the toilet or during a break, we're scrolling, scrolling, looking, poking, grasping. We are interested in, fascinated, and obsessed with all this input and can't put it down.

But now, we've tied up all our interest and fascination in this insatiable wormhole. We have nothing left to invest in something else. Our minds are too full of other stuff; our consciousness is too cluttered.

This incessant, mindless interaction with our tech is dirty fuel. We're desperately grasping at dopamine to stimulate our numbing nervous system. It's time to slow down and take a step back. As an act of O.M.O.S., try a one-week or 30-day media fast. Don't look at news feeds, headlines, or your Twitter feed.

I offered this as a challenge to people in the second level of my Mastermind program: A 30-day media fast. I'd done this over two years ago and noticed such a profound shift in my life that it turned into a permanent fast. On the call, I encouraged one of the members who was especially hooked on social media to test this out. We turned it into an invitation for the entire group, and many of the members decided to join in.

The results were amazing. At first, as you might expect, it was challenging. Some of the group members realized how addicted they were to these habits of distraction and misplaced fascination. But when they didn't feed the beast, and they stopped inputting endless amounts of volatile, disturbing, or emotionally charged information, something miraculous happened. They started to feel more alive.

More vitality and presence for their natural interests started to emerge. One group member had the mental space and focus to take a course that would greatly help him in his business. He not only took the course but did the homework and immediately started to apply new strategies in his business, which began producing results quite rapidly. Another member of the group began reading more books on topics that interested him and activated his mind. He studied more about consciousness, communication, social psychology, and energetic interactions between people. His social confidence and abilities skyrocketed, and his way of relating with others became noticeably different, even on the group calls.

Perhaps this is a game you want to play as well. Simply decide right now to disengage from as many sources of news and other media as you'd like for the next thirty days. As a man of extremes, I find that doing something "mostly" is way harder than just making a clear, bright line. Our minds will start negotiating about which sites we'll look at and when. It's like an alcoholic who is not ready for recovery yet will say, "Okay. I will only drink with others and only have three drinks at a time." Right. And how long does that last?

I prefer all the way. No media. No news in any shape or form. Heck, if you want to see something fascinating, unplug from social media for a month as well. You might be amazed at how much natural interest and fascination you'll discover that lights you up in life. And it's not surprising that it lights you up because this fascination is not only its own source of fuel; it's also an indicator of other forms of optimal fuel as well.

Inspiration

Inspiration is whatever lights you up, whatever excites you, makes your heart feel brighter, lighter, and more open and expansive. You may not always be able to explain it with your head, and you don't need to.

Instead of looking at what you "have to do" or "should do," look at what you're inspired to do. Let's ask that question right now—what are you inspired to do in your life right now? What do you feel passionate about doing?

Take a moment to reflect on this. This is not something you were passionate about a long time ago or something you "should" feel inspired to do, but something you truly feel inspired about right now.

One thing that comes to mind for me is running in the woods. I've been running regularly for several years now, but I recently discovered running through trails in the forest. My goodness, gracious, it's amazing! Running along a dirt path, surrounded by green and life, is incredible. When I'm in there, it feels like my heart is drinking nourishment directly through my chest. How much do you think I need to "force myself" to get out there and run in the woods?

Inspiration truly is a powerful, clean fuel. Notice the trend so far. Not only do these optimal fuels feel better in your mind and body, but they also provide way more power, acceleration, and sustained energy than their dirty counterparts.

Fun

> "If it's not fun, you're not doing it right."
> - Bobo Basso, or Groucho Marx, or JFK

While it's unclear who said this quote first, it's been repeated many times and for a good reason. Because nothing motivates us more than having fun. Which one do you think is more fun:

1. A serious high-intensity interval training (HIIT) workout where you do twelve sprints.

2. A pickup game of soccer with a group of friends.

For most people, the pickup game is way more fun. And guess what? Which activity do you think will involve more running and sprinting? You could end up running way more during a soccer game and not even feel as tired during or afterward simply because it's a game, and you're having fun.

Somehow, we have the idea that this can only apply to leisure time, games, and hobbies. Other things, such as work, tasks, projects, dealing with money, exercise, and other "professional activities" can't be fun. This is serious work!

But why does fun have to mean frivolous, careless, or not sincere? Can't we have fun as we do something important? If the HIIT versus pickup soccer game example applies elsewhere, which would you prefer if you were going under the knife—a surgeon who is serious and tense or a surgeon who is having fun. I don't know about you, but I'd want the guy or gal who's got their favorite music on in their headphones, completely lost in the flow of their work. I want them to be immersed in the flow, purely enjoying themselves with the challenge, skill, and artistry of it all. I want them to be letting God move through them as they carry out their purpose. I would bet good money that this surgeon would not only enjoy their work more and be able to do it for many more years but also have superior results as well.

Fun is immediately reinforcing and makes you want to do more of something. So if you want to tap into endless motivation and high-quality fuel, ask yourself this question as you do anything and everything—from work to hobbies, to fitness, to time with friends and family: "Am I having fun right now?"

If your answer is yes, then huzzah! Celebrate that and enjoy it. Take a moment to appreciate what's making it fun and how you're enjoying yourself. You can even consciously say to yourself, "I'm having fun right now. I'm enjoying myself in this moment." As strange and bizarrely A.I. as that sounds, it helps you realize that in a way that is vastly beneficial. Otherwise, it's too easy to overlook those moments of enjoyment as they flow past. And, since time flies when you're having fun, the next thing you know, you might be facing a challenging moment and think to yourself, "Man! I never have any fun. My life is always hard," which, of course, isn't true. What's true is that you don't notice when you're having fun.

If you ask yourself, "Am I having fun right now?" and your answer is no, then that's important information. Instead of barreling down, gritting your teeth, and pushing through, take a moment to reflect. What about this is not fun? How am I relating to this activity that is making it hard, stressful, agitating, or otherwise unfun?

The lack of enjoyment is not in the activity. There is someone else doing the same thing you are doing who could be having fun doing it. Yep, even that, that thing you hate doing. Someone could love it. Heck, someone out there does love it!

So instead of blaming the activity, what if you got curious about how you're holding the entire thing. Striving, attachment to outcomes, fear, and impatience can suck the joy out of any process that you're engaged in. Even things you normally love doing can instantly become unpleasant if you feel a pressure to get through them quickly to get onto the next thing or do them right or else. When something becomes a means to an end, it instantly stops being fun.

You can also ask yourself this gem of a question: "How can I make this more fun right now?" Try asking it in any situation you're in and see what comes to mind, like a workout that's feeling hard, a challenging moment with your kids, or a boring meeting at work.

The key is to become curious. Notice if you're holding onto your position, attached to your story that this situation sucks and can't be fun. Perhaps this is true, but then where does that leave you? Are you going to quit your job? Leave your kids? Stop working out? Then, you remain in a victim stance of "I have to do this, but I don't want to" and become resentful, sour, and negative.

But resentment and anger are a form of fuel. Guess which kind—dirty or clean? But old habits die hard, and sometimes, we like to stick to old fuel sources that don't work as well and pollute our habitat, like what the human race is doing with fossil fuels. Notice your small self's desire to cling to this kind of old fuel and ask yourself if that's what you really want, what will really help you feel what you want to feel.

Then ask yourself again: "How can I make this more fun?"

One final note about this idea—I'm not saying that you should have no preferences for what you do and love every activity, no matter what forever. Over time, if you are unable to find your way to enjoy an activity, then I would suggest delegating it to someone else. Over time, create your life such that you love what you do and only do what you love. Some things are easy to delegate; other things require intention over time to create the skills, resources, or relationships to make that delegation possible. And still, other things you can't delegate. In those cases, that gem of a question becomes even more important, doesn't it?

Mastery

"One of my early memories of school is wondering when they were going to start teaching me the things I didn't know, rather than what I already knew. Many years later, I began to understand how, insidiously, school had reinforced my inadequacies and had left me with what I now called 'learned incompetence' and a fear of not being able to do things 'right' the first time."

- Wendy Priesnitz

"When I lose, I learn."

- Me. After I lose at a Magic:
The Gathering tournament.

I used to dislike losing and utterly hate failure. I spent many years minimizing the former and avoiding the latter. As I've gotten older and found more confidence and freedom in life, however, I've discovered that true freedom is the freedom to fail fearlessly, to fail unabashedly, to fail repeatedly. And, if needed, fail catastrophically, publicly, and dramatically.

And none of this is bad. It's all essential and necessary. Failure is simply getting an outcome we didn't expect or want. The more outcomes we get, the more we're taking action, which means the more we're learning. So, if you want to learn something quickly, take a lot of action and get a lot of outcomes (many of which are *not* the outcomes you're hoping for).

If you've ever read a self-help book, then you know this intellectually, but when you get it emotionally and have a shift in your attitude toward failure, that's when your confidence transforms, and your life starts moving fast.

This is where you can discover an incredible source of optimal fuel in what can be described as the process of mastery. Mastery is like interest and fascination, but multiplied a hundredfold, because it's sustained, deep, and endless. Interest can change from season to season, and that's perfect. It's not meant to be permanent.

But the things we desire to master in life can remain in us for years, decades, or a lifetime. What's more, I don't think we choose what we are destined to master. Rather, it chooses us. What begins as the flame of interest turns into an ongoing bonfire of obsessive study and deep learning.

Deep inside, you feel a need to know this area, this field, this practice, this art. You are drawn to masters of it, hungering to know what they know, to be able to do what they can do. When you witness a master at work, you might temporarily feel intimidated or insecure, but there's a much stronger force inside of you that drives you forward. You want to understand how that master does what he or she does. You want to become that master. And you will.

You study, you learn, you invest, you practice. You try, and you fail, and then you try again. Each failure might hurt, embarrass you, or temporarily cause doubt or hesitation. But these don't last for long. Before you know it, you're back on that path of learning, of growth, of mastery.

This is life living through you. This is a force you cannot stop. And, again, it's not something you can determine with your head because it sounds cool. You can't choose to master something because it's practical. If you do this, then, at best, you'll be able to find a way to get motivated to learn it just enough to get some basic results.

Instead, the areas of mastery choose you. If you have one or several areas of mastery you are on the path of, then you know what I mean. Why are you so obsessed with that topic over all others? Why that sport, that martial art, that career, or that instrument over any other? That, you cannot say for sure. You can describe what you love about it and why it calls to you. But these are just reflections as you try to make sense of this force within that's guiding you on this path.

What are you called to master? Are you heeding that call and pursuing those endeavors? In your work or vocation? With your body and the ways it wants to move? In other key areas of life?

The more you do this, the more you will find an endless source of optimal fuel to overcome any obstacle in your path.

Purpose

Hands down, one of the most powerful sources of healthy fuel is having a strong sense of your why. I say sense because it often goes way beyond what you can verbalize. Like the pursuit of Mastery, your purpose is often something that you feel called or compelled to do, even if you can't quite explain why.

However, making an attempt to clarify why you're doing something does help harness this motivation and gives it more depth and staying power.

Why are you doing the job you're doing? Why are you working out? Why are you focusing your time and energy on the things you do?

Take a moment now to pick an area of your life where you feel strong motivation, where you're putting in time, energy, and focus, and engaged in the process. Perhaps it's in a facet of your work, or your dating life, or romantic relationship. Do you have that area in mind right now? Great.

So why are you doing what you're doing here? What's your purpose in this area or these activities? What does it bring to your life? Why are you so committed and motivated?

One thing I love to do is run. My purposes for running are freedom, joy, power, and expansion. No matter how I feel when I start a run, partway through, my world opens up. Problems and stresses melt away, and I feel a sense of calm, gratitude, and joy wash over me. It's also about freedom, power, and expansion. After so many years of being told by others and myself that my body is weak, injury-prone, and fragile, running provides a powerful message that I am strong and healthy. Running has also been a way for me to push my limits and see what my body can do by going further distances than I ever thought possible.

What is your why for the area you picked? When you focus on it, do you feel the energy and motivation to act in this area? Generally, people feel fired up when they focus on their why in an area they're passionate about. It helps them plug into the feelings they experience as they take action, and these positive feelings are reinforcing—we want more.

If you don't feel much energy as you focus on your why, perhaps you aren't plugging into your deepest why or the why that lights you up, the why that really matters. Maybe it served you in the past, but your purpose in this area is now stale. You might need to upgrade it and plug into why you want to do this thing now. Given that you already like this activity and feel passion in this area, it won't be too difficult to make this little upgrade.

Now, just for fun, let's pick an area where you currently feel some resistance. Maybe you're feeling some aversion to going to work or doing a certain kind of task while at work. Or perhaps working out feels like a chore, and you're fighting it inside. Or being with your spouse or kids or a certain family member is feeling difficult or burdensome.

Do you have an area or situation in mind now? Great. What's your purpose for doing what you're doing here? What's your why?

What I've often seen with clients and myself is, in these cases where we're struggling to do something, we don't have any compelling purpose to do it. At least we're not aware of and connected to that purpose. Hence, it feels like a "have to." I'm doing it because I must, or else. This is the recipe for failing motivation. Then, when our fuel starts to dwindle, we fall back on dirty sources like fear and self-hatred. Yuck.

"Having to" do anything feels terrible. It makes you feel trapped, burdened, and resentful, all surrounded by a layer of fear that something bad will happen if you decide to change something or do anything differently. A key element of living with confidence and truly being on your own side is to remember that everything is a choice. When you align with the truth of this and start to dig for your sense of purpose in whatever you're doing, you'll harness a fuel that is much more powerful than the weak charge you can get out of anger or martyrdom. You'll discover a nuclear fusion reactor inside that can drive you to do incredible feats of love, service, creation, and contribution with the effortless effort that occurs only when we're aligned with purpose.

Purpose is so powerful because it surpasses any temporary outcome. One of my clients is a highly acclaimed *New York Times* bestselling author of fiction books. He told me a fascinating story of how he struggled as an author for many years of his life. In his late thirties, he'd been writing for years and still had not been published. He went through a period of deep questioning and struggle. Should he go on? It seemed clear that he was never going to "make it" as a professional author. And then, he had a powerful insight.

"I realized that I love doing this," he said to me, "that I'd be writing until I was ninety years old, even if nothing ever got published. This is what I'm here to do."

Within a year, he was picked up by a publisher, and now, he is highly successful and acclaimed in his field.

This is one of the reasons purpose provides the most powerful fuel. It accesses a feeling deep inside of us of: *this is what I'm here to do.* That energy is not grasping for any outcome. That grasping is what our ego is all about—trying to steer and predict and control things to get what it wants in an arbitrary timeline that it creates. But your deeper purpose keeps pouring forth motivation, inspiration, and endlessly inspired action.

Many times in my own career, I've fallen back on the same bedrock of purpose. When I was transitioning from doing psychotherapy to offering coaching, I had countless setbacks, failures, and rejections. People questioned me, criticized me, and some colleagues even actively rejected what I was trying to do. I had seminars where six people showed up, teleclasses where one or zero people attended. I created and offered tons of tools, strategies, and ideas for confidence development that few people saw, and none of them wanted to work with me.

At times, it was rough. Just like the author I mentioned above, I questioned if I was on the right path. Would this work? And then, the same expression of purpose that spoke through him spoke through me: this is what I'm here to do. I'd do this for lots of money or no money. I'd be studying this and teaching this and helping people with confidence even if it wasn't my vocation. I can't stop doing this. This is what I'm here to do.

What are you here to do? It doesn't have to just be your work in the world, although aligning that with your purpose is an act of courage and confidence that few people take, but those who do thrive like no other. But beyond career, what is your why in all the areas of life that matter most? What are you here to do in your expression of love in romantic relationships and all your relations? What are you here to share, express, and contribute? What are you here to do in your physical health with this amazing gift of your body?

Continue to explore deeper answers to these questions, and you will find permanent motivation for your lifetime.

Love and Contribution

Love as motivation? Get out of here, you hippie! I know it might sound cheesy, but it's yet another source of superfuel. Think about what a parent will do for their child or what someone will do for their partner. When we love someone, the answer is anything.

In an instant, we can drop beneath the weak fuel of resentment or obligation and tune into something much more compelling and inspiring. I'm not doing this because I have to. I'm doing this because I love this person, and I choose to. That reminder alone can instantly shift you on a completely different course for that day, month, or lifetime.

Even beyond your immediate friends and family, love and a desire to contribute to the world provides some of the most impactful motivation this world has ever seen. This fuel dwarfs fear. It is the power that caused Martin Luther King Jr. and count-less others to create such major impacts on the world. Indeed it gives you the power and strength needed to overcome any fear in your path.

At one point, during the writing of this book, I bumped up against a period of writer's block, overwhelm, and confusion. I struggled to find clarity and ease in my writing. On a walk with my wife Candace, I shared my challenge with her. As we talked, I discovered the block was coming from fear. I had read a number of the most negative reviews of my previous books, and they were psyching me out. Despite the vast majority of people benefiting from the books, my mind was focusing on the small minority of people who didn't and was vocal and vicious in their criticism of me. You know, standard safety police stuff—*don't put yourself out there because look at what happens. You get rejected!*

But as we meandered down the side streets of northeast Port-land on that sunny, early spring day, Candace said to me some-thing I'll never forget.

"You're not writing for them." She was referring to the people who dislike me and the way I write. "Who are you writing this for?" She asked.

In that moment, I imagined someone finding this book who is hating themselves. Maybe they know it directly, or maybe it's more covert. Perhaps they hate their bodies and have an eating dis-order. Or they rip themselves to shreds about their performance at work, and this stress is tearing apart their relationship and family.

Maybe someone is thinking of ending their own life, lost in a sea of self-hatred, and then they find this book.

And they read it, and it helps them set themselves free in a way they never even imagined. It unlocks something and sets them down a new path that brings them confidence, power, freedom, and joy.

When I imagine them, I have unlimited courage, and my heart writes with freedom, ease, unlimited fuel, passion, and energy for sharing what I got with the world.

What source of love and contribution do you tap into in your life? How does it feel to consciously tap into that as your fuel? Where can you use that fuel on purpose, to share even more of yourself with your loved ones, people around you, and the world?

Upgrade Your Fuel Sources

Okay, which would you prefer: fear, self-hatred, and hustling to prove your worth each moment of the day, OR interest, fascination, inspiration, fun, purpose, and love?

Doesn't that second list feel better to read, let alone to live? So here's the thing–you must make this happen. Reading about these new fuel sources is interesting and inspiring. It may open up new possibilities in your mind for how you can operate. But, to make a lasting shift in how you live and feel, you must practice these new approaches to fuel.

We will get into how to do this in the next section, but as always, the decision is paramount. Are you ready to shift your fuel sources? Are you tired of running this amazing gift of life in a human body on dirty fuel? If so, I encourage you to make an internal commitment right now to fundamentally change the way you motivate yourself in this life, to put away, once and for all, the preference and dependence on dirty fuel.

That doesn't mean that you instantly switch to high-quality fuel overnight. Think about the human species transitioning off fossil fuels. That is a process, not an immediate switch. The same is true for your personal fuel system. It requires catching yourself when you resort to the cheap fuel because it's easy and fast and consciously choosing something much better, again and again. Until eventually, you'll be humming along, feeling great, with no gunk in your engine or cloud of black smoke behind you, and it will be a beautiful clear day.

THE ART OF RELAXED DISCIPLINE

As humans, we like things to be simple. Having an inner guideline that tells us to always do X or never do Y makes things clear and simple. Hence, we come up with inner guidelines such as:

Always work harder.

When you don't feel like working out, push yourself to work out.

Always get more done than you did.

Always say yes to people's requests.

These are simple instructions for your day and life. And as strange as they might seem when you read them here, you'd be surprised how many of these inner dictates are operating inside of you right now.

Of course, you are probably not consciously saying these phrases out loud to yourself. But when you observe your impulses, thoughts, and behaviors, it is clear that you feel a strong need to adhere to these guidelines.

The problem is, while you might get some measure of ease

that comes with simplicity and limited decision-making, you also get a whole host of other unpleasant side effects. For example, if you have ever attempted to live along with that last guideline of always saying yes to others' requests, then you know that doesn't end well. And if you're living under that guideline right now, hoping that it will all somehow work out in your favor, then you have to read my book *Not Nice* to free you of that suffocating cage of people-pleasing and excessive niceness.

When it comes to navigating life, I'm afraid simple can get you into trouble. The good news is, that doesn't mean you have to make things unnecessarily complicated. Instead, we want to use more intelligence to make more nuanced decisions. This is what "The Art of Relaxed Discipline" (ARD) is all about.

The best way to illustrate this point is through a story. Long ago, a climbing expedition set out to summit one of the most dangerous and mighty peaks on the planet—one that had yet to be summited by humans. The plan was to work their way up over six weeks, making a final single day push for the summit.

The first few weeks of climbing went perfectly according to plan. There were no major problems, the team was making great progress, and morale was high. They had acclimatized to the lower camp altitude and began working their way further up the mountain. Then, things stopped going according to plan.

An unexpected storm rolled in from the east, bringing high-speed winds and snow. The climbers were forced to remain in their tents, waiting out the storm for three days. Eventually, it passed, and they were able to emerge from their tents and proceed.

The climbers continued their trek to the summit, carefully navigating the treacherous terrain. In the fourth week, an unexpected break in the ice led to a loss of key equipment and supplies. This was another choice point. They now only had enough supplies to reach the summit and return if there were no further delays or alterations to the plan.

What to do? Push through and proceed? Or head back down? Had this been a more modern expedition, they may have decided to cease their climb and make an attempt the following year. However, this was the age of exploration. People were seeking to make their claim to fame, fortune, and above all, glory. To be the first ones to summit this peak was indeed a noble feat. And so they decided to continue.

Over the final weeks of the ascent, they made great progress, quickly moving toward the top of the mountain. As they got close to the summit, the skies began to turn gray, and winds began to increase. They set up camp at night, intending to make the twelve-hour push to the summit early the next morning.

When they arose, the winds were stronger. The sky was dark and ominous. Flecks of snow hit their jackets as they broke down their camp. Another choice point. What to do? Proceed as planned toward the summit? Wait out the storm for an indeterminate amount of time? And then what? Make another attempt, or head back down?

What should they do? What would you do?

Reaching the summit requires many decisions upon which much more than just climbing success rests. These decisions determine the survival of the climbers. Hence in these situations, the simplistic "just do it no matter what" approach leads to catastrophic results. Climbing history is filled with stories of people who barreled onward and upward despite numerous warning signs indicating alternatives would be better.

At the same time, if the climbers threw in the towel at the first sign of hardship, discomfort, or risk, then no one would have climbed any substantial peak, ever.

"The Art of Relaxed Discipline" is a method of trekking up your personal mountains to ascend your summits. The aim is to do this most effectively, with enjoyment and purpose.

The Five Elements of Relaxed Discipline

So what exactly is the "Art of Relaxed Discipline" (A.R.D.)? How do you practice it? There are five key elements of this art:

1. Effective

2. Sustainable

3. Relaxed

4. Joyful

5. Meaningful

A.R.D. Element 1: Effective

In the pursuit of our goals, the most effective methods are typically more nuanced. You can see this in the way that people who have practiced something a long time tend to be much more effective than beginners.

Over the weekend, I was making some wood art with my boys. We had some pieces of wood boards, some driftwood from the beach, nails, a hammer, screws, an electric screwdriver, and paint. We were ready to rock. And we had a blast, screwing all kinds of stuff together to make these large, unwieldy wood formations that we then painted an array of bright colors. While it was a fun, bonding experience, I would in no way claim that the woodworking was skilled.

As a novice, I know the basics. Line up the screws and drill them in. If they go too far and the sharp end of the screw is sticking out the back, reverse your screwdriver and pull it back out a bit. Bam.

However, if we'd been with a friend of mine who is an experienced woodworker, he would have been much more effective at building with the materials. He would know about different screws, angles, and ways things fit together. He would have built up hundreds of subtle distinctions in his mind to more effectively build something that was sturdier, more complex, better balanced, and prettier.

In much the same way, if you want to pursue your goals most effectively, you will need to learn more subtle nuances. The blunt force method of self-attack is not intelligent, nuanced, or particularly effective. Spiraling into fear, panic, and imagined catastrophe is also not effective. Even if these methods lead to a temporary burst of frantic action, there are better ways. The actions you take from this place are typically not very thoughtful, intelligent, or impactful at bringing about the result you want.

Besides, these methods often don't even lead to action, but rather to overwhelm, hesitation, and procrastination. In response to this paralysis, we typically freak out more, utilizing more self-criticism, fear, and other methods that don't work.

In contrast, when using ARD, you become highly interested in what is most effective. What is the most effective way to get the results you want? What are the steps? Who has done what you want to do? How can you find these people and learn from them? Who can you model? What are the high-leverage actions that bring about the biggest results?

A.R.D. Element 2: Sustainable

Some approaches are effective in the short term but ultimately fail because they are not sustainable. For example, starving yourself or carrying out some wacky fad diet de jour might bring about weight loss for a while. But ultimately, it proves unsustainable to eat fewer calories or only buffalo fat during a two-hour feeding window (OMAD carnivore diet for life!).

But rather than seeing that our method was ineffective because it was unsustainable, we deny this reality by blaming ourselves for being "weak" or not having enough willpower. In other words, we don't accurately take in the results of our actions. We don't see clearly. Instead, we gather data from that experience that tells us we are lazy, weak-willed, and otherwise a shamefully bad person. This misunderstanding leaves us vulnerable to repeat the entire thing in the future.

Whatever you're doing to reach your goals must be sustainable, not just for a week or a month, but for years. Unlike the metaphor of reaching the summit, there is no clear endpoint in our lives. Whatever your goals are now are your current targets. Once you hit them, you'll have new targets. You will perpetually be in the process. There is no conclusion, completion, or end.

So maybe you use self-judgment, pressure, and pride to force yourself to stick to that eating or training regiment. You grit your teeth and dig deep to become more determined than ever before. And you hold on. You reach that ideal weight and look great in your dress or in those photos on the beach, or run that race in the time you want, or even win that prestigious championship or award. Huzzah! Congratulations! Now what?

Are you done running or playing your sport? Are you forever memorialized with your beach body in those photos, so now you're done maintaining your health?

You see? There is no end. Hence, everything must be sustainable.

A.R.D. Element 3: Relaxed

Tension ruins everything. When athletes who are amazing in practice choke in the big game, it's tension. They are all psyched out, and their body becomes tense. They lose all their skills and abilities and become a rigid, clumsy shadow of their talented selves.

What about when you freeze up during a presentation? Or you don't share your opinions in a meeting because you're intimidated by the people there? Tension is to blame.

And finally, imagine this scenario. It's a beautiful, sunny summer day, and you're lounging on a picnic blanket with your gorgeous new lover who drives you wild with excitement and passion. You're lying there, soaking up the sun, side by side. But, for some reason, you feel tense.

How enjoyable is that moment now? Tension can make the most amazing moment uncomfortable, undesirable, or even intolerable. Tension sucks.

So what is it? Is it fear? Kind of. Tension is a physical contraction in your body that is a response to resistance. The thing you're resisting can be occurring in your environment or inside of you.

When that jarring car alarm goes off, your body tightens up, and you experience tension. When the person sitting next to you is wearing a copious amount of a cologne you find repulsive, your face and chest tighten up, and you begin to breathe more shallowly. You are resisting these sounds and smells.

We can also resist feelings inside our own bodies, including anger, sadness, and fear. When these feelings arise, we unconsciously and habitually clamp down the muscles in our body, bracing ourselves against the emotional sensations.

We even can tighten up in situations where we *think* we *might* feel something, sort of anticipatory tension. If this person doesn't like me, then I'll feel shame or unworthiness, so now I'm all tensed up as I meet them. I want this presentation to go well and to have these people be impressed and want to buy from me, and if they don't, I'll feel embarrassed, ashamed, and in danger of reprisal from my boss. Guess how I feel as I walk into that room?

That's right, fantastic. Fantastically tense.

Almost everyone is doing this all day long without even knowing it. Sometimes, the tension is so intense that it's obvious, as in the case of strong anxiety or anger. But most of the time, we are subtly clenching all day long, bracing ourselves against life. If I clench my guts hard enough, I'll be able to control the outcome here!

This tension is the biggest block to sustained effective action, and the main reason people don't get the results they want. As I mentioned, this tension comes from resistance, and the main thing we're resisting is our undesired outcomes.

Whenever you have a goal, you have an outcome you want. You want to earn more money, get the guy or the girl, have more passion in your relationship, have more love in your life, have less fat and tighter abs, make babies and start a family, or become the kingpin of your own little business empire. Whatever it may be, this is your goal. To play along, pick one of your favorite current goals now—one that lights you up or terrifies you, whatever you prefer.

Great. Now, for that goal, you have a main, overall outcome. That is like your mountain summit. Usually, it's some version of, "I'll get, do, or finally have X, and then I'll live happily ever after. The end." In addition, there are many smaller outcomes that you imagine are on the path to that big outcome. These mini-outcomes indicate you're making progress toward your big outcome, and all is right in the world.

To have the outcomes we want, we must, in contrast, have outcomes we don't want. These are those wretched undesirable outcomes I spoke of earlier. What are these beastly things? It turns out they tend to be everything other than your desired outcome.

In the climbing the summit example, making progress up the mountain is the desired mini-outcome toward the mega-outcome of reaching the summit. Behind that outcome may be a mega-mega-outcome of being heralded as a hero by your nation and revered across the world for your bravery, strength, and superior mountaineering abilities. Glory and all the opportunity that glory bestows upon the glorious await just beyond that summit.

A "no-summit" situation is an undesirable outcome. Anything that might lead to a no summit, no glory situation is highly undesirable. A storm is an undesired outcome. Lost equipment or shortening supplies is an undesired outcome. Anything, small or large, that in any way hinders, delays, or stops the expedition is an undesired outcome. And we can resist them all in our guts, bowels, chest, throat, low back, jaw, shoulders, neck, forehead, scalp, and anywhere else you can imagine.

We hold chronic tension in these areas as we chronically resist any undesirable outcome that occurs throughout the day. Even when nothing undesirable is happening, we can imagine that some undesirable outcome might happen in the future and start resisting it now. We then combine our physical tension with the mental tension of worry and rumination, thus creating a delightful cocktail of ineffectiveness.

In order to achieve at the highest level, you must let go. In order to achieve and enjoy yourself along the way, you just let go. And forget about achieving anything for a second. In order to simply enjoy your life and not live in a permanent state of fear and low-grade dissatisfaction, you must let go!

Ultra-Relaxed

I seem to be a man of extremes. One of my coaches encourages me to "prioritize my intensity" after she observed my tendency to try to win in every area of life, all the time.

Wait, *All I Do Is Win* isn't an anthem to live by?

While I've learned to heed this advice more in the last few years, I've still been known to grab that insanity sphere on the reg. Most recently, it was with running.

I am currently training for my first ultramarathon, which is any race longer than a marathon. I thought I'd start with something reasonable, at least as reasonable as anything with the world "ultra" in the title could be.

I found a 50-kilometer race that went along the winding Wildwood Trail within Forest Park in Portland. Perfect! It's only 31 miles; that's not too much longer than a regular marathon. Plus, it's in an epically beautiful park right in my city. Score.

And so I signed up, five months ahead of time. Somewhere along the way, however, I picked up that insanity sphere. Running for enjoyment and freedom and all that jazz went out the window. I was running to get somewhere now, dammit.

Somehow, I settled on the number 50 being significant. Running 50 miles per week seemed like an amazing achievement and meant something about me as an athlete and a human. *When I achieve X, I'll finally be somebody.*

So I set out for that outcome. This is the mini-outcome on the way to the summit. I calculated how much I'd need to run each day. I put one rest day in there because that seemed like a sane idea. Then I hit it hard. Somewhere along the way, it began to degrade from sustainable into unsustainable.

When my body was sore and felt tired, so what? Gotta run today. That's the desired mini-outcome. Not running today means not hitting 50 miles this week. Not hitting 50 somehow means not successfully running the ultramarathon. (What? I don't know. Insanity sphere, remember?)

Running began to feel harder and harder. And, oh God, it gets worse. I don't even want to tell you this part because it's embarrassing, and I feel shame about it. But, hey, you're pretty deep into this book at this point, so we know each other pretty well. Plus, shame feeds on being hidden and is healed when shared.

While I was doing this crazy running regimen, I was also intentionally slightly undereating. I was working out hard in the gym and getting leaner by the week. At this rate, I could be training for the ultramarathon and hit 10-11% body fat, thus finally being somebody, winning at fitness, and living happily ever after.

That was until it all fell apart. Shockingly, this wasn't sustainable. My body needed more food and rest to recover from all the demand. I ignored the early signs of fatigue and stiffness, only to have my body hit me with a more overt signal to bring me back to sanity.

I woke up one day feeling light-headed and weak. What do I do? Keep going for the summit or slow down and take a break. Man, F that noise. You David Goggins that shit and you run. So I did. I ran five miles to the gym and lifted weights there. But my fatigue only increased, and by the end of the day, I could barely walk.

Fortunately, I've been on this merry-go-round before. I heard the words of my coach ringing in my head, all the ways she guided me to prioritize my intensity and let go of perfectionism. I writhed around and resisted the fatigue for a few days, fighting it mentally, getting angry at the limitations, and feeling sorry for myself.

And then, I let go. I dropped the sphere, and all my awareness and intelligence returned. I had let go of needing that outcome in order to be okay.

That is the key to relaxed discipline. It's knowing that you want that outcome, and you're going to move toward it, but you don't need it. You'll be okay even if you don't get it.

Think about your goal now–the thing you want–the mega-outcome that you "must" have. Can you feel the tension around that? Do you feel the physical squeezing or tightening in your body? This is what you must let go of to become more effective, wise, and sustainably able to achieve the goals you most want.

And, yes! You might not get them. You may put effort and energy, sweat, and toil into pursuing a goal or dream, and there's no guarantee that you'll get it because there are no guarantees of anything in this life. But I do know this. Your best shot at achieving what you most desire is in using relaxed discipline. Paradoxically, it's in letting go of the craving, grasping, and desperate need that says you must have that thing or else. Because "or else" means pain if you don't get it, and pain leads to fear, and fear is a weak force in the world. It's a dirty fuel that will never get you to where you want to go.

The answer, my friend, is in letting go.

That's just what I did, after several days of thrashing around and fighting it, of course. I let go of needing to run any race. I could run it or not. I could run some and walk some. I told myself it was "just a day in the woods."

As far as "training" for my day in the woods, I could run as much or as little as I wanted. I had time carved out for running in my schedule, so if I wanted to, I could run. If I didn't want to, or wanted to run less, or take a rest day, I could do that too. I could do whatever I wanted.

I'd be okay, no matter what. I am already okay, no matter what. I am whole and complete right now, as I am. I don't need to achieve anything with running or this race. I don't need to look a certain way in my body. I don't need to try to control everything so much. Big breath, big sigh. Ahhhh. Relaxed.

Within several days, the fatigue was completely gone. I took some extra rest days and ate more. And then, I felt like running, so I did. I started running more in Forest Park, where the race was going to be. My glorious goodness, running through the woods felt amazing. Running, in general, felt way more fun with more food in my system and without the "have to" pressure. Remember, "having to" do anything feels terrible.

I stopped counting miles and planning mileage targets for the week. I ran as much as I wanted to run and no more. About three weeks before the race, I enjoyed some long, beautiful runs through the woods in Forest Park. Out of curiosity, I checked my activity stats from my GPS watch to see how many miles I ran that week: 52.

I laughed as I saw this—another reminder of the power and effectiveness of relaxed discipline. Effort less, yet do more. I remembered how much I had been striving to hit 50 miles in a week just a few months before. I had managed it several times, but it felt like a grind that took so much effort. This last week felt easy. Actually, it felt fun.

This brings us to the next element of "The Art of Relaxed Discipline"—enjoyment.

A.R.D. Element 4: Joyful

I can psychically hear the objections bubbling up in your mind, across time and space: *wait, just let go and do whatever you want? That can't work!*

I know it's counterintuitive, but only because we've been taught not to trust ourselves. We've been taught that we are untrustworthy. A common perception of children and humans of all ages is that we are lazy, greedy, selfish beasts that must be forced and coerced into being good and moral. This is a debate as old as philosophy itself, whether humans are fundamentally good-natured or not. But this isn't some stuffy intellectual concept that doesn't apply to our lives. Rather, your perception of yourself fundamentally shapes how you try to guide and motivate yourself.

Most of us do not give ourselves much space to explore and see what might emerge when we're not trying to control ourselves so tightly. We learned growing up that controlling yourself comes from force because that's what our parents used with us. Commands for good behavior were met with frequent chastising for straying off this path. We were threatened with punishments, criticized, judged, blamed, and told we were bad, both directly and indirectly.

What was your childhood like in this regard? I like to imagine children as beautiful, wild horses in an open space.[17] They need

---

17 If you're curious to learn more about being on your own side as a parent and how to help children grow up with a deep sense of O.M.O.S., or about healing your own inner child, be sure to read the Appendix at the end of this book!

room to move, run, and flex their bodies to fully be alive. They need to express, interact, poke, prod, test, feel, emote, and explore all the aspects of being in this human experience. While there is a fence keeping them within some boundaries, the space for them to run within is vast, open, green, and gorgeous. However, in many families, the space that horse can run around in is quite small. The horse is expected to remain within a tight space and threatened with physical or emotional pain if it disobeys. That horse doesn't trust herself. And if you grew up with that conditioning, neither do you.

But fortunately, what you were taught is not true. What's true is that you have a natural, inborn desire to grow, learn, be healthy, be loving, and treat others in ways that are mutually beneficial. This is your true nature. And paradoxically, when you stop trying to control yourself so much, to force yourself to be a certain way, you naturally act from this place of health and wellbeing.

Hence, you can let enjoyment guide you. It's safe to let go and see what really lights you up, and then pursue that. If you want to stop doing something or change what you're doing, it's safe to do that. You are allowed. You have permission.

I know this aspect of ARD can be quite confusing, as most of us have learned that to achieve anything and get ahead, you must exert force, willpower, and discipline by doing the things that don't feel good to get the good result later on. And there is some truth in this. Going outside of our comfort zones leads to growth, and by definition, going outside our comfort zone is, well, uncomfortable.

But there is a better way, a more skillful, wise, and nuanced way to approach this than brute force. Let me give you a few specific examples so you can see what I mean.

At Work
What if, at work, you let joy, interest, and fun guide you this

week? What projects are the most interesting to you right now? Which tasks are you most drawn to do? What pace feels best for you? Do you like focus bursts with breaks? Do you like one big chunk where you immerse yourself, get in the flow and lose track of time? If there's something you perceive you "have" to do because your boss or someone else requests it, how can you hold this in a relaxed way? Do you "have" to do it this second? Can you work on something else and get to that later in the day?

Food

What if you let go of your pressure to eat the perfect diet, just the right amount of calories, or whatever force you're exerting around food? What if you relaxed, slowed down before eating, and tuned in to your body? What if you ate the foods that felt good to you, in the quantities that felt right without measuring, counting, or tracking so much with your head? What if you let yourself eat certain foods that you've seen as "bad" and didn't beat yourself up for it. What if you didn't have to go into high-alert mode afterward to make sure you never did that again?

Free Time

What if you didn't always have to be productive or progressing? What if you let go of needing to have a perfectly clean house or organized garage? What if you checked in with yourself regularly and asked: What do I want to do right now? What sounds most interesting and engaging for me? You can ask this question even if you're with others, including children. While you may not be able to instantly do whatever you want, just the act of seeing what lights you up will bring you more joy.

Can you see how this way of being is so much more relaxed and enjoyable and how it requires more trust? If you're worried about getting nothing done at work, being reprimanded for idleness, going down the rabbit hole of uncontrollable Oreo eating, or your house degrading into a filthy den of slothery, that's okay. That's how your inner critic keeps the ongoing force tactics going—by predicting death and ruin if you do something different.

My suggestion for you would be to test it. Try embodying the "Art of Relaxed Discipline" for 30 days and see what happens. You can always go back to the old iron fist method of teeth-gritting, anus-clenching self-control. But for just one month, you can see what actually happens when you let go a little bit.

What I've discovered in myself and clients is there may be a desire to see just how wide that field is before there's a fence. So we might push off a few tasks at work, or eat a few rich meals or sweet treats. We may lounge all day on the couch, watching shows, and ignoring house responsibilities. *Ahhh! I knew it!* shouts our inner critic. *Don't you see? You need me to keep you in line!*

But, after this little period of time, something remarkable happens. Your natural drive kicks in and starts to guide you. This isn't coming from force or fear. But rather, it's coming from something much deeper within you; indeed, it's life itself moving through you. You have a natural desire to be productive, effective, and do good work in the world by contributing your intelligence, gifts, and skills. It feels good to do this, so you will want to do it. You have a natural desire to be healthy, eat healthy, and feel good in your body. Addiction to processed foods and refined sugars, or consistently overeating don't feel good, so you will not want to do them.

The more on your own side you become, the more you naturally move toward what makes you feel best, both in the short term and the long term. If you're still a little unsure of all this enjoyment, relaxation, and letting go of total control, don't worry. We'll discuss this more in the next chapter when we talk about how to deeply take care of yourself. I'll also share my cinnamon roll story, which will make everything clear; cinnamon rolls always do.

A.R.D. Element 5: Meaningful

The final element of ARD is remaining constantly connected with your deepest source of fuel, which is your purpose for doing whatever you're doing. When you let go of fear, grasping, striving, and conditional worth as motivators, then meaning and purpose become much more essential. When you stray from your sense of purpose, then your motivation begins to dwindle, the fire begins to fade.

Many people only have an intermittent connection with their purpose for doing an activity. They may have a burst of insight and inspiration when they connect with a strong reason for why they want to pursue a goal or create something in the world. Motivation comes quick and easy when we're in this state. You are directly plugged into a continual source of clean, high-quality energy.

But then, after a few days or weeks, people feel their motivation fading. They blame their lack of willpower and attempt to generate more willpower to sustain action. This might work, but willpower is a quick-burning, finite fuel. Yes, it can be replenished, and you can even increase the size of your willpower tank and capacity over time, but it's still going to be short-lived. A few days for some, a few weeks for many, and maybe a few months for the most hardened among us.

As willpower starts to wane, people will then turn to another fuel—fear and self-loathing. They will attempt to jolt themselves into sustaining action by imagining terrible scenarios of loss, pain, rejection, failure, and public humiliation. They will use self-hatred by berating themselves, calling themselves pathetic and lazy, and trying to kick themselves into action. These, too, may work for a short time but with high cost to your internal engine (i.e., your heart, nervous system, adrenal glands, and self-esteem).

Using ARD bypasses this type of dirty fuel entirely and uses willpower specifically in an intentional way, like the directional bursts that a rocket uses to guide itself in space. Hence, we need a source of strong burning, long-lasting fuel. Enter meaning and purpose. If you have a compelling purpose or set of reasons for doing something, and you stay connected with that purpose, you have infinite fuel to carry out anything and everything you want to.

On any given workday, I have dozens of different things I could be focusing on and doing. Writing books or blogs, recording videos or podcasts, creating and recording training programs, meeting with team members to discuss sales, marketing, or internal operations, working with clients, leading Mastermind calls, preparing for or teaching live events, and on and on. I love having so many different things to do!

Ever since my first monotonous and highly boring job at Longs Drugs as a cart collector in the parking lot, and then as a stocker, and then as a cashier, I decided that my career had to involve doing many different things so I would always feel engaged.

And still, I can struggle to sustain energy, focus, and productivity in a workday. I can fall into fear as fuel. *If I don't get this done, something bad will happen! I gotta do all this by the end of the week or else!* Then, things I love can become tasks to check off my list. The process goes out the window, and my day is about completing outcomes. When that's the case, my day sucks, and my energy is intermittent at best.

But my day is entirely different when I'm connected to my underlying purpose; when I'm clearly aware that this is what I'm here to do–this is my mission; when I think about the people watching those videos, reading that book, and learning from that training program; when I see the struggle and the vulnerability and the triumph in my clients as they overcome fear and step into a life of confidence. When I feel that, my fuel source is infinite. I not only take care of more tasks in a given day, but I'm enjoying myself as I do so. Optimal fuel feels...optimal!

These five elements are all well and good, but what about the "disciplined" part of The Art of Relaxed Discipline? Where does that come in?

According to Google Dictionary, discipline is "the practice of training people to obey rules or a code of behavior, or using punishment to correct disobedience."

Hmm, that doesn't sound so great. And yet, that's what most of us think of when we hear the word discipline. We think of a teeth-grinding use of force to make ourselves do something even though you don't want to. That's discipline. And that's how you achieve goals, become a good, worthy person, and win at life, right?

Maybe, or maybe not. In the next section, we will explore a more skillful, nuanced approach to this idea of discipline, discovering how to find graceful ways to do the uncomfortable, complete challenging tasks, and otherwise make progress toward the goals you value most.

MASTER AND COMMANDER

I love this term. It's a nautical term to describe a rank within the British navy of captains of mid-size ships. These ships were small enough that the captain had to lead, help sail, and help fight as well.

You, my friend, are the master and commander of your own ship. You are responsible for making high-level decisions about where you're headed and how to navigate the path to get where you want to go. At the same time, you must sail the boat, working with all the crew members (a.k.a. parts inside of you) that have different personalities, agendas, and ideas.

You may have spent much of your life trying to captain this ship from a place of force, fear, or anger. Maybe you were constantly berating crew members, shouting at them for not doing enough, blaming them for being failures. Or, you may have kept that barking at bay and instead ruled with ice-cold, callous brutality. Crew members knew not to cross you, and they did your bidding without a word, for fear of the crushing grip of your gloved hand around their neck should they disobey you. Sickness, injury, and fatigue meant nothing. Get back to your post and carry out your duties, or you shall feel my wrath.

Regardless of which approach you've been using, let me ask you this: is it optimal? I'm not asking if it works or not because brutality, coldness, and fear do work in a sense. The boat may get to where it needs to go, and this captain and crew may survive at sea for many years. But is it optimal? Are they thriving? Are you thriving? Are you joyously, exuberantly, enthusiastically alive? Are you grateful to be you? Are you emitting love?

Because there is a way to captain your ship, to be the master and commander, that is way more effective, skillful, and brilliant. There's a way to be a wise leader of yourself that will serve you so much more in this lifetime.

Deciding to adopt 'The Art of Relaxed Discipline" as your approach to achieving goals is a major step forward in this regard. Below, you will find additional aspects of optimal motivation — ways to captain your ship in the most effective, wise methods possible.

Right Action, Right Timing

Instead of the overly simplistic approach of "always do more" and "do it all now," a wise leader uses much more nuance and intelligence than this. The key to knowing what to do, how much to do, and how hard to push requires you to become highly aware of what the right action is, and when the right time to do it is.

In Taoist philosophy, there is a term "Wu Wei," which translates into "inaction" or "effortless action." This term captures the idea of taking action and efforting, without the typical kind of force we think of when we think of effort.

According to Taoist Master Bruce Frantzis, "Taoists say that until the time is right, nothing will happen anyway, so a large part of Wu Wei is the ability to be as connected as possible to the universal flows of the Tao. When all of a sudden, it becomes obvious that the time has arrived, only then do you take action."

If you are not familiar with the Tao, I would highly recommend looking up a few articles or videos online, especially anything by the British philosopher Alan Watts. Wayne Dyer has some great recordings on the topic, as well. The Tao is a way to describe the universal energy that underlies all things, that existed before matter and remains afterward.

So what does "right action" look like in practice? And when is the "right time"? Is it now? How about now? The answers to these questions are very subjective and require a nuanced assessment of your current situation. They are not the simplistic brute force methods of "always do ____" that I described earlier.

If I'm feeling tired in the morning when my alarm goes off and I don't want to get out of bed to go to the gym, is the right action to sleep more or find the willpower to get up? Is it optimal to email and call those five potential contacts to see if there's a chance to create some business, or is it better to focus on another project and do that later? Am I avoiding it because I'm scared? Don't I need to "make myself" do the uncomfortable stuff?

Our mind wants simple answers, but there are none. The answer, my friend, is wisdom. It's seeing clearly what is needed and then doing it without tension or grasping. It starts with O.M.O.S. If you are not on your own side, it's terribly difficult to see clearly because there's so much mental noise muddying the waters.

In the get out of bed to go to the gym example from above,

if your mind is cluttered with fears and beliefs about fitness and health, then it will be difficult to see clearly. If you're afraid of getting fat or think you're not worthy unless you are the kind of person who gets up early and crushes it or any thousand other stories that make the love of yourself conditional, then all you hear when you reflect inward are *those* competing beliefs.

Instead, we must start by letting go of any conditions on our worth. Remember these statements.

I am loved, no matter what.

I am worthy, no matter what.

Breathe in and out slowly, and feel the truth of that. Let go of anything that is telling you otherwise, for it does not serve you, and it's not who you are.

Then, you must find the sweet spot in the center of the river that leads to the most easeful momentum and progress–how you can flow forward gracefully, given whatever is happening.

Navigating the River

This visual metaphor can help you get a sense of what right action and timing look like in practice. Imagine you are rafting down a river. On the left side of the river, the current is slower. If you were to go all the way to the left, it gets so slow that you'd basically stop moving. As you go toward the right side of the river, the current picks up. The further you go to the right, the faster and faster it goes. If you were to go all the way to the right, your boat would be torn apart by big rocks, and you'd be grounded. (See diagram below).

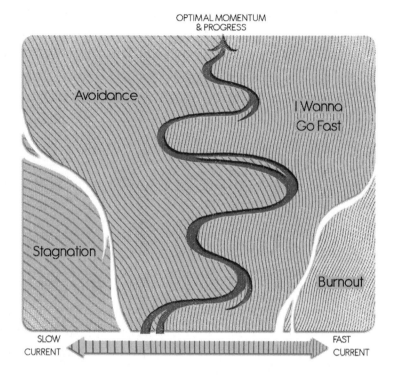

Somewhere in the middle between these two extremes, there is an optimal path that allows you to keep experiencing progress and momentum. Notice how this path is not a straight line. Oh, if only it were! That would make things so much simpler, wouldn't it? But life requires more wisdom and presence from us if we truly want to thrive. Instead, this path of optimal progress sometimes veers toward the slower current and sometimes moves toward the faster waters.

If we go too far in the slower current or stay there for too long, we enter the realm of avoidance. For example, sleeping in one day, or skipping work, or taking it easy can be great for our mental health and give us a much-needed reset. But if we were to do that for many days in a row, it starts to go south, doesn't it?

Have you ever experienced that? You skip work on Friday to take a "mental health" day. It feels fantastic. You strut around your house, feeling like an excited kid who gets to be at home while everyone else is at school or work. You make yourself some delicious food and put on your favorite TV show. Life is good. Your inner child is delighted, and your soul feels nourished.

After you finish that episode, you think to yourself, *why not?* And you throw on another. And then another. Soon it's late afternoon, and you haven't left the house. You stay up late watching TV and get poor sleep that night. Then, you proceed to cancel all commitments for the weekend, carrying out a 48-hour binge of streaming shows and food delivery. Then come Sunday evening, you are filled with a sense of mounting dread about returning to work on Monday. *I can't go back out there!* You've veered too far toward the slow current in the river, and brief respite has turned into avoidance and anxiety.

If we take this even further, we enter the realm of stagnation, which can manifest as fatigue, lethargy, agoraphobia, or depression. From this place, it can feel scary or overwhelming to take even small risks. The further we go down this path and the longer we stay there, the harder it can be to get our boat back out toward the middle of the river.

On the other side of optimal, if we go toward the faster currents, we enter the realm of what I call, "I wanna go fast!" This is the achiever's mantra and usually starts well. We are inspired, fired up, feeling powerful and strong. We're clutching the Orb of Power and feeling invincible. But at the same time, we might stay in constant motion with tasks, take on more and more, overcommit ourselves, and ignore underlying feelings or feedback signals from our body and heart. *No time for that nonsense! I'm making great progress!*

We can sustain this hyper-speed until we can't. And then we end up getting waylaid somehow. We either veer even further right into the Burnout Zone and crash against the rocks, or we fly across the river into avoidance and stagnation. Either way, our forward progress is greatly reduced or stopped altogether.

My good friend and personal trainer, Josh Sabraw, spent many years in the U.S. military. He often uses a saying he learned from his time there, which goes, "Slow is smooth, and smooth is fast." We've had many conversations about this as he's seen me try to navigate the path of optimal momentum with health and fitness. I have a tendency in fitness, and in life, to veer toward the right side of the river. After having spent so many years in avoidance and stagnation, I have a strong force inside of me that propels me toward massive action and doing whatever it takes. This is a strength and a great medicine to take in just the right doses. In too high of a dose, I'm crashing against those rocks more often than I'd like.

Josh introduced me to the concept of 8/10 at the gym, which I have now extended to all areas of life. He'd see me repeating the pattern of pushing my body hard, trying to find the line just below "too much." To me, I thought it was sustainable, but from his outside perspective, the writing was on the wall. He would say to me, "just because you are feeling energized and strong on a given day doesn't mean you have to burn it all and leave the gym empty, feeling totally spent. It's like getting a paycheck. You don't have to spend it all that weekend."

He suggested I give 8/10 level of effort, lifting 8/10 the amount of weight I think I should or want to do that day.

"What? Isn't giving it your all and operating at a level 10 how you get results in life? Isn't that how I get ahead and get those results fast?" I'd say.

"Slow is smooth, and smooth is fast." He'd reply.

"Shut up, Josh." I'd say in my head, not yet willing to relinquish my perfectionistic demands; not yet ready to let go of the Insanity Sphere and my endless pursuit of proving myself and thus earning my worth; not yet ready to let all that go and feel in my heart, staying connected with the parts of me that need my love and attention.

And then, months, weeks, or sometimes even days later, I'd crash into those rocks. My mind-body pain would flare up, and I'd be hobbling around for a week, unable to walk, let alone run. Or I'd experience intense fatigue that I couldn't "push through" anymore.

Lousy Josh, being right again.

Navigating this river is a humbling experience. There is no perfection here, and there is no way to learn other than by doing. Wisdom comes from testing things out and seeing what has you veer out of the optimal path into the slow-moving shallows.

You'll know you're there if you've been dealing with the same issue for years and have not effectively resolved it. Most likely, you've been avoiding the uncomfortable stuff, scared of getting swept up in the faster currents of the river of life. So you've stayed safe in the slow-moving waters–safe, but dissatisfied because you're not living out your full purpose here (which is *not* to remain entirely safe and risk-free until you die).

I'm sure you've also had times in your life when you jammed the gas, and it was the right thing to do. You made some major forward progress, and even though it may have been challenging or scary at times, you navigated those rapids and were moving with the flow of life in a way that felt just right. And then, perhaps you kept that foot on the gas too long, your more inspiring motivations became co-opted by fear, grasping, or perfectionism, and you steered into faster waters. And then, smash! Your boat was in pieces, and you had to spend months building a new one, not going down the river at all.

You are not alone in this process, and there is nothing wrong with you. This is universal and human. Everyone makes countless mistakes as they navigate this river, and the mistakes are ongoing. That is to say that you will never reach a point in your life when you are flawlessly navigating the river, always staying just right in the path of optimal momentum. There is no perfection here, my friend, and that is perfect.

There's just the continual learning, growing, and expansion of your awareness and capacity to love yourself and others. As these grow, you can get better at catching your boat as it veers too far and bringing yourself back more quickly.

As you read this, you may still have a nagging question in your mind, though. You may be wondering, how do we have the drive and motivation to steer toward the center of that river? How do we get ourselves to do what might feel scary or uncomfortable? Are you sure pushing through isn't the answer?

Beware "Pushing Through"

What about "pushing through"? You know, just making yourself do something that you don't want to do? Isn't that necessary, important, and valuable? Isn't that willpower, determination, and grit? We need to do that to get stuff done in the world, stick to our commitments, and generally improve in life. Isn't pushing through good?

Perhaps. It's all in what you compare it to. One of my teachers that I learned a great deal about optimal health from would have lots of people ask him which foods were healthy. Is fish oil good for you? Is meat healthy? What about maple syrup, is that healthy? His response was always a question: compared to what?

When you compare the effects of maple syrup to high-fructose corn syrup on your body, then maple syrup is healthy. When you compare maple syrup to something sweetened with whole dates, or the sugars bound with the fiber inside a blueberry, for example, then maple syrup is now the less healthy option. That question has always stuck with me, as it applies beyond our health and food choices.

So, is pushing through a good approach? Compared to what?

Sometimes a little push-through energy is just what you need to kick-start your motor and get yourself moving. We've all experienced that moment of comfort-seeking resistance to getting out of bed to go for that run or to head to the gym. Part of us wants to hit snooze, roll over, and snuggle back into the darkness of our warm, cozy beds. If we regularly do that, however, then we might fall out of the habit of exercising in the morning and experience negative consequences to our mood, energy, strength, stamina, and mobility over time.

Sometimes, you have a big project on your plate at work that you've been avoiding, and the best thing you can do is to chunk it into small steps and attack step one right now, without waiting one more second.

Remember how I said that ARD requires a lot more nuance than the old brute-force tactics? Here's another example of that. Because the more nuanced questions in this situation are — how often are you using "push-through" medicine, and what are you saying to yourself to "make yourself" do it?

The push-through medicine is a finite kind of fuel that you only have a limited supply of in your tank. It's like turbojets you flick on now and then, for just a bit. So if you're engaged in a long battle each morning to get out of bed, or wrestling with yourself day after day to get yourself to tackle those projects at work, then more of the push-through is not what you need. You don't just need to "have more willpower," and then everything would be fine.

Needing to regularly use push-through energy is a symptom that something is off. Instead of "pushing through," start experimenting with leaning in.

Leaning In

Yes, there are times when your internal crew on your boat won't want to do what's needed to get the job done. Maybe a storm is coming, and someone needs to climb up and do something with the sails (I don't know what that would be called, I'm not a literal master and commander!). When it comes to your life, perhaps the right action is to spend two hours in deep work on a particular project to make some solid progress on it. You know this is the right action because you see that what's stopping you is just fear. You're avoiding the task out of this fear, and once you dive in and do it, you'll feel so much better. Hence, the right action is to work on the project.

But how do you get yourself to do this without using fear or self-attack? Here, I like to think about leaning in. Lean into the possibility of working on the project. Imagine it and notice how you feel. Fear, overwhelm, aversion? Do you feel a squeezing in your chest? Get curious and go deeper. What's going on here? Why am I afraid of this? What am I most afraid of? What can I let go of to approach this project with more ease and joy?

Perhaps the first ten or fifteen minutes of you "working" on the project is you sitting there and doing nothing but feeling your fear and other uncomfortable feelings, facing them one by one as you let go and relax your body. This is very different than watching shows or aimlessly scrolling social media or the internet. Those are you avoiding work. Instead, facing your fear is actually doing the work. It's you leaning in.

Sometimes, leaning in also means just getting started for a short period of time. What's the first thing you'd do for this project? Is it scanning all the tasks and getting your mind back into the process? Is it doing that one specific step of creating something, editing something, communicating with someone, deciding something? Lean in by taking that first step. Don't worry about all the other steps; you're just doing this step now.

When my body is rested, and I'm healthy, and I have "running" on my calendar, sometimes I don't feel like doing it. Well, part of me does, and part of me doesn't. I know I'll feel great as I'm doing it, but it's that first moment of getting out the door in the early morning darkness or stopping my other task that gets in the way. It's the transition that's creating inertia. In that case, after I've checked in to make sure it's the right action, then I'll lean in. I'll tell myself that I don't need to run any certain distance or speed. Even if I imagined I would run ten or more miles during that run, I'd tell myself that all I'm doing is getting out the door and going for a little jog. It could be a mile or two at a relaxed, easy pace.

Some of my clients have used this kind of mental game with the gym, telling themselves that all they have to do is go into the gym. With overwhelming organization tasks, it can just be setting a timer and organizing your desk for five minutes.

The beauty of this method of leaning in is, nine times out of ten, guess what you want to do once you're running, or at the gym, or organizing your desk? That's right; keep doing it!

The key idea behind leaning in is to respond to your inner resistance with patience, curiosity, and creativity. Recently, our family was about to pile into the car and head to grandma and grandpa's house. Just before we left, one of my boys said, "I don't want to go!"

Pushing through would look like this: "What? Come on! Get in the car; we're going to be late." Or, even better, "Grrrraggh! I don't have time for this. We're leaving, and you'd better be in the car. Or do you want us to leave you here?"

That feels painful to imagine. Yet we do that with ourselves all the time, don't we? In fact, before reading this book, that may have been your default response to the parts of you that feel resistance to something.

Instead, I got curious. "Oh yeah? That's interesting. You were so excited about going earlier this morning. Tell me more. Why don't you want to go to grandma and gumpy's?"

This inquiry opened up a conversation in which my son was able to express preferences he had while being at their house–

things he liked and didn't like about being there, things he wanted to ask them but had felt scared to speak up about. If we'd used the old push-through method, we would have completely missed all that, not resolved any underlying issues, and taught him to override his own feelings and not trust himself. But other than that, it works like a charm.

Supercharged Action

Ooh! This is a good one. I'm so excited for you to discover this. I finally got this only in the last year or so, and it's been completely life-changing. Here it is:

> The results you get are less about the actions you take and more about the level of consciousness from which you take those actions.

I know, that one sounds like a neo-spiritual doozy, but it's true. Take a moment to read it again. In other words, your level of consciousness determines your results way more than the actions you take. And yet another way to say this is: actions you take from a higher level of consciousness will be way more impactful than those taken from a lower level of consciousness.

What do I mean by level of consciousness? I think the best way to describe it is by using David Hawkins' model in which he places levels of consciousness in a hierarchical list[18]. Each level of consciousness is associated with a number, which represents the level of impact and influence you have. He describes everything above 200 as "power," which impacts the world strongly and effectively brings about results. The higher up you go, the more power you wield. He describes everything below 200 as "force."

---

18 To learn more about this chart and Dr. Hawkins work, I highly recommend reading *Letting Go: The Pathway of Surrender.*

This is where you are trying to exert your will upon the world around you, needing things to be a certain way. From this place, you wield way less influence, and your actions are often less effective. In addition, force creates a counterforce, and you often experience setbacks, rejections, and other adverse reactions to your actions from these levels.

Level	Log
Enlightenment	700-1,000
Peace	600
Joy	540
Love	500
Reason	400
Acceptance	350
Willingness	310
Neutrality	250
Courage	200
Pride	175
Anger	150
Desire	125
Fear	100
Grief	75
Apathy	50
Guilt	30
Shame	20

I imagine you have seen this in your own life. Have you ever felt desperate for someone or something? I *need* this person to call me back. I *have to* get this job or else. Inside you are feeling a mixture of intense grasping (desire) and worry about it not going the way you want (fear). This potent cocktail might drive you into action—perhaps you study for that interview, call those contacts, or make those cold calls. You come up with the wittiest text to send to your crush and have your friend review it to make sure it's bulletproof. But you get no response, not even a rejection, just nothing. And the job interview seems to go fine, but you soon hear back from them that you aren't making it to the second round of interviews. What gives?

Part of you decides it was because you didn't try hard enough, didn't want it bad enough, and didn't take enough action. So you double down on your efforts, all the while being driven by a grasping need to get that result (or you're not okay) and a gnawing fear that you might never get it (and therefore never be okay inside). Yikes!

This level of consciousness might produce some results. It can lead to overanalysis, maximizing, and manipulation of others and circumstances. You can be determined to get what you want. But it pales in comparison to what is possible when you operate from higher levels of power.

When I finally understood this, I realized I had been doing it all wrong in the past. I have always been a big fan of bold action, ever since I discovered the secrets of confidence creation many years ago. And I've taken endless, repeated bold action for the last decade and a half. But now, I approach it completely differently.

Before I take action, I notice what state I am in. I determine what level of consciousness I am operating from. If I am lower on the spectrum, operating from fear, grasping, or needing to prove my worth (a.k.a. pride), then I stop and don't take any action. My first action is to let go of whatever way I'm holding the situation that is putting me in that state of consciousness. I focus on letting go of "needing" anything from this action. I remind myself that I will be okay no matter what happens, that I don't need anything from "out there" in order to feel good "in here." I am already whole and complete right now in this moment. I am worthy–no matter what, loved–no matter what, and safe–no matter what.

I focus on this and calm my body until I feel myself entering into a different level of consciousness. I focus on what I am grateful for and take time to acknowledge everything that is going right in my life, all the gifts I've received. I even focus on the problems and see how they, too, contain gifts that I can be thankful for.

Then, when I'm feeling much more relaxed and happy, I move forward to take action with love and gratitude. And guess what? That kooky old man was right! David Hawkins was a genius! The same output of one of my actions brings about ten times the result. The sales video is way more effective. The email to that potential business contact is opened and well received. In fact, I even start getting random offers and opportunities from people I didn't even initiate contact with. They are approaching me, asking to partner with me and promote my message. To which I respond with, you guessed it, more acceptance, love, and gratitude. (It's much easier to respond that way when it's the "good news.")

So if you want to supercharge your action and greatly magnify your results, I highly recommend taking on this practice. Enjoy!

Intentional Sprints

While old fuel might drive you to work long hours and manage an unsustainable pace for a surprisingly long period of time, it ultimately won't last, and you'll burn out. However, there is a technique that you can use as a master and commander of yourself that is the intentional sprint.

Using this method, you do, at times, burst longer hours or more labor on a task. But it's a specific target within a short period of time. I like using this technique when there's something hanging over my head that I've been avoiding for a while. For example, a while back, I was getting low on podcast episodes. We were only a few weeks out in our scheduled episodes, and then we were going to run out. I had many other projects on my plate between live events, coaching, leading the team, and marketing outreach, so the podcast recording project kept getting kicked down the road. As the date of "no more recorded podcasts" approached, I experienced a growing sense of pressure, thinking, *I should be working on that right now!*

After a few weeks of this, I'd had enough, and I decided on an intentional sprint. The idea of sitting down and recording a few episodes a week over the next two months to slowly get ahead didn't excite me at all. But record 25 in one week? That sounded like just the kind of insane challenge that I could get behind.

So that's what I did. I decided that I would record 25 episodes (which are about 30 minutes each) that next week. I mapped out the content, came up with the recording times, and blocked them out, and smashed. I even tried to get more done on Monday and Tuesday, so I'd be ahead of my target and could coast into the end of the week. It was a lot of work, but I absolutely loved it! Plus, I was fully immersed in podcast mode, and so I was constantly thinking about and enhancing my notes for the content for the next recording.

You can use this intentional sprint burst in any area of life. The key is to make sure it's the right time to do so, and that you are not continually doing one sprint after another. If you notice yourself thinking, "Yeah! Now this is the pace I'm talking about. I'll simply sustain this for the next three months," then watch out. That may be a sign that your old methods of perfectionism are taking over.

Also, be sure to notice if you are feeling the energy and excitement that comes from exerting yourself in a good way or the frantic, manic energy of fear. Are you engaged in and enjoying the process, or just grinding head down to get through it? That's okay if that's happening here and there for a bit. I mean, when you're out running, and you're slogging up a huge hill, it might not be all bliss and rainbows. But if your entire run is sucking, maybe you need to slow down a bit. In other words, notice if you're enjoying yourself most of the time. That's the goal here, as you also happen to crush it on this project.

Doing What Works

One final method of superior leadership involves simply asking this question: "In this situation, what is most effective?"

This can help you cut through the emotion, drama, attachments, or anything else that is clouding your senses right now. This question is great because it immediately invokes another question — effective for what? You are forced to examine what your ultimate outcome is and if what you're doing is most effective in producing that outcome.

So often, we know what we are doing on one level is not effective, but we feel compelled by emotion to do it anyway. For example, when you're angry at someone, you may feel an overpowering urge to say or do something that will hurt them. Your teeth-gritting, that'll-show-'em desire to inflict pain is oh, so enticing. But what is your outcome in that situation? *My outcome is to hurt that S.O.B.!* Right, beyond that outcome. What's your real outcome? What do you really want? What about the part of you that will be back in the driver's seat ten minutes or ten days from now. What does that part want?

When my boys are going at it in the morning, knocking over each other's towers, throwing objects at each other, and creating an environment of conflict and chaos, I notice myself becoming resistant and upset. *Ugh, I just want to be able to make some breakfast, and all coexist in peace! I don't want to have to stop what I'm doing to break up another fight over the raisin pile on the floor that no one is going to eat anyway because it's full of dirt, debris, and hair at this point* (this is just a hypothetical example here, of course).

I may want to come in with some shaming or blaming statements to try to control the aggressive behavior. I may feel anger building up inside. I aspire to be patient and loving with my boys, but in that moment, I don't feel love. I don't want to be loving. I'm pissed.

And then I remember to ask myself, "What would be most effective in this situation?" I instantly know the answer from experience–to move toward them with curiosity. "What's happening here? Let's see how we can solve the problem." Then listen to each boy share his story about what he wanted to happen. Reflect back what they are thinking, wanting, and feeling. Come up with a creative solution, and invite them to come up with solutions as well. Stop trying to clean, cook, and unload the dishwasher. In short, let go of my agenda for the moment and be present.

This is what's most effective. It may be what I want to do or don't want to do in the moment. Regardless, even if I feel like doing something else, it will not be as effective. It won't be effective at showing love, teaching them problem-solving skills, or creating more harmony in our home over the long term.

The next time you are faced with a challenge at work, in a family relationship, or anywhere else in life, and you notice strong emotions of anxiety, anger, or reactivity, pause and ask yourself— "What would be most effective here?" What would be most effective at bringing about the outcome that I truly want in the long term?

Then, take that action. Or don't. Sometimes you see the right move, the right action, the right path, and you go the other way anyway. That's okay. You will until you won't. You are worthy, no matter what. You are loved, no matter what. Welcome to the human journey, my friend!

Autobiography in Five Short Chapters[19]
By Portia Nelson

I

I walk down the street.
There is a deep hole in the sidewalk
I fall in.
I am lost ... I am helpless.
It isn't my fault.
It takes me forever to find a way out.

II

I walk down the same street.
There is a deep hole in the sidewalk.
I pretend I don't see it.
I fall in again.
I can't believe I am in the same place
but, it isn't my fault.
It still takes a long time to get out.

III

I walk down the same street.
There is a deep hole in the sidewalk.
I see it is there.
I still fall in ... it's a habit.
my eyes are open
I know where I am.
It is my fault.
I get out immediately.

---

19 Copyright (c) 1993, by Portia Nelson from the book *There's a Hole in My Sidewalk*. Beyond Words Publishing, Hillsboro, Oregon.

IV

I walk down the same street.
There is a deep hole in the sidewalk.
I walk around it.

V

I walk down another street.

Chapter 13:
Permanent O.M.O.S.

So here we are, in the final chapter of this book. What a journey we've been on together! I am so grateful to be with you and so curious to know about your O.M.O.S. transformation. You've grown so much in such a short time!

You've radically increased your awareness of your own relationship with yourself, discovering where it may have been harsh, cold, or less than ideal. You've discovered how to relate to your critic and all the different parts of yourself in a completely new and loving way, which I know without a doubt is starting to feel good and become your new way of being with yourself. And you've also looked under the hood at the machinery and patterns that have been driving all this self-judgment in the first place and began to let go of perfectionism, pride positions, and other conditions upon your worth.

There is one more thing for us to discuss, however, before we conclude. We've talked about how to identify and stop self-criticism. And we've talked about how to undermine the sources of that self-criticism, so there's less of it. But what we haven't circled back to is Level 4 of O.M.O.S. What is life like when we're no longer habitually turning on ourselves and then needing to address that? What if we were just on our own sides, all the time? What would that look and feel like? How do we reside in that place more and more? How do we make being completely, instantly on our own sides our center of gravity—the place we spend most of our time and return to quickly when we fall off? That's what you'll discover in this chapter.

To remind you, here's a quick summary of the 4 Levels of O.M.O.S. I shared these earlier in this book. Now that you're almost at the end, it might be interesting to reread them and see which level you're residing in now.

Level 1: Catch & Interrupt Direct Self-Attack

You are able to catch yourself when you fall into a spiral of direct self-attack. You notice it when you are saying mean, harsh, or critical things to yourself and actively change the way you treat yourself.

Level 2: Catch All Forms of Self-Undermining and Return to O.M.O.S.

You don't turn on yourself with direct self-attack in the same way nearly as often. In fact, direct self-attack is a more rare occurrence and is surprising and jarring when it occurs. You ask yourself, *how did I use to live like this?*

Now you are focused on identifying and catching all the other sneaky forms of subtle self-attack your critic uses. You are in the process of discovering these and healing these patterns.

Level 3: Mostly O.M.O.S.

You reside mostly on your own side. This is your center of gravity and what you naturally keep coming back to. This results in a radical reduction of social anxiety, self-judgment, and all other forms of self-doubt. You like who you are, and you are less obsessively focused on how you come across and whether people will like you or not. You are okay with you.

You generally approach your critic and all the parts of you with curiosity and acceptance. When you are suffering emotionally, you are truly empathic and looking to see what you need and what will help you.

You take more healthy risks because you are not afraid of the horrible berating that used to follow failure or rejection. You are more open to and engaged with life.

You sometimes catch ways you turn on yourself in more subtle ways. You are curious about the roots of these patterns and focused on healing them at their core. You are uncovering and letting go of long-standing beliefs about who you should be and how you should operate to be lovable and worthy. You are becoming more and more you.

Level 4: Permanent O.M.O.S.

You reside in a consistent state of love and appreciation for yourself. You are truly accepting of who you are in the world, including all of your past mistakes and painful moments. You see the magic and beauty in who you are and how your life is unfolding.

Level 4 goes way beyond just accepting yourself in spite of your shortcomings. Rather it's falling deeply in love with yourself. Loving all of who you are, including the way your face looks from that angle, the way your belly looks, your nervousness, your weak points, your longings.

At this level, you only want the best for yourself. You don't tolerate poor treatment and have created relationships that are affirming, inspiring, and loving. You are doing work that feels meaningful and fulfilling for you. In short, your life is full of love and beauty.

When there is pain, loss, heartache, change, or other inevitable challenges that arise, you are on your side throughout. You hold yourself with tenderness and patience as you feel the inevitable pains that this human life brings us.

This chapter is all about how to take your O.M.O.S. center of gravity from Level 3 to Level 4.

FALLING IN LOVE WITH YOURSELF

Who do you love in your life? I'm not talking about love as a role, or responsibility, or obligation. I mean, who do you fully, deeply, freely love? Can you think of someone right now and bring them to mind? Perhaps it's a close friend, a lover, a spouse, a child, a parent, or a pet. Picture them in your mind and focus on this person. As you do so, put your dominant hand on your chest, right over your heart, and breathe fully and deeply, as if you're breathing directly into and out of your heart.

When you imagine them, what do you focus on? Their face, their smile, or some quality of theirs? Are you remembering the magic moments you've shared together? Do you feel thankful to know them, to have them in your life? What does this love feel like in your heart? Take one more moment to expand this feeling as much as you can. Let it be as big in your chest as it wants to be, even imagining it expanding way beyond the boundary of your ribcage and your body, going out into the infinite in all directions. Even saying in your mind, or out loud, "I love you, ____" and saying their name.

Now, imagine looking at yourself in the mirror or looking at yourself from the outside as you go about your day—driving, going to work, being with your kids, talking with a friend, making some food. Send this same loving energy to yourself. Can you give yourself that gift right now? Can you extend that sweet, nurturing love to you?

As you imagine yourself living your life, let whatever scenes come to mind. Don't hold on to anything or try to force any imagery. Just witness you and your life unfolding in your imagination, sending love to yourself all the while.

You can strengthen this by saying statements like the following, using your own name instead of mine:

I love you, Aziz.
I am so in love with you.
I love this life with you, Aziz.
I love being you.
I love being me.
I am so grateful to be me.

How does this feel? It's okay to let it in. It's safe to love yourself like this. If you notice your mind getting noisy, judging this, or otherwise interfering, just smile at it and keep going. It's just noise and not to be taken too seriously. Your ego is just scared of this much love. But your heart isn't. It's right at home here, being deeply nourished by this ocean of love and appreciation.

Take as much time as you'd like to reside in this place of unconditional self-love. It may feel sweet and easy, or it may feel good yet also painful. Sometimes, we can feel nourished and filled in our hearts as we do this but then also experience squeezing in our ribs or stomachs or strong emotions of sadness, grief, hurt, agitation, or longing.

These are not bad signs or signals that somehow loving yourself like this is wrong. On the contrary, these are signs that show just how starved for love your heart and body have been. Just hold all the resistance, squirming, and other blocks to this love in your awareness with patience and surrender. No need to push them aside, manipulate them, or jam through some agenda. Just turn toward them, smiling, beaming love on them like the sunbeams light on the moist ground underneath a freshly upturned rock. The sun doesn't need to do anything or make anything happen. It will just beam its light, and sooner or later, that dirt will dry right up.

Do this for as long as you'd like, and then keep reading.

The New Normal

What if this was your new normal? What if you deeply loved yourself and felt connected to that love almost all of the time? I don't mean "coming to terms" with yourself and finding a way to accept all the aspects of yourself that you deem unlovable. This seems to be a suitable target for many. For them, wildly falling in love with yourself is unrealistic and unfeasible, and the best we can hope to do is come to terms with what we don't like about ourselves and accept it. Barf.

This is where my being a man of extremes pays off, I believe, because I don't want to settle for that as the peak of the mountain. Just like I was never satisfied in my clinical training when people talked about "managing social anxiety disorder." Manage it? Is that the best we can do? What about freeing ourselves from it? What about freeing ourselves from anxiety, low self-esteem, and grasping for others' approval entirely? What about liberating ourselves?

I see loving ourselves within the same realm of limitless possibility. I see the summit of that mountain as endless. There's always a greater amount we can love ourselves and others. And as long as we're alive and growing, we can keep loving.

What would it be like to love ourselves fully, completely, fiercely? To hold nothing back in loving ourselves? Now don't get me wrong; this doesn't mean we don't ever get annoyed at ourselves, or judge ourselves, or get angry at ourselves. This is part of loving anyone, isn't it? But when we deeply love someone, we are willing to work through these moments of disconnection, forgive quickly, and resume the joy of being together.

That's the key difference here between accepting ourselves versus wildly falling in love with ourselves. Accepting ourselves can feel a bit sterile and resigned. Yeah, I have gross looking bags under my eyes. Yep, I have wrinkles. Yep, my body is this shape and will never look like the ultrathin images I see in the media. Sigh. Well, since I'll never be beautiful, I guess I'll work on accepting myself and coming to terms with the ugly being I am.

No, no, no!

Would you want that from your lover? To see your beautiful naked body and say, "Well, it's sure not what I'd want, but I've learned to accept it, so now I'm okay with it." My, oh my. Doesn't that just send shivers of excitement and sexual anticipation up your spine? I bet you're getting aroused just imagining that smooth talker.

Wouldn't you want your lover to look over your naked body, smiling as they take every part of you in with their hungry eyes? Wouldn't you want them to walk toward you, run their hand over your smooth, naked skin, and say, "You are so beautiful to me. You are everything I could have ever wanted. I am so blessed."

This is the kind of love I'm talking about. It's a relishing of who you are—a delighting in yourself—all aspects of yourself. Yes, there are behaviors or aspects of you that sometimes might bother or irritate you, just like they would with a lover, spouse, friend, or your children or parents. But these are temporary upsets that resolve quickly, and then you return to true enjoyment of being yourself.

Expand Your Love Capacity

Our biggest block to experience this kind of deep enjoyment of who we are is not our shortcomings or that we are not quite good enough to be loved in this way. Our biggest block to this kind of joyful self-love is our own capacity to love. Each person has a current capacity to which they can give and receive love. For some, it's highly developed, and they lead with an open heart, beaming love toward everyone. These people tend to have many friends, potential partners, fans, or followers. They are magnetic to others and often rise to leadership positions where they help, guide, and inspire others.

Then, there are others who are stunted in their capacity to give and receive love. Perhaps they've been hurt and are scared or unwilling to open their hearts fully again. They may be trapped in painful emotions from the past and stories of lack and unworthiness. They may be hustling to be perfect, questing for just the right combination to unlock the safe, which holds their self-love.

Most of us are somewhere in between. In some ways, we've grown tremendously, healed so much from childhood, and become capable of loving in sweet, mature ways. And, we still have our upper limits we bump up against.

Just last weekend, my wife Candace went out of town for two full days. It was the longest she'd ever been away from our family to date. She'd done a few overnights in the last year, but those were for family illness and funerals. This was the first official mama getaway. She's given so much to our boys and me that I was excited to give back to her in this way. I really was.

But the day she left, childcare fell through, and my solo shift ended up starting five hours earlier than anticipated. I didn't want to, but I instantly threw a tantrum inside and was somewhat distant when she departed.

Over the weekend, I had the humbling experience of being solo, non-stop, on-duty dad. It was like one of those bad comedies where the two characters switch roles and have to figure out how to function. Don't get me wrong; I'm an exceedingly involved dad and love being with my boys. But being solo for days is like a whole 'nutha level of parenting fitness. About 47 times over the two days, I had moments of empathy for my wife. *Oh, this is why she gets upset at the boys for that. Oh, this is why she piles up all that stuff on the edge of the counter.*

In any case, it was a delightful, exhausting, humbling experience. I felt so much empathy for my wife and such deep gratitude for what she does every day being a full-time mother and teacher of our boys. The time of her return approached, and all seemed well until she came home.

Then—seemingly beyond my ability to control—my internal tantrum took over. I tried to restrain myself, but my energy was seething resentment and blame. It was as if part of me was saying, "How could you do this to me? You left me with my own children for 48 hours. Outrageous!"

So there I'd gone, pulling off my longest dad solo stint, giving my wife a chance to visit her sister and other beloved family members. I gave this great gift and then acted all sour-pants upon her return. If only I could have contained that part and given the gift fully, that would have been so much better!

But, alas, that was beyond my current love capacity in this regard. And that's okay. I love myself for trying and love myself for having a victim spasm at the end. It's all okay. It's in the stretching, the reaching, and the failing that we grow. My love capacity grew radically in that one weekend with so many opportunities to strengthen my muscles of patience and unconditional love with my boys (which apparently needs an endless amount of strengthening. I mean throwing huge globs of wet sand all over the windows and into the house, on purpose? Why dude, why??).

For my next act, I am planning on watching the boys solo for seven days so Candace can go to a personal growth experience. It's still a few months out. I get a little nervous in my guts when I think about it, but I got this, for reals.

It may be challenging at times, but this is what we're here to do, perhaps more than anything else. It's to grow in our capacity to give and receive love. And as you grow in your ability to love others, you can also grow in your ability to love yourself. You'll discover that loving others and loving yourself are one in the same.

When I get tight and angry with my older son because he's being extreme in his desire for mega-revenge after his brother hurts him, this is directly related to my own self-love. When I am able to see my own inner demands for things to go my way in life and to feel and empathize with the part of me that gets enraged at all sorts of people and situations, I am instantly more patient with my son's anger. In other words, the more I can acknowledge and love my own shadow parts, the more I can love others, no matter what, as well.

Whenever you notice something in yourself that you don't like, that's an opportunity to expand your love capacity. Whenever you're feeling guilty, judging yourself, or reprimanding yourself for being "bad," that's an opportunity to strengthen your love capacity through forgiveness and understanding.

In this way, you don't need to force anything. You don't get to higher and higher levels of self-love by gritting your teeth and making it happen. You don't powerslam your way to the top of this peak. Instead, you keep letting go of each block to love as it arises. Each one is a little gift to show you where you need more tolerance, or patience, or forgiveness, or lightness, or perspective, or whatever is needed. Your self-judgments are showing you what pride positions you are holding and would benefit from letting go of. Your self-hatred is pointing out exactly what parts of you need first to be allowed, then embraced, and then relished.

Love Letter

To be a master of O.M.O.S., for the next ten days, try this. Each morning or evening, write yourself a brief (or long) love letter. It could be in a journal, on your phone, or carved into stone with hieroglyphics. It doesn't matter how and where you write it, just that you write it (as opposed to "sort of thinking about it" as you drive to work, worrying about all the stuff you have to do that day).

Take three or five minutes out of your day to stop whatever you're doing or focusing on and write this little note to yourself. Make it funny, or sweet, or heartfelt. Make it whatever you most want to write, or most need to read in that moment. Just write from your heart.

Be mindful not to steer this letter into a lecture on how you need to think and feel. You can do that later in a journal where you are reflecting on the optimal mindsets and best ways to achieve X or Y. In this letter, take a moment to write about something you especially appreciate about yourself, something you really love about yourself. Write about a sweet moment that just happened, a secret win that no one knows about, a word of empathy, encouragement, or support for something challenging happening in your life.

Go ahead and try it out right now. Even if you're not going to commit to the ten days (but seriously, why wouldn't you? It's only three minutes per day!), just write one out right now. Yes, right now. Even if you're sitting down in your comfy chair and would have to get up to find a pen or your phone (but who are we kidding, your phone is within arms reach at all times, isn't it? Of course, it is! We are all one step away from implanting that sucker and becoming legit cyborgs). Okay, ready? Write it now.

My darling Aziz,

I love you so much. I love your smile. I love your humor. I love how quickly you learn and grow.

Thank you for slowing down and feeling so much these last few days. It's feeling so deeply nourishing to me. I love your courage, self-awareness, and willingness to go anywhere, face anything, and do whatever it takes to be free.

When you come to a door, what do you do? Go in it.

You are amazing. I love you. I am so grateful to be on this journey with you.

There you have it. That only took one minute. Easy as pie.

How did it feel to write it? I felt an intense surge of gratitude. I truly am so happy and grateful to be me, which, surprisingly enough, is something that I would not have been many years ago. I spent many years *not* wanting to be me and wishing I was somebody else. We'll get into that a bit later in this chapter, as it is a big component of permanent O.M.O.S.

But before we conclude this section, I want to offer you one bonus practice. If you want to earn mega O.M.O.S. points, instead of writing one letter to yourself, I encourage you to also write a second love letter each day for the next ten days. This one you will write for someone else. It can be handwritten and left for them to discover or mailed. Or you can send it in a text message, an email, or by raven. You can record a short audio or video and send it to them. The format matters not. Just find a way to express a short burst of love to someone else, and do this each day for the next ten days. You can repeat the same person multiple times if you'd like.

Doing this will not only surprise and delight others and boost your mood, but it will also help you continue to grow in your capacity to love. This, in turn, increases your self-love, which in turn increases your empathy, compassion, and ability to love others, which, in turn, well, you get my point. Ready to write those letters?

"Tired of Speaking Sweetly"
By Hafiz

Love wants to reach out and manhandle us,
Break all our teacup talk of God.

If you had the courage and
Could give the Beloved His choice, some nights,
He would just drag you around the room
By your hair,
Ripping from your grip all those toys in the world
That bring you no joy.

Love sometimes gets tired of speaking sweetly
And wants to rip to shreds
All your erroneous notions of truth

That make you fight within yourself, dear one,
And with others,

Causing the world to weep
On too many fine days.

God wants to manhandle us,
Lock us inside of a tiny room with Himself
And practice His dropkick.

The Beloved sometimes wants
To do us a great favor:

Hold us upside down
And shake all the nonsense out.

But when we hear
He is in such a "playful drunken mood"
Most everyone I know
Quickly packs their bags and hightails it
Out of town.

BECOME A CHAMPION

"We are often unaware of how inhuman, Godlike and impossible our terms for living and for self-acceptance have become. We usually have no idea that your aspirations are often totally inappropriate and incompatible with being human. Our culture produces many double-bind situations in which we are damned if we do and damned if we don't, and, even worse, damned if we *are* certain ways and damned if we *aren't.*"

                                  - *Compassion and Self-Hate: An Alternative to
                                     Despair* by Theodore Rubin (page 215)

To permanently become on your own side, you must reject the toxic messages that your culture has fed you over your entire life. You must uncover the games you're playing that don't serve you and consciously drop them. In other words, you must let The Beloved rip from your grip all those toys in the world that bring you no joy.

As long as you are buying into the major toxic messages of your culture, it will be impossible to sustain a sense of unconditional self-worth for long. All it takes is one moment of falling short, one comparison, or one glance at a photo of yourself, and your self-love can evaporate in an instant. The speed and intensity with which you can turn on yourself is not entirely an unintentional mistake, I'm afraid.

Profit From Pain

There are many industries in the world that profit from human pain and suffering. Of course, they don't say this, and this might not be the only thing they profit on, but it sure is a big piece of their pie.

Addictive substances, such as alcohol and tobacco, for example, draw a lot of their income from some form of human suffering. Even soft drinks and heavily processed foods, which are engineered to produce addictive-like patterns of consumption are known to focus their marketing on what they call "heavy users." This means they are interested in targeting not the casual soda drinker, for example, but the person who drinks 4-6 cans per day. That's their cash cow.[20]

Maybe you aren't trapped in a cycle of addiction to alcohol or tobacco, and maybe you haven't sold your soul to the sweet God of refined sugar, but you are by no means unaffected by your culture.

Every culture in the world has beneficial qualities, values, and customs that it upholds. These serve individuals, communities, and the broader environment. They may be pro-social, support those in need, and lead to healthy relationships, both professional and personal. And at the same time, every human culture on the planet has some pretty messed up stuff embedded in it as well– messages, demands, and expectations that cause people to turn on themselves and hate themselves for not being able to live up to these unattainable, unrealistic standards.

Some of these standards are distorted creations based on political or religious values–aspirational demands about how humans should be in order to create a just society or be virtuous, despite these ideals being completely unobtainable. Other times, the standards are intentionally increased and distorted to inhuman levels to create a feeling of inadequacy, failure, or insecurity. This is heavily used by advertising and mass media to induce negative

---

20   If you'd like a take a fascinating trip down disturbing processed food lane, I highly recommend reading Michael Moss' book *Salt Sugar Fat: How the Food Giants Hooked Us*. Better yet, check out the audio version, which is read by Scott Brick, who is one of the best narrators in the world. It's a most pleasant way to hear some truly shocking information.

feeling states, which can then be removed by the purchase of a product (at least so the ad tells us).

Each culture is a little different, so you will need to examine your own country, community, and family to determine which toxic messages you received that do not serve you. Below you will find some of the major messages transmitted in Western culture that can be highly toxic.

Net Worth = Human Worth

> "Let me tell you something. There is no nobility in poverty. I've been a rich man, and I've been a poor man. And I choose rich every time. Cause, at least as a rich man, when I have to face my problems, I show up in the back of a limo wearing a $2,000 suit ...and $40,000 gold f--kin' watch!"
>
> - Leonardo DiCaprio
> as Jordan Belfort in *The Wolf of Wall Street*

This one is deep in most of our psyches. Even if we aren't actively aspiring to earn more, create an empire, or achieve monetary mega-glory, we're still strongly impacted by our ideas about money.

The cultural story goes like this: The more money you can earn, the better you are. You are smarter, more disciplined, more courageous, more powerful, and somehow, just more than other people. After all, your bank account is more.

As a result of this story, we imbue wealthy people with some sort of god-like aura. Imagine you were going to walk into a room of billionaires. Ooh. You could meet these people and tell others about it. You can tell people that you met this person or shook that person's hand. Others would gasp in delight, and some of that glory would reflect upon you as well.

Not to say that someone who has earned a billion dollars or more does not have inspiring or uniquely developed qualities. They might be very smart or super perceptive in certain ways. They may have a knack for or heavily cultivated their skill sets of leadership or self-discipline. All of this might be true. But they are still just a human-animal like you and me. Their worthiness to feel loved, cared for, valuable, and happy is no different. Even if they did something amazing and contributed to the entire human race or the planet in some valuable way, this does not make them more deserving or worthy of love.

If you notice your mind fighting this, pause and ask yourself why? Why defend the philosophy that people's worthiness of love is based on money or any other criteria? Can you see how that is merely an arbitrarily chosen philosophy? That there is no one right truth around this? And how that philosophy ends up hurting you in the long run?

This is what being a champion means—we must consciously reject the messages we've received our entire lives. Something might seem true or right because you've been taught "this is how it is" for your entire life. This is what mom or dad thinks. This is what my religious leader or community thinks. This is what my college professors taught me. This is what I learned from ads and movies. Beware any philosophy, no matter where you learned it, that strips you of your power and leaves you needing to be a certain way to be "good" or worthy of love. This is usually a sign of a consciously designed method of manipulation being used by an individual or group to control others.

All I Do Is Win

> All I do is win win win no matter what
> Got money on my mind I can never get enough
> And every time I step up in the buildin'
> Everybody hands go up
> And they stay there
> - "All I Do Is Win" by DJ Khaled featuring Ludacris,
> Rick Ross, T-Pain, and Snoop Dogg

I love this song. It's so absolutely ridiculous. And it captures the essence of this unrealistic standard that our culture has for us. Basically, we should always win. We should not fail, get rejected, not get the result we want, or do anything other than win. If we don't, we feel an onslaught of embarrassment, shame, and self-hatred as we should because we are a loser.

Take a second to think about that term—loser. How loaded it is with shame, failure, and wretchedness. And it's a word that many people's critics use against them.

Hence, we have the delusional belief that we are supposed to succeed at everything we attempt. We should nail the presentation, get the sale, get the date, make the funny quip, instantly know what people are talking about, know all the current affairs, display intelligence, be fit, do everything we say we will, and always be on time. And that's all just in any given day of the week.

You might think this sounds extreme or even absurd. And it is. But that's how these toxic messages are. They are completely inhumane and ridiculous, but we buy into them, feeling bad for falling short of them, even though they are impossible. That is, until we raise our awareness and start to see them and consciously disengage, deciding to stop playing these crazy games and choosing more empowering, inspiring games instead–games that bring us joy and serve others, games that make us feel happier, more alive, and more energized.

To be free of this toxic message, we must embrace learning, which means embracing failure, mistakes, rejection, and losing. At all my live events, we have this banner up over the three days so people can see it regularly:

#DrAziz #BoldAction

The point of this banner is to remind people to fundamentally change their relationship with failure–to reject the idea that failure is wrong, unacceptable or an indication of personal inadequacy. We must instead draw a line in the sand and reject any notion that says failure is shameworthy, whether that message comes from outside or within.

You have had some painful past moments in your life in which you were shamed directly or indirectly for failing. Directly would be something like a parent saying, "How could you get a C in this class? What's wrong with you? Why are you so lazy?" Indirectly might be them getting quiet and sighing, "I don't know what it will take for you to start applying yourself." Both of these examples can leave a residue of shame around failure. They imply that the failure was due to a personal inadequacy on your part.

If you're curious about how to respond to something like that, as in, what could a parent say that wouldn't induce failure, then you'll love the appendix of this book! It's all about O.M.O.S. parenting and how to remain on your own side as a parent and help your kids do the same. O.M.O.S. for everyone! Now, after that teaser for the appendix (you gotta sell the appendix or else no one ever reads them! They just sound like homework, don't they?), the short answer is the parent would be curious.

They would be curious about their perception of their report card, curious about what's going well, curious about challenges, and what they like and don't like about school–curious about everything. Less fear and control and more curiosity is not only a great motto for parenting, but for life in general.

Hence, a parent might open the conversation with, "I saw your report card earlier today. How do you feel about it?" Then, follow up with, "What class do you like the most? Why do you like it?" Perhaps your kid got an A in that class. "I noticed you didn't do as well in English, and I'm curious to know more. How is that class for you?"

Do you see how we can lovingly move toward someone who is "failing" and truly offer support and guidance? Of course, this only applies to your child. Don't ever treat yourself this way. No, I'm kidding!

But, to treat yourself this way, you may have some healing to do. You may need to let go of some of the trapped emotions you're still holding in your body around the shame of failure. Doing so can open up your capacity to treat yourself in an entirely new way.

The One Body

This has been a recurring theme throughout this book and something I could write endlessly about, but the short of it is this: If you want to truly be on your own side, no matter what, then you must reject the cultural programming that says in order to be worthy of love, you must have a body that looks like this (insert images from the media that you have internalized as the "ideal" body image).

Rewind a few hundred years ago, heck probably even just eighty years ago, and few people wrapped their self-worth into their body shape, size, and fat-to-muscle ratio. Imagine being alive in a time when there was no media or imagery to look at, no TVs, magazines, or an endless feed of images to scroll through on your phone (Yikes! What did people even do back then?).

How many images have you seen of a "perfect body"? Have you ever seen an image of that? Perhaps you would have a friend in your neighborhood or someone you know of who you think is pretty or handsome. Of course, there were still societal standards of beauty even then, and, depending on the era, the culture may have been encouraging all kinds of weird shit (such as corsets for women). Yet, despite this, people were not exposed to hundreds of thousands or millions of images of a "perfect body."

As a result, I would make an educated guess that the vast majority of people did not spend a lot of time preoccupied with their body fat. Flash forward to the present day, and you and I have seen this perfect body a million and one times on social media on your phone, on a bus that drives by, and in a commercial during the game. This weekend, I was at a Barnes & Noble bookstore with my kids. As we paid for our items at the checkout stand, they had a rack of magazines standing beside the cashier. I glanced over and saw three *Sports Illustrated Swimsuit* magazines–not one, but three. Are they releasing three at the same time now? Did they have too many pictures for not just one but two editions? Was the *Sports Illustrated* magazine franchise now being propped up by this one yearly release of softcore swimsuit porn?

So many unknowns. In any case, in that brief second, while paying for some kids' books, I absorbed three images of the "perfect body." Oh, make that four because above that there was *The*

Men's Health Big Book: Getting Abs: Get a Flat, Ripped Stomach and Your Strongest Body Ever--in Four Weeks with a picture of (you guessed it) a dude's abs.

While the faces of these models might change, the body doesn't. We are bombarded day and night by the image of the perfect body, which always looks about the same; hence, it's "The One Body." This is the body to strive for, the body to sculpt, the body to become. If you want to feel sexy, be attractive, and win prestige and influence, then this is the way to do it. Get this body. Look like this. Be like us. And you will feel amazing, sexy, strong, powerful, desirable, and above all else, finally worthy of all the love and other goodies in life.

In order to live a life of permanent O.M.O.S., you must consciously reject this insanely toxic message. In my experience, this is easier said than done. The decision to reject this message and develop deep, authentic love and acceptance of our bodies is not a one-time thing but rather an ongoing process. It's like pulling weeds in a garden. There can be hundreds of them, and you have to pull them out by the root. You can't just hack off the top of the plant. Similarly, you must become aware of all the ways you reject yourself and your body—all the ways you strive, ache, and long to look differently. All the violent or subtle ways you try to force, starve, deprive, exercise, or otherwise manipulate yourself into looking a certain way. But only for a certain period of time, because for 99% of people, even modest changes toward "The One Body" are highly unsustainable, and we revert back to where we were within several years (or much less).

Even those who have somehow obtained the coveted "One Body" are not walking paragons of self-discipline, virtue, and sex appeal. Rather, when interviewed, many models reveal tremendous insecurity about their bodies, comparing themselves to even more perfect bodies who have obtained "The One Body" appearance even more than they have. Not to mention the host of side effects they might be experiencing in the obtainment or sustaining of those abs or general thinness, including massive hunger, irritability, amenorrhea (loss of menstruation), hyper-rigidity around food, orthorexia, anxiety, and good ol' fashioned reduced libido. Ironic for a sex symbol, isn't it?[21]

To truly liberate ourselves, we must fundamentally reject the notion that our body size and shape are related to our human worth. Just like our bank account number doesn't mean anything about our worth, the number on the scale is equally irrelevant. It means nothing about your capacity to care, to love, to laugh, to live, or to give. It doesn't even mean anything about your fitness level or health. To learn more about this, I highly recommend *Body Respect: What Conventional Health Books Get Wrong, Leave Out, and Just Plain Fail to Understand about Weight and Health At Every Size* by Linda Bacon.

Learning to be on your own side, no matter what, including no matter what your body looks like, is an ongoing journey and one absolutely worth taking, as it will help your confidence and self-esteem in ways that far exceed just body image.

Ultimately, this body you've been gifted with is temporary anyway. Even if you starved all the fat out of it and sculpted in it all the right ways, obtaining that glorious and coveted image of "The One Body" for a year, or a decade, it matters not. The definition of your muscles will fade, your skin will stretch and sag, and your body will age. Later still, you will be dust and dirt amidst rock and stone in the earth. Your time here in this body will be done. Perhaps you'll come back in a different body, or perhaps not (no one's certain about that). In any case, this is your one life with this body—your real one body. Can you love it? Can you feel the life force, vitality, and energy pulsing through it? Can you feel

---

21 To learn more about the dark side of the fitness and modeling industries, I recommend checking out Madelyn Moon's book, *Confessions of a Fitness Model: The Ugly Truth about the New Standard for Beauty*

the energy, power, and light in your heart that shines out your eyes? This is what matters. This is what you're here for.

Forever Young

An aspect of "The One Body" shape we're all indoctrinated to desire is youth–perpetual, indefinite, unwavering, permanent youth. This is the natural state for humans you see. Nevermind that all things in the world around us are born, age, and die. We, you and I, we shall live FOREVER!

Does that sound like a monologue of an insane villain in a bad sci-fi movie? Well, it turns out, it's the ad copy for the cosmetic and anti-aging industry. The standard party line is: Come on, we all know the truth. Aging is gross. It looks bad, it's not sexy or beautiful, and it's certainly not acceptable–not if you want to get ahead in life or find and maintain love. If you want to do that, then you best fix that gross aging situation with our new line of age-defying white liquid! It's only $49 per one-ounce bottle. Simply spread a small dollop on the affected area, which in your case is your face, which is where all the wretched aging is occurring. Now do that every day for the rest of your life, and you'll be set!

If it's not creams, then it's masks, or lifts, or whatever. Then it's supportive clothing to shape your body appearance to make sure it looks like nothing droops or sags. And, if you're really ready to fight the battle against aging, then you get your weapons out. You pull out knives and motors and sucking machines and slice away all that oldness with cosmetic surgeries.

And still, after all this, aging happens. Like a relentless, slow, endless river, time degrades your skin, hair, muscle tone, and all the rest. And yes, humans will keep fighting this horrid misfortune, this cosmic error. We will battle mortality with frenzied vigor, especially in this era of the new science of biotech, nanotech, telomeres, and stem cells. This may be the century we finally get it, finally achieve immortality! Or not.

In any case, there is no peace to be found there. To truly be on your own side, you must reject the cultural insanity that aging is bad. I want you to grimace when you hear messages about aging skin looking bad or old people having sex being gross. It's an insane form of prejudice, which is especially nutty because we will all eventually become the group that is being reviled!

No, no, no! Enough of this. It's time to break free, my friend. Decide right here and now that there is nothing wrong with aging; that aging is a beautiful, natural part of the cycle of life; that there is wisdom in age, beauty in the growth and maturity we develop as we live on this planet, and even aesthetic beauty in the wrinkled skin, sun spots, and breasts that sag due to gravity and feeding and sustaining new human life.

Plant your stakes in the ground here and now, and say you will be on your own side, embracing the aging process from now until you die. And each time you forget this and freak out because you see a new wrinkle, or less hair on your head, that's a reminder to come back to your senses, to remember your responsibility to fight the evil machinery that causes humans to turn on themselves, to disconnect from their own power, hearts, and sanity. You fight that machine by remaining on your own side, by finding your way to peace and self-love in the midst of aging all the way until your final breath and the end of your journey in this human life.

Fashion Police

This one is right in line with "The One Body" and trying to stay forever young so we won't spend too much time covering it. But it's yet another way people can feel an intense sense of shame when they have not done anything wrong. This shame arises when we perceive that we don't have the latest clothes, best-fitting clothes, or fancy designer outfits.

Here again, we are programmed into believing that this matters a great deal. Our outfit determines our sense of worth, lovability, and likelihood that we will be accepted, hired, promoted, invited, acknowledged, admired, and loved. There is a great deal of glamour surrounding the fashion industry that is designed to propagate this illusion. All the ads send a loud and clear message: *If you look like this, then you'll be admired, envied, loved, and accepted. You'll look like us and finally be good enough.*

Of course, the entire thing is untrue. Your human worth certainly has nothing to do with your clothing, but rather with your value, your ability to create, share, give, and do whatever you're here to do. Yet, like so many other traps we can fall prey to, this one might get you from time to time. Perhaps you judge yourself harshly when you look in the mirror, labeling your outfit as too big, not form-fitting enough, or somehow or other "making you look bad." You are scanning your environment to see what others are wearing, either temporarily feeling superior or inferior based on who you're looking at. It all seems so real, so significant.

Just the other day, I overheard a woman say this to her friend, "Yeah, I wouldn't be caught dead in last year's dress." I don't know what the context was, but this line sure stood out to me. There was such a tone of pride and superiority in her voice. She wasn't going to be one of "those people" who would wear last year's dress. Fools. Idiots. No, not her. She's one of the superior ones, the smart ones. The irony of it all makes me smile though, because she's taking pride in her intelligence as measured by her complete conformity to a system that makes her spend her money on unnecessarily new clothes every single year—a machine that, should she choose to not buy into for the coming year, would undoubtedly induce an onslaught of inferiority, insecurity, anxiety, and shame. Sure sounds smart to me.

It's yet another thing to let go of. No, I'm not saying you should wear nothing but gym shorts and t-shirts for the rest of your life. You can have nice clothes and enjoy those clothes. You can buy new clothes that delight you. Just be mindful of the entire process. Be totally honest with yourself—are you on your own side? When you're buying the clothes, are you on your own side? Are you loving your body or wishing it was different or better? When you try on that outfit, are you disappointed, not because it's not a great shirt or blouse, but because you don't look like the model did in the picture?

In other words, are you trying to get something out of the clothes that is simply not there, because it's not in the clothes? Are you trying to feel more whole, complete, or worthy through this endeavor? If so, congratulations for noticing this and having the courage to be completely honest with yourself! This building of self-awareness can be a humbling and surprising process, and it is a key aspect of becoming truly free.

Then, once you've noticed this, choose to reorient yourself. How can I get on my own side right now? If I were totally on my own side, what would I do here? Perhaps you'd buy some new clothes that fit better and make you feel more confident and outgoing. That's fine. Perhaps you see you already have a ton of clothes and don't need to grasp for anything else– that you need to focus on cultivating unconditional confidence and self-worth that has nothing to do with your shirt, pants, or jacket. Slow down and get on your own side. As you do, the answers you seek and your next steps become clear.

Flawless Sexual Performance

My, oh my, this one might cause more suffering than all the rest combined. For almost everyone in our culture, sex carries with it a certain degree of shame. Even if you didn't grow up in a household that actively shamed sex, the topic was most likely avoided, not talked about, and generally regarded as "off-limits."

I had two conversations with my parents about sex during my entire upbringing, and each one only took about 15 seconds.

Sex Conversation 1 (age 5):

I have an erection and don't know what it is. I tell my mom, and she tells me to tell my dad. Dad is sitting at the breakfast table, eating a quick bowl of cereal. I tell him something is going on with my "luli" (this is the word we used, which is Urdu for penis. The English word "penis" was for some reason dirty or not right to say). My dad has me pull my pants down, looks at my penis, and laughs.

"You're not supposed to have that until you're older!" he says, chuckling.

I stand there for a moment, confused, then pull up my pants, and dash off.

Sex Conversation 2 (age 12):

When I was a teenager, I would look through the HBO schedule to see what movies were playing late at night and if they had nudity in them. I would then set a VHS to record all night to capture said nudity. This was in the days when the internet was in its infancy, and all that was available for nudity was exceedingly slow-loading still images.

One day, I was scanning ahead on the cable channel screen and saw a channel that was entirely nudity. It was some sort of adult movie channel. Oooh, jackpot, except it wasn't because you had to pay for the movies. The screen asked me if I wanted to spend $5.99 to watch. *Hmm,* I thought. *I'd better not. I'm sure that charge will show up somewhere...*

But, on the other hand, I was a teenager with low impulse control. So I selected YES on the screen. I'd deal with any repercussions later. My initial rush of excitement soon turned to disappointment, however, when I discovered that this movie was some kind of super softcore porn. Not only were they not showing sex, but they weren't even showing much of anything. It was certainly nothing more than a sex scene from an HBO movie. Ugh!

Flash forward several weeks, and I'm sitting in the passenger seat of our sweet grey 1993 Chrysler Concorde. My mom was beside me driving, and we sat quietly, listening to the radio. My mom reached toward the command console, turned the radio down, and cleared her throat.

"So, we had a charge for an adult movie on our cable bill recently," she said.

Uh-oh.

I felt a wave of embarrassment and shame wash over me. I wanted to sink into the car seat and disappear. How fast were we going? Only 30 miles per hour? I bet I could open the car door and sort of fall out. Tuck and roll, and I'd be fine. It would be better than talking about this.

"Yeah," I admitted. "I ordered something."

"Oh." My mom said, pausing. She seemed unsure of what to say next. Perhaps she wanted to let me know it was okay. Perhaps she had hundreds of ideas, pieces of wisdom or advice, or dozens of questions she wanted to ask me. Was I dating anyone? Had I ever had sex? Would I use protection? Did I have any fears or doubts or challenges in this area of my life? Or perhaps she just felt extremely uncomfortable as well, trapped in her own conditioning of shame around sex. Regardless, she just said, "Was it good?"

"No, not really," I replied.

And that was that. We went back to silence and never spoke about that movie or sex ever again.

Meanwhile, I'm learning about masturbation from other eleven-year-olds in my middle school. I start watching porn several years later and absorb thousands of images, ideas, and perceptions about sex, sexuality, and relationships.

And I become another one of the millions of men and women in our culture who has a big ball of shame around sex with a direct pipeline to feelings of insecurity and inadequacy. On top of this completely feeble foundation of awareness of what sex, intimacy, and connection are truly about, we are then fed countless distorted messages about sex.

Here are the most common ones for men and women.

Men:

In order to "be a man" (a.k.a. worthy of acceptance, respect, and love), you must be able to meet and seduce women, have many sexual partners starting at a young age, instantly get and sustain an erection no matter the circumstances, bring your partner to orgasm, then orgasm yourself, all while appearing relaxed, confident, playful, and saying and doing just the right things to make the experience super sexy.

Women:

In order to be a valuable woman, you must be attractive to men such that you are pursued and desired. You must not sleep with partners too quickly or have too many of them, as this is unwomanly. During sex, you must be instantly wet, ready for penetration, able to orgasm relatively easily through vaginal sex without wanting or needing any other stimulation, all while looking sexy, making the right faces and sounds, and looking like you're having a great time.

This is the prescribed sequence for heterosexual sex, and it must be performed flawlessly each time, or else you must feel a crushing sense of shame and unworthiness because you are indeed shameful and unworthy. Even just the fact that we call it "sexual performance" is disturbing. Oh, and according to the dominant cultural messages, if you are gay, queer, transgender, overweight, past a certain age, or anything else that doesn't fall immediately into the two basic categories of young man or woman, then you don't count. Sex for you is weird and different, and it shouldn't be happening, or at the very least, shouldn't be talked about.

Yuck. Do you see how toxic all this is? To be permanently on your own side involves consciously rejecting this extremely narrow rulebook around who you have to be as a sexual person. The level of programming here is so thick, it's almost tangible. It's like a heavy metal that coats us, weighs us down, and pulls the joy out of sex and life.

Sex is a sacred act. The sexual energy that moves through us is the same energy that flows through the entire cosmos, that pulls planets toward stars and holds galaxies together. It is infinitely varied and expressive, like music, art, or the flowers and plants in nature. It can be so vast, so wide open, so beautiful.

And here we are, reducing it all down into a checklist of specific acts that must be performed under threat of brutal self-hatred should we fail to follow that list. Let this go now. Reject this toxic narrative and decide to do something different, to allow yourself to be something different. Let sex be about connection, expression, curiosity, and discovery. Explore what delights you and lights your partner up. And above all, let yourself enjoy it!

Fearless

Despite being one of the most anxiety-ridden cultures of all time, we have a strange delusion that we should never feel afraid of anything. We can equate fear or anxiety with a sense of personal failure as if we don't have what it takes to hack it in today's modern world. We're not tough enough, confident enough, wise enough, balanced enough, or otherwise not "together enough" to be light, free, and happy as we should be.

This has only intensified as we've spent more and more of our time, focus, and life energy on cultivating our social media personas, which, surprise, surprise, don't display much anxiety. Look, here I am at the beach having fun. Here I am at that party, also having fun. Here I am visiting my grandma, HAVING FUN! I'm always having fun. Laughing, smiling, living the good life. There, now, at least I look good to others on the internet. Whew.

But the truth is anxiety, fear, doubt, and even more intense experiences like overwhelm and panic are common occurrences—for everyone. Yes, even that famous actor, or your composed boss, or that handsome man who seems to have bullet-proof confidence at the bar. They are anxious–every single one of them, but perhaps not every moment. In that moment that you see them looking relaxed, they might truly be relaxed, or they might not be. You never know because people are highly skilled at hiding their true feelings, especially ones they feel ashamed of, like insecurity or anxiety.

But even if they are fully at peace in that moment that you witness them, they will be anxious. Later that day, or later that week, they'll be freaking out in their heads, worrying, judging themselves, wondering if they can handle something. This is normal. This is what our minds do.

To become truly on your own side is to acknowledge this reality of what it is to be a human right now. We are living in what philosopher Alan Watts referred to as "The Age of Anxiety." This is not a personal flaw or weakness—it's a product of our environment. We are living in densely populated urban areas with little to no contact with nature or the outdoors. You can spend years without your bare feet touching the soil of the earth. We spend much of our time disembodied, engaging with technology, dealing in abstract numbers, concepts, and industries such as marketing, media, and development of new consumer goods. We are completely unaware and generally uninterested in where we come from, our personal or collective roots, our connection to the cosmos, and the Three Big Questions: Who am I? Where did I come from? Why am I here?

All of this leaves us feeling unanchored, ungrounded, and unsure of ourselves. On top of this shaky foundation, we are continually bombarded with ten hours or more of screen time a day, ingesting large amounts of thoughts, ideas, philosophies, and other inputs that absorb our focus and make us more uncertain and afraid. The speed of human development is accelerating at an exponential rate, which creates even more uncertainty in our environment. Survival fear permeates everything we do. It is the Age of Anxiety, indeed.

Of course, there are many things you can do now to take care of yourself within this world. We all have so much access to information that can teach us how to come back into ourselves, rediscover our origins, and reconnect with who we are and our purpose. And still, this is a lifelong process of self-discovery and by no means eliminates all anxiety.

It's okay to feel anxious. It's okay to feel afraid. It's okay to feel insecure or doubtful or envious or inadequate. It's okay to feel whatever you're feeling.

The most powerful way to liberate yourself from this toxic cultural message is to act in defiance of what it dictates. In other words, it's to share more authentically with others about how you are in the moment. At first, this can be quite uncomfortable or scary. It can feel like revealing that you're anxious would be the worst possible thing to do. And yet, the more you do this, the more you discover it's no big deal at all. In fact, rather than turning on you, others are more drawn toward you. They appreciate your authenticity and transparency, feel closer to you as a result of it, and hunger for that kind of freedom themselves.

Fierce Love

This is but a shortlist of the toxic messages we receive from our culture every day. To liberate yourself and truly be on your own side, you must champion yourself and fight against these messages that are constantly trying to infuse themselves into your mind and consciousness.

This is not a simple flip but rather a longer-term process that requires repeated self-awareness and decisions to let go of self-hating messages that do not serve you. It entails reprogramming yourself over time to see yourself completely differently than what you were taught is true.

To do this requires strength, power, and determination. It requires a ferocity in your love for yourself and a willingness to stand up to and fight industries and systems that have hundreds of years of history and billions of dollars at their disposal. Like a mother tiger protecting her tender young, you must cultivate your inner warrior to battle this force to protect your tender, beautiful heart, mind, and soul.

As you do this, you will start to become more and more free of these poisons. You will see more clearly how inverted these messages are—how they are not only inaccurate, but they are telling you the exact opposite of what is true. Instead of being ugly, you are magnificently beautiful. Instead of being weak, you are stronger than you could imagine. Instead of being unworthy or lacking, you are infinite, fully connected, fully loved, and divine.

The more you get on your own side, the more you stop trying to conform to all these insane, inhuman, fabricated standards, and the more you start to discover who you truly are.

DISCOVER WHO YOU ARE

The path of permanent O.M.O.S. requires an entirely different approach to living, growth, and development. Most people take the standard "fix it" model and apply it to themselves, which goes something like this:

I am not living as fully, joyously, or abundantly as I could be. I could be more free, more rich, more funny, more sexy, more loved, more happy than I am right now. To become these things, I need to fix my issues–issues like anxiety, depression, niceness, insecurity, lack of education, social awkwardness, and so forth. When I fix these issues, I'll feel better and get all those goodies that I want out of life.

We discussed this mindset earlier in the book, and on the surface, it kinda, sorta checks out, doesn't it? It has a simple kind of logic to it that is appealing to our rational minds. The only problem is it treats us like an object. Much like a mechanic who wants to soup up his old Honda Civic to make it go super fast, you simply have to change a few parts, and all of a sudden, you'll be a racing superstud.

But in reality, this approach is inherently flawed because you are not an object. And you don't know what is "wrong with you" (if anything), what needs to be "fixed," and if doing so would bring you the happiness and other feelings you seek.

Happiness and fulfillment do not come in the ways we've been taught by mainstream media and marketing machinery. In that model, you are not happy because you lack something specific. Once you've acquired the specific item or experience, then you will feel happy and fulfilled.

When it comes to our human experience of fulfillment, purpose, enjoyment, and meaning in life, it works quite differently. Instead of knowing what we should be like and making ourselves that way, we gain happiness through the exploration of interesting and meaningful experiences that lead to the discovery of who we are and who we are meant to be.

In other words, you don't know how you're supposed to be and exactly who you're supposed to become. That's just an idea, often a projection of our "Fantasy Self" onto the future, in which we imagine we will one day obtain it and then experience the relief of suffering and obtainment of permanent connection, love, and victory.

Let's take a deeper look at this journey of growth and exploration by examining the Big Three Questions.

The Big Three

In his fascinating book, *Coyote Medicine*, Dr. Lewis Mehl-Madrona shares his journey straddling two worlds of healing and medicine as he trains in allopathic medicine and shamanic healing rituals simultaneously. According to the healing traditions of his Native American heritage, a key aspect of healing from an illness involves the context of the illness, not just the biomechanics of the pharmacology. To get well, someone who is sick needs to get the message of the sickness and explore three major questions:

Who am I?
Where did I come from?
What am I here to do?

While he was speaking in the context of healing from an acute medical or psychological sickness, I see the power and necessity of these questions in living a meaningful life in which we are on our own sides. Indeed, exploring these questions is part of the journey of discovering who you are and who you're meant to be.

One key distinction with these and other self-inquiry questions is that asking the question is more important than any individual answer. Getting a distilled sentence that you can repeat is not the point. It's about the way your thoughts, perspectives, feelings, and behaviors are expanded and enhanced through repeatedly asking the question.

Let's take a few moments to explore these questions together now. Each one is a highly personal inquiry, so your journey with it will be different than mine. However, discussing it will get the process going for you in a profound and meaningful way.

Who Am I?

Have you ever slowed way down and asked yourself this one? It's a doozy. There are so many different ways you can take it, aren't there? You can go simple and start listing some basic data points, such as your name, job title, roles you play, and so forth. But even as you do this, you know it's far from complete. What if you got laid off? What if you changed careers?

We can go deeper, answering in terms of biology, chemistry, physics, or metaphysics. We can bring in spiritual ideas of energy beyond matter, the soul, and much more.

Or you can examine this question through a personal psychology lens. What makes me tick? What do I love? What are my passions? What are my pet peeves, dislikes, and aversions?

The beauty of this is all of it is right, and all of it is great. There is no wrong answer here and, perhaps, no clear answer at all. And anytime you settle on something, feeling like you've gotten to the bottom of it, and you can peg "you" down to a simple verbal description, let it sit for a few days or weeks, and see if it all still feels so solid.

One of my favorite ways to work with this question is to have it running in the background as I go about my day and life. I will ask it on occasion with no goal of getting an answer in that moment or striving in any way. I let it work its magic in the background, knowing it will guide me toward more authenticity, greater choice, pursuit of what is important and meaningful, and more.

Where Did I Come From?

I love, love, love this question! For me, it instantly pulls back the thin veneer of order, predictability, and rational explanation that we have in our society. With verbal language, advanced scientific understanding of many aspects of the material world, and super powerful technology that gives us mastery over our immediate environment, it's exceedingly easy to think we have it all figured out. Mystery is on its way out, on the fringe, as our brilliant, ever-expanding base of knowledge inevitably pushes the mystery further and further back. At least, that's the default illusion we can fall into until we take just a moment to ask a question like this: Where did I come from?

Uhh. Hmm. I don't know. I mean, in the most immediate way, I came from my mother's womb. And my parents came from their mother's wombs, and so forth up the line. That, I know for sure. But beyond that, it gets a bit murky, doesn't it? Follow the human lineage back, and then, who knows? Pick your favorite theory then. Did all humans emerge from a primate species in Africa? Is our timeline on that accurate? What about all the fascinating information coming to light about Göbekli Tepe in Turkey—an advanced temple structure that existed at a time when humans were only supposed to be hunter-gatherers? Or you can take it even further back to Gunung Padang in Indonesia, where there is a pyramid that some predict is over 20,000 years old. And what about the argument that water erosion on the Great Sphinx of Giza suggests that it too may have been constructed over 10,000 years ago?

These are fascinating questions regarding the development of human civilization on this planet. What about the bigger questions about where life came from and comes from? Here, again, the reductionist explanation that random molecules collided to somehow form biological entities is interesting but by no means answers any of the deeper mysteries. Or how about this one—take a few minutes one afternoon when you're bored and lookup on your phone how water originated on Earth. Have you ever considered that one? Where did all the water come from? It didn't start on the molten ball of rock that the earth originally formed as.

These short ramblings are but a small fraction of where my mind goes when I ask this question of "where did I come from?" And we're not even delving into the utterly unknown terrain of where our consciousness comes from, how we experience consciousness at all, and what may happen after we die.

I will leave all this exploration up to you for your quest. The key action here is to merely begin asking this question. Let it pull information, conversations, and experiences into your awareness. Let the inquiry guide you as you go throughout your normal day-to-day life.

Notice how it can steer you into a deeper sense of self-discovery, wonder, and appreciation for who you are. It can help soften the chains of toxic cultural dictates of how you should be, and perhaps dissolve the sense of utter significance and reality that we give to our appearance, popularity, and fleeting successes and failures in this human game.

What Am I Here to Do?

What comes to your mind and heart when you ask this question? It may be something you've given a lot of thought or something that you have been too busy or too wary to examine, for fear of the answers disrupting your personal status quo.

Or perhaps you've only examined it within the narrow parameters of your work or career. When we examine purpose, we often immediately look at the work we are choosing to do in the world, and the two become synonymous. While this is an absolutely essential inquiry to guide the direction of your work in life, it is by no means comprehensive or complete. What you are here to do goes way beyond what you are here to contribute to a particular company, customer, or industry. That's just the tip of the iceberg.

It also includes what you're here to experience, to learn, to discover, and to do. It even includes how you are meant to be throughout your days, including the way you carry yourself, the state of consciousness you tend to reside in, and how you treat others.

When we expand this inquiry beyond vocation, you might start to realize that no one thing is inherently more important or better than any other. For example, one thing it seems that I'm here to do is to deeply explore consciousness, including dreams, lucid dreams, altered states of consciousness, and ultimately navigate the passageway from this life into death and beyond.

Hence paying attention to my dreams, deeply engaging with the dream world, and bringing more of that way of being into my waking life is part of what I'm here to do. Is paying attention to dreams and what happens in them less meaningful than completing a task at work or earning a paycheck? For most people, the default answer is, unfortunately, "yes." What we're here to do can be reduced to what we bring to the marketplace in exchange for money. At least, that is, until you begin asking yourself this third big question and discovering your own path through life.

"Used to dream of outer space
but now they're laughing at our face
Saying, 'Wake up, you need to make money'"
- "Stressed Out" by Tyler Joseph of Twenty One Pilots

Spending time with these questions in the background of your mind, guiding your focus will do wonders for not just your physical health, but your mental well-being as well. In a strange, circuitous way, these questions will also increase your sense of being on your own side. For they will help pull you further out of the delusions of our culture that demand you perform to be worthy, earn to be lovable, and look a certain way to be valuable. They will help reorient your focus with a compass that is rooted in a much deeper ground of truth, which will guide you to much higher levels of authenticity. In other words, you'll be being you more and more over time and appreciating the miraculous wonder that is the ever-evolving, dynamic consciousness that you call "me."

UNLIMITED SELF-CARE

One more key aspect of residing on your own side all of the time resides in your ability to take care of yourself. Indeed, taking care of someone is a deep communication of love that goes beyond passing feelings or desires. As a parent, you take care of your child because you love them, whether or not you feel like doing it that day. When someone close to you, such as a parent is sick, you do what you can to help and take care of them. When the situation is drastic enough, you might drop everything and give care in this way. This is a beautiful, undeniable demonstration of the power and significance of love.

And, much in the same way, when you are fully on your own side, you place a high priority on taking care of yourself or self-care. You realize that no one else can do it for you. While you might get support from others in times of need or have a friendly shoulder to lean on some of the time, the truth is no one can be there in the ongoing way that you need. No one can be there providing support, encouragement, guidance, love, and empathy twenty-four hours per day—no one, that is, except for you.

In this section, we will examine how to take care of yourself in little and big ways. This not only makes you feel better, moment to moment, it also sends a powerful message to all those parts inside of you, including your critic. A message that says loud and clear: I matter. What I think, feel, want, and need matters. And I'm going to protect, guide, nurture, and love myself because it is important to do so.

Self-Care 101

First, we must briefly cover the basics of self-care. Many of these you may already know, and others may be new to you. Regardless, reading this will raise your awareness around self-care, which will naturally lead to you doing it more. That is often the biggest challenge in taking care of ourselves—it's not that we don't know what to do; it's that we don't habitually and regularly do what we know is good for us.

Before I share more, let's do a quick pop quiz. Ready? What do you do to take care of yourself? What are your current self-care practices? Take a few minutes to reflect on this and then resume reading.

What did you discover? There is no single way to take care of yourself, just like there is no single way to love another person. So anything you came up with is part of your own way of nurturing yourself. Below are some common ways to take care of yourself.

The most fundamental form of self-care is how you care for your own physical needs–paying attention to what your body is telling you and honoring it. This includes sleep, rest, and slowing down when needed. This might seem obvious, but in today's hyperspeed, hyper-stressed culture, we can easily perceive sleep as wasting time and slowing down as an unrealistic option. For many people, creating a healthy level of activity and rest requires planting their stakes in the ground and setting clear boundaries around when they will take breaks, bedtimes, and so forth.

Another major aspect of physical self-care is how you nourish your body. Do you drink water throughout the day and minimize your ingestion of soda and other chemicals? Do you eat nourishing, healthy, real foods such as fruits, vegetables, nuts, seeds, legumes, grains, and meats—all whole foods that are minimally processed? Making this the bulk of your diet can eliminate food cravings and post-meal lethargy. Each person is different, but a practice of taking care of yourself means you study how what you eat affects you and adjust accordingly.

Do you move each day? Do you find ways to stretch and activate your body? Do you do activities that stress you physically in a good way and increase your heart rate? Self-care approaches regular exercise as something you do most days because it makes you feel better that day, rather than to obtain the perfect body.

In the next section, we'll explore that fuzzy zone of indulging in foods that satisfy your cravings. Does O.M.O.S. mean I let myself off the hook and eat what I enjoy? Or is that not being on my own side because I feel bad afterward or my body becomes less fit? We'll address this common inquiry in a moment. For now, let's keep looking at the basic ways you can take care of yourself beyond the physical.

The next form of self-care is treating yourself well within your own mind. This can be broadly described as "positive self-talk" and has been a major focus of this book. Not surprisingly, having an inner critic in there telling you that you're a no-good, rotten loser all day long is *not* taking great care of yourself. Practicing the techniques you learned in this book is a major aspect of self-care. It can make major positive shifts in your mental attitude, mood, confidence, and physical health.

A third aspect of self-care impacts every aspect of your life. However, it is invisible to many people, who wouldn't even identify it as self-care. This invisible yet obvious form of self-care is assertiveness. All of the principles I teach in my previous book, *Not Nice*, are life-changing forms of taking care of yourself in all your relationships, which directly impact your daily confidence and mood.

These principles include prioritizing your needs, asking for what you want, saying no to things that are not right for you, and expressing yourself about what's working and not working for you in any given relationship. In essence, saying "no" is taking care of yourself. Asking someone for something that you want is taking care of yourself. This kind of assertiveness is becoming your own advocate, which is an essential type of self-care.

One other type of self-care that people don't immediately recognize is what I would call generosity with yourself. Many people can have a stingy way of relating to themselves, rarely giving themselves anything, and certainly giving much less than they would to friends and loved ones. They don't buy the things they want most, labeling them as "too expensive" or "not worth it." They put off vacations or trips for the same reason.

This lack of giving to ourselves often stems from a sense of being unworthy or not deserving of the things we genuinely want in life. Giving yourself the things you desire can be a powerful form of taking care of yourself that opens your heart to more ease and joy. These things can be both small, such as getting yourself that drink you crave from the coffee shop, or large, such as a trip you've always wanted to take.

For any of these kinds of self-care, as well as the ones you came up with earlier, there is one essential ingredient for making them work: doing them. Each self-care action requires a choice to carry out that action in the moment. If you repeat that action enough, it becomes more habitual, and you reap the benefits of ongoing self-care.

Initially, setting up self-care habits takes focus and effort. Getting enough sleep, for example, might require you to look at your schedule, determine the best bedtime and wake time for you, and then commit to a schedule. Even still, you may discover it's an hour past your bedtime, and you're deep in a wormhole on your phone instead of going to sleep. Now your eyes are all zapped out from the blue light of your phone, and you're agitated and have a hard time falling asleep. These setbacks require you to study your behavior and make adjustments, discovering what lead you off course and what you might do to solve those problems.

The thing about a lot of self-care practices is they feel fantastic once you're doing them regularly. However, getting into the practice is sometimes uncomfortable, and we can have resistance to change, physical effort, or abstinence from indulgent behaviors that ultimately don't make us feel good (such as staring at our phones for an hour before bed).

The best way to start is to see what you're currently doing and what's already working. Then, focus on strengthening those practices, making them more consistent. If you want to add something else, pick one change at a time, and implement it. For example, if you want to alter your diet, focus your energy on that. You can determine the kinds of foods you want to eat, look up recipes, determine when you'll go shopping during the week, and generate a meal plan. Resist the urge to make multiple changes at the same time, like altering your sleep schedule, working out more, and, and, and... Pick one thing and focus on that.

As you do this more and more, it becomes a kind of game that is rewarding to play. You can see how many areas of your life you can be managing well at the same time. Remember to let go of perfectionism and the need to "do it all just right," and instead, find the enjoyment in taking great care of your diet, health, emotions, and mind. The more you do this, the more you'll want to do it, and the better you will feel.

Indulgence and Self-Care

Is it good to indulge? Is that part of being on your own side?

This is a question that often comes up with clients and in my own life. For many, the path of self-control with diet, exercise, work ethic, and more comes from a harsh inner tyrant that whips you into shape. Hence, if you eat the donut, that part makes sure that you hate yourself for eating the donut. Your "donut" (a.k.a. dopamine hit) can be many things—processed sugar, alcohol, cannabis, tobacco, porn, escaping into the internet or streaming media, flicking, poking, and scrolling impulsively on your phone. By punishing yourself in this way, you'll never, ever do it again. I mean, why would you? Look how bad you're making yourself feel. You'd never subject yourself to that again, until you do.

Wanting that dopamine hit comes from feeling restless, agitated, sad, scared, empty, or anything other than feeling whole and complete in this moment (which you always are). So there we are, feeling some sort of bad inside and wanting to feel better. *I know! I'll eat the cinnamon roll dipped in cannabis oil while I binge-watch my favorite show and scroll on my phone at the same time!* And so you go for it to reduce the pain inside and temporarily feel better.

But then, in comes the punishment pit crew. Your critic goes to town on you, berating you for your weakness, your lack of willpower, your wretchedness. It also hits you with fear about how bad this is and how you'll never fix it, and you'll get fat, sick, and gross because of your transgressions. So, in response to this emotional version of getting repeatedly punched in your stomach, you vow to never do it again.

But what does this kind of self-treatment do to your mind, body, and heart? Does it fill you with love, confidence, and self-esteem? Or make you feel some form of inadequate, flawed, or bad, which in turn makes you feel restless, agitated, sad, scared, empty, or...uh-oh, I know where this is headed.

And around and around we go on this merry-go-round, always repeating the same pattern, even though it's clearly not working for long. The way out is not through more self-attack or punishment but, paradoxically, through forgiveness and letting go.

I made a little study of this earlier this year with a particularly delightful indulgence— cinnamon rolls. There's this little vegan bakery near my house that serves a variety of delicious treats, including some wicked awesome cinnamon rolls. I had spent months doing a particularly regimented diet routine (as part of some Insanity Orb nonsense to get lower body fat percentages) and had decided to relax a little.

I was out on a date with Candace, and we walked by the bakery. *Why not?* I thought. Less rigidity and more fun–let's live a little! Candace got a pear galette, and I got my favorite pastry of all time, the cinnamon roll. We sat down at a little table in this cozy little shop, and I looked at my confection on the table. My heart rate slightly increased, and my mouth salivated. This is going to be awesome! And it was. The outside was a little crunchy, and the inside was a little gooey. As you worked your way into the middle, there was more sweet cinnamon frosting coating the sides of the heavenly spiral.

Why had I restricted myself for so long? How stingy. How uncaring. How cruel. This was where it was at. I finished the cinnamon roll and took a big sigh of relief. Absolutely delicious. It was a decent size roll, and my stomach felt pleasantly full. My mouth, on the other hand, was not on the same page. It wanted more–more pleasurable sensations now! In addition, my heart seemed to also be wanting more. I could feel a craving, grasping energy for more cinnamon roll, more stimulation. I noted these sensations as we left the shop and carried on with our date.

Over the next few days, I found myself thinking about that dang roll again. I wanted it to be the next Sunday date so I could get another one. I find this is the way it goes with me. When there's something I delight in that gives me that dopamine hit, be it sugar or cannabis, I will want more the next day. Then begins a long, protracted battle within myself between the part that wants to indulge and the part that wants to resist.

So what does this have to do with you and indulgence? I don't know, but you do! What's your experience? Are you able to dabble a little here and there, or does your hunger for sweets, porn, drugs, or alcohol take over quickly? So, is an act of O.M.O.S. to let yourself indulge or to resist? That is a personal inquiry that has different answers for each of us, depending on the substance in question and the time in your life.

In this particular case, I rode the cinnamon roll wave for about seven weeks. Like a trained rat hitting the pedal for a pellet of cocaine, I repeated the same behavior every Sunday for almost two months. I was determined to get that cinnamon roll. In fact, one Sunday, we went, and they had run out earlier in the day. I was utterly devastated. We went to another bakery in town, and I got a cookie, but it didn't suffice–a lesser drug–I mean food.

Interestingly enough, I watched as my perception of the downsides of the habit began to outweigh the benefits. I saw how I felt a strong craving ahead of time but then a dissatisfaction upon finishing the roll. I also noticed how it made my other foods, such as my daily smoothie, chock-full of vegetables and sweetened with banana and blueberries, wasn't cutting it. I kept adding more of those two fruits, trying to make it have more pop, but there's no way around it; a vegetable and fruit smoothie ain't gonna taste like a cinnamon roll.

I've found this is the most powerful way to unhook from a habit that is no longer serving you. Simply bring mindful awareness to the entire experience over a period of weeks. Study how it feels before, during, and after. Notice the benefits and any adverse effects over time. Your inner critic has a sense of urgency, fear, and condemnation. You'd better stop this or else! In truth, you can let that habit run for a while longer. It's probably already been going for months or years anyway. So let it continue but with more attention, mindfulness, and self-love.

Is this serving me? Is this enhancing my life or making it more difficult overall? These are great questions to ask yourself. They will help you navigate this particular craving you're working with, as well as deepen your discovery of yourself.

I've found, for myself, that the old adage, "One hundred percent is easy; 99 percent is a bitch," rings true. In other words, deciding I'm not going to do something at all is way easier than doing it occasionally because then, there's always this nagging question of "is now the occasion?" As a result, I don't eat chocolate, drink caffeine, eat refined sugar of any sort, or drink alcohol. I use cannabis infrequently and only purchase enough for one use, to prevent the "I have it so I might as well smoke it" phenomenon. While this might seem spartan or restrictive, I find it delightful and relieving. Given my extreme personality, I find the ongoing craving for one thing or another annoying.

But what about when you are reducing or eliminating a behavior or substance, and you experience that craving? What do you do? You know it's not in your best interest, and it doesn't serve you long term, but who cares about later? I want it now!

Below is a technique I've used many times to navigate cravings to sidestep them without getting sucked in when I don't want to.

Ride the Wave of Craving

When there's something you find yourself craving but know it's not best for you, here's a powerful technique you can apply. About two years ago, I decided to stop all use of pornography. I had been exposed to it at the age of eleven and had used porn regularly since that time, even while in romantic relationships.

After a period of deep investigation of the impact of porn on my life, including my relationship, sexuality, and brain chemistry, I decided I no longer wanted to use it. So one day, I made the final decision to never use porn again.

But I found that this compulsion had a form of intensity that was much stronger than an urge for a particular food. This makes sense, as the rush of dopamine from using porn is most likely stronger than from say, processed sugar.

I began to bring mindfulness to the process and developed a technique that I call "Riding the Wave," in which you take careful note of the experience of the craving. Here's how to do it.

When you notice the craving arise, pause what you are doing, and pay attention to it. Cravings can come on strong and fast and sometimes lead to immediately acting on them without even thinking about it as if your body has been taken over. Do your best to pause, breathe, close your eyes, and ask yourself: "how strong is this craving on a scale from 1 to 10?". Rate the craving in its intensity and the time since it began. Also note what the craving is "saying"—as in, what it is urging you to do, and how your mind is urging you to do it. For example:

Desire level: 8/10

Time: 0 min

Do it! Do it now! It will be so bright and shiny and gratifying. Do it now. Don't wait!

I've found this is often the case with cravings. There is an urgency to them and a feeling that you must do it, and do it now. Interesting, as most likely, you could do it in an hour or so. But that's not how cravings work. This part of you wants you to do it now, so it creates a false sense of urgency. There can also be a strong sense of aching or longing or missing out if you don't do it now. Just ride the wave and hang on. It's building.

You can either sit there in a form of meditation, observing the craving, or busy yourself with something else, such as a work project or washing dishes. Check again in a few minutes. How strong is the craving now? I've noticed that sometimes, within as little as two minutes, the craving can be significantly less. Keep checking back every few minutes to see what the intensity level is, and jot it down somewhere. Writing down the numbers and seeing how the craving arises, peaks, and falls can give you a great sense of mastery over the process. You know that all you have to do is wait it out, even though that craving voice inside tells you that the feeling will never go away until you indulge.

During this process, you can also remind yourself of your reasons for not wanting to indulge in this behavior or substance. You can project into the future and imagine how you'd feel after indulging. This can create a sense of aversion that gives you fuel to resist the urge to cave in and do it.

I've found that after seven to ten minutes, the craving is almost always gone. Of course, when I check back in at that time, it can resurge a little, back to a three or four. But if I keep focusing on something else, it will disappear entirely.

The more you practice this technique and successfully dodge the craving impulse, the less intense the cravings will become. I often remind myself that indulging now will only make me want it even more tomorrow, and it will be even harder then because I'd just indulged. Over time the cravings become less intense and less frequent to where they appear only on rare occasions and are easy to resist.

Of course, in this process, if you do end up caving in and going for it, what are you going to do? That's right! Beat yourself mercilessly. No! Instead, practice instant forgiveness. Soothe the judgmental part inside of you that is angry at you for doing it and scared of bad things happening. Reassure yourself that you're okay, and that forgiveness, self-love, and understanding are the keys to making the change over time.

Say to yourself and any part of you that is upset: I'm sorry. Please forgive me. Thank you. I love you. Repeat these phrases again and again as you breathe in and out slowly. It's okay. You're okay. The most important thing to do now is to remain on your own side.

And that truly is the most important thing my friend. Not just with cravings, or productivity, or goals, or relationships. In all things, what if your highest priority was to be on your own side first?

Epilogue:
The Gift of Failure

I stopped running less than two blocks from my house. The pain searing through my back and leg felt like my nerves were on fire.

"I can't do it," I said out loud in the silent, predawn air.

I turned back toward my house and limped home. This was failure. I was registered for my first ultramarathon that was in less than two weeks. I'd been training for the last four months, running throughout the winter, through rain and snow.

I'd overcome my mind-body pain, inspired others, and told lots of people about this upcoming race. But about three weeks before the race, I experienced an intense flare-up of pain that severely limited my ability to move and walk, let alone run.

I took a few days off from running and looked inward as I'd learned to do. What message did my body have for me? Where was I pushing too hard, being too perfectionistic, and building up tension or unconscious anger through stress?

The first message I received from my body came back loud and clear in an instant: *Slow down.*

Where? In what ways? I asked myself. But even then, I was guiding the answer because I didn't want to hear the truth. Slow

473

down at work? At the gym? Certainly not with running, that was out of the question this close to the race. And so, I took some steps to slow down in other areas, but these proved ineffective at relieving the pain.

I gave it a week, stressing about the race, trying to let go of needing to run it. But so many stories were popping up in my mind. What would people think? I said I was going to do it, but maybe I'm not?

Behind the fear of others' imagined disapproval (bonus points if you can remember which kind of self-criticism that is) was a greater fear of what failing would mean about me.

Hence, the forced run attempt in the early morning. *The race is ten days away. I haven't run for a week. I have to be able to run now to show myself I'll be able to run that thing!*

But my body was saying "NO" loudly. As I turned and hobbled home, I felt discouraged, sad, and frustrated. I could feel the stories in my mind start to churn. And then, in an instant, it all stopped. It was so sudden and so relatively effortless that I felt confused for a moment. And then I laughed.

I felt a wave of gratitude for this book, for the gift of being able to write about being on my own side for almost a year. I felt grateful for you, for, without readers, I would not spend this much focused, deliberate time writing on this one topic. But thank goodness, I did.

Because in that instant of relief, all the teachings and healing messages in this book flooded back to me.

I saw the perfectionism, the drive to prove something, to show that I was good, impressive or enough in some way. I saw how I was trying to prove to myself that I was healthy and strong by doing these feats of strength. I saw how extreme they were. *I'm not just going to run, or run some races, or even just a marathon. I'm going to run ultramarathons! That's how healthy and ultra-strong I am.*

This was the game I was playing. It was a game of my choosing and something that people around me didn't care much about. All the significance was in my own head.

"Aziz," I said out loud. "I love you, no matter what. You're worthy, no matter what– whether you do this race or not–whether you even run or not. Running is just an activity. It has nothing to do with your worth. I love you, regardless."

But, but... My mind grasped. I could feel the sadness, aching, and longing underneath. I felt disappointment at the idea of not running through the woods doing this race I had dreamed about. As another act of O.M.O.S., I felt the sadness fully and empathized with that part of me.

"Of course, you want to run free and strong through the woods; how amazing that would feel. I know it would be disappointing if we didn't run the race. You'd feel tremendously let down. I hear you. And I'll be with you through that disappointment and sadness.

"I'll be with you as you experience all those feelings, loving you no matter what. I'll defend you from fabricated, critical stories about what this means about you. I am proud of you, no matter what. I love you, no matter what. I think it's amazing how far you've come with your body. Regardless of this one particular race, your story of physical healing and liberation is inspiring. And I'll keep on loving you through it all, to when this pain episode recedes, and we run again, through the woods. Maybe not at this race, but you will run again soon. We will run for fun, run for joy, run as a celebration of gratitude for a healthy body that can move freely after so many years of pain and perceived limitations. And it will be glorious."

I breathed deeply into my chest in the damp morning air. The sky was starting to brighten, and I could see all the flowers that cluttered the bushes near my house. The air smelled sweet. The feeling of deep relief in my chest was sweet. I felt a wave of gratitude growing in my chest and felt tears in my eyes.

I felt grateful for my body, grateful for the pain. I'd been striving so much to be who I thought I was supposed to be–an "ultra" man of sorts doing feats above and beyond what average people (mere mortals) would do on a path that seemed right, that sounded good, that gave me pride. But it was time to veer off that path. It wasn't the wrong path to take before, because all paths move us forward. It just is no longer the right path to stay on. For it was still me trying to become something I thought I needed to be in order to be good enough.

Despite letting go in a deep way that morning, I apparently needed to learn the lesson at an even deeper level. As the race approached, I noticed myself fretting about my inability to run without pain. Completely letting go and withdrawing didn't feel right, but I didn't know why. Was it just my ego? Could I not fully let go for good? Or was it something else? Was I guided to run this thing for some reason?

Who knows? But I felt called to do it, so I did. So there I was, standing in the wet early morning air at the starting line of the Stumptown 50K at the edge of Forest Park, surrounded by a hundred other people who think running for 30 miles in the woods seems like a fun way to spend a Sunday.

My body hurt. I hadn't even started running yet, and my body hurt. I managed a four-mile run earlier that week, but that felt like a struggle. Yet here I was, open to learning whatever it was I was guided here to learn.

The gun sounded, and off we went, running up into the hills of Forest Park with incredible green, lush beauty on all sides. Yet the joy I often feel running in the woods was not present in that moment. All I was aware of was the tight, stabby feeling in my low back and buttocks as I ran. Ugh, this was going to be a long race.

I had secretly hoped that getting out there and just running it would somehow send the right message to my subconscious—

that the pain was not physical in nature, not "real," and therefore could be pushed through or ignored. Apparently, the part of me generating the pain had a different idea. Over the next five miles, the pain intensified, reaching peak levels of intensity. Each step shot waves of nervy, pinchy, burning sensations up my leg and spine. My pace slowed. More and more people passed me. Ow, my pride.

But I kept trucking. I made it about thirteen miles in that state before something snapped inside of me. *I can't do this*, I thought. Or rather, I don't want to. I could somehow will myself to keep gutting it out for the remainder, but sweet Jesus, did that sound brutal. And for what? For who?

So I decided I'd quit. Only there was just one problem. This wasn't a major city marathon where I could dart off the main road, sneak into a deli, order a sandwich, and be done with the whole thing. We were way out in the woods. I didn't even know where the next checkpoint was. Doh!

Eventually, we came to it at mile fifteen, where there was a small folding table with three volunteers and a jug of water. I came up to them and slowed to a walk as other runners busied themselves, filling water bottles and such. I stood there, hesitating. *Other runners would hear my sad admission of failure and judge me...*

"So," I began. "What would be the best way to stop at this time, if I wanted to do that."

"Oh," one of the volunteers said, looking confused. Apparently, no one else had asked that this early in the race. We were only halfway through. Shame. Shame. Shame.

He put his hand on his chin and furrowed his brow. Then, he opened his mouth as if he were about to speak, paused, and closed it again. Then, he turned to his compatriots, and they talked amongst themselves. I stood there sheepishly as runners came by, filling their water pouches, snacking, talking about how hard it was. But they kept going. Not me. I was quitting. Loser.

The three men at the aid station all turned toward me now, apparently having determined the correct answer. I had two options, apparently. I could go to the top of this one-mile steep ascent and turn right, making it to the next aid station in three miles. There, I could sit out the rest of the race and drive in with them after they broke down that aid station in three or four more hours. Barf. I had to get out of dodge faster than that. So it will be option two then.

Option two was to go up that same damn one-mile ascent (there was no avoiding that apparently) and turn left at the top. This would take me to a trailhead where people park and go for hikes. I could find some unsuspecting, wilderness-loving family and pounce on them, beseeching them for a ride back to town. Sold! I chose option two.

By this point, my body was toast. My lower back had completely seized up, and a slow jog was excruciatingly painful. My body hobbled from side to side as I attempted to jog. Walking would take forever, so I tried to press on more quickly, but about halfway up the steep ascent, I began to walk. Runner after runner passed me. Even the ones who were walking walked faster.

I felt flooded with shame, embarrassment, and failure. I felt so weak, so broken, so incapable. And then, in an instant, I again remembered this blessed book and the phrase on the cover: O.M.O.S.

"Hey!" I said to myself. "I have a choice here. I can choose to hate myself for this and make it the worst thing ever. Or I can choose, right here and now, to not turn on myself, to be on my own side, no matter what, especially right now!"

And then, with the full force of every word you've read in this book, the message of O.M.O.S. burst into my heart. The shame and anxiety and judgment melted away instantly. I looked around at the ancient trees around me, covered in moss, the fields of ferns on either side of the trail. I watched a middle-aged woman huff and puff as she jogged up the steep hill, passing me on the narrow trail. What was her story? What was she running this for? How hard had the journey been for her to get here? I felt curiosity, empathy, and love.

I saw the truth that she was not judging me. Heck, she was deep in her own process and probably only barely noticed me, mainly as an obstacle to run around on the trail. No one cared. In the best possible way, no one cared. The only one that cared was me. But, then, I realized even that wasn't true because this part of me didn't care. It was my ego that cared, my ego that was embarrassed and bruised. But I was just fine in that moment.

I laughed as these insights burst forth on that one-mile ascent. It was the most amazing experience of deep O.M.O.S. I'd ever had in my life, right in the most intense moment of judgment and self-hatred. To be able to have that torment break so quickly and shift so readily was nothing like I'd ever experienced before. I am so grateful for the gift of this race and the gift of the failure within it.

As you've been on this journey with me, I imagine you have had similar moments of self-love expand in your heart. And if you have not, keep practicing, and you will! Available to all of us right now is the deepest relief that comes from the moments when you profoundly let go, when you are able to see clearly with your mind and know in your heart that you are whole and complete right now–that you don't need to achieve more, earn more, do more, or be more to be worthy of love and joy, and that you don't need to do or achieve anything more to feel relaxation and peace.

Peace is available right now. And the path to experiencing it is not in tackling more projects, getting someone else's love or approval, or getting somewhere "out there" in the world. It's bringing your attention "in here," inside of yourself, and finding whatever part is dissatisfied, demanding, scared, or hurting. Tap into your deepest sense of self-compassion, and even a source of compassion and love way bigger than any of us. Let this divine love pour through your own heart and into and around all these parts of you. Bathe every single part inside of yourself in this ocean of acceptance and soothing love–infinite acceptance, patience, and love for no reason other than because you decided to give it and receive it.

Do this consistently, and you will feel a joy that is so much greater than the temporary high you feel at the attainment of a goal–a joy that is not fleeting or dependent on everything going your way out there, a joy that lasts.

This is the gift you can give yourself, again and again, moment by moment, in your moments of failure and moments of triumph. In every moment for the rest of your life, you can be on your own side.

Thank you from the bottom of my heart for taking this journey with me. I love you. And I can't wait until our paths cross one day, and you can tell me with enthusiasm in your voice and tears in your eyes about how much you love yourself.

How to Connect With Me

Thank you for reading my book. If you are interested in going further with your confidence journey, I would be delighted to support you on that path. There are a number of ways to connect with me and continue your journey toward ever-increasing O.M.O.S. and confidence.

Coaching Programs and Live Events:

The most impactful way to make rapid changes in your confidence and life is through immersive experiences. These can be one of my three-day live events or an ongoing coaching program with me or a hand-selected confidence coach from my team.

Unstoppable Confidence Mastermind

An exclusive group program with Dr. Aziz designed to produce radical and rapid transformation in your confidence in all key areas of life. In a deeply supportive environment, you will receive direct coaching and guidance from Dr. Aziz and his team of coaches through group coaching calls, mastermind retreats, live events, daily videos, and much more.

To learn more, visit

www.SocialConfidenceCenter.com/mastermind

Rapid Confidence Immersion

A deep coaching program with one of Dr. Aziz's personally trained, hand-picked confidence coaches. You will be guided through proven strategies with an expert on the subject to hold you accountable and ensure you get the confidence you need in relationships, at work, and in all areas of your life.

Dr. Aziz Live Events

Over the course of three days, you will be immersed in an environment that is inspiring, supportive, and refreshingly authentic. Through dynamic teaching, engaging exercises, and bold action, you will not only learn how to build confidence, you will actually build your confidence muscle real-time at the event.

Live events focus on key areas of life, including:

- Conversation Mastery
- Relationship Confidence
- Career & Professional Confidence
- Core Self-Confidence

To find out about upcoming live events with Dr. Aziz, visit: www.SocialConfidenceCenter.com/Events

Online Training Programs and Books

Confidence University
Progress through the most powerful, dynamic, and systematic confidence-building program in the world. You'll make consistent weekly progress through interactive teaching, activities, and Action Steps in the real world. Imagine knowing exactly what to do each day and week to build unstoppable confidence, step-by-step.

www.theconfidenceuniversity.com

Five Steps to Unleash Your Inner Confidence
This ebook contains powerful and proven techniques used by the world's top psychologists and coaches to help you overcome your fears and self-doubts. Whatever area your lack of confidence is impacting, this ebook can help you. It gives you the basic tools and strategies you need to start mastering your confidence today.

To download your free copy today,

go to www.SocialConfidenceCenter.com

The Solution to Social Anxiety
In this inspiring, breakthrough book, Dr. Aziz guides you on the path out of social anxiety into lasting confidence. You will discover why you feel anxious around others and the steps you need to take to develop social confidence in all areas of your life.

To get your copy today, visit

www.SocialConfidenceCenter.com

The Art of Extraordinary Confidence
This book playfully and ruthlessly shreds through the stories, excuses, and self-doubt that hold you back, showing you the core reason you aren't taking bold action in life: fear. Dr. Aziz expertly guides you through any fear that is in your path so that you can live with more boldness, power, confidence, and freedom.

To learn more about this book, visit:
www.SocialConfidenceCenter.com

Not Nice

This popular book gives you complete permission to stop pleasing others, avoiding direct conversations, and being so... nice. You'll discover why "nice" is different than kind and loving, and learn essential skills for sanity and healthy relationships, including: Having boundaries, asking for what you want, saying no, speaking up for yourself, and many more.

To get your copy today, visit
www. SocialConfidenceCenter.com

APPENDIX:

O.M.O.S. Parenting: How to Be on Their Side and Yours

Throughout this book, you've discovered dozens of new ways of treating yourself with more empathy, kindness, and love. Nowhere is this more needed than in the realm of parenting. Parenting is a full-spectrum experience that stretches and challenges you way beyond your perceived limits. It evokes a wide range of emotions and can bring out your most immature, undesirable behaviors. Because of its demanding nature and the deep significance of nurturing another being, being a parent radically increases your own emotional, psychological, and spiritual growth. This appendix will provide you with some key ideas on how to approach this life-altering, monumental task with more love for you and your children.

Even if you do not have children, you may find the following appendix highly valuable. To become fully on your own side requires reparenting yourself inside of your own mind and tending to the parts of you in a different way than they were tended to when you were young so that you can move toward, reassure, and love all of yourself, including the scared parts, angry parts, immature parts, and so on.

Who this appendix is for:

- Parents who want to know how to help their children love themselves, have high self-esteem and feel more confident.

- Parents who want to be more O.M.O.S. with themselves about their parenting, releasing ongoing judgment, shame, perfectionism, and relentless demands to "do more" and "be better."

- Anyone who wants to have a deeper understanding of how to treat their own inner child, thus greatly improving their own O.M.O.S. skills.

The topic of how to raise your children is enormously vast, with thousands of authors, teachers, and experts each providing a perspective. This short appendix is by no means a comprehensive look at parenting with all of its intricacies. And I do not stand behind these ideas as the "right way" or "only way" to parent your child. Only you can determine that for yourself.

My main goal for this appendix is to help you open your heart even more—both to yourself and your children, thus creating more forgiveness, ease, harmony, sweetness, and magic in your life now.

Diamond Hunting

One way to think about life is as a series of moments. There's this moment right now as you're reading my words. Then, there's another moment in which you are doing something else, feeling something else, experiencing something else, and on and on. We live moment to moment, to moment, until the very end of our moments on this plane of existence.

I like to imagine this progression of moments as beads and stones on a string. Some moments are mundane and seemingly ordinary. Those are like plastic white beads that don't captivate you much. Organizing your mail pile, responding to basic emails, preparing a meal you've made a thousand times before—while you may reside so fully in the moment that you find joy in these moments, often times they feel like "nothing special."

Other moments are new, exciting, fun, different, or beautiful. These are pleasurable moments, and we often wish they would last longer. In the necklace analogy, these moments would be like a luminescent crystal, sparkling in the sunlight.

Of course, no moment lasts, and so it passes right by, and you are back to some more beads. Then, something awful comes down the pike. Oh no! A wretched stone that you can't even look at. Someone rejects you, you hear that your company is going to do layoffs next month, and you don't know who's going to make it, or your child gets sick.

In these moments, you wish time would speed up so this discomfort would end quickly. You may even proclaim to others via complaints out loud or silently in your head, "I don't like this! It's all wrong!" You are making it abundantly clear that you never want a moment like that to happen again. *Are you listening, God? You got that??*

Parenting takes this string of moments and radically turns up the dial on the intensity knob. Each passing moment becomes even more fully experienced to a much greater degree. The plain, ordinary moments might take on an endless quality to them. When reading a story that you've read a hundred times before, you may struggle with boredom or the repetitiveness of it all. When there is struggle or strife amongst your children or between you and a child, it can seem awful and unbearable. Your mind might instantly resort to intense complaining about not liking what's happening, not liking your child, not liking your life.

Here's a series of snapshots from just one morning to show what I mean:

It's 4:30 a.m. In this moment, I am calm. It is before my boys wake up, and the house is quiet and still. During meditation, I realize how rigidity is the cause of so much suffering in me. I want things to be a certain way and get anxious or angry inside when they are not. I enjoy the feeling of insight and the sense of possible liberation from letting go and being more flexible. I think, *Today, I'm going to be like water. I am going to flow and adapt.*

It's 7:30 a.m. In this moment, Candace is out for a run. I'm taking care of our two boys and two puppies. Yep, we got two puppies a few months earlier. I know, what on earth were we thinking? It made everything exponentially more challenging. And yet, we felt inspired and guided to do it, so we heeded the call. But that decision was months ago and old news.

This moment is loud and chaotic. Zaim and Arman are fighting over whose turn it is to rotate the oat grinder handle. I play referee and help come up with a workable solution. I glance back repeatedly at the puppy area—they seem good. It looks like a potty accident is a low likelihood in this moment. I'm managing everything well.

It's 8:05 a.m. In this moment, I am enraged. Arman is putting a puppy on the couch and then jumping next to him. The dog is cowering and clearly frightened. This kind of thing has been happening for months. I want to make him stop it once and for all. I want control so bad. I hate my life.

It's 8:30 a.m. In this moment, the boys are in the bath, fighting again. The fight escalates, and I need to step in to help them solve the problem. I am handling it with patience, but inside, it grates on me–the noise, the irritation, the drama. But then, right there, in that moment that seems "bad," something miraculous happens.

"Wow," I exclaim. "That's a really deep bath!"

Arman's face shifts from upset regarding the conflict with his brother and instantly brightens. "Yeah!" he says, as his eyebrows go up. Snot, which had dribbled out of his nose from a cold he is still recovering from, has been smeared towards his left cheek. His hair is wet and bedraggled. His essence is so bright, so luminous, so charged. Lifeforce seems to be emanating out from him in all directions, beaming like the rays of the sun. I feel a deep, awe-inspiring amount of love for him. The power and depth of that love seem to obliterate my small self with all its petty concerns and demands for control, ease, and for things to go my way. I am instantly aware of the impermanence of this moment and our entire lives and how singularly important love is in this existence. This moment is a diamond in the rough.

I've seen this again and again in parenting. Right there, mixed in with the noise, irritation, demands, overwhelm, and anything else that might be going on, there is a moment that is so sweet, so poignant, and beautiful that it can take your breath away. And then, that moment passes.

"Hey Mani, watch this," Zaim proclaims. "Do you see this wet towel?" he asks as he holds up a small wet washcloth.

"Yeah," Arman replies.

"Okay, close your eyes for ten seconds," Zaim commands in his magician tone. Arman complies, at least for a second or two. As he closes his eyes, Zaim swoops the towel over his head and behind his back, spraying water all over me, the mirror, and several bathroom walls. The towel makes it behind his back into the bathwater just in time, as Arman opened his eyes after two seconds.

"Wow!" He exclaims with genuine surprise. "Where did it go?"

Does the water on the mirror and wall matter? I guess, in one way, it does. We'll need to clean it up to prevent marks, or mold, or damage. But in another way, it doesn't. This moment is what matters, the depth of joy and connection that is accessible only when I am in this moment fully, letting go of rigidity, ideas about right and wrong, and needing to control anyone, especially my kids.

NAVIGATE THIS LIFE

What is your main purpose as a parent? Have you taken the time to step back and reflect on that question? It can be so easy to get sucked into the day-to-day, responding to inner and outer demands without even knowing what you're doing and why. But there's a purpose behind all this, a guiding principle. And if you don't consciously reflect on it, then you will most likely carry out the principle by which you were raised.

For some, parenting is about making your child good in the eyes of your community, religion, or some other system. For some, it's about molding children to follow in your footsteps, believe in what you believe in, and live as you have lived. And for others, it's about training them to be intelligent, capable, and successful in this world so that they can earn money, support themselves, and survive.

For me, parenting is about helping my children navigate this life experience. I personally start with as few belief systems as possible and look from the ground up. Here's what I know: We are hyper-intelligent, magnificent creatures that are mysteriously conscious, living on a planet full of other miraculous creations. This planet is one point in a vast, seemingly infinite cosmos. The Great Mystery of it all is so palpable, so ever-present behind a thin veil of understanding and certainty that we humans erect with our labels, taxonomy, and ability to predict aspects of the world around us.

This is the world that my children and I came into. I would not presume to know why they are here and what they are born to do. Only they can discover that, in all its depth and beautiful unfolding for them over the course of their lives, just as my purpose continues to unfold in my own life.

First and foremost, I am deeply grateful for the gift of being able to bring another human being into this world. I am in awe at the intelligence of my wife's body to create this human from the unpacking of codes within microscopic bits inside of single cells. I find the idea that the children are "mine" laughable. First off, they came through Candace, with a single cell contribution from me. She did all the heavy lifting of bringing their physical bodies into this world.

I am responsible for caring for them and giving them what tools I can to navigate this existence, but they are by no means mine. They are their own. They are the Creator's creations, just like me. The only thing I have over them is that I happened to pop through the portal into this world thirty years or so before them. That's the only difference, thirty years more experience than them, which, if you think about it, is not that much at all. In the big scheme of things, it's infinitesimal.

And yet, it's enough of a headstart for me to have some things I can provide that will help them. I can provide for them physically and monetarily. I can take care of their basic needs for shelter and comfort and warmth. I also want to do my best to help them be able to navigate this life experience. Because while parenting might seem like a forever job when you're in the middle of it, it's relatively short. Yes, you're their parent for their lives, but your period of full, active engagement lasts at most twenty years. And even in that period, there is a significant decrease in the amount of dependence they have on you.

So in that short time, what can we do to help them navigate this life in the best way possible? What do they need from us? Also, it can be helpful to ask this question: What is my outcome? What kind of beings do I want my children to be and become? If we don't consciously reflect on these questions, we will often get sucked into daily control battles and power struggles, and our purpose seems to be about making them obey and be the way we want. But when we take a step back and imagine what kind of humans we want our children to become, we are able to see the big picture, the ultimate outcome.

Here's my outcome for our two boys:

My vision for my children is for them to be awake, aware, compassionate, empathic, strong, expressive, alive, passionate, enthusiastic, confident beings of light who trust themselves and discover who they are, where they come from, and what they're here to do. Then, they have the courage to do it.

They have an internal code of morals and live in high integrity with that code. They are on their own sides and have a great capacity to love themselves and others and receive love. They are assertive, able to take care of themselves, have boundaries, say no, know what they want, and advocate for it. They are interpersonally effective. They are emotionally aware, intelligent, and mature. They have focus and relaxed discipline to pursue projects that are meaningful to them while enjoying themselves along the way. They are aware of their many gifts and grateful for their blessings and their lives.

What do you want for your children? What kind of adults do you want them to become? Take a few minutes to reflect on this and write it down. The act of writing will help you clarify and solidify the vague desires that operate in the background of your awareness. This by no means has to be complete or permanent, as your ideas and desires may change over time. This is merely a version 1.0 vision of what you want for your children.

The next step is to ask yourself: *What will help them become this? What do they need?* For me, it seems like, regardless of the outcome, the most powerful foundational component that I can give my children that would serve them above all else in this life is love.

(Almost) Unconditional Love

What seems to create the most shame in children is when they are judged and rejected by a parent. The parent yells, rejects, or displays disgust or aversion in a direct or subtle way, and the child feels this painful shriveling inside. They are bad, unworthy, unlovable.

This shame makes it harder to navigate life, as they become

more risk-averse, fearing failure, setbacks, and rejection, all of which reinforce the feeling of badness already in place. Thus, it would seem ideal to avoid this if we are attempting to instill self-confidence and O.M.O.S. in our children.

Easier said than done, right? Let's face it, at every age, your child is going to repeatedly do a half-dozen or more things that really push your buttons. In some of these situations, you might have a cognitive understanding as to why their behavior upsets you so. In other instances, you will have no idea why you get so triggered.

When both my children were infants (under six months old), I had a recurring experience of intense overwhelm and rage that would explode out of nowhere when certain conditions were met. If one of my boys was crying uncontrollably, and I was responsible for calming him down because Candace was unavailable, then, on certain occasions, I would feel an intense wave of panic and rage shoot through my nervous system. I simultaneously wanted to run away screaming or throw the baby at the ground. I did neither of these things, but I was disturbed at the intensity of the feelings that would course through me. I would feel guilty, despite not acting out any of the feelings. I imagined their little sensitive nervous systems could feel my energy, and it disturbed them even more.

I still don't know what that was about. Fortunately, as they grew, that trigger seemed to subside. My best guess is that something about the way I was treated as an infant led me to experience intense feelings of fear or terror. These feelings are still in my nervous system and were activated when exposed to my kids' experience. But who knows?

At the time, I thought: *Man, when they get a bit older, it will be way easier. I won't have to deal with this trigger anymore.* Sure enough, that was true. But guess what's waiting for you in the next stage as a parent. That's right, more triggers! Huzzah!

Flash forward five years and a dozen stages later, and now I get to work with a different set of triggers inside of myself. For example, one current pattern that can push my buttons is when my older son Zaim gets upset about something minor, such as his younger brother wanting to play upstairs with me. He doesn't want to play that game upstairs and doesn't want to join in. He also doesn't want us to play. He then proceeds to go upstairs and interfere with the game, while threatening and pushing his brother. Eventually, this escalates into a physical confrontation with his brother in which, if he gets hurt, he will explode with a strong desire for vengeance, even though he was the one who instigated the entire thing.

In general, I approach the situation with empathy, patience, problem-solving, and humor. But sometimes, I don't. Sometimes, I am able to see the scared, needy boy underneath and move toward him with love. And other times, my aversion inside makes it hard to move toward him lovingly.

Can you relate? Are there certain behaviors, habits, tendencies, or personality characteristics of your child that grate on your nerves? If so, you're not alone. And there's nothing wrong with you! Parents can feel so much shame about sometimes feeling dislike or aversion toward their own children. There is a subtle feeling of failure or shame for not being loving enough, patient enough, or a "good enough" parent. Unfortunately, this shame can flip into blame in which we stand behind our judgment of our child. We can then get locked into a fixed perspective of "he's like this" or "she always does that" and start to react to the undesired pattern with more force, attempts to control, punishments, and harshness.

Of course, that never feels good either, does it? When the dust of the conflict settles, and we've been too cold, harsh, or punishing, it feels pretty bad in our hearts. We don't want to be that way; it just happens too fast. We get hooked, and we end up dropping lower in our own maturity level, often behaving inflexibly ourselves. We become stingy with our love and want to withhold it, as a part of us inside says: "I don't want to love you when you behave like that."

When we act from this impulse, we are doing two things, neither of which work. First, we have a fantasy wish that if we withhold love and treat them with coldness or harshness, that our children will feel so bad and remorseful that they'll shape up and start complying with our wishes. This rarely works and often backfires into increased escalation. If it does work, usually it's temporary at best and is often a fear-based reaction in your children that they will lose connection with you, which is terrifying. That doesn't work out so well for long-term self-confidence and O.M.O.S. either.

The second thing we're doing when we become stingy with our love and withdraw it when our kids are being "bad" is acting out our anger and aggression. There are so many hundreds of moments in the day in which we must, as a parent, give to our children. Cooking, cleaning, care-taking, providing, helping— basically the entire time you are with them. At times, this can feel sweet and bonding. And other times, it can be enraging to the small part inside of us that doesn't want to do so damn much for others, doesn't want to accommodate a picky eater, doesn't want to break up another fight, doesn't want to clean up another mess! But we want to be loving and patient, so we push those feelings down and keep operating with a loving and chipper attitude.

But then, when our kid does that one thing that really pushes our buttons—you know the thing I'm talking about—it's the final straw. Usually, there is some feeble justification for our anger like they did something willingly, or hurt their sibling on purpose, or made a big mess because they didn't listen to our direction. Whatever the reasoning, we use it as an excuse to pour out a percentage of our slush fund of suppressed annoyance and anger. Our tone gets cold, harsh, and judgemental. Or we raise our voices and say things that we don't mean.

I want to assure you as you're reading that all of this is okay. It's normal and generally unavoidable. Yes, you can become more self-aware, patient, and conscious. Yes, you can be more mindful and slow to react. And still, it seems highly unlikely that you will make it through a day or a week without getting your buttons pushed and sometimes acting with less love than you are capable of. Welcome to being a parent and human. There's no perfection here, only forgiveness, humbleness, and do-overs.

HUMBLENESS, FORGIVENESS, AND REPARATIONS

So no matter how great of a parent you are, sometimes you are going to flip your lid. When you do, it may look scary and dramatic, with lots of red-faced huffing and puffing. Or it may be tightly contained in display, but the words coming out of your mouth are dripping with acerbic judgment and rejection. Or you may slap your kid's hand, set them down too hard, or grab and yank them by their arm—all things you would not be delighted if they were to be recorded and posted on social media.

When this happens, what do you do? Think about the last time it occurred for you. What did you do? How did you treat yourself inside after the fact? For many, the default response is one of shame, judgment, and self-reproach. *What is wrong with me? Why did I do that? I'm so bad.* This is the old punishment mentality coming back 'round again with its weak-sauce logic of: If I beat myself up enough, then I'll learn to behave and never do it again.

But that doesn't work. That's just using fear to try to exert more control over yourself. But the solution isn't more control. Control is like the lid on a yogurt container. If stuff is bubbling up in there and creating pressure, a lid is helpful. But when the pressure inside gets great enough, no lid is going to be able to keep everything down. You will flip your lid and explode yogurt all over the place—the sour yogurt of rage and rejection. Okay, I think I've taken this metaphor as far as we can. Moving on.

Do you see my point? The solution here is not judgment and self-hatred. It is a more nuanced, intelligent, deeper working with the parts inside of you. It's in giving time and space to the part of you that gets frustrated, impatient, and enraged, and listening to that part, journaling from that part, and venting or expressing that part when you're away from your kids. The solution also involves, as do all solutions, more O.M.O.S., even when you are mean to your kids, even when you don't behave how you want. That is especially a time for O.M.O.S.

A powerful aid to O.M.O.S. as a parent lies in humbling ourselves. Without knowing it, it can become so easy to be slightly superior and arrogant. I noticed a pattern in myself when I would see parents struggle with something, and I'd think to myself: *Pssshh. That won't happen to me. I'd do things differently.*

Flash forward a month, or a year, or five years later, and I'm facing the exact same challenges as those parents I'd judged earlier. Sigh. Nothing shatters that feeble sense of superiority like being a parent.

I no longer feel such a strong conviction that I'm "better than my parents" or that I even need to be better than them. They did the best they could and chose the way they wanted to raise me. I can make decisions to do things differently, and yet I will still make mistakes, fall short of my ideals, and cause pain in my kids. So yes, I am different in some ways than my parents, but am I superior? Is that even relevant? Does that even matter?

Something profound happens when you let go of needing to be better than anyone as a parent. You can let go of the incessant judgment of others and how they're doing it worse than you. Instead, you can feel the relief of just being an advanced primate in an insanely complex cultural milieu that has evolved at lightning speeds on a planet that we don't even begin to understand truly. Given the awareness of that, what else is there to do other than to love as best we can as we navigate this life and help our kids do the same?

This humbleness paves the way for forgiveness, which is an essential practice for any parent—forgiveness of yourself and forgiveness of your children. The faster, the better, be as generous as you can with your forgiveness; it's safe.

Often, when we are angry, hurting, and acting from our small selves, we reject the idea of forgiveness. *If I forgive him right away for hitting his brother, he won't feel my dislike of him, and he'll just do it again. I must temporarily hate him so that he feels how bad it is to hurt someone else and thus be transformed into an angel who never does it again.* So absurd! Yet this is how that part of us thinks.

When you can access it, rapid forgiveness works wonders. It can quickly turn a negative situation of conflict and distance into one of connection and peace. In fact, when you truly forgive and love, your level of influence skyrockets in the situation.

I know this one is a tall order and can go counter to so much programming inside of us. The urge to reject and punish, either physically or emotionally, is so strong that it can almost feel wrong not to do so. But how is all that punishment and petty resentment working? Does it feel great inside of you or your child? Is it creating love and enjoyment in your life?

I know it can seem challenging to pull this off, but sometimes, all it requires is a decision.

S.L.D.

Several weeks ago, my wife attended her first in-person parenting class. She's a brilliant life-long learner and has been reading books about child-rearing and development since before our first child was born. But this was an opportunity to work directly with a counselor and a group of other parents to learn about how to help a child who struggles with flexibility, adaptability, and problem solving, as our oldest child does. These lagging skills manifest as rigidity that can lead to intense emotional explosions at things that seem minor, such as not getting a certain spoon for his cereal or just the thought that his brother might have more of something than him.

It's a Monday evening, and I'm on daddy duty, planning to take care of the boys and dogs and put everyone to bed solo. I got this.

And yet, there I am in the kitchen feeling stingy with my love. I'm resentful that I have this on my plate after a long day at work. Actually, I don't even know the real reason. An immature part of me is just angry that I have to do more work and have more responsibility. Waah!

So I'm acting pouty with Arman. He wants another item from the fridge, but he already has three different foods out, each in their own bowl. I don't want to get him anything else until he eats some of those. He climbs up on the counter and threatens to throw a spoon. I get even more hard and angry and command him not to. He looks me right in the eye, breathes out hard through his nose, and holds the spoon over his head. I am so pissed.

That moment passes, and the boys are in the bedroom a few minutes later. Their wrestling game has quickly devolved into someone hurting someone else, and I hear crying from the bedroom. "Uggh!" I mutter to myself in total exasperation. I am in total resistance to the moment. I am hating my life, hating my kids, hating this moment. And it feels absolutely awful.

Then, I am gifted with a moment of sanity. Thank God!

This isn't working, I say to myself. *I'm fighting them and this moment and resisting it like crazy, and it feels awful. It's not going to change anything, but rather, just keep making it worse. Let's try something else.*

So, in that moment, I made a decision to do something else.

I walked into the bedroom and saw both boys splayed out on the bed, kicking at each other. Arman was screaming and red-faced; Zaim was laughing.

"Guys!" I said in a loud excited tone.

They both paused their kicking "game" to look at me.

"Guess what?" I asked, building anticipation. Arman stopped crying.

"What?" he asked, still frowning.

"I am going to transform!" I said, waving my arm in front of me in a grand gesture.

"Into what?" asked Zaim.

"Into Super Loving Daddy!" I exclaimed. I reached into the closet and pulled out a new t-shirt. I took off my old one and put the new one on. "Now, behold, I am Super Loving Daddy."

They both stared at me, slightly confused. At least the kicking had stopped. I took the moment and ran with it. I dove into the bed and began to hug and kiss each of them, saying the most loving things. I really hammed it up, and they loved it, laughing as they tried to get away from the daddy that was almost too loving.

The rest of the evening, I surrendered and gave generously of my love. Arman wanted to try mixing salt into his coconut water. Yes, let's try it and see how it tastes. Zaim wanted his own bowl of grapes on the couch when we read stories, instead of sharing with Arman. Yes! I can see why. Let me get you that bowl.

For the rest of the evening, there was no fighting between the boys, no conflict, no upset. They were laughing and giggling. Zaim told me he loved me a half-dozen times. He even brought up a moment from a week earlier in which I had been cranky, and he had felt hurt. I am certain he would not have been able to bring that up had he not been residing in a field of unconditional and generous love.

It was a beautiful evening and a powerful reminder that how we approach our kids can radically transform how they behave and how quickly we can change from one part of ourselves to another.

Do-Overs

While I do have moments of dramatic heart-opening that allow me to shift a conflict with my kids immediately, I certainly do not always do that. Sometimes, I'm too frustrated, stubborn, or attached to a rigid idea to let go and parent with more love. In those moments, I will say or do things that make the situation worse, that hurt my kids' feelings, and end up hurting my heart as well.

As we discussed earlier, the immediate answer here is forgiveness—of yourself and your child. This can occur as soon as you can let go of stubbornness or pride and access it. As we do this, we open the door for softening of our egos, humbleness, and reconnection with our hearts. Then what?

Then it's time for a do-over. I am a huge fan of do-overs, and my wife and I regularly use these to repair connection with our children after a rupture. A do-over is a fun and simple way to make amends and make things right with your child. Once your energy has shifted, and you are humble enough to be willing to be wrong, willing to see that you could have handled it differently (and dare I say better), then you can suggest a do-over.

I will say something like, "Hey, can we do a do-over?"

Then, I will ask them to pretend to do the thing they were doing just before the conflict. For example, the other morning, my son Zaim was feeling agitated inside and barking commands in the kitchen.

"Get me this!"

"Noooo!"

"You're wrong, Mani!"

Sometimes, these were specific demands of what he wanted, and other times it was telling his brother not to do something, like drinking soy milk from a cup. It just so happened that this morning, I was feeling low on patience. I had a short night of sleep and was feeling a bit agitated, like father, like son.

As he fired off another command, I made a snide, judgmental comment comparing Zaim to King Derwin. He is a character from two Dr. Seuss books, who is a bossy, immature king who frequently makes unreasonable demands and is easily enraged. It was one of those moments of using humor to cut someone down—something that I am highly skilled at from my younger years but something I don't do much at all now, less, but not never apparently.

He instantly felt hurt and even angrier. He began knocking over the doggy fence that kept our puppies confined to their section of the house during this potty-training stage. I hardened inside and felt even angrier. Someone had to break the cycle.

Fortunately, Candace was there, and she swooped in with the compassion and skill that she seems to have an endless reservoir of.

"You felt hurt when daddy said you were like King Derwin," she reflected.

"Yeah. BAD DADDY!" he yelled, waving a finger in my direction.

I felt more anger surge up, but then something shifted. It was a moment of insight and empathy. Tomorrow, Zaim was going to be starting Trackers. It was an outdoor class once per week, where he would spend five hours away from home, away from his mama. He was starting several new classes this week as part of our approach to self-directed learning, all of which he was excited about but scared of as well. I imagined his barking commands and wanting to control what was happening in the kitchen was an attempt to get certainty when he felt so uncertain about tomorrow. In that moment, I remembered my primary purpose as a parent—to help my son navigate this life, to be on his team, not against him, no matter what.

So I moved toward him, got down on my knees on the kitchen floor, and looked up at him. His face was constricted with anger and hurt, and underneath, I could feel his fear and uncertainty. "I'm sorry, Zaim. I'm sorry I said you were like King Derwin."

We talked for a moment about how I was feeling irritated (yellow zone) and said something I didn't really believe. Then I suggested, "Hey, can we do a do-over?"

So we had him say a few commands in the kitchen, and this time I stopped what I was doing and turned toward him and swooped him up in my arms and held him close. "I hear that you want some things," I said, looking at him. "Let's help you get them. I got you."

And that was it. He smiled, the energy shifted, and the storm had passed.

Do-overs and any other sort of repair are incredible news. They reveal that you don't need to be perfect as a parent (as if you could be). You can drop the subconscious expectation that you will one day never be triggered, never get upset, and always respond with the compassion and mindfulness of an enlightened zen practitioner. A much better and more realistic goal is to get better at identifying when there's a rupture, softening inside of yourself afterward, and then moving toward your child with a genuine desire to repair and reconnect, making it better for all.

THE MAGIC POWER OF EMPATHY

Do you remember way back in Chapter 3 when we discussed the origins of your inner critic? In that chapter, I shared "The Essential Four." These are the four things that children need to develop a healthy sense of self-esteem and an ability to be on their own sides. To recap, they are:

1. **Physical Safety:** Children need consistent access to food, shelter, and a stable living environment. Receiving this creates a sense of predictability and control that allows children to relax and feel safe in the world.

2. **Witnessed and Known:** Children need at least one adult who is able to be present with them, observing them as they cry, crawl, walk, and eventually, talk, dance, and play games. Through this witnessing, the parent deeply knows the child, including their personality style, preferences, fears, strengths, and quirks. This allows the child to feel deeply seen, preventing loneliness, and providing a sense of belonging and worthiness of connection and love. This "being seen" also creates safety and relaxes the nervous system.

3. **Seen as Significant:** Children need to feel like their thoughts, desires, perceptions, and feelings matter–that *they* matter. They need a parent who relates to them in a way that communicates that their effort, struggle, accomplishments, failures, interests, thoughts, feelings, and desires are worthy of attention. Getting this need met allows the child to see themselves and their life as meaningful and worthwhile.

4. **Loved for Who You Are:** Children need to feel loved and accepted for who they are. This requires maturity and growth of the parent's capacity to love with fewer conditions and demands, not just when the child conforms to their preferences. This leads to looser control of the child and greater respect for their individuality and sovereignty. Through this, the

child learns that they, in all their colors, are worthy of belonging, connection, and love. This leads to a capacity to take risks, be authentic, share openly, and create mutually rewarding relationships based on honesty and respect for other people's individuality.

Thus far, we've talked about how to approach your children and yourself with more love. This is an essential gift that plants the seed of O.M.O.S. within your child. Yet being loved (which is number 4 on the list above), does not automatically mean your child receives number 2: being witnessed and known.

It's possible for a parent to feel a lot of positive regard for their child but not deeply know them. They might not spend that much time with them, or they might not be that present, observant, or emotionally available. This leads to a sense of aloneness in the child, as well as a background feeling of lack of safety, and that something vague within themselves is just not quite right.

To avoid this and instead, give your child a deep sense of safety and belonging in the world, empathy is the answer. Empathy is such an amazing tool and one that we all could stand to use more of in all of our relationships. Put simply, empathy is your ability to imagine the experience of another to really "get" them and their experience.

Empathy leads to better romantic relationships, more productivity within teams at work, and more harmonious relationships with your children. And, as you've seen throughout this book, it happens to be a foundational component of getting on your own side, which requires you to have empathy with the different parts within yourself.

Let's explore some ways you can increase empathy and use this magic tool in your life starting today.

Increasing Empathy

A while back, I was on an afternoon date with Candace. It was a cold, wet day in the late fall, and we were eager to get out of the rain into a local tea shop in our neighborhood. The quaint shop always had a long line, and we stood in the back, grateful to be indoors and dry. Within moments, we realized they had the heat pumping in there, and we removed our wet outer layers and settled into the cozy atmosphere.

As I was talking with Candace, and no doubt sharing some highly fascinating story as I'm known to do, I noticed she kept glancing past me as I spoke. I turned to see what she was looking at, and I saw a woman toward the front of the line with her baby in a stroller. Candace's spidey sense must have been tingling because, within seconds, the baby let out a loud cry of discomfort. As the baby cries, her mother slowly rocks the stroller back and forth, reading the menu.

"It breaks my heart," said Candace. "She's too hot in all those clothes. She wants to be picked up."

As I looked over at the baby, I could see she was right. The baby was dressed for the winter outside, not the overheated teahouse.

"Why do you think she isn't picking her up?" I asked her.

"She's not tuned in, not open in her heart. If you're open and connected, you feel their pain and want to keep trying things to help them feel better."

That was true. I'd seen her do that thousands of times with our boys. I remember hours of us bouncing on a large yoga ball, playing music, experimenting with different holding positions, and dozens of other attempts to soothe Zaim as an infant, who tended toward being colicky and harder to soothe.

This mother in the teahouse wasn't bad or cruel or mean. She just seemed to have lower empathy. Candace would've instantly noticed the temperature change and taken off her baby's layers.

And if he continued to be upset, she would find a way to soothe him. She wouldn't be able to do otherwise.

Let's reflect on this together for just a moment. Look how easy it is to become less sensitive, less empathic with both ourselves and others. Look at how we can become armored and hardened in our hearts without even knowing it. Remember the objections to O.M.O.S. we discussed earlier in this book and how the thought of loving ourselves more is met with mistrust as if it's some sort of weakness that we must remain vigilant to not fall prey to. How little empathy we have.

And yet this kind of thinking runs deep in our collective psyche. World-renowned psychologist and author of numerous popular books on child-rearing in the first half of the 20th century, John B. Watson taught parents that displaying too much love and affection would lead to coddling and later relationship problems. Hence, he advised:

> *Let your behavior always be objective and kindly firm. Never hug and kiss them, never let them sit in your lap. If you must, kiss them once on the forehead when they say good night. Shake hands with them in the morning. Give them a pat on the head if they have made an extraordinarily good job of a difficult task.*[21]

While you may read this with slight bemusement of the sterile advice of yesteryear, make no mistake that this kind of thinking is still deeply lodged in many of our most common parenting methods, or, at the very least, in the way you parent yourself. Hence, we have the fear of showing ourselves too much love or affection, lest we be coddled and be unable to perform later in life. And as we harden toward ourselves, we must harden toward

---

21 Watson J. B., & Watson R. R. (1928). *Psychological Care of the Infant and Child.* New York: Norton & Co, Inc.

others, including our children. The armor around our hearts is not selective. It blocks our ability to empathize with both self and others deeply.

So how can we shift this? First and foremost, you can do so by doing your own inner work, as you have throughout this book. Relating to different parts of yourself with more empathy and curiosity is a significant and impactful first step. Going toward the places within that are wounded and inviting them to show you everything they got not only strengthens empathy for yourself but makes you less reactive and judgmental to others. And then, you extend this outward to others—your partner, friends, colleagues, parents, and children.

When you notice someone doing something in your life that you judge, choose to become curious. I wonder what's happening for them. I wonder what needs they're trying to meet. I wonder why they act in that unpleasant way. Each time you notice your mind labeling someone as "bad" or "wrong" and your heart closing, that is an opportunity to soften your fixed perspectives and build empathy.

With your children, you can instantly increase empathy by adopting this belief:

Children want to do well.

They want to follow the values of your house. They don't want to hit their siblings or try to hit you. They don't want to yell or break things, or otherwise, be destructive. They want to live in peace and harmony. They want to feel connection and love, rather than conflict and strife–just like you.

Thus, when they are not behaving well, this means they cannot. They do not have control over themselves and their impulses, even if it looks like they do because they sometimes have this ability. In truth, their self-control is quite variable and highly intermittent. And yet, isn't the same true of you and me?

When they are not doing well, they need something. Hence, when you see your child struggling, and you notice judgment and aversion arising rapidly inside you, you can ask yourself, "What does my child need right now?"

Other powerful questions to increase empathy and effective responses include:

- What might be bothering my child under the surface?
- What problem is he or she trying to solve?

Simply by reflecting on what could be bothering them, you will start to see the vulnerability beneath the acting out. You don't necessarily have to say the thing that you imagine is bothering them, although sometimes this can be helpful if done with curiosity rather than accusation. For example, you might say, "You seem agitated right now. I wonder what's going on. We're seeing a friend later today, and I know that sometimes it can be hard to wait. I wonder if you're feeling restless."

This is just your best guess, and you don't need to be attached to being right or making your child agree. Even if it is what's bothering them, they may not have the awareness to see or know this. Often times, you simply pondering the question is enough to evoke more empathy, which leads to a more loving response, which makes everything better.

Another inquiry is wondering what problem they are trying to solve. This helps you realize that something is not going the way your child wants, either out there in the world or "in here" inside themselves. Exploring what the problem is and then highlighting the ways they're trying to solve it can bring more empathy into the interaction and build their self-awareness over time.

There are many more methods than I can list here to shift your mindset to one of more empathy. The key is not in the strategy, but in your desire to approach your children, and other beings on this planet, with more empathy. With this as your intention, you will find countless ways to grow.

Jedi Empathy

We've discussed how increasing empathy can improve your connection with your children and give them a deep sense of being seen and known in the world. But did you know that empathy can also give you virtual Jedi mind powers? Here's what I mean.

Approaching your children with simple empathy when they are upset can shift their state incredibly quickly. It can also put you in such a great rapport with your child that they will happily follow your requests. I've seen empathy shift Zaim from an angry, pouty state into being a super-helper extraordinaire in just minutes. Here's an example.

Arman, my boisterous three-year-old, decided to go in for the attack. He ran past me and kicked his older brother Zaim's tower, causing the blocks to scatter all over the floor. Arman knew this would bring on wrath and revenge, so he ran behind me onto the couch. Zaim was undeterred by these maneuvers and lept into full-on retaliation mode, grabbing the hard plastic blocks and throwing them with all his might at Arman. The second attempt made contact and hit Arman hard in the arm, causing him to scream in pain as he thrashed his legs and cried.

That was just another ordinary morning in the Gazipura household. But one thing I absolutely love about my work is that helping others heal helps me heal. When I am writing a book on a subject, I grow and am healed just as my readers are. As a result, my sense of being on my own side has never been stronger. And the more O.M.O.S. we are, the more loving we can be with others.

So I noticed my impulse to chastise Zaim but did not say anything. While Arman did antagonize him, Zaim escalated it to an intense level quickly. I noticed myself feeling upset by his attack and wanting control. But instead of acting that out, I did this.

I said, "Oh Zaim, those blocks are rock hard. I think that really hurt Arman." He looked at me defiantly and stamped his foot, indicating he was angry and stood behind what he'd done. I picked Arman up and put him on my lap as I sat on the floor. I reached my arm out toward Zaim and said, "Come here, buddy. It's okay." He hesitated for a second, then darted toward me, jumping into my arms.

I sat there on the floor, rocking slightly as I held them both. I could feel Arman's hot tears as he sobbed against my chest.

"Arman, you didn't like what bro-bro was doing, so you knocked over his tower. Zaim, you got really angry when he knocked over your tower, so you threw a hard block and hit him. Arman, when he hit you, that really, really hurt."

I'm not sure where I learned this technique—from one of the many parenting books Candace has read and told me about. I've used it hundreds of times with great impact. I simply reflect back what occurred without loading it with my judgments or evaluations. It provides a deep sense of empathy and being seen and can often quickly deescalate tense situations and fights.

"I'm sorry Arman knocked over your tower," I said, as I kissed Zaim on the head. "I'm sorry Zaim hit you with the block," I said, kissing Arman on his hot, sweaty hair.

And that was that. Within seconds, the boys were up out of my lap, playing with blocks. In fact, without my demanding one apologize to the other or trying to control the situation in any way, here's what happened next.

Arman declared he would help Zaim build a new tower. As they began building together, Zaim paused and said in a sincere voice, "Arman, I'm sorry I hit you with the block."

"That's okay," his little bro replied.

I couldn't help myself from laughing and crying in that moment. It was so sweet to watch. It's so powerful to be reminded of how much goodness there is in our hearts, and how that goodness naturally emits when we are nourished with empathy and unconditional love.

The next time your child is in conflict with a sibling, a friend, or you, practice physically moving toward them. Get down on their level, so your eyes are at the same height as theirs or slightly lower. Look at them and narrate what happened exactly as you saw it, without any judgmental interpretations. Simple statements work best, such as, "You didn't like it when she did ____" and "When he took your toy, you got angry and pushed him down."

Sometimes, you will need to narrate the entire exchange a second or third time. If you're doing it right, you will find that the children involved will stop acting out and start listening. Being clearly seen without judgment has a hypnotic, trance-inducing effect. We've even busted out a whiteboard and drawn the scene like a football coach drawing out a play with his team.

As all parties involved are seen and validated and not judged, the need for conflict often disappears. Play and harmony can resume. And you, my friend, return to the other adults who were observing in awe at your superhuman powers of persuasion.

GIFTING YOUR VALUES

What values are important to you in life? What ways of being do you think are better? Perhaps it's kindness, humor, love, compassion, generosity, courage, or adventure. Each human has a different set of values in a different order, and these shape how we approach life. Most parents believe their way of approaching life and their values is a good, sensible, and smart way to go about life.

I mean, that's the way I'm doing it after all, so it must be smart!

Parents attempt to instill their values into their children. This is not inherently problematic, especially since many parents want to instill their best values and highest virtues. The problem often arises, not in what is being passed on, but in the manner in which it is attempted. Sometimes unwittingly, and sometimes consciously, many parents attempt to install their values into their child with the expectation that their children should be the way they want. If they aren't, then the parent dislikes and rejects the child until they acquiesce and adopt the "right" values. Needless to say, this rigid approach creates great suffering in both parents and children and often leads to distant family relationships that have a pretense of togetherness during a family holiday, with no real depth, intimacy, or connection.

In this final section, let's look at how you might gift your best values to your children so that they can use them to lead a better life.

The Ultra-Long Game

Do you have control over your child? No? Well, you should!

At least this is how we feel, isn't it? If your child is doing something unpleasant in a public setting, such as yelling or having a tantrum, you can feel a sense of embarrassment, social anxiety, and shame. It feels like it reflects poorly on you as if you should have more control over your child.

And there are plenty of people who believe that and will even tell you that, directly or indirectly. They might say your child needs more discipline or consequences or that you need to be firmer with them or let them know that you are in charge.

Control is not only appealing to those on the outside but is rather appealing to you on the inside as well. Of course, we want to control our children! We want control because we don't want agitating behaviors that irritate us or make our lives more challenging. We want control because we don't want to feel the feelings that get triggered when our kids push our buttons. We want control because we want more ease and autonomy in our lives. And we want control because we want to look good and not be judged.

And, at the same time, if we reflect on our overall purpose as parents and our ultimate desired outcome for our children, we'll see that control doesn't lead there. Control is about making this moment easier, often with a cost in the long term. For example, gaining control over your child's expressiveness so that they don't raise their voice inside, interrupt you when you're speaking, or otherwise blurt out unwanted things might seem nice in the moment. Your child is now obedient, polite, and quiet. But what did you have to do in order to obtain that level of control? Most often, it involves a fair amount of threat and fear in order to make them comply. Hence, they don't interrupt you because they are terrified to do so.

"Good!" Your parents might say. "You are teaching them to respect their elders."

But flash forward to when they're in school, and a group of kids is excitedly talking all at once. What does your child do? He or she sits there quietly, of course—that's what he or she has been conditioned to do. What about during the teenage years when someone pushes them toward something they don't truly want, perhaps involving cheating on a test, doing drugs, or sexual activities. Do they speak up for themselves? Are they able to be outspoken, expressive, and assertive? That depends, to a degree, on what they were conditioned to do when they were young.

While the promise of control is appealing, and the desire inside of humans to gain this control is seemingly endless, it is not optimal for creating confident children who are on their own sides. What works much better is a form of guiding that I refer to as the Ultra-Long Game.

This refers to an approach to help steer your children toward your values over many years, without exerting coercion to make it happen in any time frame, or ever. It is my preference than my sons will adopt my values around courage and kindness, for example. But I am open to them developing those values over many years, indeed their lifetimes, as I am still developing those qualities to greater degrees in myself.

Hence, when one of my kids displays something that is unkind, I do not move in with force, saying, "What is wrong with you? Why did you hit your brother like that? How awful of you. Apologize this instant!" And then, should he refuse to apologize, I would escalate my coercion in order to gain dominance and control. I may punish him in some way to make him apologize. Are you familiar with this approach? Did your parents use it with you? Did you like it?

Do you use this approach with your children? Sometimes people back this style up by saying kids need the discipline and need to be trained or else they will become spoiled. However, a deeper understanding of child development will reveal that young children have limited empathy and impulse control.

So, if I want my son to be more kind, I'm much better off using the empathy-style skills I shared in the section above. This is the ultra-long game for building kindness. I am looking at over the next ten years, not the next ten minutes, days, or weeks.

Control always comes with a cost. I have witnessed parents who use force and control and have obedient and polite children that followed all their commands. The grandparents approved. Aunts and uncles and teachers approved. They were good parents who knew what was what. And then their children reached adolescence, and all hell broke loose. They no longer had the same amount of control because of the growing autonomy of their children. They physically couldn't control them any longer. Worse still, they had lost a deep sense of mutual rapport and connection over the years of dominance and control. Their children were rebellious, distant, peer-oriented, and over it. Their parents had lost them without even knowing how or why.

Then, in the face of their dwindling influence and disappearing child, these parents would do the only thing they knew how to do—exert more control. They would attempt to ground them, forbid them from doing things, or take away things they loved. As the divide grows greater, the parents become more desperate and dramatic in their attempts. In the case of one parent, he took his son's gaming system console, smashed it in the driveway, and then burned it in the backyard in a metal barrel. What values are we trying to pass on again?

There is a better way. Within the frame of the long game, there are two extremely powerful ways to positively influence your child while increasing connection, trust, and rapport, with all upside and no downside.

Modeling

Modeling is the most direct, lasting, and influential form of teaching you can ever do with your children. What you verbally say to them, while important, is a far second to the impact you'll have on them by how you behave.

Your children will observe you and adopt your habits, patterns, styles, and behaviors in the world. How do you eat? Do you drink coffee? Alcohol? Do you smoke cigarettes? Do you get up early and take care of yourself? Do you exercise regularly? How much do you use your phone? How much do you watch TV and stream video? What do you talk about? Are you vocal with your judgments and condemnations of others? How compassionate and forgiving are you? How empathic are you? How motivated and self-disciplined are you? What's your work ethic like?

This is just a short list of questions that will illuminate your habits, lifestyle, and way of being in the world. And this is what your children will emulate. Hence, if you smoke cigarettes, they are extremely likely to do the same (even if you think you're hiding it). It is possible that a child who grows up around addiction develops such an aversion to it that they become extremely anti-substance use and avoid it forever. But in many cases, children will emulate what they witnessed growing up. They will do whatever was "normal" in their family.

So the best way to influence your children over the long term is to up your game, my friend. Want your children to eat healthier when they become adults? Clean up your diet! Do you want them to be focused and disciplined in their work ethic? Live that way yourself, even when they're not around. This is yet another beautiful gift our children give us—a powerful motivator to level up and live as our best selves.

In addition to the day-to-day way of being, you can also consider how you want your children to handle specific events in life. For example, if you want your children to be relaxed in the face of mistakes so they can keep a cool head and solve the problem, guess what? That's right, time to work on your mindfulness! When you freak out in exasperation about losing your keys or something not going your way, your kids observe this and learn that's what you're supposed to do when something "bad" happens—freak out!

I made a conscious decision last year to model for my children how to deal with conflict. The conflict in our home between Candace and me is extremely peaceable, and we resolve all issues with respectful conversations. We don't yell at each other, threaten, or throw things. So far, so good. But then a strange thing happened one summer.

Over several months, I had three encounters with men who

approached me out in the world with anger and aggression. Each one seemingly came out of the blue for minor infractions. In one case, my children and I were waiting outside our car as my wife went into a restaurant to pick up some take-out. We were standing on the sidewalk and watching two children in front of a nearby house trying to use a pogo stick. The little boy was reasonably good at it, but his older sister seemed to struggle with it.

As we watched, Zaim asked me questions about pogo sticks. Had I ever been on one? Yes, once. Was I good at it? Definitely not. Could he bounce on one? Yes, but it would take practice. The moment felt sweet and easy.

And then, all of a sudden, the man on the porch of the house who'd been sitting there chatting with a friend as his kids played out front stood up and moved toward us.

"Excuse me!" he yelled, with his hands out to his sides as if to say, "How could you think this is okay??"

We just stared at him, unsure of how to respond. I was waiting for more input.

"What the hell do you think you're doing?" he asked.

"Watching the pogo stick situation," I replied. At this point, I felt curious but unperturbed.

"What the hell is wrong with you? You've been watching us for fifteen minutes, creeping us out. What makes you think that's okay?" He proceeded to go on a mini-rant about how awful it was and what a bad father I was–projection city.

But somewhere along the way, I got hooked, not to the point that I wanted to fight him, as that would only end badly with me getting beaten up in front of my kids, thus modeling what NOT to do in a situation like this. But I did get hooked enough to where I wanted to antagonize him. That's something I've done since I was a little kid and always been relatively good at. I could come up with smart-ass responses that would goad the person even more.

So I started saying things to mess with him, which really got his blood boiling. His voice rose, and so did mine. His kids had long ago stopped bouncing on the pogo stick and watched the exchange. My kids stared in silence, probably never seeing their dad heatedly argue with a stranger before.

Candace came out of the Mexican restaurant carrying a big bag of delicious rice and beans. As she got closer, her smile faded, and she watched in confusion as our exchange continued. The whole thing was so immature and absurd. I got in the car, and we drove off, and I was so angry. I kept wanting to replay the scene and vent how unfair his accusations had been.

In short succession, I experienced two other occurrences similar to this one where someone came at me aggressively, and I took the bait. One of these almost led to a physical altercation at 5 a.m. as I was going for a run in the dark. I stopped myself from pushing the guy because I thought he or his friend might have had a weapon. What the hell was going on? I live in a safe, cozy neighborhood in Northeast Portland. I'm not in Judge Dredd's Mega-City One, for God's sake.

One day, I decided I would fundamentally change the way I approached conflict. I would respond with overwhelming empathy, deference, apology, softness, and love so much so that it would disorient the aggressor. I made this conscious choice and went about my life.

A few months later, I was walking down a neighborhood sidewalk with my two boys. Arman, our three-year-old, was trailing a few steps behind. All of a sudden, I heard a distinct crack that sounded like a small piece of glass being broken behind me.

Just as I heard the sound, a woman's voice yelled: "You broke it? Well, that's just great!"

I turned to see an elderly woman outside her house on the sidewalk. She had the edge of her garden lined with little bits of colorful ceramics, seemingly from old teacups and pots and such. Arman was frozen in place, terrified.

I moved toward him and her and crouched down to look at the broken little piece of ceramic.

"Well, he just broke it." She said loudly with frustration and anger in her voice.

I stood back up, holding the pieces of broken ceramic. "I'm sorry," I said in a sincere tone.

"Yeah, I don't know what you were thinking," she continued. Not enough apology yet, so I did it again.

"Yeah, he did. I'm so sorry about that." I placed the little broken pieces back along the edge of her garden. She stood there for a minute, unsure of what to do or say next. And then something shifted in her. She saw Arman hiding behind me.

"Well, at least you're showing them how to handle it in a good way! He probably thinks I'm an old B-I-T-C-H." She spelled out the last word, so as to not say it in front of the boys. I laughed and said, "You just got upset is all. No big deal."

We carried on our way, and my boys had a dozen and one questions about the situation. This time I felt peaceful in my body, full of ease and love. I happily discussed the incident to their hearts' content.

Interestingly enough, since this incident and one more following it, I have had zero confrontations in public. This, once again, reminds me of the real power we have to create our experience out of this quantum soup. Something in me was itching for those conflicts, and when I shifted to a more humble stance, the need for them disappeared–a lesson that I apparently needed to learn and model for my boys.

What do you want to model for your children? What specific situations do you want to handle in a different way? The more specific you can be about those kinds of situations and how you want to handle it, the more likely you'll be able to execute on that vision in the moment.

Conversations

We remember certain conversations for a lifetime. Can you remember moments where someone said something that you remember to this day? It could be with a friend, a mentor, or one of your parents. No matter how old you get, it's burned into your memory. We all have that.

But here's the thing. You don't necessarily choose which conversational moments get etched into your long-term memory. And the same is true for your children. In all your conversations with them, you won't know what they will hold onto consciously and remember, or what will go into procedural memory in their subconscious, or what they will drop entirely (What? But everything I say is pure gold!).

As a result, my suggestion is to have those conversations whenever and wherever you can. You can work little moments into daily life without making a big deal of teaching them something. In fact, it often works best when you casually give them a profound lesson in a random moment that doesn't feel like a "teaching" at all.

The other day, I was out for a hike with Candace and our boys. We were in a small patch of woods in the city of Portland, which has some amazing segments of preserved forest land nestled in between housing and neighborhoods.

This particular section of woods resided on a hill. We started at the top, and the boys were eager to keep going down to see where the trail led. On the way down, some patches were steep, and Zaim was scared of falling. At times, I held his hand, and a few times, I said, "I think you can handle this section on your own. I'll be in front so you won't fall. The worst thing that can happen is you'll slip and hit your butt. But if you're not holding my hand, you'll see that your body can handle the slope and knows what to do, even if your mind says you don't."

He did a number of sections himself, and I could see his growing confidence in the smile on his face, although he did fall on his butt once. I made a big show of brushing his pants off, and he made a big show of how much it hurt (which he does when things don't hurt that much). This is a way of him communicating "This is challenging for me, but I'm ready to do it," and me communicating, "I'm right here with you, supporting you, and I know it's a stretch for you."

Lessons in courage, failing, and getting back up, resilience, and trusting in yourself by doing it numerous times. Damn, I'm good. But then Candace started throwing in her magic, and I was once again humbled by her skill and wisdom to teach our boys (and many other people).

She shared about facing fear and how there are moments when we feel fear, and it would serve us to do the thing that scares us and moments when it wouldn't be a good idea to push through our fear.

"Like when?" Zaim asked.

"Like if a friend wanted you to jump off a fifteen-foot drop," she said. "He might say it would be fun and exciting, and you might feel fear inside that was telling you that it was dangerous and not a good idea. In that case, you could find me or another adult."

"Yeah, because I could break a bone!" he said.

"That's right. Knowing when to face your fear and when to move away is wisdom," she said. I smiled and thought, *I love this woman.*

One final teaching moment occurred on the way back up the trail. I realized this one was as much for my boys as for my wife and me. We were hiking back up to the top of the hill, and both boys were in protest. It was too steep, they were too tired, they needed to be carried. At one point, Zaim stopped on the trail and sat down. The whole thing was humorous as the entire route was several hundred feet. We could see the top just ahead.

"Watch this," I said as I moved a few feet ahead of them. "We all have to get to the top of this hill on this trail. There's no other way to get back. So we have two choices for how we do the trail. We can do it like this…"

I slowly plodded along the trail, my body wavering with mock exhaustion. I stopped in between each step and moaned, saying I couldn't do it, that it was terrible, that I hated it.

"Or, we could do this." I snapped my body upright, took a deep breath in, and hit my chest with the palm of my hand three times. "For Wakanda!" I yelled as I stormed up the trail with long, powerful strides.

My boys were both obsessed with a Black Panther action figure who would say random clips from the movie, including "For Wakanda!" They had not seen the movie and had no idea what Wakanda was, but they sure loved that phrase.

As soon as I finished my demo, both boys yelled, "For Wakanda!" and began stomping up the trail. Arman really went for it with the stomping, yelling, "For Wakanda!" with each step. They made it about ten steps and then fizzled. I laughed and ended up giving them both "boosts" up the hill, in which I put my palm on their backs and lightly pushed them up the hill as they walked.

I'm not sure if any of those would stick for a lifetime, but they might. Who knows? Just keep looking for fun, interesting, and creative ways to share those moments with your kids. As they age and mature, your conversations will deepen and evolve to include topics that your parents may have avoided with you—topics like sex, drugs, racism, life path, and more. Shy away from nothing and welcome everything. You have so much guidance to give; please do not hold back out of fear.

MELT AWAY

When my body won't hold me anymore
And it finally lets me free
Will I be ready?
When my feet won't walk another mile
And my lips give their last kiss goodbye
Will my hands be steady?

When the jealousy fades away
And it's ash and dust for cash and lust
And it's just hallelujah
And love in thoughts and love in the words
Love in the songs they sing in the church
And no hard feelings

- "No Hard Feelings" by The Avett Brothers

There will come a time when your life will be reaching its conclusion. It may come suddenly and sweep you away in an instant, or the end may be looming for a long time due to illness or age. Regardless, when it comes, there is universally one thing desired by all humans as they depart this life and this world—to be with those they love.

When people are faced with those final moments, and if they are lucid enough and open enough, something profound happens. As they go through the physical pain and discomfort and the emotional intensity of preparing to depart their body, they can see with such clarity what matters most: love.

One mother said this to her daughter as she was dying: for many years, I worried about my appearance, desiring to be thinner, thinking I was not beautiful enough, not good enough. Now I see how foolish that was, how meaningless. All I want is another year with you and my granddaughter.

This powerful perspective shift can come when the loss of ego is impending and can create a kind of sacred opening and healing for both the departing and those around them. While you and I may not be close to our final breath today, we can still tap into that deep wisdom that comes from those who have gone before us.

Imagine for a moment that the end is near for you. Perhaps you are old, ancient, gray, and wise—however you like to imagine it. But there you are, on your deathbed, looking at your children who are there to love and support you as you go onto your next adventure. What do you feel?

Take a few moments to really settle into this visualization. Slow down, breathe, and let it inform you, teach you, and alter you. Take your time and let your imagination create and show you anything about this scene.

~~

One afternoon, when I was doing this during meditation, I had a most beautiful combination of feelings and images come to my mind. I began the meditation reflecting on how I could open my heart even more, becoming unconditionally loving of myself, my children, and others.

I felt the depth of love I have for my two boys and how much I want to create a deep sense of home for them. I could see how it's easy as a parent to get caught up in right and wrong and what kids should be doing, from the most minute detail of what they should be watching or eating to major life decisions such as career, relationship partners, and ways of being in the world.

Underneath all this, I felt a powerful desire to create a deep sense of home for them, of belonging to a wolf pack so profoundly that no matter where they go, they would always be a part of it. And in that moment, I could see how the most important thing in creating that was love. But my words do not do it justice.

In my mind's eye, I saw a long, deep shaft going deep into the earth. The walls of the shaft were made of brown rock and had many small structures in them, like small wooden ramps and bridges and such.

Up above were the blue sky, fluffy white clouds, and bright sunlight. And then came a churning, torrential mass of moving water, flowing from all directions toward the mouth of the shaft. Like a flash flood, this churning water spilled over the edge of the lip of the entrance to the shaft, cascading down, down into the depths below.

As the massive amount of water surged down, it easily smashed through and swept aside the little structures that had been in the shaft. These little constructions felt like my conditions on love — my rules, ideas, demands, and requirements. *This is how you need to be in order for me to love you. If you do this (which I don't like), then I'll do that (which will teach you).*

The cascading water, which felt like infinite and divine love, washed away all these demands and attempts to control others. It felt as if this shaft went straight into my heart, where the water pooled and gathered, sloshing and spilling out in all directions.

After that vision, I felt a profound shift in my relationship with my boys. I opened my eyes and decided that I would love them no matter what. I wouldn't retreat or recoil or contract. Even when they did something I didn't like, or threw something, or scratched, or hit.

I saw, clear as day, that the answer in those moments was not less love or the withdrawal of love, but rather *more* love. Like the water surging in my vision, love could pour out through me even in those instances. I would win them over with love. If I were to err, I'd err on the side of being a "softie."

Things changed in beautiful ways after this moment. I have not achieved any sort of perfection, and I still get contracted inside, but my willingness and desire to move toward my boys, no matter what, reached a completely new level.

And I love the growth, so I'm sure there's another level after this, which is absolutely delightful and amazing, isn't it? The parenting game is set up in a way that you are deeply bound and bonded to your child. You will do anything to keep them safe, support them, and help them thrive in this world. You want it so badly for them, and this is built into your mammalian DNA.

And at the same time, they do the wildest, most outrageous, obnoxious, hilarious, sweet, challenging, enraging stuff. So it's a relationship you can't escape. You can't break up with them or distance yourself and see them on holidays. And if for some extreme reason you did, it would feel awful inside. There's no escape.

These conditions require growth, specifically, growth in your patience, wisdom, and capacity to let go, growth in the size and depth of your heart so that you empathize more fully and give more love than you receive. What a gift these little (or big) teachers are.

This brings us to the end of this appendix and our time together in this book. I want to deeply honor you as a parent, as a brother or sister on this same path. You have taken on a challenge that seems so commonplace, but is nothing short of the most transformative, expansive, challenging, amazing, and heart-opening journey there is. May you travel the path with light feet, a smile on your face, and your heart open wide. Until we speak again, may you have the courage to be who you are, and know that you are awesome.

About the Author

Dr. Aziz is a psychologist, author, and coach who is internationally known as the world's leading expert on confidence. Through his coaching, books, videos, and online media, he has helped thousands of people break through shyness, social anxiety, and self-doubt to create richer, happier, more confident lives.

What is most remarkable about Dr. Aziz is his own personal struggle with self-doubt and social anxiety. After reaching a low point in his own life, he made a powerful decision to do whatever it would take to get the confidence he always wanted. This led to a passionate pursuit of studying confidence from every source, including books, audio programs, seminars, and a doctorate degree in clinical psychology from Stanford and Palo Alto Universities.

Dr. Aziz is the author of the best-selling books, *The Solution to Social Anxiety*, *The Art of Extraordinary Confidence*, and *Not Nice*, as well as over a dozen ebooks, including *Five Steps To Unleash Your Inner Confidence*. He is the host of the podcast "Shrink for the Shy Guy" and the YouTube channel, "Get More Confidence." Dr. Aziz is most passionate about his direct work with individuals and groups in coaching programs and weekend seminars. To find out more about all of the resources Dr. Aziz offers, go to www.SocialConfidenceCenter.com.

Dr. Aziz lives in Portland, Oregon, with his wife and two boys (and now two dogs). To find out more about his personal story and inspiring journey to confidence, visit the "About" section of the website listed above.

Made in the USA
Las Vegas, NV
02 December 2020